# THE ARCHITECT

# THE ARCHITECT

## Chapters in the History of the Profession

Edited by
SPIRO KOSTOF

Foreword and Epilogue by
DANA CUFF

UNIVERSITY OF CALIFORNIA PRESS
Berkeley · Los Angeles · London

University of California Press
Berkeley and Los Angeles, California

University of California Press, Ltd.
London, England

First California Paperback Printing 2000

Published by arrangement with Oxford University Press, Inc.,

Library of Congress Cataloging-in-Publication Data

The architect : chapters in the history of the profession / edited by Spiro Kostof;
foreword and epilogue by Dana Cuff.
    p.    cm.
    Originally published: New York : Oxford University Press, 1977.
    Includes bibliographical references and index.
    ISBN 0-520-22604-6 (alk. paper)
    1. Architecture—Vocational guidance.  I. Kostof, Spiro.
NA1995 .A73 2000
720'.23—dc21                                              00-025827

Printed in the United States of America

08  07  06  05  04  03  02  01  00
9  8  7  6  5  4  3  2  1

The paper used in this publication meets the minimum requirements of
ANSI/NISO Z39.48-1992 (R 1997) (*Permanence of Paper*). ∞

# Contents

# Foreword

The fundamental purpose of the architectural profession has evolved to mediate between its practitioners and the culture in which they practice. The architect, in history or in the present, is defined to a large extent in relation to a larger social context. Without denying the architect's creative, individual contribution to the work of architecture, this volume edited by Spiro Kostof locates design in society. In *The Architect: Chapters in the History of the Profession*, Kostof fundamentally dislodges the autonomous individual artist and the biography as primary explanatory constructs of design. Instead, Kostof reasons that the architect is substantially governed by the historical conditions of practice. Inspiration and genius, long considered almost supernatural requirements for architectural production, are displaced by social forces like economics and politics. The structure of office practice, the working relationships among building trades, the nature of architectural training, the profession's status—all hold significance in the life of any individual architect or building.

Historically, architects have assumed varying stations in the social hierarchy dependent upon cultural differences as well as shifts in notions about the architect's technical expertise, building safety, and the role of aesthetics. For example, in his description of the ancient Egyptian architect William MacDonald states "In a culture such as Egypt where the building of monuments had an extraordinary social and economic impact, the post of chief state architect clearly belongs at the very peak of the governing hierarchy." (Kostof, p 6). The same point is made by

Gwendolyn Wright explaining why women architects are situated in the lower reaches of the social pyramid: "The issue of women's place in architectural practice was obviously influenced by Victorian society's rigid sexual stereotypes. . . . In the middle-class cult of domesticity, spirituality and sensitivity were personified by the woman—as long as she stayed in the home; the competitive philosophy of laissez-faire encouraged masculine assertiveness in the commercial environment." (Kostof, 281). From ancient Egypt to Victorian society, cultural patterns conscribed opportunities for architects and set the bar for their social standing.

Professional education exists to enhance the architect's social status, but ironically the academy's inherent task is to override social norms at the same time. Thus architecture school provides a vehicle for novices to access professional training previously held close to the aristocratic chest. Education can overcome the predetermimation of birth. But schools also embodied the means to reform the profession from the inside; schools could operate as institutions of social change. As Joan Draper points out, through an emphasis on art and scholarship, the Ecole des Beaux-Arts had as its ultimate purpose "to raise the status of the profession."(p 214). Architect Joe Esherick describes how the University of Pennsylvania, following the Ecole intended to mold its apprentices, himself among them: "Training in established skills, indoctrination into an established profession, and the development of an understanding of commonly held architectural perceptions were explicit formal tasks for the staff; less formal and less explicit was the task of introducing us to a broadly cultured intellectual life." (p 243).

The late Spiro Kostof, educator, scholar, and historian, molded his share of architecture students at the University of California, Berkeley, where he taught for twenty-six years. Writing and lecturing about the architectural profession from within the architectural academy, Kostof was simultaneously an agent of change and a mirror of received wisdom. To document the history of the profession in this volume, Kostof and his fellow authors analyzed a wealth of information, drawing portraits of architecture and its practice at various moments in time. The "facts" are refracted through the lens of Kostof's scholarly apparatus.

If there was such a thing as a "Berkeley school" in architecture in the seventies and eighties, it was critically shaped to a large extent by Spiro Kostof. A formidable intellect, he had a bracing command of history from ancient times forward, spanning geographies and cultures across the globe. His incisive wit might have proven deadly were it not for the expansive foundations of his character. He was a teacher of the highest caliber, who mentored many doctoral students during his decades at the University of California, while inspiring hundreds of undergraduates in his lecture courses. The breadth of his knowledge was evident in the range of topics undertaken by his advanced students, from ancient to modern, near-eastern to Italian, vernacular to high art. Before settling into Art History, Kostof's graduate studies at Yale began in Dramatic Arts, which comes as no surprise to his students. Like Vincent Scully, Kostof had the ability to set a tempo and spin a yarn that would hold the attention of even the most disaffected undergraduate. Like Robert Stern, Kostof was willing and able to stand in the pulpit to bring the American landscape to the public's living room. But beyond other architectural historians, Spiro not only brought historical places to life, but brought life into architectural history. His broad understanding of economic, sociological, and political forces brought cultural studies to architectural history. He defined all buildings as architecture, keeping popular places and their makers within the ken of architectural history. When he died in 1991, he bequeathed to posterity his writings, but also his students who have continued to teach and study and publish in his absence.

Like all good pedagogues, Kostof knew that a seminar room full of bright advanced students was a gold mine for one's own work. Academic careers were launched when some of the students in Kostof's graduate seminar on the history of the architectural profession authored essays for the text you now hold in your hands. They were joined by Kostof's colleagues at Berkeley and beyond, brought together to write *The Architect*. The volume came together at a particular time and place—Berkeley in the 1970s—which lent a special patina to the project.

Indeed, the intellectual context for *The Architect* was one part Berkeley, and one part the state of scholarship on professions. In the 70s, UC Berkeley was still very much influenced by the protest movements in the prior decade, and People's Park held particular relevance for its design faculty. The College of Environmental Design represented an interdisciplinary marriage of architecture, landscape, and planning. These departments, and Architecture in particular, were hotbeds of the new focus on "man and the environment," as it was then classified. Joe Esherick, the department chair, along with architect and planner Roger Montgomery (who would later become Dean) were instrumental in this social remaking of the field. But a sizable group of the Berkeley faculty had its social agenda clearly staked out. So did other schools across the country which employed social scientists, primarily psychologists, on their faculties. More than social scientists teaching architecture, what was unique at Berkeley were the historians who came to their task with a cultural overview. Led by Spiro Kostof who arguably set the intellectual tone for the department, the architectural historians included Norma Evenson, Steven Tobriner, and most recently Dell Upton.

At Cal, an interdisciplinary social emphasis carried across fields and departments. Senior academics there framed the current discourse: Donald Appleyard, Clare Cooper Marcus, Mel Webber, and Alan Jacobs. J. B. Jackson motored in each year to teach his incomparable cultural land-scape courses, while Horst Rittel developed his theory of design method-ology. Christopher Alexander, having completed *Notes on a Synthesis of Form*, was working on *A Pattern Language* with a growing band of student acolytes. A younger faculty that included Lars Lerup, Russell Ellis, Mark Mack, Anthony Dubovsky, and Galen Cranz were experimenting with cultural implications of everything from drawing to bathing. And doctoral students in architecture, planning, and landscape came to be part of the intellectual climate that emanated from Berkeley.

The general climate of environmental design at Berkeley might be characterized as a critique of formalism. Standing in contrast to the art historical traditions at schools of architecture like Yale and Princeton, the object of analysis was not the building per se. Instead, intellectual bear-ings were sighted upon the building in its human context: the city, the society, the cultural history, the inhabitant, the client, and indirectly then, the architect. Whereas the history of architecture favored the object and the development of its form, the Berkeley school was gathering in-terdisciplinary steam to reshape an understanding of buildings and their role in society. This way of thinking existed elsewhere, as at the Univer-sity of Wisconsin, Milwaukee and City University of New York, primarily as a critique from social scientists conducting empirical research about the significance of physical space on behavior. Berkeley, like MIT, was reshaping architecture toward humanism not only by drawing faculty from the social sciences, but by attracting like-minded architects, plan-ners, and historians as well.

But nearly all this well-intentioned scholarly effort had focussed upon the "user," as the objectively scrutinized subject was termed. Among social scientists, populations like prisoners, guards, asylum patients, and school children were the people worthy of study. On occasion, a psychologist would study the creative design process, as did Berkeley's own Kenneth Craik. But it had to wait for historians to redirect attention from buildings to the architectural profession and its means of production.

*The Architect* was produced under the general influences of UC Berkeley, but also at a time when professional studies had just begun to flourish. In 1977, when this edited volume appeared it was, as Kostof points out, the first scholarly text to examine the architectural profession since Martin Briggs's 1927 book, *The Architect in History*. Although *The Architect* is not a comprehensive survey, the individual chapters spanning ancient to contemporary practice are intended to tell a continuous story. Though some chapters are interwoven more carefully than others, each provides a valuable portrait of a particular time period or issue in the profession. While previous scholarship had illuminated the professional lives of individual architects, Kostof was the first since Briggs to make the profession itself the object of study.

Actually, since the middle of the nineteenth century, the architecture profession had been studying itself at first informally, then in earnest. Proceedings of the American Institute of Architects from its annual meetings were a source of professional reflection, if not empirical rigor. In particular, *The Architect at Mid Century* (Bannister, 1954) was an important milestone gauging the profession and its future directions. The American Institute of Architects, while never as strong as its medical or legal counterparts, undertook sporadic studies of its incomplete membership. That organization's annual meeting (the first was held in 1867) was a *de facto* record of the changing status of the architect and the uneven building economy. In addition, journalists' articles in the professional press and the occasional survey have given practitioners a mirror, albeit hazy, to view themselves.

Indeed, scholarly fascination with professionalism was in a nascent phase when Kostof published this book. This was a field that would evolve and grow through subsequent decades. Professions, sociologists reported, bore structural similarities. Doctors, lawyers, school teachers, clergymen, as well as architects were equipped with training that separated them from the hoi polloi. Professional knowledge was beyond lay understanding—both in terms of cultivated, mysterious sensibilities (like diagnostic powers or design creativity) and a technical expertise (such as legal precedent or structural engineering). That knowledge and how it would be imparted was controlled from within professions granted permission to regulate themselves. This right was conferred by the state because of a profession's primary responsibility to protect public health, safety, and welfare. While this recipe remains fundamental to professions' role in society, there was, in the early 70s, a significant redefinition of that role.

Academic interest in professions was framed by a general public challenging assumptions about professionalism as a whole. From *Our Bodies, Ourselves* (Boston Women's Health Collective, 1973), to Do-It-Yourself-Divorce workbooks, a growing body of publications undermined the traditional authority professions had assumed in society. These populist activities paralleled investigations by academics, and historians in particular, into the evolution of individual professions and their professional institutions such as schools, firms, and professional organizations. The historians were joined by sociologists, anthropologists, and practitioners who turned their collective (if not collaborative) attention to the study of professions. From the 1960s through the 70s, a profusion of literature reexamined professions in society, Kostof's among them.

As Kostof noted in his introduction, studies of architectural education were more prevalent than studies of the architecture profession as a whole. The same can be said for other professions. *Boys in White*, a seminal study of medical school training, was published in 1961 by Howard Becker, followed by Sociologist Eliot Freidson's model study (1970) of the medical profession. Studies of law school and the distinctions between "schoolmen and practitioners" (Johnson, 1978) complemented larger works on the profession as a whole, like *The Lawyer in Modern Society* (1976; first published in 1966). Not only were specific professions reflected in the light of history, but professionalism itself received close socio-analytic scrutiny. In the same year that *The Architect* appeared, Magali Larson published her Berkeley dissertation *The Rise of Professionalism* (1977) which followed a year after Burton Bledstein's *Culture of Professionalism* (1976).

Within architecture, some of the sociologists and psychologists who had been brought into the discipline primarily through academia were now turning an eye not to the buildings' occupants or clients, but to their makers and to the process of making. UC Berkeley, having strong programs in architectural history, social and cultural factors, and design theories and methods, was ripe for spawning new studies of the architecture profession. Perhaps only MIT paralleled this interdisciplinary exploration of practice. There, a series of studies of the design process was initiated by the philosopher, Donald Schön, and colleagues from architecture and engineering. With significant funding from the Mellon Foundation, Schön, Bill Porter, and others undertook the Architectural Education Study (1981). Building upon Argyris and Schön's disquisition (1974) on the disparities between theory and practice, or espoused and in-use theory, studies concerned design thinking and communications. Schön's later book, *The Reflective Practitioner* (1983) encapsulated some of that research.

The first major text on women in the profession appeared the same year as Kostof's (Torre, 1977). Sociologist Judith Blau and colleagues edited a collection of essays on design and planning professions called *Professionals and Urban Form* (1983). Soon thereafter Blau published her important text, *Architects and Firms* (1984). At Princeton, sociologist Robert Gutman turned his attention to architectural practice to become the primary spokesman for professional studies. Gutman's 1988 book, *Architectural Practice: A Critical View*, was the most thorough encapsulation of the state of the profession and has not since been supplanted. (I discuss this work in more detail in the epilogue.) Gutman enumerates ten basic trends shaping practice, offering brief historic context to current data. His work corroborates general trends that Bernard Michael Boyle and to some extent, Gwendolyn Wright, had identified in *The Architect* ten years earlier.

By the late eighties, a small but growing community of scholars could be identified with the history and sociology of the architect's practice and profession. Now there are scholars across the globe thinking about the widest range of issues concerning architectural practice: Robert Prost, Francois Ascher, Elisabeth Campagnac, and Jean-Pierre Epron in France, O. Sluiser in the Netherlands, C. McKean in Scotland; in Britain, John Worthington, Francis Duffy, Graham Winch, Martin Symes and Joanna Eley; in Australia Garry Stevens. Magali Larson's subsequent book on architecture, *Behind the Postmodern Façade*, was published in 1993. Gwendolyn Wright edited a work on teaching history in architectural schools in the United States (1990). My own book on the culture of American architectural practice appeared in 1991. Harvard University, under the stewardship of Dean Peter Rowe, launched a series of symposia about the architectural profession which eventually evolved into a series of essays on practice in the 1990s (edited by William S. Saunders, et al., 1996).

In the wake of *The Architect*, there have been many studies of individual architects and firms. These include Paul Baker's study of Richard Morris Hunt (1980); Jeff Ochsner's book on H.H. Richardson (1982), Leland Roth's study of McKim, Mead and White (1983), and Diane Balmori's essay on George B. Post (1987), to name but a few. An excellent work by Mary Woods (1999) examines the architectural profession in nineteenth century America, with a particularly fine study of Latrobe.

Spiro Kostof did not sustain his focus on the profession. He was first a scholar and teacher, and secondarily a public intellectual. In some ways, the texts he wrote after *The Architect* demonstrate that his chosen public was the undergraduate population. First came A *History of Architecture*, then the book that accompanied his television series, *America by Design*, then *The City Shaped*, and posthumously, *The City Assembled*. He is best known for his sweeping survey, A *History of Architecture*, and for his urban studies, a territory he had staked out by the mid-seventies according to William MacDonald (1992). In a sense, the study of architectural practice and professionalism was one more way that Kostof contextualized architecture itself. While his comprehensive surveys of architecture and urbanism are grounded in a socio-cultural context, they make little reference to the profession and professionals who were the creators. This is somewhat surprising, except insofar as few texts existed outside of Kostof's own, to offer guidance on matters professional during the great march through history.

When Kostof was diagnosed with cancer in June of 1991, he spent his last months completing the final chapter of *The City Assembled*, about the process of urban growth and change. He makes the sentient argument that cities are never static, or they would no longer live. He closes, in the last paragraph, with a description of what he calls the urban process.

"The urge to preserve certain cities, or certain buildings and streets within them, has something in it of the instinct to preserve family records; something of the compulsion to protect a work of art. . . . Cities] are live, changing things—not hard artifacts in need of prettification and calculated revision. Cities are never still; they resist efforts to make neat sense of them. We need to respect their rhythms and to recognize that the life of city form must lie loosely somewhere between total control and total freedom of action. Between conservation and process, process must have the final word. In the end, urban truth is in the flow." (p 305).

That urban process also describes the scholarly process which led to the reissue of the present edited volume. It is not meant to be a reliquary, nor a memorial; instead, it is bringing back into circulation the essays which are still pertinent and new chapters constructed to extend Kostof's original project of understanding the architectural profession. Within the urge both to preserve and transform this valuable work of scholarship, there is truth in the flow.

BIBLIOGRAPHY

Alexander, Christopher. *Notes on the Synthesis of Form.* Cambridge: Harvard University Press, 1964.

Alexander, Christopher, Sara Ishikawa, and Murray Silverstein. *A Pattern Language: Towns, Buildings, Construction.* New York: Oxford University Press, 1977.

Argyris, Chris and Donald A. Schön. *Theory in Practice : Increasing Professional Effectiveness.* San Francisco: Jossey-Bass Publishers, 1974

Baker, Paul. *Richard Morris Hunt.* Cambridge: MIT Press, 1980.

Balmori, Diana. "George B. Post." *Journal of the Society of Architectural Historians,* Vol 46, December 1987, pp 342–355.

Bannister, T. C. (ed). *The Architect at Mid-Century.* Report of the Commission for the Survey of Education and Registration of the American Institute of Architects (1950 survey). New York: Reinhold Publishing, 1954.

Becker, Howard S., B. Geer, E. C. Hughes, and A.L. Strauss. *Boys in White : Student Culture in Medical School.* Chicago: University of Chicago Press, 1961.

Boston Women's Health Book Collective. *Our Bodies, Ourselves; A Book By and For Women.* New York: Simon and Schuster, 1973.

Briggs, Martin. *The Architect in History.* Oxford: Clarendon Press, 1927.

Countryman, Vern, T. Finman, and T. J. Schneyer. *The Lawyer in Modern Society.* Boston: Little Brown and Company, 1976.

Cuff, Dana. *Architecture: The Story of Practice.* Cambridge: MIT Press, 1991.

Johnson, William R. *Schooled Lawyers: A Study in the Clash of Professional Cultures.* New York: New York University Press, 1978.

Larson, Magali Sarfatti. *Behind the Postmodern Façade: Architectural Change in Late Twentieth-Century America.* Berkeley: University of California Press, 1993.

Larson, Magali Sarfatti. *The Rise of Professionalism: A Sociological Analysis.* Berkeley : University of California Press, 1977.

MacDonald, William L. "Spiro Konstantinos Kostof, 1936–1991." *Society of Architectural Historians Newsletter,* June 1992, pp 2–3.

Oschner, Jeffry. *H.H. Richardson: Complete Architectural Works.* Cambridge: MIT Press, 1982.

Roth, Leland. *McKim, Mead and White, Architects.* New York: Harper and Row, 1983.

Saunders, William S. (ed) with Peter G. Rowe. *Reflections on Architectural Practices in the Nineties.* New York: Princeton Architectural Press, 1996.

Schön, Donald A. *The Reflective Practitioner: How Professionals Think in Action.* New York: Basic Books, 1983.

Wright, Gwendolyn and Janet Parks [eds]. *The History of History in American Schools of Architecture, 1865–1975.* New York: Princeton Architectural Press, 1990.

# Preface

Architecture cannot be the world's oldest profession—tradition has decided that issue long ago—but its antiquity is not in doubt. The presence of architects is documented as far back as the third millennium before Christ. Graphic conventions of architectural practice make their appearance even earlier, as for example the plan of a residential cluster in a wall painting of the seventh millennium B.C. at Çatal Höyük in Asia Minor. Indeed even without documentation it can fairly be postulated that architects were abroad from the moment when there was the desire for a sophisticated built environment. For buildings of substantial scale or a certain degree of complexity must be conceived by someone before construction of them can begin.

This is what architects are, conceivers of buildings. What they do is to design, that is, supply concrete images for a new structure so that it can be put up. The primary task of the architect, then as now, is to communicate what proposed buildings should be and look like. The architect does not initiate buildings, nor necessarily take part in the physical act of construction. The architect's role is that of mediator between the client or patron, that is, the person who decides to build, and the work force with its overseers, which we might collectively refer to as the builder.

These are not of course rigidly distinct identities. When architects undertake to build their own houses they become, additionally, clients, and non-professional clients sometimes dispense with the services of an architect and simply produce their own designs. Even more frequently, builders put up standardized buildings for a general market without benefit of the architect's skill. Finally, the great majority of buildings, so-called vernacular architecture, is the result of individual efforts—people who decide to build, settle for the common look of the community, and produce buildings in the accepted local way.

In this book we are not concerned with anonymous architecture of this kind, nor with the rare cases where architects act as their own clients and the reverse. We are dealing with the profession of architecture, the specialized skill that is called upon to give shape to the environmental needs of others. How did architects get to be architects in any given period of history? How were they educated and trained? How did they find their clients and communicate with them? To what extent did they supervise the execution of their designs? What did society think of them (as against what they thought of themselves, which is another matter)? What honors and remuneration could they command? These are some of the questions that underlie the chapters collected here.

The book came out of the classroom. In the spring of 1974 I offered a new course on the history of the architectural profession at the University of California, Berkeley, and invited several of the contributors to this volume to participate. Since the heady sixties, students of architecture at Berkeley, as in other schools around the country, had been grappling with doubts about the relevance of their venerable calling. Unease about the future of architecture was general, in fact, although it was felt and expressed differently by different segments of the profession. While the American Institute of Architects sought dispassionate advice from its established membership by creating the Committee for the Study of the Future of the Profession (headed since the fall of 1967 by the chairman of the Department of Architecture at Berkeley), the disaffected voice of many young aspirants was embodied in a little book by Herbert Muschamp called *File under Architecture* (Cambridge, Mass., 1974). The Committee's report (G. M. McCue et al., *Creating the Human Environment*, Urbana/Chicago/London, 1970) reviewed "the range of possible futures" for an expanding, proliferating presence of the design professions. Architecture was here to stay. "The future of the design professions and the building industry is an integral part of the future of our society" (p. 255). Muschamp, on the other hand, saw no professional future at all. "I am an architect who has neither designed nor built any buildings nor has the inclination to do so. I call myself an architect purely out of the comic conceit which is all that remains of our Western architectural tradition" (p. 1).

It seemed to us that as historians we could help to focus the differences between confident establishment and doubt-ridden neophytes in the way of our own discipline—a look at the past. The new course was the first step. The interest that its discussions generated confirmed our view that the story of the architect, aside from being a good one to tell, would be a useful exordium to the contemporary debate on the health and prospects of the profession. We decided to reach beyond the classroom.

No attempt had been made since M. S. Briggs's *The Architect in History* (Oxford, 1927) to survey for the English-speaking world the fascinating career of what has often been thought of as the Mistress Art and its practitioners. The history of architecture in this century has tended to be centered primarily around the product of architecture. It is interested in architects, in the main, only as the makers of this product. The education and training of the architect at different times and in different cultural worlds, the *process* of architectural practice, the structure of the profession and the social standing of the architect—such topics have been of secondary importance. Yet their bearing on the understanding of the canon of past monuments that is the handiwork and charge of architectural historians is undeniable. As pertinent as the history of the profession is to those who carry on its traditions, it should equally be a constituent concern of the general study of architectural history.

In view of the absence of any comparable successors, the decision to reissue Briggs in 1973 is easy to understand. But the book, still a good read and not without its uses despite the intervening decades, clearly needed updating. The emphasis of *The Architect in History*, as behooved an author who had been a prominent member of the Royal Institute of British Architects, was on England. The professional scene in America, our own special focus, was entirely absent. For the rest, sporadic but significant scholarship in the last forty years had filled in the historical picture and revised our estimate of the better-known portions of it. Lastly, the success of the Modern Movement and attendant developments had not only added a new chapter to the story, but had changed as well our perspective on the entire post-Industrial episode of the profession. The long-lived Beaux-Arts tradition, to mention one instance, came to be discredited, and then, once it had ceased to be the dominant philosophy of architecture and receded into decent obscurity, was gradually rehabilitated as a phenomenon of history. All this, it seemed to us, justified a fresh account of the architect's progress through the centuries.

This history does not aspire to be exhaustive. To attempt to say it all would have been too ambitious and protracted for the goal we had set for ourselves: to produce as expeditiously as possible and for a general reading audience an up-to-date chronicle of the profession, principally in the West. If there is no pretense to universality, neither has the effort been made to fit the chapters into a predetermined mold. The book is meant to read as a continuous story, and not a series of isolated essays. But beyond that, the authors were free to set their own approach. Some chapters are critical syntheses of present knowledge, others contain original research not available elsewhere in print. Chapter 9 is a memoir contributed by a distinguished architect and teacher of design whose career spans the culminating phase of American architecture, from the determined rise of the modern idiom in the thirties to the ambiguous seventies.

In line with our intention to produce, above all, a readable story, the scholarly apparatus has been modified. The burden of documentation is in the bibliographical notes at the ends of chapters, where we have chosen to be descriptive of our sources instead of merely itemizing them. Footnotes have been eliminated by and large, in preference for brief citations in the text; readers who wish to do so can locate the full references in the bibliographical notes. Illustrative material, some of it published here for the first time, has also been kept to a minimum. A broader selection will be found in L. Vagnetti's *L'Architetto nella storia di occidente* (Florence, 1973), which, despite its title, is also about a lot of other things.

*The Architect: Chapters in the History of the Profession* is a genuinely collaborative work. Each chapter has been circulated among contributors to give them a chance to suggest improvements. In addition, we have drawn upon some outsiders for expert advice, among whom I should personally like to thank Professors Jean Bony and Richard G. Carrott. Acknowledgment of help in procuring illustrative material is made in the List of Illustrations. In the preparation and production of the book, we are all indebted to two fine associates: our editor at Oxford, James Raimes, who took the project very much to heart and gave it benign supervision; and Ms. Wendy Tsuji, to whom goes the chief credit for overall editorial assistance. The index is due to the gallant effort of Virginia Beane.

*Berkeley*                                                                    S. K.
*June 1976*

THE ARCHITECT

# 1

## The Practice of Architecture in the Ancient World: Egypt and Greece

SPIRO KOSTOF

Through the centuries, only a fraction of the built environment has ever been affected by the architectural profession. Its summons has come from clients who had need of special buildings, buildings with a disposition and refinement of form that was out of the ordinary, and who could afford to pay for them. Traditionally, therefore, architects have been associated with the rich and the powerful. Their services were required by the state and the church, the wealthier classes, administrative bodiés, and affluent business concerns such as guilds and corporations. This association did not always assure the architects a favored standing in the social hierarchy, but it sufficed, at the very least, to set them apart from the laboring classes. They were not workmen but rulers of workmen, as Plato puts it; they contributed knowledge, not craftsmanship (*Politicus* 259E).

The knowledge, starting with the legendary heroes of the profession, was understood to embrace two qualities, learning and the gift of invention, what used to be called cunning. In Egypt, the prototypical architect Imhotep was revered for his great wisdom as a scribe, astronomer, magician, and healer. As healer, he was later deified. Architecture for him represented one of the fields of learning he commanded, as well as the canvas of his cunning. He devised the stepped pyramid for the tomb of his patron King Zoser by piling up several mastabas (the mastaba was the common burial platform of early Egypt) into a monumental tower that rose 195 feet above the west bank of the Nile at the necropolis of Saqqara. What is more, the pyramid and the entire complex that surrounded it were built of cut stone—the first of the great masonry structures of the Old Kingdom, of which the pyramids of Giza are the best known. The change from an architecture of brick and wood to one of stone was nothing less than a constructional revolution. It required, to succeed, a range of new and highly specialized technical skills. The traditional materials of sun-dried or baked brick and timber were easy to shape, transport, and use. Stone is different. Whether it is soft or hard—alabaster, sandstone, limestone, or granite—it has to be quarried laboriously, cut, transported with great difficulty and hazard over land or on water, and then used and dressed with precision and a full understanding of its properties and behavior. Egyptian building methods and tools are still, in part, a hypothetical subject. To see the superb workmanship of the pyramid of Zoser, where the cutting imitates logs and papyrus leaves, helps to explain why the architect who introduced this advanced building mode without the aid of much local precedent should be honored for his cunning as much as his erudition.

Daedalus, the legendary first architect of the Greek world, was an inventor of both form and contraptions. He is credited with the labyrinth of Crete where the Minotaur lived (perhaps the first palace of Knossos), the plan for which Daedalus is said to have acquired from the tomb of an Egyptian king. From Egypt he also learned the art of statuary, specifically standing figures with legs apart and eyes open, so that they looked real. He made a machine to enable Pasiphaë to mate with the bull she loved, the offspring of the strange union being the Minotaur. Homer refers to a dance floor "which Daedalus once fashioned in wide Knossos for fair-haired Ariadne" (*Iliad* XVIII, 590). And when things got bad and Daedalus fell into disfavor, he invented wings for his son Icarus and himself to flee Crete. The son did not make it very far, but Daedalus flew all the way to Sicily, where he pleased his new patron King Kokkalos with such things as an underground steam bath and a reservoir. The very name Daedalus means "the cunning worker" or just "the skillful one."

There was one category of building that brought the first architects extravagant praise—or total obscurity. In the ancient world, the urge to provide homes for deities was felt keenly, especially during the initial phase of transition from a nomadic to a settled way of life. The onus attached to this divine provision was overwhelming. How could mere mortals presume to know the kind of built environment that would please the gods, so that they would consent to dwell there, at least from time to time? It is the classic doubt of King Solomon at the Temple of Jerusalem: "Behold, the heaven and heaven of heavens cannot contain thee; how much less this house that I have builded" (I Kings 8:27). To a number of ancient cultures, the answer was obvious. The form of the temple must be god-given, and the recipient must be the highest representative on earth of divine authority. This often meant the king. In Mesopotamia, specifications for the temple at Lagash, for example, were revealed to its King Gudea in a dream. As late as the Babylonian period, the kings were supposed to keep measurements secret, and themselves lay out the dimensions of the temple and initiate construction. The divine overlord, client and architect at once, deigned to use the king as his builder. That was the presumption. In truth the client was the king, and a genuine architect undoubtedly prepared the designs for the temple within the established norms of religious architecture. It was only because of the high sanctity of the commission that the architect's identity was preempted by the king, who would also often assume credit for all other major buildings of his reign as his due. So it is that the fertile minds that conceived the ziggurat of Ur, the Temple of Jerusalem, or the great palace at Persepolis have remained anonymous.

In other cultures, notably Egypt, the execution of sacred or prestigious public works elevated the office of the architect instead of forcing it into obscurity. Plans and other pertinent information about the design of temples were preserved in archives. The same was true for all official institutions, such as law courts, public works of various kinds, palaces. These written instructions, divinely inspired and contained on rolls of papyrus or leather, would have to be consulted by the state architect in remodeling extant buildings or replacing them with new ones. Senmut, the famous architect of Queen Hatshepsut, boasted of this privilege in these words: "I had access to all the writings of the prophets; there was nothing which I did not know of that which had happened since the beginning." And when Akhenaten founded his own religion based on a form of solar monotheism, he had to train architects personally since there was no written tradition for the temples required by the new faith. His chief architect, one Bek, records on a wall of his tomb, among his other titles, that he was "the assistant whom His Majesty Himself taught."

The principal deity of architecture and reckoning was the goddess Seshat, known as "Lady of the builders, of writing, and of the House of Books." She assisted the king in the laying out of new buildings, through the ritual act of driving a tall stake into the ground with a mallet. She was sometimes replaced by Thot, the god of science, or Ptah, the god of crafts: a constellation that neatly scans the total scope of architecture, from pure theory on the one hand to the practical knowhow of construction on the other. Imhotep had served as chief official of the cult of Ptah. In Ptolemaic times his legend included authorship of "The Book of Foundation for Temples," which had to be consulted by king and priests for every major building program of the official religion. The book had been carried up with the gods when they chose to withdraw from the earth, but Imhotep was believed to have let it fall from heaven, somewhere north of Memphis.

Several things may be deduced from this body of tradition. In the first place, the education of architects was closely tied to the priestly class, as indeed was all schooling in pharaonic Egypt. Secondly, the architect was bound by precedent in the performance of his calling. Extant monuments from Egypt's long history testify to this preponderant architectural conservatism and the slow pace of formal innovation. Thirdly, the existence of trade secrets that were passed on encouraged a family adherence to the calling of architecture. Sons of architects learned the recondite language from their fathers and taught it to their own sons. A professional dynasty, if not perhaps strictly lineal, could thus be traced among the practitioners of architecture, much like the recorded order of royal dynasties. We have the list of twenty-five generations of architects as supplied by Khnumibre in the fifth century B.C., starting with Kanofer, the father of the great Imhotep, and ending with Khnumibre himself.

These state architects were, to be sure, exceptional men. In their capacity as learned persons entrusted with the prerogative of delving into sacred books, they shared the high company of the king and the ranking priesthood. It is little wonder that most of them were powerful administrators in the land; for to them were consigned not only the conception but the supervision and disposal of all major public projects. Their professional title denotes "master builder" and "overseer of works." In a culture such as Egypt where the building of monuments had an extraordinary social and economic impact, the post of chief state architect clearly belonged at the very peak of the governing hierarchy. At times, there was no more powerful official after the king. Imhotep describes himself as "the Chancellor of the King of Lower Egypt, Chief under the King of Upper Egypt, Administrator of the Great Mansion, Hereditary Noble, Heliopolitan High Priest, Imhotep." Senmut's proximity to the person of the remarkable queen Hatshepsut is unparalleled even for Egypt. In addition to being "architect of all the works of the Queen," he was "Chief

Guardian of the King's Daughter . . . Governor of the Royal Palace
. . . Superintendent of the Private Apartments," and so on. Portraits of
him in stone show him holding the royal princess in his lap. His portrait
also appears behind every door in the queen's mortuary temple at Deir
el Bahri.

Hundreds of lesser architects must have worked under such luminaries
of the profession. We know nothing about them, but their working methods are slowly being pieced together by Egyptologists. A handful of surviving architectural drawings illustrate the graphic language of Egyptian
design. Pictorial sources, i.e., representations of built environments in
wall paintings and reliefs, supply additional information. Drawings were
made with reed pens on such surfaces as papyrus and leather. These materials, being expensive as well as fragile, were used for the more important
drawings, such as the master schemes maintained in institutional archives.
Only rare fragments have survived. Durable materials—stuccoed tablets,
panels of wood—were also used to draw upon. And cursory sketch-plans
were incised on flat flakes of limestone, called *ostraka* in Greek, as a
working guide for the foreman on the job.

The instruments of design were the ruler, the square, and the triangle.
Rulers were made of wood, and divided into cubits; the cubit, the major
unit of Egyptian architecture, was in turn subdivided into 7 palms, and
each palm into 4 digits. These were measurements of human derivation.
The royal cubit stood for the length of the forearm from the elbow to the
tip of the middle finger, and a smaller cubit, used up until the Twenty-
sixth Dynasty, for the length of the forearm to the tip of the thumb.
Palms were derived from handbreadths, digits from the length of the finger. Of the other instruments, the square has been recovered in numbers
from excavated tombs, and triangles of various kinds are known to us
from small-scale hematite or gold reproductions which used to be buried
as amulets in the foundations of Eighteenth Dynasty temples.

Plans and elevation drawings, often used in conjunction, were governed
by a central axis line and the rule of bilateral symmetry. They were over-
laid by squared grids. A famous instance can be seen in one of the very
few papyrus drawings in existence, now in Turin, showing the front and
side elevations for a shrine. The line itself is in black, the grid in red (Figure 1). Similar grids were known to have been applied to walls and blocks
of stone, to control the carving of figures in relief and in the round. The
practice may have corresponded to the modern conception of *mise aux
carreaux:* the squared grid, invented in the Renaissance as an "optical

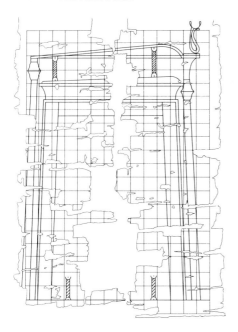

Figure 1. Side elevation for a shrine; Egyptian papyrus drawing from Ghorab, probably from XVIII Dynasty. The squared grid in red superimposed on the black-line drawing may have served to control the proportional inner structure of the design.

veil," on the basis of which an image can be enlarged to any size while holding to the same proportions. But possibly the grid may have served the Egyptian designer in a different or related way, having to do with the inner structure of the pictorial composition or the scheme of architecture. The grid, to put it differently, may have come first, as the structural basis of the original design, rather than being imposed upon the design as an aid to proportional reproduction.

The theory of architectural design was seemingly empirical, and only minimally indebted to mathematics. According to one scholar, A. Badawy, the architect employed simultaneously a modular system and a geometric system. The module would be derived from a major dimension in the building under design, the width of the inner room in a temple for example, which might be, say, 10 cubits. Multiples and fractions of the module would then determine all the other dimensions of the building, as well as the placement of columns and piers. Dimensions were also calculated at times in the so-called Fibonacci series, wherein every number is the sum of the two preceding numbers—3 : 5 : 8 : 13 : 21 : 34 : 55, and so on. The geometric system depended on a few simple figures, mainly the square and a specified number of triangles, among them the so-called Osiris or sacred triangle, where the height is to the base in the relation of 4 to 3;

isosceles triangles with the height equal to the base, twice the base, 8 times the base; and, most common of all, the isosceles triangle whose height is to its base as 5 is to 8, a ratio approximating the golden section.

Relying on a set module and a combination of two or more of these basic geometrical figures, the Egyptian architect prepared a ground plan and a set of outline elevations for all parts of the building in question. Perspective views, in our sense, did not exist. What the building would look like in its totality was probably conveyed through images like the representations of architecture in pictorial art. These were ideationally rather than optically composed, and sought to record the conceptual rather than the physical reality of the building. Thus, in the frontal view of an Amarna palace (Figure 2), what is behind is shown *above*. The object is to show all important aspects of the building additively, one next to the other, much in the way that actual buildings were made up of set parts, added on to the initial core in the course of time along the same longitudinal axis. The lowest register highlights the three gates of the outer court; the next register depicts the principal facade of the palace, with a pavilion of appearances in the middle flanked by colonnades; the third register shifts to an interior view of the Hall of Appearances (apparently set for a banquet) and side aisles; then, some sort of service corridor; and at the top—that is, in the farthest distance—storerooms and the king's bedroom, with a ventilating mechanism on the roof. Clearly, there is no

Figure 2. Bird's-eye view of an Amarna palace in a painting from the tomb of Mery-Re, high priest of Aten; XVIII Dynasty. The main sections of the palace in depth are shown as registers placed one on top of the other, with the bottommost register representing the three gates of the outer court and the topmost, in the farthest distance, some interior rooms.

attempt made to create a visual impression of the palace, as this might be had from a single vantage point. And the picture includes those essential features that characterize the concept of a palace, and not specific details of the number of rooms, the disposition of columns, and the like.

The next step after the completion of the design would have been to transfer the building onto the site. This was done by reference to something called the "plan-net" (Badawy's translation), the original word being related etymologically to the verb "to plan, to project" and the noun for "cord." The procedure seems to have involved staking the ground and stretching a cord to delineate the outline of the building and the formative axis. The length of the building was predetermined and laid out accordingly; the width was then established proportionally to it, in accordance with some recognized rule. "Its length is exact," a text from Dendera states, "its width according to the formula, its norm is in excellent work [?]." The initial phase of this laying out of the plan-net was a solemn ceremony presided over by the king and overseen by the goddess Seshat. The details would then be filled in under the direction of the architect, and in reference to working drawings. The main instrument for the entire procedure was a cord knotted at twelve equal intervals. With it one could fix a right angle, or even a catenary curve. We have a statue of Senmut holding such a cord, neatly rolled up (Figure 3). It is also the standard attribute of land surveyors, who measured fields and plots and affixed the official boundary stelai, removal of which was a serious crime.

Then construction began. The degree of the architect's involvement in the procuring and transport of building materials and the day-to-day supervision of the work on the site is not known. The phrase "overseer of works" seems to suggest close surveillance. There were obviously foremen who led the effort of the hundreds of masons, stone-carvers, plasterers, painters, and the like engaged on any single project. But the architect was "foreman of foremen," as for example Ineni, chief of works at Karnak under several kings of the Eighteenth Dynasty, describes himself in his tomb. And the architect Haremsaf of the Twenty-second Dynasty is praised for working around the clock "building [the Great Pylon of Bubastides at Karnak] without ceasing."

This is as much as can be gleaned about the profession of architecture in ancient Egypt from the limited evidence at our disposal: funerary inscriptions, textual references, artifacts, portraits and other works of art, architectural drawings like the Turin papyrus, and of course what has lasted

Figure 3. Portrait statue of the architect Senmut; XVIII Dynasty. He holds the cord with which buildings were laid out on the site. The head which surmounts the roll is a later reworking of a ram's head, symbol of Chnoum-Shou, the patron deity of surveyors.

of the buildings. With Greece, we are on more familiar territory. The time is less remote, the culture less alien, information about the architect both fuller and more enlightening. The sources for this information are also dissimilar to Egypt's. For one thing, there are no monumental tombs of famous architects with self-proclamatory texts on their walls. And even though the excellence of Greek draftsmanship is blazoned on thousands of vases, not a single architectural drawing has come down to our day.

This curious gap has prompted one scholar, J. Bundgaard, to advance the thesis that the Greek architect never made plans or elevations for the buildings he undertook to design. He did not, strictly speaking, design buildings, the way Senmut or Rabirius or Michelangelo did. He was rather a master craftsman, like the shipwrights responsible for the Greek triremes. Indeed, the Greek term *architekton* meant, at least initially, nothing more than master-carpenter; it was in this sense, rather than *master-designer*, that it was used to refer to shipwrights and temple-builders alike. According to this view, both the form and construction of a Greek temple were traditional enough to allow the architect to settle issues on the site as the building went up. The central agent of the art of architecture was the stone-mason, and he worked from detailed verbal descriptions set down by the architect, usually referred to as *syngraphai*.

For these, we have ample evidence. Two instances in particular are illuminating. One, dealing with a new monumental porch for the Telesterion of Eleusis, is a technical document seemingly intended for skilled workmen. The text is complete, and yet it gives no indication of the total structure. There is no mention of the columns and their disposition, for example, nor of the ceiling, nor the roof. It describes in detail individual blocks of stone needed for construction, in terms of their quarrying and rough-hewing at the quarry, their transport, and their finishing at the building site. According to Bundgaard, different parts of the document would be consulted by different contractors depending on which pertained to their own responsibilities, just as a contractor might consult pertinent parts of working drawings. The order of the blocks described does not, in fact, correspond to the order of their erection, but to the distance from which the stone was to be brought, beginning with two of the most distant places, the island of Aigina and Mount Pentelikos just outside Athens. Here is how this inscription reads in part:

Blocks shall be quarried from the soft stone of Aigina, of uniform structure, length 4 feet, breadth 3 feet, thickness 1½ feet, and be hewn plain on all sides, having the necessary surplus on all sides. They shall be transported undamaged to Eleusis. Number: 44. . . . Moldings shall be made of the soft Aigina stone for the full length of the wall . . . all of equal length . . . to be hoisted up and joined without damaging them and in such a way that they fit closely everywhere, and they shall be connected with clamps and dowels in molten lead where the architect directs and the upper face of the course shall be levelled off. Number of moldings: 42. . . . Three capitals shall be made of Pentelic marble according to the *anagrapheis* to be provided by the architect, and hoisted up onto the columns, and the joints made so that they fit and are flush. . . . The state shall supply lead and iron for connecting the stones, and a complete pulley.

The word *anagrapheis*, used several times throughout the document, is crucial. It may mean either *drawings* or *descriptions* (i.e., specifications), since both are implied by the same verb, *grapsai*. Bundgaard takes it to mean the latter, in support of his thesis that the practice of architecture in Greece had no need of graphic aids.

Figure 4. Reconstruction drawing of the naval arsenal at Piraeus, the port of Athens, built between 340 and 330 B.C. The architects were Philon and Euthydemos. The building, which does not survive, can be recreated with some surety on the basis of specifications inscribed on a stone tablet.

The other inscription concerns a naval arsenal at Piraeus, the port of Athens (Figure 4). It refers to a celebrated building actually erected in 330 B.C. to hold the tackle of the Athenian navy. The building was burned to the ground by Sulla; its site is no longer known. The principal architect was Philon, a native of Eleusis and author of the porch we have just discussed. In the inscription, he is coupled with one Euthydemos. It was not uncommon for Greek architects to work in teams of two (or more, on occasion) on the same building, although the exact division of labor is unclear; there is no good cause to assume, as some scholars have done, that one member of the team attended to the artistic end of the project and the other the business end. At any rate, the arsenal inscription, on the basis of which the lost building can be entirely reconstructed with some degree of certainty, serves a different purpose from the Eleusis inscription we have quoted. We have no information here about specific constructional details, least of all for the upper parts of the walls. Instead, we can visualize what is impossible with the Eleusis inscription, namely, the general outline of the whole building. We are told of the site, the overall measurements, the thickness of the foundations, and the material and standard size of the stone blocks, but not their exact number, or details about their quarrying, transport, and final dressing. The document is as follows:

The Gods: Specifications (*syngraphai*) of Euthydemos, son of Demetrios of Melite, and Philon, son of Exekestides of Eleusis, for the stone arsenal to be used for the storage of naval tackle. An arsenal shall be built in Zeia for naval tackle, beginning at the Propylaea of the market place and running behind the ship sheds which have a common roof. The length shall be four *plethra* [about 405 feet], the width 50 feet or 55 feet including the walls. The ground of the site shall be cut down 3 feet where it is highest and levelled off in the other parts. On this area the course masonry of the foundations shall be laid to an even height, the whole being dressed by the level. The foundations shall be extended so as to support the piers, to a distance of 15 feet from the walls, including the thickness of the pier. There shall be 35 piers in each row, which will be arranged so as to leave a passageway for the public through the center of the arsenal. . . . Two doorways shall be left open at either end of the arsenal, each 9 feet wide. And a center wall shall be constructed at each end between the doors, 2 feet wide and running 10 feet into the interior. . . . The height of the walls shall be 27 feet, including the triglyph under the cornice, with the height of the doors being 15½ feet. Lintels of Pentelic marble shall be set into position, 12 feet long, wide as the walls and two courses high; this shall be done after doorjambs of Pentelic or Hymmetian marble and thresholds of Hymmetian marble have been put in. There shall be windows all around, in every wall, opposite every intercolumniation, and three along the width at each end. And into each window there shall be fitted bronze shutters of the proper size. . . . The epistyle shall be made of wood and shall be fastened to the top of the piers. . . . That there may be ventilation in the arsenal, when the courses of the walls are laid spaces shall be left open at the joints of the blocks wherever the architect shall direct. All these things shall be carried out by the contractors in accordance with the specifications and the measurements and the model which the architect shall provide, and they will make delivery at the times agreed to in the contract for each of the jobs.

If Bundgaard's thesis is accepted, this document belongs to an earlier stage of the building process than the Eleusis inscription, and is intended for a higher authority than the work force, probably the person in general charge of the construction. But the document strongly suggests that it was the architect himself who was the director of works. Why would he need a detailed set of specifications such as that provided by the arsenal inscription, Bundgaard asks, if he has already drawn the plan and elevations of the building? The answer must be that the drawings never existed.

It is hard to follow this conclusion, especially as reflective of general practice in Greek architecture. However standard Greek temples may appear to the untrained eye, the much-praised visual subtlety of the elevations alone, the so-called Greek refinements, would be extremely difficult to achieve without preliminary drawings to scale. The very standardization of form was a process in which architects participated; to think that their proposed solutions over time, and the treatises some of them wrote about these solutions, went entirely unillustrated seems unlikely. That some need was felt for visual presentation is evident from the reference to "the model" in the arsenal inscription. In fact, there is no doubt that wax models, at least for details, were indeed current practice, at the latest by the late fifth century B.C. The Erechtheion accounts show payments to the sculptor Agathanor, who made a wax model for the acanthus of the coffer lids of the ceiling, and to the wood-carver Neseus for the rosettes of the ceiling. In one other instance, a drawing is clearly implied. A decree dated about 400 B.C. speaks of the doorway of the temple of Athena Nike on the Akropolis; it invites suggestions from the people, and asks that "anyone who wishes make a drawing [*grapsai*] and exhibit it, not less than a cubit [long or wide]. . . ." Now the verb here cannot logically be understood to refer to a description, since the metric dimension specified clearly makes sense more for a drawing than a piece of writing. Finally, there is Vitruvius. More will be said, in the next chapter, of this Roman architect and writer of the late first century B.C. Since his famous *Ten Books of Architecture* was an attempt, in part, to summarize the professional knowledge of his day, much of which derived from Greek precedent, his testimony is vital. Vitruvius is explicit about the graphic conventions of Classical design: plans, elevations, and perspective views. He includes drawing among the subjects of the liberal education he outlines for the would-be architect, and instructs him to be "skillful with the pencil" (1.1.3). It is very improbable that a chronicler so anxious to record the traditional knowledge of his profession would neglect to point out the peculiarity of an exclusively verbal communication between architect and builder if this had been the case.

The arsenal inscription and the one from Eleusis, rather than being practical working documents exclusively, were probably part of that public record it was customary to keep for all projects that made use of public funds. Setting down particulars for every transaction entailed by the building process amounted to a passion in the Greek centuries. Full instructions for contractors and crews and other relevant day-to-day information would be posted as work progressed, probably on wooden notice boards.

But selected aspects of the project, of interest to the average citizen, were elaborately carved on stone tablets and set up as public monuments. The many fragments that have been uncovered in modern times demonstrate that the inscriptions covered a broad range of legal, financial, and practical matters, from the intent to build and the tenders for contracts to the quality of workmanship, the length of a working day, fines for overrunning set time limits of production, and the regulation of lawsuits. They are the basic source of our knowledge of the practice of architecture in the age of Greece.

The architect is not preeminent in this public record. His own side of his professional contribution was presented more fully, and presumably more self-importantly, in trade books and treatises. These also aided in the education of future architects, which seems to have been both practical and bookish. An early work we hear about is the volume brought out by Theodoros of Samos, a sculptor, architect, and metalworker of the sixth cenutry B.C., dealing with the temple of Hera in his homeland, which he had designed jointly with the architect Rhoikos. The fame of the huge building spurred commissions from abroad. Theodoros was consulted by the Ephesians on the problems of stability of their temple of Artemis on its marshy site, and he advised them to put a layer of ashes (packed charcoal, according to another source) beneath the foundations, to keep the stone blocks from sinking. And he was summoned to Sparta to take charge of the temple of Athena there, at the completion of which he stayed on to run a private school of architecture. Chersiphron, the architect of the Artemis temple at Ephesos for which Theodoros had been consultant, also wrote a book, in collaboration with his son Metagenes. In it he explained his new mechanical devices for transporting heavy columns and epistyle blocks from the quarry to the site and hoisting them into position. The sixth century saw the wholesale adoption of cut stone as the principal building material for temples, in the place of wood and terra-cotta, which had been in currency since the beginning of this monumental form about 800 B.C. The challenge that confronted Chersiphron, therefore, was similar to that which Imhotep had met so spectacularly at Saqqara two thousand years earlier.

The architectural initiative rested during the seventh and sixth centuries B.C. with the Aegean colonies and with Corinth on the mainland. But after the traumatic Persian wars, Athens rose to be the undisputed center of activity, with a massive program of public works that included the rebuilding of the sacked Acropolis. Skilled labor, always at a premium, was concentrated for several decades in the great city of Perikles; much of it undoubtedly came from abroad. The experience of the Parthenon led to a book by one of its architects, Iktinos, written in collaboration with one Karpion.

Several other monographs by architects about their important buildings are enumerated by Vitruvius. Since all of these books are lost, we have him and later Latin authors to thank for the knowledge of their existence and something of the nature of their contents. It would seem that until the fourth century B.C. architectural books dealt both with theory—that is, the proportions and properties of the Orders, ornament, and the like—and with technical matters of construction. In the fourth century the discussion settled into a battle of the styles reminiscent of the aesthetic side of the polemics of revivalism in the nineteenth century. Doric diehards like Philon, the architect of the naval arsenal at Piraeus, defended that venerable Order against the sweeping popularity of the Ionic. Pythios, author of the temple of Athena at Priene, extolled the superiority of the Ionic Order in a book called *Commentaries*, where he apparently also proposed that architects should show proficiency in "all the arts and sciences," in contrast to practitioners of other professions who "bring a single subject to the highest perfection" (Vitruvius 1.1.12).

With the advent of Alexander the Great, the profession came to be in great demand. New cities were being founded everywhere in the lands of his spectacular conquests, and older towns, with swelling populations, engaged in extensive programs of face-lifting and expansion. For the next three hundred years, the period called Hellenistic, architects would enjoy the profits of this building boom, and the challenge of new building types. The spectrum now included—in addition to the traditional repertory of temples, treasuries, theaters, stadia, and assembly buildings—libraries, princely tombs, mercantile exchanges like the Hypostyle Hall at Delos, baths, stoas, formal squares and colonnaded avenues, clock-towers like the famous Tower of the Winds at Athens, lighthouses, and other port facilities. The Corinthian Order, tentatively introduced in the mid-fourth century B.C., became the norm; with it, an architecture of rich pictorial textures came into its own. Arkesias, architect of a temple of Asklepios in Tralles, wrote a treatise on the proportions of this new Order. The scale was now explosive. Monumental axes led up to public buildings elevated on massive platforms. The capitals of the Alexandrine kingdoms—Pergamon, Antioch, Alexandria—led the fashion in an urban opulence and pomp unknown to the tough Greek world of earlier days. There were palaces for the rulers and their families, and luxurious homes for the rich that kept private practice alive.

This aspect of the profession in antiquity is poorly understood. There is little information to go on. It is sometimes assumed that the architect was exclusively confined to the design of public buildings; that houses were built by masons and carpenters. But the absence of documentary proof notwithstanding, this view is hardly tenable. First of all, in total schemes of urban design the architect's involvement in the disposition of private houses came naturally. The Egyptian worker colonies at El Lahun and Akhenaten's capital of Amarna were both planned ensembles; they obeyed the same principles of design that applied in the temples. What Aristotle calls "the modern manner" of residential architecture stemmed from the application of the checkerboard layout, an urban solution of great moment, to cities such as Miletus, Priene, and Olynthos. Beyond general planning, the architect undoubtedly received private commissions. The wealthy classes have always been consumers of the art of architecture; this was also most likely the case in Egypt, Mesopotamia, and Greece. The difference between a royal palace, which was a center of public administration as well as a residence, and an upper class house was, to speak formally, only one of scale. Idealized house plans drawn on clay tablets have come to light at Tell Asmar, a city of northern Mesopotamia (Figure 5). They may have been architects' exhibits to would-be clients of what was possible. Even in the democratic environment of Classical Greece, some houses were larger and more elaborate than others, and would plausibly require the special care of an architect—or at least the distinction of having been "architected." In Hellenistic towns such as Delos on Apollo's sacred island, surviving mansions with their formal courtyards and wall paintings announce plainly that they were not mere builders' recipes. Finally, it should be observed that Vitruvius devotes one section of his book to "the theoretical principles and symmetrical proportions of private houses"; one chapter deals with the Greek house.

By all accounts, the demands made on the architectural profession in the Greek world were broad in range, and the practitioners versatile and ingenious. Individual architects might choose to specialize in one or another of the categories embraced by the profession. Temples and related buildings were the major commissions from the seventh to the fourth centuries B.C. The elite of the profession made its mark through association with one or more of the principal temple sites. But of the seven greatest

Figure 5. Clay tablet from Tell Asmar (Iraq), the ancient Eshnunna, later third millenium B.C., bearing an ideal house plan which may have been an architect's exhibit to a would-be client. It is reproduced here in its actual size.

Greek architects, according to a list current in the late Hellenistic period, only two, Chersiphron and Iktinos, were primarily temple-builders. Daedalus headed the list as the legendary hero-architect. Philon, the chief architect of the Attic school in the early part of the fourth century, was on it; his work included, as we saw, both religious architecture (the portico of the Telesterion at Eleusis) and civil architecture (for example, the famous arsenal of Piraeus). Of Menekrates, who appears between Iktinos and Philon on the list, we know nothing. An inscription mentions one Menekrates as the architect of the Great Altar of Zeus at Pergamon, but it is uncertain if this is the same man. The last two names are Archimedes and Dinokrates. Both had unorthodox reputations for architects. Dinokrates, the favorite architect of Alexander, brought himself to the attention of the king with a project that would have shaped Mount Athos into the figure of a man holding in one hand a fortified city and in the other a huge vase into which the streams of the mountain would be collected and poured from there into the sea. Alexander admired the project, as Vitruvius tells us, but turned it down on the grounds that the land surrounding the proposed city would not sustain it. He engaged Dinokrates anyway, and had him build, instead, the city of Alexandria at the westernmost mouth of the Nile. Archimedes was foremost a mathematical genius. His place on the list was won, it would seem, for the war engines he invented for the defense of Syracuse—in other words, as a military engineer.

In fact, no clear-cut distinction was recognized in Greece between architecture, engineering, and city-planning. The architect's responsibility went beyond the design of public and private buildings, which is what Vitruvius calls *aedificatio*, one of the three branches into which he divides architecture. The others are *gnomonice*, the construction of sundials and other devices for measuring time, and *machinatio*, which means engineering or mechanics and included proficiency in the erection and equipment of military defenses (1.3.1). Herodotus, who first uses the term *architekton* in the fifth century B.C., applies it both to architects in the modern sense and to the likes of Eupalinos (3.60), who devised an underground canal to bring water to Samos, and the engineers who bridged the Bosphorus for Darius' expedition against Greece and the Hellespont for Xerxes' (4.87-88). The same term is used by others for designers of siege engines and ships. And then there is the question of city-planning. The involvement was undoubtedly an old one. In the founding of colonies abroad, architects probably went along with the civic and religious leaders of the mother city. Were they distinct at this stage from the *harpedonaptae*, or official surveyors? Most of the later planners of Greek cities were architects by profession. Dinokrates is a good example. The one exception is also the most prominent planner of Classical Greece, Hippodamus of Miletus. Aristotle, who tells us of him, is somewhat at a loss to characterize him. He comes out sounding like an eccentric political theoretician who became interested in city form through his concern with social organization, and ended up by inventing one of the most popular schemes of urban design, the checkerboard or grid. Actually he was not so much its inventor—it was in use as early as the seventh century B.C.—as the first person to write about it. He lived in Athens for a while, and replanned the irregular Piraeus on the new method. Tradition has it that he was also asked to draw up plans for the cities of Rhodes and Thurii in South Italy. Here is what Aristotle has to say about him.

Hippodamus, the son of Euryphon of Miletus, invented the partitioning of cities, and laid out Piraeus; in other aspects of his life, he was rather ostentatious in order to draw attention to himself, so much so in fact, that he seemed to some, what with his flowing hair and expensive jewelry and in addition the cheap but warm clothing that he kept on not only in the winter but during the warm parts of the year, to lead a very peculiar life. He aspired to excel in the whole of natural science, and was the first person not actually involved in politics to advance theories about the best form of government. He assigned his ideal city a population of ten thousand, which he divided into three classes—one of artisans, one of farmers, and the third those who would fight for the state in case of war and bear arms. The land too he divided into three parts: sacred, public and private; sacred land where the customary offerings to the gods could be made, public land that would sustain the military, and private land for farmers [*Politics* 2.5.1-2].

On the subject of the education of the Greek architect there is little to go by. Architecture was, on the whole, an upper-class occupation. Often the inspiration came from within the family, where the father or a brother might be practicing architects. In a number of recorded cases, it seems that the would-be architect started off in one of the arts or building crafts, in which he might continue even after the shift to architecture. Skill in carpentry was specifically looked for in the salaried state architects of cities like Athens and Delos. The architects of the temple of Hera at Samos, Theodoros and Rhoikos, both had experience in metalwork; they were credited in antiquity with the invention of the hollow casting method for bronze statues. There is some evidence for close professional ties between architecture and sculpture in architectural settings and on the buildings themselves. Skopas, the celebrated sculptor of the later fourth century B.C., designed the temple of Athena at Tegea. Polykleitos the younger, who is given credit for the elegant round structure, or *tholos*, at Epidauros, was almost certainly the same Polykleitos of Argos known, also in the fourth century, as a sculptor and bronze-worker. Perhaps the most exalted of Greek sculptors, Pheidias, was selected by Perikles to be the general director of all the work for the rebuilding of the Akropolis at Athens.

But there was also a theoretical side to the education of the architect. Though it did not approach the ideal curriculum set down by Vitruvius (see Chapter 2, pp. 38-39), the general education of the would-be architect was bound to include, as befitted a young Greek gentleman, exposure to one or more private instructors. He might also attend in the same vein a professional school of architecture, or rather atelier, run by a practicing architect. We have noted above that in the sixth century B.C. Theodoros of Samos had started just such a school in Sparta. And then there were books, headed by the monographs and treatises written by architects.

We must assume for the beginning architect some kind of apprenticeship alongside of a master. He might be set to overseeing construction or assigned a physical task suited to the practical knowledge he brought with him. In the accounts of Delphi for the years 343 to 340 B.C. there is record of a *hyparchitekton*, an assistant to the official architect of the sanctuary. At Delos, one Phaneas was employed, according to the documents, first as workman and later as architect. This particular case might indicate, however, the occasional man from the lower classes who may have entered the profession directly from building. Actually, architecture was never altogether distinct from building. Some architects clearly did contracting on the side. One instance is Kallikrates, one of the architects of the Parthenon, who contracted for the building of the Long Walls of Athens, a gigantic job.

When the architect came into his own, he was employed in one of several ways. He might receive a commission, independently or in association with other architects, for a major building in his city or outside it. Or he might be appointed to be the salaried architect of a city or one of the principal religious sites where work was constant. There were official state architects at Athens at least from the fourth century B.C. onward; they were elected rather than appointed by lot. Hellenistic cities usually had a regular building works department within the municipal administration. Its tasks included anything from the inscribing and erection of stelai to the maintenance of fortifications and engines of war.

The salary of an official architect was not high. Often it did not exceed what a skilled workman was paid. But of course as in all public offices, it was the civic honor as much as the profit that would be coveted. And the salaried architect was surely not restrained from accepting commissions on the side, or engaging in other gainful occupations such as contracting or sculpture. The top architects commanded high fees. "You could buy a craftsman for five or six *minae* [i.e., 500-600 drachmas]," Plato says, "but a first-class architect not for 10,000 drachmas." Apart from the implication that an architect could be bought as a slave, which must have been extremely rare, the passage is interesting in its distinction between the relative values of workmen and master architects, of whom "there is a scarcity throughout Greece" (*Erastae* 135C).

In the design of a public building such as a temple, the architect worked closely with a building commission. At religious centers like Delphi or Eleusis, the commission consisted of the temple overseers. Elsewhere, members were responsible citizens appointed by the state to supervise the creation of the building, from the initial stages of design to the final details of its execution. The commissioners (*epistatai*) were drawn from the business and political worlds and the professions. They were not required to have practical experience in architectural matters, except perhaps a cultured taste; what was expected of them was financial and administrative competence. An under-secretary, salaried like the architect, served as the commissioners' accountant, recording the labor and wages.

The commission was not, strictly speaking, the client. The decision to build was made by the city council or assembly, or a finance board in the case of a religious center. These governing bodies set the budget for the projected building, authorized the expenditure of funds, and appointed the building commission. The money came from special administrative appropriations and through public subscription. The cost of a new temple was considerable. It has been estimated that the Parthenon cost between 460 and 500 talents, exclusive of the gold and ivory statue of Athena by Pheidias, a cost whose magnitude can be appreciated if it is set against Athens' internal revenue for one year, about 400 talents.

The first task of the commission would be to collaborate with the architect on the business of procuring designs suitable to the aesthetic preferences of the day and in line with the allotted budget. If there was a salaried state architect, he would be *ex officio* a member of the commission. More often the architect was distinguished from the commission, which he served in the capacity of technical adviser in matters of form and construction. The design method was modular. Since each of the Orders had revered traditions and the basis of propriety was the alignment of the various elements of the building, the architect's habits tended to be conservative. Proportions of general length to width were largely determined by convention, and so was the relation of triglyphs and metopes in the Doric frieze, the lining up of these with the exterior colonnade, and so on. The principle, therefore, was akin to that of Egyptian design: the form came about not through an external standard of measurement, but in terms of some arbitrary unit derived from within the building itself—in the case of a Doric temple, for example, the width of the triglyph. Tradition then dictated how many of these units would determine the various dimensions of the building. The building was original or unusual to the extent that the architect manipulated these conventional relationships for some special effect that was to be achieved.

Once the design of the building had been agreed upon between the architect and the commission, together they would put out the work to contract. The practice was to assign the work piecemeal, rather than entrust the entire project to a general contractor. The sale of each contract began with a public announcement by the herald in the marketplace. The architect and the commission would then review the tenders and make the award to the best bidder. It was up to the architect to draw up detailed specifications for each job, and the contractor would thereafter be responsible for hiring the labor and buying the materials called for in his contract. Each contract was backed by a guarantor, appointed on the strength of his financial and social standing. Since there is no clear indication of profit, the guarantors seem to have participated in the process of putting up a public edifice as a form of civic service. There was some overlap among commissioners, contractors, and guarantors, and a measure of altruism would appear to have been a general motive.

The remaining task of the building commission was to administer the contracts and ensure the public accounting of the appropriated funds. For a limited number of special purposes the commission would procure commodities directly, without contract (glue, ivory, iron for clamps and dowels, timber for scaffolding, pulley wheels, etc.), and would also hire labor independently, on the basis of day work, including painters, tile-layers, and letter-cutters. Sawyers working on the parts of the ceiling and roof were paid either by the day or by the foot. Sculpture was commissioned by the piece, and paid for according to some standard rate. This applied to friezes, where the unit was one of length, as well as to attachable figures of relief, such as those for the pediments, and free-standing statuary. For the white marble figures to be affixed to the blue-black limestone band of the Erechtheion frieze on the Akropolis, the going rate was sixty drachmas for the figure of an adult (about 26.5 inches tall) and thirty for that of a child, with some adjustment for unusual cases. It is unclear, although of definite interest for our understanding of the profession, whether the total scheme of sculptural decoration was supplied by the architect or by a different person engaged especially for the purpose.

The Erechtheion accounts show that citizens worked on the building side by side with metics (non-Athenian residents) and slaves. The slaves, most of them owned by citizens and metics in the same work force, were skilled and drew the same pay as their masters. They were employed only in two major trades, as masons and carpenters. Much of the work on the building would be done away from the site. Blocks were cut and shaped at the quarry, often some distance away from the client city. But the architect's engagement with the building process was continuous. He presided on the site, where the plot was leveled and readied and a workshop of modest materials, usually mud-brick over a rubble-stone base, was built for the masons and carvers. Here the blocks delivered by the individual contractors were trimmed down for proper fitting. The assembly of the hundreds of premade parts was the most exacting responsibility of the architect. The setting of the blocks in place, the jointing, the last touches of smoothing and finishing were all technical matters that demanded expert care and precision. A good deal of work had to be done on the building itself: the fluting of the columns, for example, the painting of the sculptural decoration, and the finish of the ceiling. In at least a supervisory sense, the architect led an army of craftsmen and specialists in the manufacture and grand assembly of the stones that made the gleaming marvels of the Greek landscape. Plutarch vividly recalls this huge and motley crew in his discussion of the building of the Akropolis:

The materials to be used were marble, bronze, ivory, gold, ebony and cypress wood; the craftsmen required to do the job and work such materials were carpenters, molders, bronze workers, masons, dyers, gilders, ivory carvers, painters, inlayers, turners; and the people who provided and transported the materials were merchants, sailors and pilots by sea; and on land, cartwrights and cattlemen and drivers, also ropemakers and weavers and leather-workers and roadmakers and quarrymen and miners. And since each craft had its own body of unskilled labor, practically every able-bodied man was employed [Chapter XII].

To orchestrate this prestigious enterprise toward a prior vision was no common task, and the architect who had been called to it would be right to feel proud of his profession. Yet there is not much praise for the architect in Greece. Despite the broad scope of professional practice, no Greek architect ever attained to the high position of an Imhotep or Senmut. The aspect of occult consultations that bonded the Egyptian state architect to the ruling class was missing from the straightforward world of Greece. There is a body of early legend that may imply a privileged status for the architect at one time, akin to the experience of Egypt. Trophonios, who designed the temple of Apollo at Delphi with his brother Agamedes, was believed to have been swallowed up by the earth and transformed into a god; his oracle was famous throughout Greece. But in historical times all mystery had vanished from the architect's profession. Its practitioners were not especially prone to be lionized by the public, perhaps because the product they were associated with had such mixed and confusing authorship. Painters and sculptors whose skill in relation to their product was direct found much wider admiration. For all that, the mark of men like Iktinos and Philon and the great planners and designers of the Hellenistic cities survives to this day, and points plainly to the subtlety and splendor of the built environment in the Greek centuries.

BIBLIOGRAPHICAL NOTES

I    Egypt
In spite of its recognized shortcomings, the best introduction to this subject is still E. Baldwin Smith, *Egyptian Architecture as Cultural Expression* (New York/London, 1938), especially Ch. X, "Egyptian Architects and Their Methods." But it should now be supplemented by A. Badawy, *Ancient Egyptian Architectural Design: A Study of the Harmonic System* (Berkeley/Los Angeles, 1965). Useful information is also contained in S. Giedion, *The Eternal Present, II: The Beginnings of Architecture* (New York, 1963).

On the career and legend of Imhotep, see J. B. Hurry, *Imhotep: the Vizier and Physician of King Zoser* (Oxford, 1926). The statue of Senmut illustrated here is discussed in J. Vandier, *Manuel d'archéologie égyptienne*, Vol. 3 (Paris, 1958), pp. 476-77.

For Egyptian architectural drawings, see A. Badawy, *Le Dessin architectural chez les anciens égyptiens* (Cairo, 1948).

For a Turin papyrus with the plan of the tomb of Ramesses IV, see H. Carter and A. Gardiner in *Journal of Egyptian Archaeology* 4 (1917), 130-58. See also N. de G. Davies, "An Architect's Plan for Thebes," in *Journal of Egyptian Archaeology* 4 (1917), 194-99.

For building materials and techniques in general, see A. Lucas, *Ancient Egyptian Materials and Industries*, 3rd ed. (London, 1948), pp. 61-98, and S. Clarke and R. Engelbach, *Ancient Egyptian Masonry* (London, 1930).

II    Greece
The documentary sources are conveniently collected in J. J. Pollitt, *The Art of Greece*, Sources and Documents in the History of Art series (Englewood Cliffs, N.J., 1965).

On the Greek architect in general, consult the following: A. L. Frothingham, "Greek Architects," *Architectural Record* 23 (1908), 81-96 (use cautiously); M. L. Clarke, "The Architects of Greece and Rome," *Architectural History* 6 (1963), 9-22; R. Scranton, "Greek Building," in *The Muses at Work*, Carl Roebuck, ed. (Cambridge, Mass., 1969), pp. 2-34.

The building process for the temple of Zeus at Olympia, the Parthenon at Athens, and the tomb of Mausolos at Halikarnassos is discussed by B. Ashmole, *Architect and Sculptor in Classical Greece* (New York, 1972). The situation of the sanctuary at Epidauros is analyzed in detail by A. Burford, *The Greek Temple Builders at Epidauros* (Toronto, 1969). For the buildings of the Akropolis at Athens, see also: A. Burford, "The Builders of the Parthenon," *Greece and Rome*, supplement to vol. X, 1963, 23-35; R. Carpenter, *The Architects of the Parthenon* (Harmondsworth, Eng., 1970); R. S. Stanier, "Cost of the Parthenon," *Journal of Hellenic Studies* 73, 1953, 68-76; G. P. Stevens et al., *The Erechtheum* (Cambridge, 1927), Ch. IV; R. H. Randall, Jr., "The Erectheum Workmen," *American Journal of Archeology* 57 (1953), 199-210.

J. A. Bundgaard's thesis is found in his book *Mnesicles: A Greek Architect at Work* (Copenhagen, 1957), where you will also find the texts and translations of the inscriptions for the porch at Eleusis and the arsenal of Piraeus. On this subject see also: R. Scranton, "Greek Architectural Inscriptions as Documents," *Harvard Library Bulletin* 14 (1960), 159-82. The question of architectural drawings in Greece is reviewed in a recent book, but with no important new theses: A. Petronotis, *Zum Problem der Bauzeichnungen bei den Griechen* (Athens, 1972).

For city-planners and city-planning, see J. B. Ward Perkins, *Cities of Ancient Greece and Italy* (New York, 1974), and F. Castagnoli, *Orthogonal Town Planning in Antiquity* (Cambridge, Mass., 1971).

# 2
## Roman Architects
WILLIAM L. MacDONALD

The remains of major buildings, standing and excavated, that can be seen and studied today in twenty-odd countries are the chief source of our knowledge of the profession of architecture in Roman times. Though very numerous, they are only a fraction of what once stood, the witnesses of professional work from a period of several centuries. And as a fully trained Roman architect was also expected to be expert in construction, hydraulic engineering, and surveying and planning, the profession was obviously a significant and influential one. For the Romans architecture, both functionally and symbolically, was the mistress art, and an architect was someone of consequence. Cicero ranks architecture with medicine and teaching (*De Off.*, 1.151); Vitruvius speaks of "so great a profession [*disciplina*] as this" (1.1.11).

Vitruvius—an architect met with on every side in the history of the art—might seem to hold the key to our subject in his writing. But, imbedded though his name and work are in the study and practice of architecture, this is not the case. The reasons are, first, that he wrote from a rather conservative point of view conceived within a particular theoretical framework, and, second, that he wrote before the profession had wrought some of its most significant triumphs. Indeed Roman architecture is to a considerable degree a post-Vitruvian phenomenon. This is not to say that Vitruvius' celebrated work, the *Ten Books on Architecture*, does not contain a great deal that is valuable. Quite the contrary—it is invaluable. It is the only treatise on architecture that has come down to us from antiquity.

Filled with information both practical and theoretical, it contains much historical material as well; most of this we would not otherwise have.

But Vitruvius wrote around 25 B.C., early in the reign of Augustus, the first Roman emperor, and well before the careers of the creative masters of the first and second centuries A.D., such as Severus, Rabirius, Apollodorus, and others—architects who built very different kinds of buildings from those Vitruvius knew. Self-made to a considerable degree, Vitruvius took pains to show his book-learning, and his work has, in the parts dealing with historical matters, the flavor of the library. His practical advice, his descriptions of materials and methods of building, give us our only view into the day-to-day world of a Roman architect, many of whose details and procedures would not have varied much in subsequent times. Still, in reading him, one finds no awareness of the originality and the prophetic qualities of buildings he could not have been ignorant of, such as the great Sanctuary of Fortune at Palestrina near Rome of about 100/ 80 B.C., or the Tabularium overlooking the Forum in Rome itself, of 78 B.C. Perhaps their very originality offended his traditional mind. In short, one should bear in mind *when* Vitruvius wrote and what his predilections were, while remaining aware of his influence on architecture through the Middle Ages and on into Renaissance and post-Renaissance times. Later architects and theoreticians had many difficulties with him because so much Roman architecture they could see was built after his time. Alberti, for example, sometimes found it difficult to equate what he read and studied so carefully in Vitruvius with what he saw still standing in and near Rome, and no wonder, for some aspects of Roman architecture changed radically after Vitruvius wrote, and most Roman architecture Alberti saw was of post-Vitruvian date.

There were other ancient writers on architecture before Vitruvius—we often know of them only because he mentions them in what has been called his "parading of hard-won knowledge"—but their treatises are lost. In antiquity after Vitruvius there was of course more writing on architecture, but only a little of this has survived—there are two shadowy late antique quasi-Vitruvian manuals, for example, by Faventinus and Palladius. Architects are mentioned now and again by Roman historians, poets, and biographers, but not in a number proportionate to the obvious size of the profession, a size we can infer from our modern knowledge of Roman architecture. These writers rarely speak of work in the sense of the use of the hands, of the products of craftsmen and artisans, and almost never of shop life. Their subjects were thought more elevated; architecture is not

Figure 6. Casts of architects' tomb inscriptions. Such inscriptions abound, testimony to the size of the profession and its practitioners' pride in it.

the only profession they overlook. Inscriptions naming architects, usually from their tombs, are fairly common (Figure 6), and once in a while a name can be gleaned from some other source. But these last-named simply produce lists, and tell us little else. Quantifying the data as to place, date (when known), names, and the like yields little or nothing of use because the data are both sporadic and insufficient.

And it is not common, even when an architect's name does appear from one or another source, to be able to attach it to an actual building sufficiently well preserved to allow of close analytical study, though luckily there are a few outstanding exceptions to this, as we will see. Because of this state of affairs a surprising number of very well known Roman buildings, for example the Colosseum, the Pantheon, and the Baths of Caracalla, go unattributed, though a good deal has been made by modern students of the possibility of attaching one of the rather few names we *do* have to great buildings here and there. Surely Roman patrons, commissions, and officials, ever orderly and methodical, kept careful records; but with rare and minor exceptions, such as those on fragments of papyri from Roman Egypt, these have perished.

Additional information about Roman architects and their work comes from other sources. For example, treatises have come down to us that deal with related subjects such as water supply and aqueducts, surveying, and aspects of mechanics, engineering, and mathematics. Drafting tools have been preserved, and field instruments are well understood. Some architectural models exist, and though they may often have been made not to show to a client but to be placed in an architect's tomb, or in the tomb of a person who had commissioned a temple or some other building, they seem to be quite good evidence for model-making. Architectural plans are also rare, but they do exist, though probably most are not working plans, which would have been made on ephemeral materials. What we have are either surveyors' plots, fragments of city plans (prepared not by planners but made as surveys of established localities; [Figure 7]), or, now and again, fragments of plans of buildings executed in mosaic or paint, perhaps also originally placed in tombs.

A mosaic plan preserved in the Capitoline Museum in Rome is very interesting (Figure 8). It is dimensioned, with the figures given in Roman numerals (the Roman foot was equal to 0.295 m., or about 11⅝ inches), the mosaicist having copied an architect's drawing. The plan is that of a bath building because of the shapes of the rooms and the fact that the pools or plunges (marked V feet in longitudinal depth at the ends of spaces VIII feet square) are shown in green tesserae. The fitting of curving rooms into a rectangular outline, brought to maturity by the great architect Severus in his palace in Rome for the emperor Nero, the famous Golden House, is common in imperial architecture in the second and third centuries A.D.

There are many famous, splendid Roman wall paintings and mosaics that depict architecture, both viable and fanciful, and though they need more study from the point of view of what they can tell us about architecture specifically, they clearly record aspects of architectural draftsmanship. There is a most useful example for study at the Metropolitan Museum of Art in New York City, where a room from Boscoreale, near Pompeii, is installed (Figure 9). There is in the Bardo Museum in Tunis a tomb mosaic of a late Roman architect and his assistants (Figure 10).

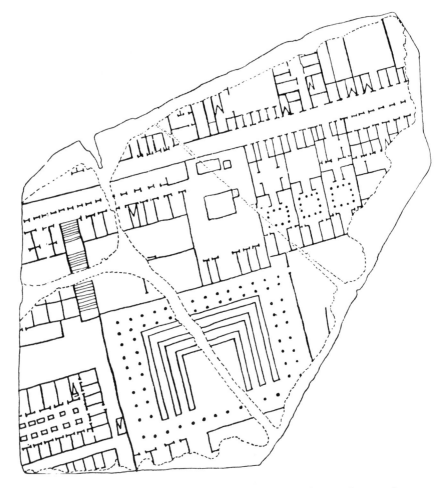

Figure 7. Fragment of a marble plan of Rome, ca. A.D. 200, showing houses, shops, and tenements. The original, mounted on a wall in the Forum of Vespasian, showed most of the city at a scale of about 1 : 300.

Formally dressed, the architect holds a five-foot measuring stick, and nearby are a square and a plumb bob and line—the insignia, so to speak, of his profession. His assistants flute a colonnette, make mortar, and bring a column to the job. And there are tomb paintings showing simple buildings under construction (Figure 11), and an occasional text mentioning work in progress.

Finally, with respect to our sources, there is the evidence of the build-

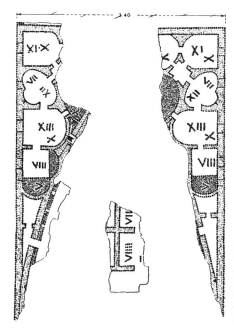

Figure 8. Fragment of a bath plan in mosaic. The dimensions of the rooms are given in Roman numerals, the bathing niches (V) are shown in green tesserae, and, the rather baroque character of the rooms notwithstanding, the plan is bilaterally symmetrical.

ings themselves. From about 200/150 B.C. onward we have fairly complete physical evidence for all major and many minor building types of Roman times, some of Greek provenance, others purely Roman. Numerous minor structures did not of course require architects, and there were builders and contractors who were prepared to carry out various commissions. But the sources we have just canvassed make it clear that major public and private buildings, scores of new towns and new city quarters, and the readily supplied public urban buildings of municipalities throughout the empire were usually the work of professional architects.

Who were these men? What were their origins, their training? For answers to these questions the evidence is rather thin. Cicero allows that the profession is suitable for persons of non-aristocratic standing (in theory members of the senatorial class could not engage in trade). Vitruvius was obviously a self-made man to a considerable degree; he apparently came from fairly humble origins, though it should be noted that his parents were able to give him a basic education. Many architects in the Roman world were ethnically Greek, or deeply influenced by Greek culture, but this does not mean that they designed buildings in a traditionally Greek manner by then long since become historical. The Roman administrator Pliny the Younger, writing from an eastern province to the emperor Tra-

Figure 9. Detail of a painted wall from the Boscoreale cubiculum in the Metropolitan Museum of Art in New York. Roman painters were fascinated by architecture and were masters of a cavalier but effective perspective.

Figure 10. Mosaic of an architect and his assistants, in the Bardo Museum, Tunis. The wreath should have enclosed an architect's name, either that of the standing figure or his master.

Figure 11. Wall painting from the tomb of Trebius Justus, Rome. The mason's pointed trowel is clearly visible; at the lower right a workman mixes mortar.

jan in Rome to ask for an architect to come out and evaluate some work where there had been a serious cost overrun, is told by the emperor that

> You cannot lack architects: every province has skilled men for this work. It is a mistake to think that they can be sent out more quickly from Rome when they usually come to us from Greece [Pliny the Younger, *Letters*, 10.40.3; ca. A.D. 110].

And Vitruvius' text is thick with Greek names; Latin ones appear less often. But not too much should be made of these apparent ethnic distinctions, which are partly due to Vitruvius' predilections. Greek artists and intellectuals served the empire well, and the imperial system, begun in the later first century B.C., tended increasingly as time passed to blur certain of the ancient distinctions between Greeks and Romans. In architecture this can be seen in the stylistic near-homogeneity of so many buildings East and West from Augustus' time onward, especially in the large typology of public buildings that appeared in every city and town ruled by Rome. In other words, baths of the second century A.D. in Athens were stylistically, structurally, and functionally like their counterparts in Rome itself, irrespective of the geographical or ethnic origins of their architects.

None of the aristocrats we know so well, either through their writings or through public careers that attracted great attention, were architects. But it is clear that the privileged usually knew something of the art and that some were much taken up with it. Many retained professionals permanently. One is reminded of the English aristocrats and gentlemen of a later time for whom architecture was part of a proper life. Thus architects were probably mostly from the lower social strata, and there is evidence to suggest that liberated slaves attained professional standing; this should be viewed in light of the fact that a slave might not only have very considerable authority in a city administrative office but could even be the head of one of the great bureaus of the imperial administrative machine.

There seem to have been three avenues to professional status: training first in the liberal arts and then through service with an established master, that is, a private career; training in the army, beginning with rudimentary engineering, construction, and experience with the artillery, and thence by steps to a senior engineer/architect post, with or without a practice later, in retirement; or an ascent through the graded levels of the imperial civil service. Only the last-named route, presumably, would have been open to slaves, and our precarious evidence seems to indicate that such men were liberated before they attained professional standing.

Vitruvius' career is really the only one we know much about. Most of the few great Roman architects whose names we know—and whose buildings we know something of—appear in the literature as acknowledged masters, and little or nothing is given about their training and previous careers; they caught attention because of some great palace, forum, or religious building they designed, or because they were close to an emperor whose story was being told. In Vitruvius' case his early education, for which he blesses his parents, obviously helped his public career. Public, because he was a military engineer for quite a while, either actually in the service, or as a partner in a successful contracting firm that made and maintained war engines (he names his associates, but without saying if they were all in the army together or formed a civilian firm). Eventually he got preferment, and directly from Augustus and his family. When, after 31 B.C., the world became more secure, he sat down to write, in a straightforward and well-organized if somewhat pedantic way, a systematic exposition of architecture and its rules, together with chapters on building techniques, water engineering, astrology, and the construction of a variety of machines and engines military and otherwise.

At first he says little about being, or having been, a practicing architect, but as he writes on he mentions a town hall, or basilica, that he built in the town of Fano in Italy, and it quickly becomes evident that he had had a great deal of experience with every aspect of design and construction. This extensive practical material is quite distinct in tone from his exposition of rules and theory, his rather touching and—luckily for us— careful record of his research, studded with the names of the authors of the past whose works he has read. The mixture of the two gives the *Ten Books* an attractive flavor. Vitruvius comes through as an honest, hard-working man, one who has succeeded at work he loves, has earned the favor of the emperor himself, and can say that now, as he writes, he is free from want for the rest of his life. It may be that aside from the circumstances of the preservation of his work, his later influence may be due in part to the kind of man he was. His effect on architecture, for good or bad (his attempt to fix the proportions of the Orders, and the effect of this on Renaissance and subsequent architects, may be an example of the latter) is all but incalculable. The unending influence of his contemporaries Virgil and Cicero comes to mind, and one can wonder what Vitruvius' story would have been like had he been a grand intellectual.

The degree to which his career and his attitudes were typical is hard to gauge. Probably his career was not atypical; probably there were many such self-made professionals, both before and after 25 B.C., of his stamp: competent, serious, at home with rules and set solutions, well versed in the traditions and methods of the shop and scaffold, but without the artistic and intellectual equipment of the great architect. Yet Vitruvius had no doubt about what an architect ought to know. His words are worth pondering:

only persons can justly claim to be architects who from boyhood have mounted by the steps of their studies and, being trained generally in the knowledge of arts and sciences, have reached the temple of architecture at the top [1.1.11]. The architect should be equipped with knowledge of many branches of study and varied kinds of learning, for it is by his judgment that all work done by the other arts is put to the test. This knowledge is the child of practice and theory. Practice is the continuous and regular exercise of employment where manual work is done with any necessary material according to the design of a drawing. Theory, on the other hand, is the ability to demonstrate and explain the productions of dexterity on the principles of proportion [1.1.1]. [An architect ought] to be both naturally gifted and amenable to instruction. Neither natural ability without instruction nor instruction without natural ability can make the perfect artist. Let him be educated, skillful with the pencil, instructed in geometry, know much history, have followed the philosophers with attention, understand music, have some knowledge of medicine, know the opinions of the jurists, and be acquainted with astronomy and the theory of the heavens [1.1.3].

The last sentence has provoked skepticism and even ridicule, though in his succeeding paragraphs Vitruvius makes a good practical case for the education he specifies, detailing his reasons and giving examples of the need for such broad knowledge. Furthermore, it has been shown that the whole burden of his work was to demonstrate that architecture was one of the Liberal Arts, with its own perimeters and governing definitions; that he saw architecture "as the whole artificial environment of man" (F. E. Brown). As practitioners of one of the Liberal Arts, architects had to be well and properly educated, and Vitruvius explains how this education would help those possessing it reach the desired goal of an architecture at once pleasing, functional, and safe. He saw a truly Roman order in his subject. Architecture was a necessary and fitting part of that peaceful rule his great patron had achieved and that had helped make his research and composition possible. For him, architecture was indissolubly a part of the "immense majesty of the Roman peace."

Now and then, in subsequent times, we have a glimpse of a sort of Vitruvian polymathy among Roman architects. Nero's audacious team of specialists, Severus and Celer, designed and built a palace, the Domus Aurea (late A.D. 60s) in Rome in a radically new style. They also began at the young emperor's instance a stupendous canal through low-lying land stretching far northwest of Naples, and it is likely that they laid out new parts of the capital after a truly disastrous fire that occurred the summer of A.D. 64. In one historical text there is an abbreviated version of a new building code published by the government after the fire, and though it is not certain that Severus and Celer were directly involved in its formulation, it does represent a kind of urban architectural thinking clearly in harmony with the design and construction of their extant work. And in the early second century A.D. the great master Apollodorus, architect-in-chief to the emperor Trajan, was a renowned engineer, a vitally creative designer equally at home in traditional or modern design, and very possibly a sculptor of the highest rank as well.

Something of the Roman architect's duties and methods of work can be pieced together from various sources, including those described above. Vitruvius writes briefly of what was done in the drafting room:

The ways of setting things out [*species dispositionis*] are these: plan [*ichno-graphia*], elevation [*orthographia*], and perspective [*scaenographia*]. A plan is made by the proper use of compass and rule, through which the proper out-lines are set for the building. An elevation is the image of a standing facade, properly drawn to show the finished appearance. Perspective is the method of drawing the façade together with the retreating sides, the lines all meeting at the center of a circle [1.2.2].

In another place we glimpse office work again:

An architect must be a man of letters that he may keep a record of useful works. By his drafting skill he will readily be able to make shaded drawings to represent the effect desired . . . by arithmetic the total cost of a building is summed up and measurements are computed; but the difficult problems of design are solved by geometrical rules and methods [1.1.4].

In the same section he says that

Geometry, also, furnishes much assistance to architecture. It teaches the use of rule and compass, and thus facilitates the laying-out of buildings on their sites by the use of set-squares, levels, and plumb lines.

Another ancient writer refers to "the suitable method of drawing images of buildings" (Heron of Alexandria). Much of this work was based on Greek experience, and in particular upon the development of graphic methods of expounding Greek studies in geometry, which in turn had cer-tain roots in very ancient practices in the Near East. It is clear that dimen-sioned plans and elevations, perspective drawings, shaded and colored renderings for the client, and, probably, models, were all in common use. Of course most of them, if not indeed all, would have to be. Major Ro-man building projects could not have been approved of or built without them. Minor dimensioning was probably done on the site, for it seems unlikely that detailed working drawings were made. One cannot be sure, however.

Roman craftsmen and workmen were organized into groups according to their specialties. The sources for this aspect of building and construc-tion are good and have been quite thoroughly studied. Associations of men of the same trade probably began as social clubs whose purposes in-cluded mutual assurance of a proper funeral and care of the deceased craftsman's family. As the influence of the state spread and deepened, these organizations became larger and were increasingly brought under government control. They apparently became subject to government as-signment, at least for major projects in big cities, and they were one of the chief instruments of an imperial architect's will. Most of the specialties connected with building had a *collegium*, as such an association was called: blacksmiths and ironworkers, potters and brick-makers, carpenters, stone-sawyers, and the like. There was a *collegium* of general construction workers, and one of demolition experts. The mosaicists, fashioners of stucco, bronze-workers, and other craftsmen were similarly organized. This orderly division of workmen facilitated the planning and construction of the immense projects the Romans so frequently undertook.

The supply of materials, both raw and finished, seems also to have been arranged in an orderly fashion. This is certain in the case of the great brickyards and with regard to certain marble quarries and marble shippers; for the latter the government had the ready example of the state-operated mines, which had a long history. Bricks were made in standard sizes, at least in and near Rome, where for three centuries and more they were used by the millions. Standard bricks were what we would call large tiles, one or two feet square, and a variety of other terra-cotta building parts were made to more or less consistent dimensions. For a century or two a proportion of the bricks made at Rome were stamped with the names (much abbreviated) of the reigning consuls and the name of the brick-yard and the master potter in charge (Figure 12). Since the dates of the consuls are known, these stamped bricks can be of considerable help in dating buildings in which they are found. The full style, in this case from a brick made about A.D. 204, is as follows:

Brick from the estates of His Excellency C. Fulvis Plautianus, Prefect of the Praetorian Guard, twice consul, from the Terentian Brickyard; made by L. Aelius Phidelis [OP DOL EX PR C FULV PLAUT PR PR C V CO II FIG TER A L AEL PHIDEL].

Brickyards could be owned by members of the senatorial class because brick-making was classed not as a trade but as a traditional branch of agriculture.

Marble quarrying, dressing, shipping, and finishing was also a very large industry in Roman times, and the supply of at least some of the more exotic stones—Egyptian porphyry, for example—was in government hands. But of course much of the actual structure of Roman imperial buildings at Rome and in its environs was for a long time chiefly of concrete, which was also often used in the provinces. Brick-faced concrete of great durability was the structural material of the triumphs of Roman interior space-making from the first century A.D. onward. Because of its use, the artists who would have made, say, the marble capitals and entablatures of a

Figure 12. Casts of Roman brickstamps of the first and second centuries A.D. The much-abbreviated Latin of these stamps frequently helps in dating buildings; perhaps they were connected in some way with inventory or taxation.

classical temple were bypassed as far as bearing structure was concerned, and this brought the architect into more direct control of the overall effect of the finished building than he had been when designing a traditional building composed, both visually and structurally, of the Orders. The latter continued to be used, and regularly, but in vaulted-style buildings they were frequently non-structural, and took on new, non-traditional, visual and symbolic roles.

Roman workmen are described by the poet Statius, writing in the late first century A.D. of a trunk road to Naples which he saw under construction in the Volturno marshes:

The first work was to prepare furrows and mark out the borders of the road, and to hollow out the ground in a deep excavation; then to fill that up with other material, and to make foundations ready for the road's arched, bridge-like surface, lest the soil give way and a treacherous bed provide an unstable base for the heavily loaded stones; then to bind it with blocks, set close on either side, and with frequent wedges. How many gangs are at work together! Some cut down the forest and strip the mountain sides, some shape beams and boulders with iron tools; others [cement] the stones together . . . others work to dry up the pools and [dig canals] to lead the minor streams far away. These men could cut the Athos peninsula . . . [*Silvae*, 4.3.40-58].

Such well-organized gangs were crucial to success in making large vaulted buildings of concrete. The timing of pouring, the traffic on the ladders and scaffolds, the orderly progression of brick-laying, and the proper availability of the right materials at the right time and place all had to be regulated by the architect, who by the first century A.D. had to be an administrator to a greater degree than previously.

For post-Vitruvian times we have no text that describes an architect actually at work, but we do have a detailed description of the staff, equipment, organization, and aqueducts in the charge of the Water Department of Rome, written by Sextus Julius Frontinus about A.D. 100. Frontinus had been consul, and governor of Britain, and was the author of books on military tactics and surveying. He was one of those men who made the empire work, and obviously one with the kind of education Vitruvius had prescribed. In fact he mentions Vitruvius, saying that Vitruvius, "the architect," had been active in the field of hydraulic technology. Frontinus seems to have been called out of retirement by the emperor Trajan to take on his new, and very serious, responsibilities. His description of his office and staff suggests something of the kind of assistance, and the orderly staffing, available to a great state architect in the noontime of the empire.

There were, in the *statio aquarum* or Water Commissioner's Office, in addition ·to the *curator*, Frontinus himself, twenty-odd categories of administrators and specialists. There were assistant directors, architects, engineers, and a flock of secretaries and clerks. There were gangs of slaves publicly owned. Measurers, levelers, pipe-makers, plumbers, keepers of reservoirs, and inspectors appear. The men who re-paved streets disrupted during the laying or repairing of water mains are mentioned, and even the workmen who chipped and pulverized terra-cotta for use in waterproof cement. This is the kind of division of labor typical of Roman times, the sort of organization that would have executed the projects of a major architect. A text of the eighth or ninth century which says that the sixth-century church of Hagia Sophia in Constantinople was constructed by ten thousand workmen divided into hundreds, with each hundred captained by an experienced builder (master), describes the legacy of the Roman tradition of orderly, almost paramilitary, organization of workers and craftsmen. The text adds that fifty master craftsmen with their people were building the right-hand side, and the other fifty were likewise building the left-hand side, so that the work would proceed quickly, in competition and haste [*Narratio de S. Sophia*, 7; ed. Th. Preger, *Script. orig. Const.* (Leipzig, 1901), 82].

Thus Roman order.

The designation "architect" embraced a number of specialties, and a Roman town, or private client, could have asked an architect for surveying work, many kinds of hydraulic engineering—dams, ports, jetties, reservoirs, and the like, in addition to the securing of a water supply—and for town-planning as well. There were specialists in all of these fields, but architects quite normally included them in their practice. Often this would have been the result of military service, in which legionary architects were re-sponsible for a wide range of activities: laying out camps, designing mili-tary buildings, many engineering matters, and even the planning of whole towns, as for example Thamugadi, now Timgad, in Algeria, built for the Third Augustan Legion about A.D. 100 (Figure 13).

After Vitruvius' time we have the names of Severus, Nero's architect, spoken of above, and of Rabirius, probably somewhat younger, who built for the emperor Domitian the palace of the Caesars on the Palatine Hill in Rome in the 80s and 90s of the first century A.D. The texts, and the extant buildings, are rather more comprehensive for the former, though in neither case do we begin to have the information we would wish, given the remarkable talent clearly evident in the remains of the relevant build-ings of Nero and Domitian. Severus and Rabirius have to stand for all the other architects working in and near Rome in the first century. Of those in the provinces we know next to nothing.

Because of this scarcity, the name and career of Apollodorus stand out strongly. We probably know more about him than about any architect between Vitruvius and Brunelleschi, unless perhaps the detailed, exact data now being given us about the Hagia Sophia in Constantinople re-veals, when taken with his mathematical writings, more about Anthemius, who is discussed below. Our information about Apollodorus is of a dif-ferent order, in any event.

He is said to have come from Damascus in Syria, and this has been made the basis of a good deal of profitless speculation, running along the lines of how he brought Hellenistic architectural ideas to Rome, how his provenance proves the ascendancy of Greek art in the High Empire, and the like. But names alone, in the study of Roman art, mean nothing; it is

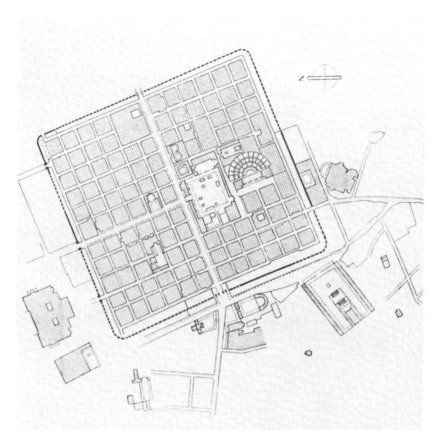

Figure 13. Plan of Timgad in Algeria. Typical of the right-angled or orthogonal Roman plan, presumably of military origin, Timgad also displays the entire building repertory of the Roman civil architect.

only the works of art themselves that count. And by Trajan's time (A.D. 98-117) no Greek architecture was being built, in the sense of the principles of the fifth and fourth centuries B.C. Hellenistic architecture, the style of the third and second centuries B.C. in the Greek-speaking east, had become an ingredient in the Roman imperial style, major or minor according to place and patron, and had already been fully adapted by the Romans by Vitruvius' time, as the *Ten Books* clearly show. So Apollodorus, who rose to be Trajan's chief architect and engineer, and whose name continued to be known for at least four hundred years by educated men, was not in respect of his designs a *Greek* architect. He may have

Figure 14. Trajanic bridge, Alcántara, Spain. The larger arches have a span of 110 feet and the bridge rises 210 feet above the river; though somewhat restored, the major part of the original massive granite construction has survived.

been a Greek by birth or by education and culture, but he was a *Roman* architect, as at least one, and perhaps two, of his great buildings show beyond any doubt. He did design in what can be called the Hellenistic-Imperial manner, it is true, but the very fact that he was equally at home in the vaulted, space-shaping manner of Severus and Rabirius and the more traditional modes of his homeland simply emphasizes that he was a Roman architect, one who exhibited in his person and his work that synthesis of Greek and Roman culture that *was* the Roman Empire. He knew Hadrian, an intellectual kinsman of Trajan's and that emperor's eventual successor, and though the two men apparently did not get along it is worth noting that Hadrian of all the Roman rulers after Nero was the most philhellenic.

Apollodorus was born probably not before A.D. 50, for he was alive in the 120s. He was certainly in Rome about 105/110, when the palace built by Rabirius and the huge Flavian Amphitheatre (the "Colosseum"), were quite new. A few years before that he had built a celebrated bridge over the Danube to facilitate Trajan's conquest of Dacia (roughly modern Romania); he wrote a pamphlet or book about it that has not survived. However Dio Cassius, a senator and historian who wrote early in the following century, bothered to notice it (the attribution to Apollodorus, correct beyond doubt, is found in another text):

Trajan constructed over the Ister [the Danube] a stone bridge for which I cannot sufficiently admire him. Brilliant indeed as are his other achievements, this surpasses them. For it has twenty piers of squared stone one hundred and fifty feet in height above the foundations and sixty feet in width, and these, standing at a distance of one hundred and seventy feet from one another, are connected by arches. . . . Yet the very fact that the river in its descent is contracted from a great flood to such a narrow channel, after which it again expands into a greater flood, makes it all the more violent and deep, and this feature must be considered in estimating the difficulty of constructing the bridge. This too, then, is one of the achievements that show the magnitude of Trajan's designs. . . . [*History*, 68.13].

The Trajanic bridge at Alcántara in western Spain, built in A.D. 105 by Caius Julius Lacer, though smaller is well preserved, and gives a sense of Apollodorus' accomplishment (Figure 14). The arches of the Danube bridge, however, were of wood, as the abbreviated version of it on Trajan's Column in Rome makes clear (Figure 15; Figure 16 is a model of one of the spans).

In Rome Apollodorus built Trajan's Forum (Figure 17); with its im-

Figure 15. Apollodorus' Danube bridge as seen on the Column of Trajan, Rome. The artist has shown only a part of the structure, whose stone piers and complex wooden superstructure are quite clearly recorded.

mense wooden-roofed basilica, the Ulpia (after Trajan's family name), as well probably as the still-visible vaulted Markets of brick-faced concrete beyond. He also designed and built an odeion or concert hall, which has disappeared entirely, and the huge Baths whose fragmentary remains can still be seen on the Oppian Hill above the Flavian Amphitheatre. The passage in Dio Cassius that records these data contains much useful additional information. The version that has come down to us is in a condensation of Dio's text prepared in the eleventh century in Constantinople, and presumably the Byzantine monk who made it selected stories he thought would most interest his contemporaries. Certainly the anecdote in question is a striking one. Dio, who disliked Hadrian, set out to reduce his reputation even though the emperor had been dead nearly a century. He alludes to Hadrian's supposed ruthlessness and then says:

But he first banished and later put to death Apollodorus, the architect who had built the various creations of Trajan in Rome—the Forum, the concert hall, and the baths. The reason assigned was that he had been guilty of some misdemeanor; but the real reason was that once when Trajan was consulting him on some point about the buildings he had said to Hadrian, who had interrupted with some remark: "Be off, and draw your pumpkins. You don't understand any of these matters"—it happened that Hadrian at the time was pluming himself on some such drawing. When he became Emperor, therefore, he remembered this exchange and could not endure the man's freedom of speech. He sent him the drawings of his Temple of Venus and Rome by way of showing him that a great work could be accomplished without his aid, and asked Apollodorus if the proposed structure was satisfactory. The architect stated in his reply first, in regard to the temple, that it ought to have been built on high ground and that the earth should have been excavated beside it, so that it might have stood out more conspicuously on the Sacred Way from a higher position, and might also have accommodated the [stage] machines in the basement, so that they could be put together unobserved and then brought into the theatre [that is, the Flavian Amphitheatre hard by]

Figure 16. Model of a portion of Apollodorus' Danube bridge in the Museo della civiltà romana, EUR, Rome. The timberwork suggests the abilities of Roman carpenters, whose work was essential in carrying out their architects' designs, especially those for grand vaulted spaces.

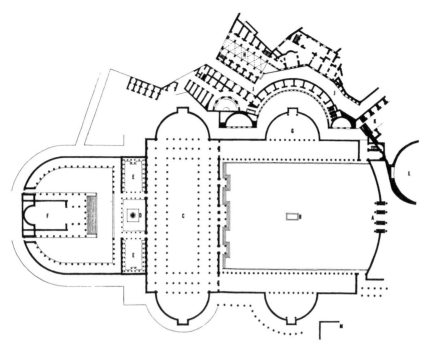

Figure 17. Plan of Trajan's Forum, Basilica, and Markets, by Apollodorus. The apogee of Roman monumental civic design, encompassing both symmetrical, classicizing principles (the Forum and its adjacent Basilica) and asymmetrical, vaulted, concrete space-making (the Markets, at the top of the plan).

without anyone being aware of them beforehand. Secondly, in regard to the temple's statues, he said that they had been made too tall for the inner chambers. "For now," he said, "if the goddesses wish to get up and go out, they will be unable to do so." When he wrote this so bluntly to Hadrian, the emperor was both vexed and exceedingly grieved because he had fallen into a mistake that could not be righted, and he restrained neither his anger nor his grief, but slew the man . . . [History, 69.4].

Now the frame of the story—Hadrian's execution of Apollodorus—is almost certainly a calumny, the result of Dio's bias. But within that frame the whole passage has the ring of truth, even the remark about pumpkins, as will be seen. The architectural facts are perfectly circumstantial, and fit properly with present-day knowledge gained from studying the buildings and other sources. It can be shown that the meeting took place about A.D. 104, when both the gigantic Forum and the Baths were just begun in Rome, or about to be begun. The passage gives, together with the others

about the Danube bridge, the only works of which we are certain Apollodorus was the architect; his name, like that of Rabirius before him, has
been attached to a dozen or more additional buildings by modern writers.
In what might be called social terms, the scene is at first glance rather exceptional: the emperor is consulting an architect; the emperor, the architect, and Hadrian (a man of the highest rank) are meeting on a quite
equal footing; and the architect makes free with Hadrian and treats him
almost more as an inferior than as an equal. When one realizes how accessible Trajan was, and that the better Roman emperors really did run
the Roman Empire and took their responsibilities with the gravest sincerity, then it becomes apparent that such a consultation would be quite normal. Thus the text makes it clear that Apollodorus moved easily in the
very highest circles.

We are not told what Hadrian said when he interrupted the consultation, but obviously it did not sit at all well with Apollodorus. Perhaps it
was a display of knowledge that put the architect off, or tactless criticism.
In any event Apollodorus let himself go even though he was in the presence of the emperor himself. Often it has been thought that the "pumpkins" referred to some still-life or other that Hadrian had drawn. But recently a most attractive suggestion has been put forward: that Apollodorus
was referring to drawings of domical vaults of pumpkin-like shape; that is,
of gored and undulating surfaces of a kind that are still to be seen in the
remains of a half-dozen Hadrianic buildings—in Rome, at Baiae near Naples, and above all at Hadrian's great villa near Tivoli outside Rome. In
any event, the passage confirms the exalted rank of the architect-in-chief.
More importantly, it certifies that Apollodorus designed Trajan's Baths in
Rome, enough of which remain to show that he was responsible for the
definitive version of a building type that was to be built far and wide
and that was to have an enormous influence on the future course of
architecture.

The inspection by Apollodorus of Hadrian's drawings for the immense
Temple of Venus and Rome also emphasizes the architect's standing, no
matter whether Hadrian's intentions were truly professional, or were just
a way of boasting to Apollodorus. It has often been pointed out that at
least one of the architect's suggestions was taken up, for the Temple rests
on a high vaulted platform of poured concrete, the chambers of which
open toward the Flavian Amphitheatre across the way. As for the sizes of
the statues, nothing is known. The temple design is unusual in its proportions and in the dispositions of its parts. It was all Hadrian's design, and

is a major part of the clear proof of his deep commitment to architecture. He was an architect beyond doubt—talented, very knowledgeable, and able to build whatever he wished.

It must have happened often, this intimate association of the most senior people with the best architects. The Romans were forever building, and often on an immense scale. They built new cities, and added to and refurbished older ones, as a continuing policy. Apollodorus can stand for those members of the profession who made the cities and towns of the empire look as they did, and who enriched Mediterranean and European architecture not only with new building types but with fresh and original uses of the vocabulary of design they had inherited from earlier times. Apollodorus, like Frontinus, comes through to us as a creative civil servant, a man whose career was made possible above all by his own talents as an artist and his abilities as an engineer and administrator, but also to a degree by that curious quasi-democracy of the high imperial system, wherein men could rise, almost irrespective of their origins, through ability even to a place beside the throne itself.

It is not known when Apollodorus died. The Temple of Venus and Rome was begun sometime in the mid 120s, and he was certainly alive just before then. At some point Hadrian moved a colossal statue of Nero, keeping it upright, with the aid of a certain architect named Decrianus, but he remains a shadow. Twenty-four elephants were used for the work, and it sounds like the kind of project Apollodorus would have welcomed. He is not mentioned, however, and it may be that the work was put in hand after his time.

In the Late Empire (the third and fourth centuries A.D.) the profession continued to flourish; the quality and number of major monuments from this period make that clear. There was a shortage of architects in some areas in the time of Constantine the Great (A.D. 306-37), due probably to the numbers needed to design and oversee the building of his extensive new capital, Constantinople, on the site of ancient Byzantium by the Bosphorus. In an edict posted at Carthage in A.D. 334 Constantine addressed his chief financial officer, the Praetorian Prefect Felix, as follows:

There is need of as many architects as possible, but since there are none of them, Your Excellency shall encourage to this study those men in the African provinces who are about eighteen years of age and who have had a taste of the liberal arts. In order to make this attractive to them, it is Our will that they themselves as well as their parents shall be immune from those services that are wont to be imposed on individuals, and that a suitable salary shall be appointed for the students themselves [the *Theodosian Code*, 13.4.1, trans. C. Pharr (Princeton, 1952)].

In the next entry, 13.4.2, of A.D. 337, architects and almost all artisans and workmen concerned with building and decoration are exempted from all public services, in order to have more time to improve their proficiency and to train their sons. A later Roman emperor had few more welcome gifts to bestow on his subjects than to remit their obligations to the state and to their towns, not just their taxes proper but the even more onerous and expensive obligatory public offices and duties, or "services," that they were required to fill and furnish. To include architecture students' parents in these exemptions, and to add scholarships as well, would seem to indicate that the shortage was acute indeed. The prerequisite of "a taste of the liberal arts" recalls Vitruvius.

It is in this century, the fourth, that Faventinus and Palladius, those shadowy followers of Vitruvius mentioned earlier, belong. In their handbooks the elaborate rules for the proportioning of the Orders have gone, but something of the practical flavor remains. Much is made of materials, and a good deal of the supply and purity of water. A few minor new matters are brought up, but these late antique architectural writers are not of great importance; their short treatises contain nothing theoretical or analytical. On the other hand they do demonstrate the persistence of architectural literature, the long reach of Vitruvius' *Ten Books*, and the continuing need for manuals in the current idiom, suited to the requirements of the landowner and the builder. Little, however, of Vitruvian pride appears, though some of his antiquarian learning survives.

The profession, as far as can be ascertained, did not change substantially with the advent of Christianity as one of the legal religions in the Roman Empire early in the fourth century. The direct influence of the monarch upon major building programs was as strong as ever; perhaps stronger, given the zeal of the Christian Roman emperors for building grand churches. Consider Constantine's instructions to Macarius, Bishop of Jerusalem, in the matter of the design and construction of the Holy Sepulchre there:

It befits, therefore, Your Sagacity to make such arrangements and such provision of every necessary thing, that not only shall this basilica be the finest in the world, but that everything else, too, shall be surpassed by it. As regards the construction and decoration of the walls, know that we have entrusted that to the care of Our friend Dracilianus, deputy to the Praetorian Prefects, and to the governor of the province; for they have been instructed by My Piety to furnish forthwith by their providence both artificers and workmen and everything else that is necessary for the building after consulting with Your Sagacity. Concerning the columns and marbles of whatever kind you consider to be most precious and serviceable, please inform Us in writing after an estimate has been made, so that We may learn from your letter what quantity and kind are needed, and that these may be conveyed from every quarter: for it is fitting that the most wondrous place in the world should be adorned according to its worth. As for the vault of the basilica, I wish to know whether in your opinion it should be coffered, or finished in some other fashion; for if it is to be coffered, it may also be adorned with gold. It remains for Your Holiness to inform with all speed the aforementioned magistrates how many workmen and artificers and what expenditure of money are needful, and to report to Me directly not only concerning the marbles and columns, but also concerning the coffering, if you should consider the latter to be preferable [letter of about A.D. 328, quoted by Eusebius in his *Life of Constantine*, 3.31-32].

Another source gives the architect's name as Zenobius; he seems to have been assisted by an ecclesiastical architect sent to Jerusalem from Constantinople, one Eustathius. They were able to depend, in planning for a major project such as this, on the cooperation of the bureaucracy, directed from the palace itself, and on receiving columns and marbles "conveyed from every quarter."

The last architect in the imperial tradition we shall discuss is in many ways the most interesting: Anthemius, from Tralles in western Asia Minor, the designer of the Great Church in Constantinople, the Hagia Sophia or Holy Wisdom (Figure 18). He is mentioned in some detail by several contemporary writers, and he enjoyed a considerable reputation in his day and subsequently. His family was distinguished. His father Stephanus was a physician of note, as were his brothers Dioscorus and Alexander. A third brother, Olympius, was a lawyer who may have practiced in Rome, and another, Metrodorus, was a student of literature. Anthemius was an architect, engineer, geometrician, and physicist; he may have studied in Alexandria, which in many ways was the intellectual center of the later Roman world. He died probably about A.D. 535 or 540.

Some of Anthemius' writings on mathematics have survived, and they were known to medieval mathematicians both Arab and western. He was very advanced in his knowledge of the properties of cones and parabolas, and apparently was the first to describe the construction of an ellipse by means of a string looped around two fixed points. He studied mirrors closely, and a fragment of his quite sophisticated work on the subject sur-

Figure 18. Hagia Sophia, interior. In some ways an architecture of perforated shells, the building is by any test one of the grandest and yet most subtle of architectural creations, and in great part a triumphant end-product of centuries of Roman architecture.

vives; it was given wide currency in modern times by publication in France in 1777 and has since been studied in print more than once. He belongs in the front rank of those who studied, interpreted, and built upon the works of Euclid and the other great theoreticians of geometry and mathematics from an earlier age.

Another side of Anthemius' character is provided by a writer of Justinian's time (A.D. 527-65), who tells several anecdotes about him. At Constantinople a certain Zeno, a successful orator, incurred Anthemius' wrath when he worsted Anthemius in litigation. The architect then secretly gained access to Zeno's cellars and built under his floor a steam-pressure device that shook the building. Zeno fled, fearing an earthquake. Anthemius further harassed him, and Zeno managed to bring his persecutor before Justinian himself. The emperor is supposed to have said that he could not stay the force of Zeus, who made thunder, or Poseidon, who made earthquakes. Another writer makes it clear that Anthemius, though enormously skillful, was also considered somewhat crafty.

Procopius, a court historian and civil servant, describes at length the construction and qualities of the Hagia Sophia, which was begun in 532 and dedicated in 537. The passage begins thus:

The Emperor, disregarding all questions of expense, eagerly pressed on to begin the work of construction, and began to gather all the artisans from the whole world. And Anthemius of Tralles, the most learned man in the skilled craft which is known as the art of building, not only of all his contemporaries, but also when compared with those who had lived long before him, ministered to the Emperor's enthusiasm, duly regulating the tasks of the various artisans, and preparing in advance designs of the future construction. Associated with him was another master-builder, Isidorus by name, born in Miletus, a man who was intelligent and worthy to assist the Emperor Justinian. Indeed this also was an indication of the honor in which God held the Emperor, that He had already provided the men who would be most serviceable to him in the tasks which were waiting to be carried out. And one might with good reason marvel at the discernment of the Emperor himself, in that out of the whole world he was able to select the men who were most suitable for the most important of his enterprises [*Buildings*, 1.1.23-26].

The Hagia Sophia, which in Procopius' words "exults in an indescribable beauty," is admitted on all sides to be one of the great creations of architecture. Isidorus seems to have been to Anthemius rather as Celer had been to Severus, more of an expert on building methods and materials than a designer; his nephew, Isidorus the Younger, rebuilt the great central dome of the church, raising it higher and making it more stable, when

Anthemius' daring original creation fell in 558. Curiously, some modern writers have denied that Anthemius was truly an architect. He has even been called a sort of amateur, a description impossible to credit upon viewing the great building itself. That he was sometimes daring beyond his resources may be true, though we do not really know the reason for the collapse of his central superstructure—there are several possible causes that would have been beyond Anthemius' control. And it may well be that he designed other buildings in Constantinople—SS. Sergius and Bacchus, for example—a possibility which would if true suggest strongly that in addition to being a mathematician and a physicist he was also a *practicing* architect. But the proof of his genius and his professionalism is secured by the colored shells of light and space that he created at the Hagia Sophia, whose superstructure Procopius found "not to rest on solid masonry, but to cover the space with its golden dome suspended from Heaven" (*Buildings*, 1.1.46).

Other architects' names appear in Procopius' writings—Evaris, John, and Theodorus—but no details are given about them. As in earlier periods, we have information only about the major figures of the time, architects whose careers must stand for those of their nameless contemporaries. It is important to point out that the great figures, about whom we do have some knowledge, are also those whose buildings unequivocably record the originality of their talent: Severus and the Golden House of Nero; Rabirius and Domitian's Palace; Apollodorus and Trajan's Baths, Forum, and Markets; Anthemius and Justinian's Hagia Sophia. They were not only great artists, but members of a proud profession. Their works, standing for centuries, outlasted their culture, until in much later times they became in their several ways sources of new inspiration and rediscovered knowledge.

BIBLIOGRAPHICAL NOTES

The ancient writers—Pliny, Frontinus, Dio, Procopius, and so on—are collected in the numerous uniform volumes of the Loeb Classical Library, where the original Latin or Greek texts and English translations are given together. Vitruvius appears there also, but there is a better English translation by M. H. Morgan, without the original Latin (Cambridge, Mass., 1914, and reprinted New York, 1960); however, because of the advances made in the study of Roman architecture in the last sixty years, some of Morgan's interpretations need revision (see for example *Art Bulletin* 33 [1951], 136). For Vitruvius see also A. Choisy, *Vitruve*, 4 vols. (Paris, 1909); A. Boëthius, "Vitruvius and the Roman Architecture of His Age," *Dragma: M. P. Nilsson . . . dedicatum* (Lund, 1939), 114-43; F. E. Brown, "Vitruvius and the Liberal Art of Architecture," *Bucknell Review* 11 (1963), 99-107; K. J. Conant, "The After-Life of Vitruvius in the Middle Ages," *Journal of the Society of Architectural Historians* 27 (1968), 33-38; P. Frankl, *The Gothic* (Princeton, 1960), pp. 86-105 and 890 (Vitruvius and Gothic architecture); and R. Wittkower, *The Architecture of Humanism*, 3rd ed. (London, 1962), references on p. 173 (Vitruvius and Renaissance architecture).

For Frontinus see also C. Herschel, *The Two Books on the Water Supply of the City of Rome . . .*, 2nd ed. (New York, 1913), and O. A. W. Dilke, cited below, pp. 227 and 255.

For bibliographies of the general subject, see the article "Architetto" in the *Enciclopedia dell'arte antica*, vol. 1 (1958), pp. 572-78, and the articles in the *Enciclopedia* under the names of the major ancient architects.

General works: M. S. Briggs, *The Architect in History* (Oxford, 1927), esp. pp. 28 ff.; M. L. Clark, "The Architects of Greece and Rome," *Architectural History* 6 (1963), 9-22; G. Downey, "Byzantine Architects, Their Training and Methods," *Byzantion* 18 (1946/48), 99-118; A. L. Frothingham, "The Architect in History, II, Roman Architects," *The Architectural Record* 25 (1909), 179-92 and 281-303; C. Promis, "Gli architetti e l'architettura presso i romani," *Reale accademia delle scienze di Torino, Memorie* 27 (1873), 1-187; J. M. C. Toynbee, *Some Notes on Artists in the Roman World* (Collection Latomus, vol. 26; Brussels, 1951); and W. L. MacDonald, *The Architecture of the Roman Empire*, Vol. 1: *An Introductory Study* (New Haven, 1965), Ch. 6.

For some of the matters touched upon here, see the following.

Architects' plans: G. Carettoni et al., *La pianta marmorea di Roma antica*, Vol. 1 (Rome, 1960), pp. 207-10, and Tav. Q.

Instruments: H. W. Dickinson, "A Brief History of Draughtsmen's Instruments," *Transactions of the Newcomen Society* 27 (1949/51), 73-83 and Plate XVI.1; E. M. Stone, "Roman Surveying Instruments," *University of Washington Publications in Language Literature* 4 (1928), 215-42; and Matthews, cited below.

Hydraulics and aqueducts: Frontinus, as above; K. D. Matthews, "Roman Aqueducts: Technical Aspects of Their Construction," *Expedition* 13 (1970), 2-16; and *Oxford History of Technology*, Vol. 2 (Oxford, 1956), Ch. 19.

Surveying: O. A. W. Dilke, *The Roman Land Surveyors* (London, 1971).

Urban planning: F. Castagnoli, *Orthogonal Town Planning in Antiquity* (Cambridge, Mass., 1971); and J. B. Ward-Perkins, *Cities of Ancient Greece and Italy: Town Planning in Classical Antiquity* (New York, 1974).

Paintings of architecture: P. W. Lehmann, *Roman Wall Paintings from Boscoreale* (New York, 1953); and A. M. G. Little, *Roman Perspective Painting and the Ancient Stage* (Kennebunkport, Maine, 1971).

*Collegia*, etc.: J. P. Waltzing, *Etude historique sur les corporations . . .*, 4 vols. (Louvain, 1895-1900, reprinted Hildesheim, 1970), esp. Vol. 2.

Military works: R. MacMullen, "Roman Imperial Building in the Provinces," *Harvard Studies in Classical Philology* 64 (1959), 207-35, and *Soldier and Civilian in the Later Roman Empire* (Cambridge, Mass., 1963).

Materials and construction: M. E. Blake, *Ancient Roman Construction in Italy . . . to Augustus* (Washington, D.C., 1947), *Roman Construction in Italy from Tiberius through the Flavians* (Washington, D.C., 1959), and *Roman Construction in Italy from Nerva through the Antonines* (Philadelphia, 1973); and MacDonald, cited above, Ch. 7.

"Pumpkins": F. E. Brown, "Hadrianic Architecture," in *Essays in Memory of Karl Lehmann* (New York, 1964), pp. 55-58.

Bricks and brickstamps: H. Bloch, "The Roman Brick Industry and Its Relationship to Roman Architecture," *Journal of the Society of Architectural Historians* 1 (1941), 3-8, and *I bolli laterizi . . .* (Rome, 1947).

Technology: A. G. Drachmann, *The Mechanical Technology of Greek and Roman Antiquity* (Copenhagen, 1963).

Quarrying and the marble trade: J. B. Ward-Perkins, "Tripolitania and the Marble Trade," *Journal of Roman Studies* 41 (1951), 89-104, and "Quarrying in Antiquity: Technology, Tradition, and Social Change," *Proceedings of the British Academy* 57 (1972), 1-24.

Faventius and Palladius: H. Plommer, *Vitruvius and Later Roman Building Manuals* (Cambridge, 1973).

Anthemius' technical writings: G. L. Huxley, *Anthemius of Tralles, A Study in Later Greek Geometry* (Cambridge, Mass., 1959).

# 3

## The Architect in the Middle Ages, East and West

SPIRO KOSTOF

As a topic of research and speculation, the architectural profession in the western Middle Ages does not suffer from neglect. More has probably been written about the medieval architect than his counterpart in other periods of history. The record is varied and plentiful. There are hundreds of extant drawings of all kinds, at least from the later centuries, from large-scale general schemes to molding profiles; the notebook of one practicing architect, Villard de Honnecourt; texts describing architectural programs or arguing points of aesthetics and symbolism; verbal pictures of contemporary buildings; constitutions of masons' lodges; building accounts and minutes of building commissions; portraits of architects; and a variety of representations, in the arts, of structures being put up by work forces of masons and builders. And above all there are the buildings themselves—the cathedrals, monasteries, and castles—prodigious efforts that have inspired awe in the modern beholder, together with the romantic urge to see them as miracles of the collective will. Irrespective of the record, and the constructive reality of buildings as big and complex as medieval churches, some of the modern literature has been wedded to the proposition that architects in the accepted sense were not of any major consequence in their creation. Credit for the buildings is to be shared, in this view, by the learned patron and the anonymous master-mason, whose joyous craft had no need for the cerebration of the architect.

Some support for such an interpretation of the architectural scene in the Middle Ages resides in two general conditions: the attitude of the time toward the built product, and the notable shift of the profession since the collapse of the Roman Empire—from an intellectual pursuit that required a liberal education as a base, to an empirical skill that could be learned within the restricted compass of apprenticeship.

The first point involves a reluctance on the part of sponsoring agencies, primarily the Church, to acknowledge the specific identity of professional experts in charge of structures it commissioned. This attitude is not altogether new. We have seen it in pre-Classical antiquity, in areas other than Egypt, where the architect's part in the intricate human equation that underlies every building of consequence was subsumed in the person of his powerful master, the patron-prince, or in the glory of the gods. In the western Middle Ages, abbots and bishops and kings often took full credit for what they had ordered put up, and the fame, at least in the case of ecclesiastical buildings, redounded in the end to the Christian God, the ultimate architect. He was shown with compasses in hand setting out the shape of the universe (Figure 19), and Scripture referred to Christ as "the architect of the Church" (*architectus ecclesiae*) and to St. Paul as the wise master-builder (*sapiens architectus*) who laid the foundation of Christian faith. In this sense, and this sense only, does the record speak of leading churchmen as having "built" a church or a monastery. When we encounter in documents descriptive words such as *fecit, construxit, aedificavit*, the referent as a general rule is the patron. To interpret these passages in any further way, either that the architect was not essential in the design of the building, or that the patron in question embraced the role of the architect, leads to a serious distortion of actualities.

The second point is also a matter of the proper reading of the sources. What is indisputable is that, after the seventh century, the term *architectus* appears with less and less frequency in extant medieval writings, and that when it is used it refers by and large to masons regardless of any special professional distinction. What should not be deduced from this philological pattern, however, is the notion that architects became somehow obsolete during the Middle Ages, leaving building to be conceived by bookish clerics and realized under able masons. The fact is that the term *architectus* fell into disuse precisely because the Classical concept of the architect as it is represented in Vitruvius faded and was replaced by something else: the architect as master-builder. For Vitruvius, the theoretical aspects of the profession and a thorough grounding in the Liberal Arts were as important to the architect as expert knowledge of building technology. Not so in the case of the medieval architect, who rose from the ranks of the building crafts, carpentry or the working of stone or commonly both, and took part in the actual process of construction alongside the building crew as one of their own. What changed was not fundamental to the traditional task of the architect, the conception and supervision of buildings. The change was rather one of social standing. And, reflecting this new role of the medieval architect, his titles came to be drawn from the world of the masons' lodge: *Caementarius, lathomus, magister operis, capudmagister,* and their equivalents in the languages of Europe.

To speak of "the medieval architect" is of course simplistic. The general period spans a thousand years, from the collapse of Roman order to about 1500, when the fresh vision of that revival of Classical antiquity we call the Renaissance had spread outside Italy, the locus of its origin, toward the north. Three power blocs shared the Mediterranean basin during this millennium: the Byzantine Empire in the east; the western successor-states of Rome; and the vast might of Islam, which rose as a fervent religion of the desert in the early seventh century and took over most of the Middle East and North Africa, where it prospered through a chain of brilliant states. The history of the architectural profession in the Middle Ages must perforce encompass Byzantium and the Muslim territories, not only because of the geopolitical fissure of the once-unified *mare nostrum* of the Romans, but also because the professional practice of the West was repeatedly inseminated by these two other sources.

In fact, there was greater mobility in the medieval world than is commonly admitted, and more contact among the architectures of East and West, both direct and through less immediate cultural seepage. In the first place, conquest delivered some Christian architects into Muslim hands, and the reverse also occurred. The earliest buildings of Islam were indebted to designers of the Byzantine provinces that fell in the spectacular early offensive of the new faith. Cities of the Levant changed masters more than once during the Crusades, and with them their architects exchanged one set of patrons for another. Secondly, artists and architects sometimes traveled voluntarily from culture to culture. There were Byzantine mosaicists at Muslim Cordoba in Spain in the tenth century and at Montecassino in Italy in the late eleventh. Also in the late eleventh century a Greek architect, Busketos by name, was altering the design of the cathedral of Pisa that went back to 1063, while at the same time John the Monk and his brothers, from Edessa in Syria, were engaged in the building of new fortifications for Fatimid Cairo. Thirdly, images of famous buildings in distant lands, and sometimes their measurements, were brought back by travelers and put to practical use. For associational or aesthetic reasons, entire pieces of architecture or selected motifs cropped up in areas far remote, geographically and culturally, from their places of origin. Free renditions of the Holy Sepulchre in Jerusalem stood in Pisa and Cambridge, in Fulda and Paderborn. The Dome of the Rock, the first architectural masterpiece of Islam, inspired the Templars, who used it during the Latin occupation of Jerusalem in the twelfth century, to adopt it as their church form in the West. Features of Muslim architecture show up in otherwise distinctly western contexts, such as the flat arch with joggled jointing, common in Fatimid and Mameluke Egypt, used in Fountains Abbey and Conisbrough Castle. Finally, modes of architectural thinking were transmitted, directly or indirectly, across cultural borders. The spread of Euclidian geometry in western Europe owes a debt to the civilization of Islam, since the first Latin translation was made about 1120 from an earlier Arabic version of the Greek text. Indeed, whichever way the current flowed, the preoccupation with geometry was common to both western medieval and Muslim architecture. The ground plan of the Dome of the Rock was evolved according to a geometric progression, and much ornament in Muslim design, from the window grilles of the Great Mosque at Damascus onward, is based on astounding, almost unanalyzable constellations of basic figures of geometry.

And yet for all the evident signs of cross-fertilization, very little has been done to document professional links among the three spheres of the Old World during the Middle Ages. We do not know one hundredth as much about the architect in later Byzantium or in the Muslim countries as we know of the medieval architect in the West. The fault lies, in large measure, with the sources. After the great era of the emperor Justinian when Anthemius and Isidorus were active, Byzantine architects are scarcely ever mentioned in the texts, and nothing of substance is said about the profession from the later sixth century to the fall of Constantinople in 1453. The Muslim situation is only slightly better. In 1956 L. A. Mayer published a "roll of architects" active in all regions of Islam up to 1830. Some 330 names are listed—very few for a period of more than a thousand years. And nothing more is known about the great majority of them except the name itself and some building it is connected with, often because both pieces of information are derived from an inscription on the building. Archival material is very scant until the Ottoman period; not accidentally, most of the fuller portraits of Muslim architects come from this period—Esir Ali, the great Sinan, and his pupils Kemalettin, Davud Ağa, and Dalgïç.

The early centuries of Byzantium belong with the history of the Roman Empire. William L. MacDonald properly ends his chapter on Roman architects with the designer of Hagia Sophia, Anthemius of Tralles. It would seem that during this formative phase of Byzantine civilization the architect continued to aspire to the status of learned gentleman, informed both about the theoretical groundwork of his profession and the technical know-how it demanded. According to the treatise of the geometer Pappus of Alexandria, written probably about A.D. 320, the ideal education of the architect comprised a theoretical part made up of geometry, arithmetic, astronomy, and physics, and a manual part that involved work "in metals, construction, carpentering, and the art of painting, and the practical execution of these matters" (Preface of Book VIII; the translation is by I. Thomas, as revised by G. Downey). The remarkable thing about this definition of architectural studies is that it appears in a book on geometry and that the outlined curriculum—which is said to be based on the doctrine of Heron of Alexandria, an expert on stereometry and the author of a book on vaulting—is referred to as "the science of mechanics." The person who mastered the curriculum became a *mechanicus* (or *mechanikos*), a term applied to a number of late Roman and Byzantine architects, among them Anthemius' colleague Isidorus of Miletus. It is clear that this term had by now superseded the Classical denomination of the architect, i.e. *architekton* or *architectus*, which in turn began to be applied to those practicing architects who lacked the theoretical schooling outlined by Pappus.

Indeed, Pappus himself recognized, in the passage just cited, the possibility of a strictly technical route to the profession. "But when it is impossible for the same person to familiarize himself with so many academic studies and at the same time to learn the above-mentioned crafts, they instruct a person wishing to undertake practical tasks in mechanics to use such crafts as he already possesses in the tasks to be performed in each particular case." In other words, one could become an architect either through a formal education at the university or through a trade school of some kind. The title *mechanicus*, far from being used pejoratively to describe the architect as a mere technician, which it was once thought to do, indicated rather a higher academic discipline and a more prestigious standing. The *mechanicus*, to turn once more to Pappus, had studied "the stability and movement of bodies about their centers of gravity, and their motions in space, inquiring not only into the causes of those that move in virtue of their nature, but forcibly transferring others from their own places in a motion contrary to their nature." He was the conceptual man who probably did not have to be a practicing architect in the strict sense, but whose architectural ideas, however diagrammatic, could be carried out by the master-builder, or *architectus* in the new meaning of the word. The mechanicus might hold a government office and merit appropriate honorific titles. In an inscription from Syria, Isidorus is styled "Most Magnificent and Illustrious."

This distinction between learned designers and master-builders may have held until the end, at least for officially sponsored architecture. Monasticism, often at odds with the religious policy of the state, undoubtedly spawned its own designers and builders. The Rule of St. Basil recognized building as one of the permissible occupations for monks, along with other useful activities such as agriculture, cobbling, carpentry, and smithing. But whether schooled or monkish, Byzantine architects functioned within a strictly regulated tradition, especially after the Iconoclastic Controversy when the arts were forced to serve the Church and the state under rigid guidelines enunciated as official policy. But then the architect has rarely been free to invent forms with impunity. What we call "program" comes laden with restrictions of various kinds: functional, stylistic, economic, intellectual. The architect's mettle is as much in the way he handles convention as it is in creating new solutions for unique challenges. The nameless masters of later Byzantium did both. They helped to shape the forms that could accommodate the changing demands of post-Iconoclastic liturgy. The cross-in-square and allied church plans were devised to contain a strict hierarchy of religious images determined by the Church. But beyond obvious innovation, the architects were also able to sustain a brilliant spectrum of variants on the established themes, all the way to the sunset years of the Byzantine Empire.

The story of the architect in medieval Islam, so far as it can be retrieved, follows a different line. Several trends can be detected in the slim record. With few exceptions, the architects had little theoretical training. Ibn Haldun speaks of the importance of geometry for architects (*Muqaddima*, Ch. 25), and there are distinguished men, such as the mathematician and astrolabist Alamaddin Qaisar, or Maslama b. Abdallah, the geometrician of the tenth century at the court of Cordoba, who were practicing architects. But on the whole, like his Christian counterpart in Europe, the Muslim architect started out in one or more crafts—masonry, cabinet-making, faience, metalwork, and the like. In an architectural tradition that thrived on decorative effects, this early training made good sense. Yet for all the splendid ornament that sheathes the palaces, mosques, and tombs of Persia, Egypt, North Africa, and Spain, the structural stability of the frame was a chief obligation of the architect. Buildings like the mosque of Sultan Hassan at Cairo or the tomb of Oljeitu in Sultaniya cannot have been achieved without seasoned, albeit entirely empirical, experience in construction.

Even so, there was no clear line between a foreman mason and an architect, and no very pronounced or consistent respect for the profession. The three terms commonly used to designate architects—*mi'mar, banna, muhandis*—though not synonymous, do not seem to carry explicit distinctions. *Mi'mar* was probably the lowest-ranking category, at least during the Middle Ages. Whatever they might be called, architects were often qualified as "master" (*Ustad, mu'allim, sahib*), an honorary title that denoted some special ability or respect. At any rate, with the exception of a few architects, mostly in the Ottoman period, who held a high position in the court, the profession belonged to the lower strata of society and its practitioners were classified with the servant class. Where there is evidence, the salary of a resident architect at a mosque appears no higher than that of the marble mason, and lower than those of the minister or even the gate-keeper. A master would exceptionally be rewarded by his patron for a particularly satisfying performance. The gift of a robe of honor is mentioned several times in the texts. The ultimate compliment, to credit the same anecdote told of several architects, was to have one's hands chopped off upon the completion of a masterpiece (if not to be killed outright), so that the design could not be repeated for another patron.* This brutal fiction may be taken to indicate, at the least, that the Muslim architect prepared drawings for his buildings.

Legends about architects, as a matter of fact, are few and unedifying. As Mayer points out, they are mostly stories not so much about architects as about their patrons. In the same way, inscriptions on the structures themselves commemorate primarily the patron or the official who supervised the work, and only secondarily the architect. The frequent locution

---

* Similar stories circulated in the West. The Norman architect Lanfrey was said to have been beheaded in 1094 upon completion of the castle at Ivry to keep him from building a similar or better castle.

*ala yaday,* "by the hands of," usually introduces the supervisor or "Super-intendent of Buildings" and not the architect. The superintendent was an administrative official—a military officer of junior rank in the case of Mam-eluke Egypt, a civilian in Spain. The architect, when he did sign his name, which was rare, did so inconspicuously at the end of the inscription honoring his patron, after the date. The time span of the Muslim Middle Ages and the diversity of the states it encompassed are too great, how-ever, to allow safe generalizations. Thus the names of some Seljuk archi-tects appear boldly in medallions flanking the main inscription, or on some other visually prominent feature of the building, and in a number of Spanish inscriptions the architect's name precedes that of the Superin-tendent of Buildings.

In at least two significant ways the story of the medieval architect in Islam differs from that of his western counterpart. In the first place, the close identification of the architect with the religious establishment, so characteristic an aspect of the profession in the West, does not apply in the Muslim territories. To quote Mayer, "although the bulk of public buildings in Islam were either devoted to religious use (like mosques, ma-drasas, kuttâbs, zâwiyas, cemeteries) or founded out of a religious impulse (like hospitals or sâbils), with very few exceptions they were constructed by order of laymen. Economically they were entirely the work of the gov-erning classes, military or civilian, and independent of any ecclesiastical authority" (*Islamic Architects,* pp. 22-23). Secondly, the rate of com-pleting buildings, even ones of considerable size, tended to be fast. In con-trast to the protracted execution of Gothic cathedrals, where one architect succeeded another in the course of several decades or even centuries, in Islam most important buildings could be conceived and executed by their original architect.

Against this paltry record of Byzantium and Islam, the case for the West is remarkably well documented. We should distinguish three approximate periods in the development of the profession during the Middle Ages: an early period of transition from late Roman to medieval forms, and from the Vitruvian ideal of the architect as the humanist planner to the medi-eval concept of him as master-builder; a second period during which a dis-tinctly medieval architecture with its own iconography and building tech-niques had come to full bloom, roughly 800 to 1150; and lastly, the Gothic period, which in form as well as in the approach to the architect's profes-sion introduced and nurtured a fresh tradition. The third period is also the richest in terms of documents, both visual and literary, which in itself may be a comment on the status and methods of the architect in the late Middle Ages.

I. The Roman Empire had been good for the architect. There were dozens of big cities within its borders, ranging from 10,000 inhabitants to over a million in the case of Rome, and public building was their pride and the first among municipal responsibilities. The state supported costly public-works programs; buildings were commissioned through the munificence of wealthy patrons and administrators, led by the imperial court; and appeals went out frequently for public subscription.

But with the decline and ultimate collapse of the empire in the West, the architect's fortune plummeted. Cities shrank as the general economy reeled under the impact of an interlinked series of adverse conditions. With the declining size and revenue of the once-prosperous cities, civic pride and munificence declined as well. Political power shifted to the triumphant Church, in whose new building programs the architect found his principal patronage. The fall of the empire spelled the end of slave labor upon which building, like all other dominant technologies, heavily relied. Major building industries that made the vast imperial program feasible— brickyards, quarries, the overseas levy of marbles and other stones—could no longer survive; they yielded to a village economy of small-scale craftsmanship and the limited supply of local materials. Brick-faced concrete, the supple cloth out of which so many of the great Roman monuments had been cut, was soon abandoned. Its production made sense in terms of bulk; its need had been created by a scale in building that could not now be entertained. It gave way to humbler methods of construction that required a smaller and less complicated work force. And the architectural profession lost numbers rapidly; we saw in the preceding chapter the efforts of Constantine the Great to spur the study of architecture by special dispensations.

The prestige of Roman architects stood high, as did that of Roman monuments. The Gothic princes, to whose care the West was consigned with the waning presence of Roman *imperium*, took up for a time the tradition of official state patronage, and some attempt was made by them, in the general spoilage of the built patrimony of Rome, to preserve and restore the more celebrated of the Roman structures. King Theodoric (491-526) typifies these attitudes. He sponsored a fair amount of building both in his capital city of Ravenna and outside it, and when he visited Rome in the opening years of the sixth century, he appointed a body of professional men, under the direction of an *architectus publicorum*, to oversee the repair of public monuments, including the Colosseum and the theater of Pompey. Anxious for the rehabilitation of the ancient monuments through alternate use or urban renewal, he approved a project that involved the building of houses on a site immediately adjacent to the Roman Forum. What is more, the idea that ancient architecture should be respected and emulated in contemporary construction took hold during his reign. We have evidence of this in a document where the palace architect is exhorted to see to it that his "new work harmonises well with the old." This document comes from the *Variae*, or correspondence, of Cassiodorus, who was secretary to Theodoric, and is worth quoting in full. It is a set formula to be used when appointing a palace architect, and conveys the lingering grandeur of the profession as it had been in the days of Rabirius and Apollodorus of Damascus.

Much do we delight in seeing the greatness of our Kingdom imaged forth in the splendor of our palace.

Thus do the ambassadors of foreign nations admire our power, for at first sight one naturally believes that as is the house so is the inhabitant. . . .

Take then for this Indiction the care of our palace, thus receiving the power of transmitting your fame to a remote posterity which shall admire your workmanship. See that your new work harmonises well with the old. Study Euclid—get his diagrams well into your mind; study Archimedes and Metrobius.

When we are thinking of rebuilding a city, or of founding a fort or a general's quarters, we shall rely upon you to express our thoughts on paper. The builder of walls, the carver of marbles, the caster of brass, the vaulter of arches, the plasterer, the worker in mosaic, all come to you for orders, and you are expected to have a wise answer for each. But, then, if you direct them rightly, while theirs is the work yours is all the glory.

Above all things, dispense honestly what we give you for the workmen's wages; for the laborer who is at ease about his victuals works all the better.

As a mark of your high dignity you bear a golden wand, and amidst the numerous throng of servants walk first before the royal footsteps, that even by your nearness to our person it may be seen that you are the man to whom we have entrusted the care of our palaces [T. Hodgkin, *The Letters of Cassiodorus* (London, 1886), pp. 323-24].

With the decline of Rome, architectural patronage shifted to the north. Ravenna and Milan were major centers of activity for a while, and there was also work beyond the Alps thanks to the determination of some ecclesiastics to import the Roman way of building. Later medieval tradition speaks of Bishop Wilfrid of Hexham, who brought builders from Rome in the seventh century to do his abbey. According to William of Malmesbury, Wilfrid supervised the work in person, but it was their skill in masonry (*magisterio cementariorum*) that produced the unusual results. By the seventh century, too, Lombardy had developed a reputation for proficiency in masonry. Building masters from this north Italian region, known as *magistri comacini*, came to be in great demand. The term *comacinus* was once thought to derive from the town name of Como; more likely it should be read as *co-macinus*, and interpreted as *co-mechanicus*, i.e., one of a group of associated architects, or co-mason. That there was an active masons' guild in Lombardy at an early age is not in doubt. It is mentioned in 643 in the charter of King Lotharis, in relation to liability for fatal accidents. In 714 it is once more the subject of royal regulation when a diploma is issued by King Liutprand with respect to a fixed price scale for architectural and building work.

Medieval guilds may represent another aspect of the Roman heritage in the medieval West. There is good reason to think that their ancestral origin is the Roman *collegium*, or craft guild. The *collegia* had started as voluntary associations, but were taken under state control in late antiquity along with all other trades and professions. The state legislated regulations of membership, permissible profits, and even the siting of shops and factories. Membership in the *collegia* was hereditary. There was undoubtedly also an architects' guild. The Theodosian Code includes an edict by Constantine the Great (quoted in part in the preceding chapter) in which architects, ceiling-makers, and plasterers, along with some thirty other trades and professions, are exempted from all obligations "in order that they may acquire the leisure for studying their arts and so may be the more inclined to obtain greater skill themselves *and pass on their knowledge to their sons* [my emphasis]" (Theodosian Code 13.4.2). With the passing of the Roman Empire the nature of the guilds must have changed, but there may have been no break in the practice of professional association as such. The hereditary basis for the building trades seems to have been in effect until the thirteenth century, when the system of apprenticeship gained currency.

Still one more contact with Roman practice was Vitruvius. The famous treatise continued in use uninterruptedly. A fair number of copies circulated among the intellectuals and in the lodges. On the whole, Vitruvius was looked to for practical advice on matters of construction, engineering, and surveying. A Vitruvian compilation with this emphasis, called *De artis architectonicae liber,* was made by M. Cetius Faventinus. There was, in addition, one other book of practical use to the medieval builder, the dissertation on military affairs by Flavius Vegetius Renatus, produced in the late fourth century. But it is inaccurate to assert that the other side of Roman theory, the rules of design so pedantically insisted upon by Vitruvius, were of no interest to the Middle Ages. The five Orders, to be sure, had lost their paradigmatic validity. Yet here and there one or another of his precepts is obeyed. For example, both the fourth-century atrium of Old St. Peter's in Rome and the much later narthex of the third abbey church at Cluny have been shown to be proportioned like a Vitruvian atrium of the third class (6.3.3), where the length is equal to the diagonal of a square whose sides are derived from the width—the relationship designated by the neologism "diagon." Similarly, the Vitruvian concepts of Eurhythmy and Symmetry appear to have been heeded in the design of a number of well-known medieval buildings. There is some evidence that Vitruvius was not totally absent from the geometrical curriculum of monastic schools, when these got going in earnest.

But Christian thought permeated this aspect of Roman survival, as it did all others. Numbers for the medieval mind were fraught with complex symbolism, and numbers initiated the essentially geometric process of architectural design in the Middle Ages as they did in ancient Egypt. That is, some unit of measurement was first selected as the module of the building under design, before the forms were generated through geometry. That the module should be commensurate was clear, since it would serve as the basis of proportional relationships. As Vitruvius puts it in his discussion of Symmetry: "There is nothing to which an architect should devote more thought than to the exact proportions of his building with reference to a certain part selected as the standard" (6.2.1). But for the Christian architect the module, in addition to serving design convenience, was capable of expressing messages of faith. The key dimension of the monastery of St. Gall, of which we shall say more presently, is forty feet, the width of the nave and the transept. But to the monkish audience forty was also a number rich in Biblical associations, having to do with periods of expectation and penitence: the forty days of the Flood, the forty years the Hebrews wandered in the desert, the forty-day vigil of Moses on Mount Sinai, etc. That complicated numerology was beyond the ken of ordinary architects and church-goers is not sufficient reason to doubt its importance. We must remember the symbiotic nature of the relationship between patron and architect, and the fact that the patron was commonly a high-ranking churchman whose thought was firmly founded in Scripture and its exegesis.

The point to be stressed is that, whatever the professional continuity between Classical antiquity and the Middle Ages, Christian content could not but condition the practice of architecture. Already as early as the seventh century, the particular amalgam of the pagan and the Christian is reflected in the description of architecture offered by Isidore of Seville in his *Etymologies* (19.8-9). The Classical inspiration of the passage is unmistakable, with its mention of the legendary first architect Daedalus and the acceptance of the Vitruvian triad of architecture, i.e., commodity, firmness, and delight (*dispositio, constructio, venustas* in Isidore). But the meaning is tempered by the reference to St. Paul as the wise architect. In terms of the development of the profession too, Isidore strikes a middle posture between the antique notion of the architect as the planner and the medieval notion of him as the master-builder. *Architectus* and *caementarius* are taken as synonyms; architect and mason are already one. On the other hand, the principal job of the architect is said to be the design of the ground plan (*disponere in fundamentis*), as distinct from construction.

II. The lean centuries of the so-called Dark Ages came to an end about 800. The consolidation of Europe under the rule of Charlemagne and the rise of the monasteries as the backbone of European economy alongside the diminished cities provided the stability and means that are needed for large-scale architectural projects. Carolingian architecture, therefore, represents the first major leap since antiquity for the architectural profession, which had been significantly weakened in the intervening period of political uncertainty and social disorder. The policy of Charlemagne to revive Roman authority by emulating Roman forms encouraged the study of older buildings, especially the great early structures of Christianity like Old St. Peter's and the Lateran Palace in Rome and the church of S. Vitale at Ravenna. The designers of the monastic church at Fulda, the palace group at Ingelheim, and the palatine chapel at Aachen were clearly conscious of these famous predecessors, as well as of the earlier foundations of the emperors. The broad confident layout of the monastery plan of St. Gall, for example, evokes the scale and order of the imperial fora in Rome.

This plan is remarkable (Figure 19). It is the earliest architectural drawing of the western Middle Ages to survive, and it says much about the state of the profession at the Carolingian juncture. It is an exceptionally

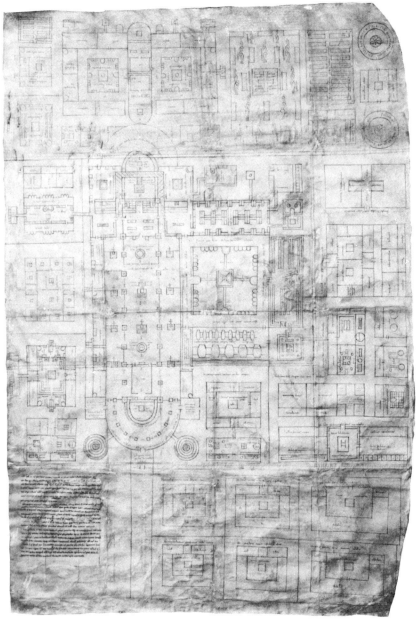

Figure 19. Monastery plan of St. Gall, ca. 820. This remarkable architectural drawing is a rare survivor from the earlier Middle Ages. It represents an ideal monastery complex of forty buildings centered around the church, the cloister, and the refectory.

large drawing, about 30 by 44 inches, made up of five separate sheets of calfskin sewn together. Its survival was accidental, due to the fact that the parchment had been folded and reused for a Life of St. Martin. The drawing is actually a freehand copy of an earlier original, as can be ascertained from a close examination of the surface. Among other things, it lacks the framework of auxiliary lines and reference points which it was customary to press into the parchment with a fine stylus or silverpoint before tracing the drawing in ink. The copy was made for Abbot Gozbert of St. Gall by one of his superiors to apprize him of decisions taken at the second of two meetings held at the palace of Aachen in 816-17, from which the abbot had been absent. The meetings concerned the reform of the monastic movement, and the drawing shows an ideal monastery complex that incorporated the official policies enunciated at Aachen.

The vision of the St. Gall plan is expansive. Designed for about 100 inmates, the monastery comprises forty buildings centered around the church, the cloister, and the refectory, including the hospital, dormitory, and bathhouse, the school for the novitiate, a house for the abbot and one for distinguished guests, workshops, granary, bake and brewhouses, animal pens, and a cemetery. All these are carefully labeled, and the precise delineation of furniture—beds, stalls, barrels—proves that this was no mere sketch of an architectural idea but a fully developed master scheme that could be used for any new monastic installation. Drawn to a scale of 1/16th of an inch to one foot, the plan conforms to a module of 40 feet, subdivided into 16 units of 2½ feet, a unit derived through the simple process of continuous halving. In the church, the additive regularity of space based on sub-modular squares prefigures the standard Romanesque procedure a couple of centuries later.

We have no knowledge of the architect. He may in fact have been an ecclesiastic, or an educated courtier with the training of a Byzantine *mechanicus*, since the plan is a conceptual arrangement that does not presuppose constructive involvement on the part of its maker. That such "programs," both graphic and written, existed is certifiable. K. J. Conant has analyzed a written program for the second abbey at Cluny meant to accompany a similar linear diagram. This document, called Customs of Cluny or Farfa (a Cluniac daughter-house in Italy), gives all the measurements of the extant parts of the complex as of about 1040 and of the parts yet to be constructed. In contrast to the ideal solution of the St. Gall plan, the Cluny text is a specific inventory of one monastic institution. Somewhere between these two types of programs lie the written specifica-

tions that the patron submitted to the architect as the contract of architectural intentions. Finally, there were generalized outline specifications
for classes of buildings, such as those laid down for castle-builders by
Alexander Neckam in his encyclopedia of terminology written about 1190.

The exceptional drawing of St. Gall and the existence of written programs acquire special significance in the face of the hypothesis, cham-
pioned most recently by Robert Branner, that the medieval architect had
abandoned his dependence on project drawings as such—Vitruvius' *ichno-
graphia* (plan), *orthographia* (elevation) and *scaenographia* (perspective).
Branner maintains that the return of this graphic apparatus is to be dated
no earlier than the thirteenth century. In the meantime, the architect relied on programmatic layouts such as the plan of St. Gall, routine lodge
practice, and the kind of mental procedure that Guillaume d'Auvergne,
thirteenth-century bishop of Paris, calls *cogitatio* and describes as the first
step in architectural design. The ground plan, in other words, was conceived in the architect's head; he would then go directly to the site, and
use it as a full-scale drawing board to lay out the design. Intermediary
parchment drawings were not called for, and that is why they do not survive until the later medieval centuries. In fact, the oldest extant project
drawings are those in the Rheims palimpsest, which date from about
1240/60. By this time, the technique of construction had become too complicated to be handled intuitively, and full-scale detail drawings engraved
on the structure itself had made their appearance. The most prodigious
example of these is the group of drawings on the terrace above the ambula-
tory of the cathedral at Clermont-Ferrand, showing the archivolts and
gable of the north transept portal and two sets of flyers for the nave buttresses. With the habit for graphic aids thus established, according to this
hypothesis, project drawings that could be consulted during the actual
building process came into their own. The evidence for architectural
models is ambiguous. The model of the church of St.-Maclou at Rouen
is the only example we have for the medieval period outside of Italy, where
the practice seems to have been common. But the model of St.-Maclou
seems to represent a stage *after* the construction of the church and not
before; that is, it was not used as an aid in the design process but as a subsequent memorial. In the ninth century, when the abbey of St.-Germain
d'Auxerre was to be built (or rebuilt), a model of the whole complex (*con-
cepti operis exemplar*) was made in wax, according to a contemporary text.
This might seem to prove the active use of architectural models, were it
not for the fact that such an early instance may just as easily be viewed

as the tail end of antique practice as held to initiate a medieval tradition.

The contrary opinion argues that the absence of drawings may be a fortuitous accident of survival; that it is inconceivable for buildings of the scale of Romanesque churches to have been constructed without graphic delineation. This is especially so for those which display complicated design concepts, whether arithmetical or geometrical or both, such as the church of St. Michael's at Hildesheim and the abbey churches of Cluny and Fontenay. The interest of working drawings was limited to the task at hand; they would be discarded when their usefulness was over. The notion of preserving samples of an architect's draftsmanship as works of art is quite late. Indeed, some of the medieval drawings that survive do so because they were reused, as valuable parchment, for something of a more permanent nature, such as bookbinding or the copying of an important text (such as the Life of St. Martin on the reverse of the St. Gall plan). Used parchment, melted down, makes good glue; this may have been the fate of some medieval drawings, as it was the fate of marble statues of Classical antiquity to be burned down to lime. Perhaps craft secrecy may also have had something to do with the disappearance of working drawings.

By the time of Cluny II, Europe was entering an era of confident reconstruction. The dread millennium had passed without ushering in Doomsday. The relief and renewed faith poured into new construction, a fevered campaign of church-raising along pilgrimage routes and in the reawakening cities. The famous account of the monk Raoul Glaber talks of the world casting off her old age and draping herself "in a white mantle of churches." The size of the new and the renovated older structures was extravagant. Since the Carolingian revival, size had been a symbolic issue. To some, the ambitious scale of religious installations smacked of enormity; to others, it sang of proud faith and the glory of the Almighty. On the St. Gall plan, the church was initially intended to be 300 feet long but was subsequently reduced to 200 feet, as an explanatory note on the drawing makes clear. The abbey church of St. Remi at Rheims, begun by abbot Airard in 1005 "under men skilled in architecture" (*qui architecturae periti ferebantur*), was similarly reduced by his successor Thierry: even so it has a central nave of 43 feet, a prodigious space to span even though it was never intended to be vaulted in stone.

The architects who undertook the erection of post-millennial Romanesque churches had to be seasoned masters of construction. Some were undoubtedly schooled in the monasteries; most were laymen who rose through the ranks of the mason's lodge with some acquired trade secrets of geometry and much practical experience in the handling of cutstone and the statics of masonry construction. The work force consisted of traveling bands of masons, stuccoists, glass-makers, mosaicists, and the like. They came to the site of a major project, often from a long distance away, and set up shop. Such a team of experts in the building trades, once assembled, became established as a resident workshop, trained local talent, and in time sent out craftsmen elsewhere. The masters who rose out of these ateliers as professional designers and clerks of the works now began to acquire a high status and command wide respect. Names before the Gothic period are rare, but the evidence of the buildings and documentary sources is incontestable. The term *architectus*, which had been subsumed by masonic designations, began a slow comeback, as the architect was more and more distinguished from the body of craftsmen. Illuminations show the architect directing the workmen and not himself using his hands. To be sure, it was not until the thirteenth century that the emergence of the new image of the architect is complete, but by then the intellectual detachment of the designer from the work force was so commonplace that it could be decried as excessive. In the famous words of Nicolas de Biard, the Dominican preacher and writer of Paris, "The master masons, holding measuring rods and gloves in their hands, say to the others, 'Cut it here!' and they themselves do nothing; but yet they get the greater fees. . . ." He likens them to clerics who are long on words but short on deeds.

The practice of the architect went beyond church programs. His commissions included palaces, wealthy homes, gardens, castles, military installations, and the design of cities. We have record of a house designed ca. 1120 by Louis de Bourbourg in the castle of Ardes, Flanders, for Arnold, steward of Eustace, count of Boulogne. The three-storey house, we are told, had a labyrinthine entrance, provision stores, granaries, cellars, and a chapel. The living quarters were on the second floor, and the third floor accommodated the children and the servants. Louis is praised as being "not much inferior to Daedalus in his skill."

In the design of fortress towns and military installations, Flavius Vegetius Renatus must have served as a popular sourcebook. Geoffrey, count of Anjou, is pictured as reading *De re militari* during the siege of Montreuil-Bellay in 1151 and profiting from it in the improvement of his siege engines. The count is said to be "skilled in engineering and carpentry" (document cited by Harvey in *Mediaeval Architect*, p. 209). The fortress towns founded by Edward the Elder between 913 and 924 to defend South England—Hertford, Bedford, Nottingham—were undoubtedly laid out with professional help. (The term *ingeniator,* most commonly encountered in English documents, may apply to an architect who specialized in military engineering.) So also with Dunstable in the time of Henry I, and the new town of Salisbury when the cathedral site was moved in 1217 from Old Sarum. From the early twelfth century onward there were planned cities on the gridiron scheme, built *ex novo* in the countryside. The earliest among them—Freiburg, Leipzig, Lübeck—were founded as trading centers. But after 1200 the purpose of the foundations was almost exclusively military, to insure control of the surrounding country. These so-called *bastides* had a rectangular enceinte and a formal marketplace, and were obviously modeled after ancient Roman colonial settlements. The practice seems to have been made popular by St. Louis of France, and there were soon *bastides* all over Europe. Edward I built some fifty of them in France. In 1296, he ordered the citizens of London to elect four men who knew best how "to devise, order and array a new town to the most profit of Us and the merchants," and who were ready to follow him around the country for that purpose. The document is in French: the critical words are *deviser ordiner et arayer. Ordiner* goes ultimately back to Vitruvius' *ordinatio.* The other two are new words. *Deviser* derives from *devis* or *devise,* meaning design or drawing. In late medieval documents from England, it is sometimes what the patron is said to supply the architect, which apparently meant both advice and an architectural drawing.

III. This discussion has already moved into the Gothic period, to which we might now properly turn. "Gothic" is a style, a convention of form. As such it is, in its buildings, the product of architectural imagination. So complex and dazzling is this product that the minds responsible for its inception and subsequent development could not but be extraordinary minds, able to rise above the single block or stone statue and conceive with faultless precision shells of masonry that stood to dizzying heights and were made up of myriads of parts. The notion that Gothic cathedrals were the triumph of anonymous teamwork or the conjuring of scholarly churchmen cannot seriously be entertained. Contemporary thought knew better. Credit was given where it was due. Although the acknowledged birth of the style at the abbey church of St. Denis has no professional name attached to it but only the self-glorifying record of its patron, the Abbot

Figure 20. Portrait of the architect Hugh Libergier on his tombstone at Rheims Cathedral; thirteenth century. The inscription says: "Here lies Master Hugh Libergier, who began this church in the year 1229 and died in the year 1267." The architect is shown with the instruments of his profession: the rule, the square and the compass.

Suger, hundreds of architects burst into public prominence in the next three centuries. They were buried with honors in the churches they designed, and shown holding models of their work in their hands (Figure 20). Statues of them appeared here and there on the bodies of the churches. Their names are found inscribed upon the giant structures, as at Rouen Cathedral or the Portico de la Gloria of Santiago de Compostela, as if the artist were signing his painting or the author his book. Their Daedalic origin is stressed by labyrinths on the floors of cathedrals like those at Rheims and Amiens (Figure 21). Pierre de Montreuil, the architect of certain parts of St. Denis and of the south transept of Notre Dame in Paris, was described on his tomb slab at St. Germain des Près as *doctor lathomorum*, professor of freemasons, as clear an indication as we might wish of the dominance of the designing master over his crafting colleagues. Lafranc, architect of the cathedral at Modena, is called *architector* and *mirificus aedificator*, and is shown, in a scene of the translation of the body of S. Gimignano, holding the lid of the coffin together with the bishop of Reggio. All this is not ambiguous.

Public recognition reflected the architect's own pride in his calling. He arrived at his high position through hard work and native talent, rather than any predetermined social distinction. Often he came from the lower levels of medieval society; his profession was thought by some, Hugo of St. Victor for instance, to be suitable only for commoners and the sons of the poor. (Migne, *Patrologia latina*, CLXXVI, 760). But at the lodge he was taught that building had an honorable origin. Christ was a carpenter's son, and the apostle Thomas could make "in stone, pillars and temples and court-houses for kings" (*Apocryphal New Testament*, trans. M. R. James [Oxford, 1924], p. 366). Intellectual thought reinforced this image by characterizing God as the artful architect (*elegans architectus*) who made the universe as his palace, harmonizing all creatures by means of musical proportions (Alan of Lille, *De planctu naturae*, cited in von Simson, *Gothic Cathedral*, 31-32).

Now such rarefied erudition may have been outside the normal opportunities of all but the most exceptional architects. Nonetheless, what was intellectualized by the philosopher had its own humble reality in the lodge. Most notably, it was the shared belief that geometry was both the aesthetic and technical basis of the universe. To the educated mind which had mastered the quadrivium, most commonly the privilege of clerics, geometry was a theoretical science wedded to the other three Liberal Arts, astronomy, music, and arithmetic. The applied geometry of the ordinary

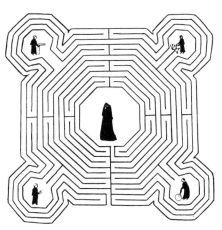

Figure 21. The labyrinth at Rheims Cathedral; once imbedded in the pavement of the nave, it was destroyed in 1779. The four corner octagons contained the names of four architects who supervised the construction of the cathedral in the thirteenth and fourteenth centuries—Jean d'Orbais, Jean Le Loup, Gaucher de Reims, and Bernard de Soissons. The device was meant to bring out the relation of the Gothic architect to the legendary Daedalus.

master mason stood on a much humbler plane, but it was, for all that, the vernacular of the same language that was used by the intelligentsia. And in the end what distinguished the architect from the master mason would be exactly this mastery of the theoretical implications of geometry, which is why the architect could find no loftier portrait for himself than to be represented as a geometrician with compass and measuring rod in hand.

The usual apprenticeship was for seven years, beginning at age thirteen or fourteen. This was followed by three more years of improvement as a journeyman, a time spent on the job gaining practical experience in different types of work. It was also the time to travel and observe. To be qualified, one had then to present, at least in Europe, a masterwork, which would be either an actual job completed satisfactorily or else a model demonstrating the skills required of a master. Once graduated, the master would open his own studio if he had enough means to be able to take on commissions; or else he would be attached to a princely house or to a church or abbey large enough to maintain a works department. At court and in the monasteries, the architect found the chance to intermingle with the upper classes and absorb their learned ways. Although generally not a nobleman himself, he was well thought of, allowed to eat at the prior's or prince's table, and paid adequately.

In a brief summary such as this, it might be wise to review the vast amount of knowledge that has been amassed about the Gothic architect by modern scholarship within the typical framework of his relation to the building process of a church. Bear in mind that the type stands for three hundred years during which the profession was hardly static; that individual commissions as well as national habits varied considerably; and that there was as wide a range of quality among practicing architects then as there is today.

The patron for whom the architect worked was a bishop, the chapter of a cathedral or collegiate church, or the abbot and brethren of a monastery. Rarely, as in the case of the reconstruction of Sta. Reparata (now Sta. Maria del Fiore) in Florence in 1294, or of the religious foundations of Siena, the commission came through a vote of the people. In most cases, representative committees dealt with the architect in the name of such corporate patrons as chapters and communes. But there are cases of systematic involvement with the building process on the part of individual bishops or abbots, to the extent that the church in question should be properly called an effort of true collaboration between patron and architect. We have already mentioned Suger, whose account of the rebuilding of St. Denis manages to obscure the role of the architect entirely. Suger sends out for building crews, questions the advice of his master carpenters about the necessity of going to Auxerre for timbers of the size required by the construction, and finds them in his own forests nearby; has columns brought from a quarry near Pontoise; personally makes sure, "by means of geometrical and arithmetical instruments," that the nave of the old church lines up with the new choir; and supervises every detail of the decoration, from the design of stained glass windows to the workmanship of the gem-encrusted golden crucifix. Another patron, Bishop Evrart de Fouilloy, is linked with the architects in the labyrinth of Amiens Cathedral. The bond between the architect and his patrons is most strikingly portrayed in the commemorative plaque of the cathedral at Ulm (1377): it shows the mayor and his wife resting the model of the church on the shoulders of the architect, who stoops to receive it (Figure 22).

The undertaking was momentous. It meant a long building campaign that would disrupt the normal function of the church, if it were a matter of a significant reconstruction, and would run the risk of intermediate disaster. Suger describes the great storm that rocked his new church after the walls but not the vaults were complete and the centering had already been removed from the freshly made ribs. He was lucky; other patrons were not. The case of the collapse at Beauvais is well known. But the chief concern was money. Great sums were needed for a major building campaign, the drying up of which would mean long, costly delays and embarrassment. Material was more costly than labor, and one of the talents to be looked for in an architect was ingenuity in the conservation of resources, especially in minimizing the use of timber for scaffolding.

Funds came from a variety of sources. In the first place, there were the chapter's or abbey's own holdings and the income derived from the performance of its religious duties and the popular pilgrimages to its relics. Secondly, there were princely donations, which could be very generous, as well as more modest offerings from the public. From the thirteenth century onward, indulgences would be proclaimed for donors to the building fund of a major church. Thirdly, there were loans, for which treasures of the church, including relics, would be advanced as securities. Relics were also sent abroad on money-raising tours. Still, things could be difficult. In the 1250s, after some forty years of construction, the chapter at Rheims was 7000 pounds in debt.

Clearly, the funding of new structures could not be left to chance, or handled routinely as part of the treasurer's responsibility. Special confra-

Figure 22. Relief commemorating the founding of Ulm Cathedral in June 1377. The mayor of the city, Ludwig Krafft, and his wife rest the model of the building on the shoulders of the architect.

ternities were established to raise money systematically; the best-known instance is the *Maison de l'œuvre* founded at Strasbourg in 1290. To administer the daily operation of the works the chapter also selected an able person from within, or engaged a lay expert. The documents refer to this administrator as *magister operi* or *magister fabricae*, terms which are confusing since they also apply at times to the architect himself. Perhaps the distinction was not firm, at least not until the fourteenth century and onward, when the "master of the works" was nothing more than the administrator.

Much depended on the wise choice of an architect. He would be put in charge of a tremendous enterprise, and would be responsible, in the end, not only for the form but also for the stability of the building. That is, he would act as his own builder, and the way he conducted his assignment would undoubtedly affect how well the patron's money was used. Often, the choice was a local architect, especially if he had served as assistant to the previous master. But the chapter often looked further afield, to find the architect with the safest record or the most attractive reputation. French architects were much sought after with the invention of Gothic, especially in the north where the *opus francigenum* was soon popular. Master Henri was at Leon, Spain in 1209; Etienne de Bonneuil, at Uppsala in 1287; Jean Mignot, at Milan in 1401. If Gothic became a genuinely international mode of building, credit is partly due to the mobility of the masters.

Sometimes a competition would be held among possible candidates for a job, or rather professional opinion would be solicited from several architects to see which one appeared to be the soundest. At Canterbury, the question was how best to repair the choir of the cathedral which had been burned down in 1174. "They called together both French and English architects [*artifices*], but they disagreed among themselves." Some counseled judicious restoration, others declared the structure unsafe and proposed to replace it with a totally new choir. William of Sens, a Frenchman, impressed the chapter best, and they engaged him. Actually, this "most clever artist in wood and stone" was also a clever judge of human behavior. He bided his time by surveying the burnt walls with the monks until "they were somewhat more cheerful" and receptive to the idea that the wreck should be demolished to make room for something new. Four years later, with the new choir building and the vault not yet in place, William fell down fifty feet from the scaffolding and was seriously hurt. For a time he guided the work from his bed through a young monk who had served him as warden of masons; but in the end he had to resign his commission and return to France, with an Englishman replacing him on the job (Harvey, *Mediaeval Architect*, 210 ff.).

The choice was not always happy. In 1195, twenty years after Canterbury had settled for William of Sens, the monks of St. Albans hired a master, Hugo de Goldclif, because of his "good reputation." But he turned out to be "a deceitful and unreliable man" who added unnecessary carvings to the facade and left the half-finished walls uncovered during the rainy season, with the result that the stones cracked and the walls came down.

The architect having been selected, a contract was drawn up to specify his charge. Examples surviving from the late Middle Ages show that a principal concern was that the architect devote himself to the task wholeheartedly and not have other employment on the side. Jacobus de Favariis (Jacques de Fauran) of Narbonne was made architect of the cathedral at Gerona, Spain, about 1325, with the stipulation that he was to make at least six visits yearly from Narbonne to oversee the project. A contract to build the nave of Fotheringhay Church, dated 22 September 1434 and drawn up between a building commission on the one hand, consisting of the Duke of York, William Wolston, squire, and Thomas Pecham, clerk, and William Horwood, freemason, on the other, stipulates the type of work to be done, the pay (300 pound sterling) and by what installments it is to be paid, and penalties should Horwood neglect to pay a workman or be unable to complete the job "within reasonable time." For the latter breach he goes to prison, and all his "movable goods and heritances" are confiscated. (See E. Holt, ed., *A Documentary History of Art*, I, 115 ff.)

The extraordinary power the architect exercised over the project should not be interpreted as boundless. There were many restrictions as to what he could and could not do. He was, for one thing, bound by the wishes of the patron, which could be very specific and demanding. Sometimes, as some late English documents show, the patron set himself up as determiner of size and proportions of the whole building or parts of it. Sometimes the architect was told to imitate this or that extant building. He was also obliged to tolerate outside consultants at various stages of the work; in the contract of Fotheringhay just mentioned, Horwood's work on the foundations of the nave was to be "overseen by masters of the same craft." There are cases of documented consultations, such as the famous debate at Gerona over whether the proper spanning of the gigantic church was best solved with a three-aisled scheme or an aisleless nave. In the case of Milan Cathedral at the end of the fourteenth century, native Lombard masons were forced to consult with a string of French and German architects, as annual reports show.

Beyond this direction from patron and colleague, there was much else that conditioned the design of the church. The religious thinking of a particular monastic order, Benedictine or Cluniac, was expressed in drawings and descriptions of intent which guided the architect. Aesthetic choices were equally affected by what might be called architectural politics. A good example of this is the celebrated disagreement between two prelates, Suger and Bernard of Clairvaux, toward the middle of the twelfth century, one extolling ornate building as a tribute to God, the other decrying it as vanity. There were, besides, regional and national tendencies, often with political connotations; we might mention the ostentatious rejection of pronounced exterior buttressing by the English as a consciously anti-French statement, or the "merchant Gothic" of Germany reflecting religious independence and an image of rational citizenship.*

The design method of the Gothic architect had shifted significantly by the thirteenth century. Much about Carolingian and Romanesque practice still remains inexplicable. It seems that in the earlier period design method may have been caught in the conflict between systematic ordering and the inconstancy of local traditions. How the conflict was resolved in the course of time is, for the most part, unclear. Strictly modular layouts, such as that of the St. Gall plan, appear at present to have been of limited currency. In these, the design was ordered on the basis of a rational, additive progression. The simple applied geometry of the plans and elevations yielded subdivisions of the module that were reasonable yardstick measurements. In mature Gothic design, arithmetical tidiness in the much more sophisticated geometry used was not always of prime concern. The design process evolved from a geometric progression that started with basic figures, such as equilateral triangles, circles, and squares, ending up, through a series of simple geometric steps, in elaborate constellations of form. In this dynamic manipulation of geometry the module had, as it were, to fend for itself. Measured drawings were exceptional. Proportions were not fixed according to a respected general canon, as with Classical

* I owe this observation to F. Bucher, whose paper read at the 1974 annual meeting of the Society of Architectural Historians, "Aesthetic Imperatives and Restraints in Medieval Architectural Patronage," was amply suggestive. For an abstract, see the *Journal* of the Society for October 1974, p. 232.

architecture. There is a standard relationship between the diameter and the height of a Classical column, say, and an organic response between the column and the height of the building which will determine that the column would be proportionately taller as the total height of the building increases. In Gothic architecture, proportions are more abstract; the individual elements have no accepted set of proportions in themselves or in relation to the overall dimensions of the building, but rather follow a system of interrelationships grounded in the consistency of geometric formulae.

It is sometimes said that the dependence of the medieval architect on geometry came about because of the absence of generally applicable measuring units. It was therefore convenient to be able to spin the design of the building through the immutable discipline of geometry. Actually, standardization of measures and weights had started by the thirteenth century, at least within each country. The strict submission to geometry was not merely a matter of exigency, but rather one of distinct preference. Only those buildings that obeyed the laws of this discipline were thought to be structurally sound and aesthetically pleasing. In the minutes of the architectural conferences held in Milan from 1391 to the early years of the fifteenth century to determine the progress of the new cathedral, the issue is neatly encapsulated by the dictum of the French master Jean Mignot, *Ars sine scientia nihil est*, or "Art without science amounts to nothing." *Ars* here meant practical building knowhow; *scientia*, the rational theory of architecture based on geometry. The foreign experts from the north were critical of the native Lombard masters for neglecting the geometrical rationale of Gothic design and relying too much on constructional common sense. They had been called in, one by one, after the foundations of the cathedral had been laid. The issue was to determine whether the design for the cathedral proper as drawn up by the local masters could be safely realized. Northern opinion held that it could not, because the height of the nave and the aisles, and other lesser dimensions, had not been established through sound geometric deployment, but too much emphasis had been placed on the arithmetical order of a governing ten-*braccia* unit. The main debate was whether the section of the cathedral should be derived *ad quadratum*, that is, on the basis of a square subdivided into a grid of smaller squares (Heinrich Parler of Gmünd); or *ad triangulum*, on the basis of a series of triangles, equilateral (Gabriele Stornaloco) or Pythagorean. In the first case, the height of the building would be equal to its width; in the second, equal to the height of the triangle and therefore less than the width. The question that the Gothic designer considered important was not "How high should the building be in terms of the strength of the foundations and the structural possibilities of the whole?" but rather, "Within what figure shall it be designed?" This was so because of the belief that with the proper geometric formula decided upon by the architect, both the aesthetic *and* the structural correctness of the building could not help but be assured. This perspective must be kept in mind in reading those modern accounts of Gothic architecture that see in the cathedrals a manifestation of the rationalist doctrine "Form follows function." Since the days of Viollet-le-Duc, this school of thought has insisted that every detail of Gothic design is a response to a structural necessity. But the point about the Gothic architect is that he sees form and structure as one, and both as engendered through theoretical reasoning—that is, in accordance with geometric formulae. *Ars*, or the craft of masonry, guarantees that the theoretical construct will be executed in a predetermined, correct way.

The drawings prepared by the architect during the building process at this later stage of the Gothic style were numerous. Some were meant for the patron, others were the product of the architect's own arrival at design solutions, still others were working drawings to be consulted by the masons on the job. In the first category, we might cite large presentation plans and elevations, carefully rendered drawings on special skin to convey to the building committee the impression of the finished church. Magnificent drawings survive for the west elevation of Cologne Cathedral, the north tower of Vienna's St. Stephen, and the west elevation and tower of Ulm Cathedral (Figure 23). One recorded incident reflects the importance attached to these formal documents. In 1497 the City Council of Stuttgart took Master Niclas Queck to court for absconding with a large plan for the cathedral tower when he moved on from his post as Chief Master in Frankfurt to work in Mainz; he was forced to return it in due time. In the second category belong quick sketch plans dashed off by the architect to see how something might look. The third category is the richest. We might mention first the "key-plan," on the basis of which all the parts of the church were correlated in a complicated way that remains unexplained. The idea was to derive all structural and decorative members from each other in a concatenated pattern based on lodge practice. Linear diagrams of working drawings were also in use to indicate where such things as ornamental keystones would be affixed in the course of construction. F. Bucher calls them "placement or positioning plans." Full-

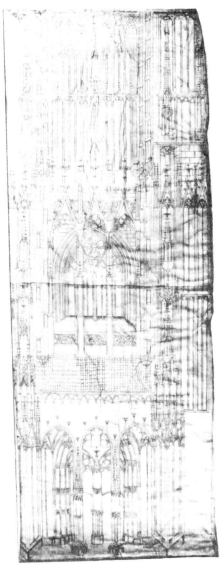

Figure 23. West elevation and tower of Ulm Cathedral, parchment drawing in the Victoria and Albert Museum, London; fifteenth century. This extraordinarily fine drawing shows the level of sophistication of late Gothic practice.

size drawings for architectural or sculptural details were scribed on the actual stonework, traced on a plastered floor, or derived from templates— that is, cutout molds made usually of thin panels of oak that fixed the profiles of architectural members and their moldings so that they could be traced on the stone and repeated as many times as necessary. The preparation of templates was considered a major responsibility of the architect.

They were delivered with some formality to the master mason after having been drawn and cut in the tracery house, the architect's own office on the construction site.

Much of this design process rested on established tradition. Behind every architect stood the education of the lodge and the zealously guarded formulae of the trade. Distinguished practitioners added to this core knowledge by setting down exemplars derived from their own experience. The thirteenth-century album of Villard de Honnecourt is a treasured specimen of these pattern books. A master mason of Picardy, he traveled extensively during his career, as far as Hungary, recording the more notable bits of architecture he encountered. Included in the album are elevations of Rheims Cathedral, a plan and elevation of Laon Cathedral, and rose windows from Chartres and Lausanne. But much of it is given over to drawings of animals and human figures and diagrams of building tackle (Figures 24 and 25). The extent of a Gothic master's skills is outlined in the note of Plate II: ". . . in this book one may find good advice for the great art of masonry, and the construction of carpentry; and you will find therein the art of drawing, the elements being such as the discipline of geometry requires and teaches."

Such model books were not meant for general circulation, but only for the teaching of the initiated. Lodges were enjoined not to divulge trade secrets to outsiders. The Regensburg Convention of 1459, for example, expressly states that "no workman, nor master, nor journeyman shall teach anyone, whatever he may be called, not being one of our handicraft and never having done mason work, how to take the elevation from the ground plan." It is little wonder that no professional treatises were produced in the Middle Ages along the lines of Vitruvius' for Roman antiquity. The only work of a technical nature actually published is very late, toward the close of the fifteenth century when Renaissance treatises in Italy—by Alberti, Filarete, Francesco di Giorgio—had already made their appearance. The work in question is a pamphlet dealing with the problem of plotting a pinnacle in correct proportion from its ground plan. Its author, the Chief Master of Regensburg Cathedral, Mathias Roriczer, invokes in his dedication to Bishop Wilhelm the latter's frequently expressed wish "that such an art of general utility should be thrown open and clearly exposed" (Holt, Documentary History, I, p. 96).

But to return to the architect's involvement in the design of our typical church. Having produced the preliminary drawings and had them agreed to by the building committee, he would proceed to set up the work force.

Figure 24. Page from the notebook of Villard de Honnecourt (Bibliothèque nationale, Paris); thirteenth century. The notebook was meant as an aid for the practitioner, teaching him techniques of carpentry and masonry and the art of drawing. This page shows a drawing of two wrestlers, and plans for the church of the order of Citeaux and for the east end of the cathedral at Cambrai.

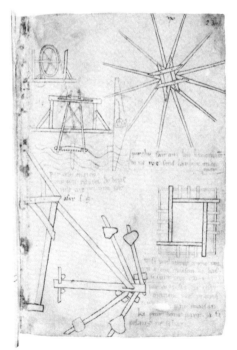

Figure 25. Another page from the notebook of Villard de Honnecourt, showing various engines and instruments. Such pattern books recorded the accumulated knowledge of the mason's lodge and the author's own professional experience. They were not meant to circulate beyond the closed circle of the trade.

His immediate staff would consist of a number of master craftsmen whom he would personally hire and pay. There was the master quarryman and the master stonecutter, the master sculptor and the master mason, the master carpenter and the master glassmaker—each running a workshop staffed with his own apprentices and assistants. Most of the heavy work— digging foundations, piling up earth for ramps or vaults, lugging stones around—was done by laborers, men of no particular skill and minimal pay. The master carpenter would be in charge of procuring the vast amounts of timber needed for scaffolding, shoring, centering, and the hoisting machines. The master quarryman would set up shop at the quarry itself where much of the preliminary chipping and even shaping of the cut stone would be done, to reduce the overall load that had to be transported. The individual block was marked to show its future location in the cathedral; the particular quarry it came from, so that the quarryman could be paid for the number of blocks he extracted; and the particular mason who had worked it.

Meanwhile, at the site, the ground was cleared, the workshops for the craftsmen built, and forges set up to make new tools as they were worn or broken in the course of construction—adzes, chisels, levers, dividers, and so on. The outline of the church was laid out by the architect by means of a cord and marked by wooden stakes or metal rods. The cords were stretched and restretched as the building proceeded from bay to bay, causing the slight shifts of axis and other irregularities that are apparent today only in careful surveys of the churches. Then the laborers began to dig the foundation ditches, as much as twenty-five feet deep for thick foundation walls. The clay at the bottom of the ditch was coated with a bed of small pebbles, and on this bed the foundation stones would be lowered after an impressive corner-laying ceremony attended by church and political dignitaries and huge crowds from the town.

In supervising the construction of the church, the Gothic architect would be under one main imperative: the need to keep the floor as unencumbered as possible, so that the church could begin to be used once the walls and a temporary timber roof were in place. This and the urge to economize in materials rather than men encouraged the use of minimal scaffolding. Towers would be set up, for example, for the construction of each nave pier, then dismantled and moved to the next. These timber structures were lightly built of thin poles lashed together with ropes; for platforms to stand on, "hurdles" were used, composed of straight rods interwoven with withes, like mats, resting in part on the stone construction already in existence. In fact, the building as it rose became scaffolding for what was to be built above. For this reason, one of the most extraordinary elements of a Gothic cathedral was a system of passages and stairs built along and in the thickness of the walls, facades included, to serve as a circulation network for the crew and as the substructure for higher scaffolding. The stairs, narrow and spiral, were called *vices* and could be put up with no scaffolding at all—just one step resting on another and the mason climbing with the rising stair and building the skin around it as he climbed. Working drawings for the *vices*, which were to be found at the transept ends, in the bell towers of the west facade, and other such places, were supplied by the architect.

When the walls had been raised up to and including the clerestory level, the building was shored with cross-beams within, and the nave walls stabilized by the flying buttresses without. Then a roof with a very steep pitch would be built high above the crown line of the rib vaults that were to be put up later. The shaping, notching, and test-assembling of the roof beams was done on the ground; then the truss assemblage was taken apart so that the members could be hoisted and reassembled at the top. In time the vaults would follow built on formwork, one bay after another with the help of movable centering. The tracery, cut from the architect's templates, would be assembled in the windows at some point in the later stages of the construction, and the sculpture put in place.

The great sculptural programs of Gothic cathedrals are an integral part of the architectural frame and its experience. They were, in the same way, an integral aspect of the architect's responsibility, and not the province of a separate mastermind. The medieval architect had come out of the same training as the mason and the sculptor. All had to master the working of stone, from the splitting of the block out of the native rock and its cutting and shaping to the specialized skill of carving moldings, capitals, and sculptural figures, at which stage one deserved to be called freemason. The architect rose to prominence from freemasonry. Having gone through all the stages of treating stone that were called for in the building process of the church, he was therefore fully qualified to oversee every aspect of this process.

This sketch provides only a superficial look at the construction of Gothic cathedrals. The full story is infinitely more complex and still not free of mystery. If we have gone into it at all, it is to demonstrate how indispensable the architect was to the making of the fabric. Despite some contemporary criticism, the comments of Nicolas de Biard for example, that the architect had divorced himself from the workshop content to lead with words rather than by example, the truth is that he was at all times intimate with the stones and timber that were molded under his direction into transcendent theaters of Christian faith. Above and beyond the conceptualization of the drawings, his hand was to be found everywhere on the actual fabric. The design of all important details was executed on the building site itself. His sketches of the outline of the piers can still be seen on the granite slabs covering the side aisles of Limoges Cathedral. And he took chisel and hammer in hand to carve a tricky bit of tracery or the heads of the more important statues of the facade. The actual separation of the architect-conceiver from the reality of the building process did not occur until the Italian Renaissance. That is the subject of the following two chapters.

The Gothic architect had many associates and collaborators. Some of his responsibility was relegated to, or at times preempted by, agents whose contribution has been variously assessed. This contribution has either gone unsung because of the difficulty of pinpointing it; or else exaggerated to lend credence to favorite hypotheses about Gothic building. They include determined attempts to read the great cathedrals as the product of an inspired communality, the intellectual miracle of symbolism and numerology, or the ineluctable result of the time-spirit. All of this special pleading is tinged with the romantic impulse. But romanticism tugs the other way as well, in urging the declaration of supremacy for the Gothic architect, his canonization; the attraction of the architect as hero is heady stuff for the lay person and of obvious self-service for the professional. It is essential to be dispassionate, to avoid alike niggardliness and inflation. There is still much that we do not know about the Gothic architect. What we know is nevertheless enough to prove that architecture in the later Middle Ages was a demanding and respected profession, and that its practice was, for the most part, in able hands.

BIBLIOGRAPHICAL NOTES

There is not much to read on the Byzantine architect. See G. Downey, "Byzantine Architects: Their Training and Methods," *Byzantion* 18 (1946-48), 99-118; and H. Meek, "The Architect and His Profession in Byzantium," *Royal Institute of British Architects, Journal* 59 (1952), 216-220. For aspects of construction A. Choisy's *L'art de bâtir chez les byzantins* (Paris, 1883) is still useful; see especially Ch. XV on building crafts.

The bibliography for the architect in Islamic countries is also limited. See primarily L. A. Mayer, *Islamic Architects and Their Works* (Geneva, 1956).

The bibliography for the Western Middle Ages is vast. A good place to see it all listed is J. Harvey, *The Mediaeval Architect* (London, 1972), which is also the best current summary of our knowledge on the subject. Note especially the recent articles by L. R. Shelby in the Harvey bibliography. Also useful as a general handbook is P. du Colombier, *Les chantiers des cathédrales* (Paris, 1953); and for the Gothic period O. von Simson, *The Gothic Cathedral* (Harper paperback; New York, 1964). Documents in translation will be found in E. Holt, ed., *A Documentary History of Art*, I (Princeton, 1957); C. Davis-Weyer, *Early Medieval Art, 300-1150*, and T. G. Frisch, *Gothic Art, 1140-c.1450*, both published by Prentice-Hall in 1971 in their Sources and Documents in the History of Art series.

For terminology, see especially two articles by N. Pevsner: "Terms of Architectural Planning in the Middle Ages," *Journal of the Warburg and Courtauld Institutes* 5 (1942), 232-37; and "The Term 'Architect' in the Middle Ages," *Speculum* 17 (1942), 549-62.

The best account of Gothic building techniques in English is J. Fitchen, *The Construction of Gothic Cathedrals* (Oxford, 1961). For its lively visual material, see also a popular book by D. Macaulay, *Cathedral: The Story of Its Construction* (Boston, 1973).

For principles of Gothic design and design theory, see: J. Ackerman, "*Ars sine scientia nihil est:* Gothic Theory of Architecture at the Cathedral of Milan," *Art Bulletin* 31 (1949), 84-111; P. Frankl, "The Secret of the Mediaeval Masons," *Art Bulletin* 27.1 (1945), 46-65; K. J. Conant, "The After-Life of Vitruvius in the Middle Ages," *Journal of the Society of Architectural Historians* 27 (1968), 33-38; and F. Bucher, "Design in Gothic Architecture: A Preliminary Assessment," *Journal of the Society of Architectural Historians* 27 (1968), 49-71.

The bibliography for medieval castles is considerable. As a good introduction, the reader is referred to the English examples analyzed in R. A. Brown, H. M. Colvin, and A. J. Taylor, *The History of the King's Works: I, The Middle Ages* (London, 1963).

On Villard de Honnecourt, see T. Bowie, ed., *The Sketchbook of Villard de Honnecourt* (Bloomington, Ind., 1959); and R. Branner, "Villard de Honnecourt, Reims, and the Origin of Gothic Architectural Drawing," *Gazette des Beaux-Arts*, series 6, vol. 61 (1963), 129-46. See also R. W. Scheller, *A Survey of Medieval Model Books* (Haarlem, 1963).

The Plan of St. Gall has been studied, most recently and thoroughly, by Walter Horn. Until the definitive volume appears, these articles by him should be consulted: "On the Author of the Plan of St. Gall and the Relation of the Plan to the Monastic Reform Movement" and "The Plan of St. Gall—Original or Copy," both in *Studien zum St. Galler Klosterplan* (St. Gall, 1962), pp. 79-128; "The 'Dimensional Inconsistencies' of the Plan of Saint Gall and the Problem of the Scale of the Plan" (with E. Born), *Art Bulletin* 48 (1966), 285-308. For Cluny, see especially K. J. Conant, *Cluny: Les églises et la maison du chef d'ordre* (Macon, 1968). For Suger and the abbey of St. Denis, see: E. Panofsky, *Abbot Suger on the Abbey Church of St. Denis* (Princeton, 1946); and S. M. Crosby, "The Plan of the Western Bays of Suger's New Church at St. Denis," *Journal of the Society of Architectural Historians* 27 (1968), 39-43.

# 4

## The Emergence of the Italian Architect during the Fifteenth Century

LEOPOLD D. ETTLINGER

Any discussion of the architect's profession in Italy during the fifteenth century has to begin with a paradox: practice of architecture, as we today understand it, was not yet a recognized profession, and unlike the painter or sculptor, the designer of buildings did not have his clearly defined place within the trades. There was no standard training for those wishing to engage in architecture, there was no guild devoted specifically to the professional interests of architects or to supervising their education, and the men who made the plans for churches and palaces were now ranked with humble artisans, now with scholars putting their knowledge to practical purposes. At best we may claim that the architect as a specialist or professional man began to emerge during this period, so that by 1550, when Giorgio Vasari published the first edition of his history of Italian artists, he could call it *The Lives of the Most Excellent Painters, Sculptors and Architects.*

But even so, among over one hundred artists listed by Vasari between Cimabue and Raphael, only seven are simply designated as architects, and of these five worked in the late fifteenth and early sixteenth centuries. The list is rather interesting. At the head stands Arnolfo di Cambio, the first architect of Sta. Maria del Fiore, the cathedral of Florence, and his *vita* is preceded by a longish disquisition on the anonymity of medieval architects and the scant knowledge about a few working in the thirteenth and fourteenth centuries. Yet it is made quite clear by Vasari that Arnolfo is allowed to make an appearance because he had designed the cathedral of

Florence, and even more because there had to be an imposing figure in architecture at the outset of his story just as Cimabue opens the story of painting and Nicola Pisano that of sculpture. There is no other "architect" mentioned until we come to Alberti, who according to Vasari is better known by his theoretical writings than by his other works, and the point—typical of a humanist's argument—is made that Alberti was a scholar who liked architecture. This to Vasari the Renaissance historian is an ideal combination: "When theory and practice are united in one person, the ideal condition of art is attained, because art is enriched and perfected by knowledge, the opinions and writings of learned artists having more weight and more credit than the words or works of those who have nothing more to recommend them beyond what they have made, whether it be done well or badly" ("Life of Alberti"). Next come two minor figures, Baccio Pontelli and Chimenti Camicia, the former working for Sixtus IV and the latter for Matthias Corvinus of Hungary; both combined simple architectural tasks with military engineering. Donato Bramante, not surprisingly, is accorded the title "architect," and so are Giuliano and Antonio da Sangallo. But all others, whose buildings Vasari lists and often discusses in some detail, are listed as "sculptor and architect," "painter and architect," or even "painter, sculptor and architect." Brunelleschi falls into the first category, and his training as a goldsmith, his participation in the competition for the Florentine Baptistery doors, and the wooden Crucifix he carved, are all treated in great detail. Michelozzo's contributions to sculpture and architecture are both assessed, and while Bramante's work as a painter is neglected, Raphael's work as an architect is duly credited. Clearly Vasari, a careful historian who documented his biographies as best he could, knew that those masters of the fifteenth century who were responsible for designing architecture were usually trained in one of the other arts and continued practicing their original métier even after they had become well-patronized designers of buildings.

In the Middle Ages any architect, whether he bore that title or not, was an artisan, usually a stone-mason, and if he was head of a workshop he would be called "master mason," though a number of other terms were also in use. (See preceding chapter.) But all this began to change in the early fifteenth century in Italy, and the humanists played a decisive role in redefining the functions of an architect. Their unbounded admiration for Classical models in literature also stimulated the study of Roman remains, and they understandably expected that this newly discovered formal vocabulary would be used in contemporary architecture. But that was not all. As far as ideas about the architect's profession were concerned, one particular event was of special significance.

In 1415 the Florentine scholar Poggio Bracciolini, attending the Council of Constance, found in the library of the monastery of St. Gall in nearby Switzerland a manuscript of Vitruvius' treatise on architecture, the only surviving ancient text of this kind. While Vitruvius had never been entirely forgotten—his book was copied many times during the Middle Ages (see above, p. ooo)—this manuscript was a particularly fine one dating from the Carolingian period. Poggio might easily have mistaken it for a copy made at an even earlier date. Moreover at that particular moment, when Classical texts were being eagerly collected, this find can only have helped to enhance Vitruvius' reputation. Here was an authentic handbook of ancient architecture in which could be found not only useful information about buildings and their decoration, but also a precise description of the tasks of the architect. And these were rather different from those of the traditional medieval master mason. Architecture to Vitruvius was a "science." Or rather, he was at some pains to explain that an architect had to have both theory and praxis. How is he to combine the two? Vitruvius argues that a mere practitioner cannot give sufficient reasons for the forms he adopts, while a theoretician "grasps a shadow instead of substance" (1.1.2). Only the fully trained man, who understands what he wants to do and at the same time knows how to do it, will carry out his plans properly. This means that anybody embarking on the career of architect must be something of a scholar before he can design, let alone execute, a building. Such views were well received in an age when new aesthetic ideals increasingly required from artists a certain amount of theoretical knowledge, say of anatomy, perspective, or proportion. When, in the middle of the fifteenth century, Leone Battista Alberti (1404-72) wrote a treatise on architecture (*De re aedificatoria*), he clearly echoed Vitruvius in his preface: "An architect is not a carpenter or joiner . . . the manual worker being no more than an instrument to the architect, who by sure and wonderful skill and method is able to complete his work. . . . To be able to do this, he must have a thorough insight into the noblest and most curious sciences."

Obviously Vitruvius' text was studied by progressive architects and patrons for many reasons other than his definition of the learned architect. Nevertheless, he seemed to justify scholars like Alberti turning to the praxis of architecture. At the same time, in the eyes of any student of Vitruvius, the master mason was no longer sufficiently educated to deal adequately with the tasks of building with knowledge and understanding. The new attitude becomes perfectly clear in Antonio Manetti's biography of Filippo Brunelleschi (1377-1446), written in the early fourteen-eighties. Brunelleschi, he writes, wanted to rediscover "the excellent and highly ingenious building methods of the ancients and their harmonious proportions" (Saalman ed., p. 51). Manetti describes these studies in great detail—perhaps greater detail than the truth—but it becomes quite clear that he wishes to stress Brunelleschi's twofold aim: he studied Roman ruins both as a technologist and as a mathematician. His concerns were construction and proportion in order to benefit from these researches in his own work. He wished to understand the principles of Roman architecture, not just to copy it.

Brunelleschi was only the first of a long line of Renaissance architects for whom the remains of Roman antiquity became a means of education and a source for the compilation of a new kind of pattern book. It was not antiquarian interest which sent him to Rome, but the architect's desire to fill his notebooks with measured drawings after capitals, bases, columns, and so forth, the wish to investigate vaulting techniques and to measure plans or elevations in order to obtain the proportion of actual buildings, which might be compared with the rules given by Vitruvius. Unfortunately, Brunelleschi's drawings, which certainly did exist though some scholars have expressed doubts, do not survive. They were his most important working material when it came to his own designs, and it is precisely for this reason that, together with much similar material from the fifteenth century, they were not carefully preserved once they had served their purpose. For such drawings were not archaeological records but workshop patterns for the present, and like all such patterns they were discarded or forgotten after use. What we still have of architectural drawings of the Quattrocento is only a fraction of former riches, but therefore all the more important for our understanding of architectural practice of the period.

The Vatican Library owns a sketchbook by the Florentine architect and engineer Giuliano da Sangallo (1445-1515), which was started in 1465 and kept for many years, while constant additions were made. It is significant that this book contains not only drawings which Sangallo, in his own words, "measured and took from the antique," but also several which he saw in other pattern books, found useful, and therefore copied. Conversely, there is evidence that his collection was available to others who took material from it.

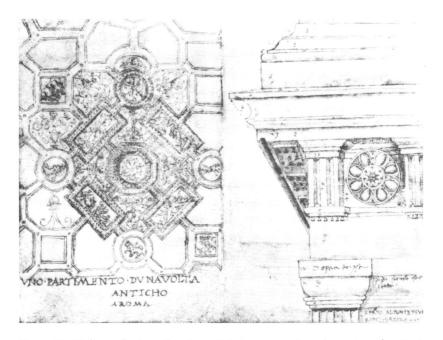

Figure 26. Giuliano da Sangallo, decorated Roman vault and cornice of a Doric building; Public Library, Siena. The drawing of the cornice is particularly interesting because measurements of the various parts have been entered, demonstrating that Giuliano did not only draw what he had seen, but that such fragments of ancient architecture were also carefully measured in order to determine their proportions.

The nature of Sangallo's approach is demonstrated by a marked difference between his two types of drawings (Figures 26-28). Some are accurate and sharply delineated copies of the actual appearance of a ruin, a cornice, a capital, etc., while others show only half the building as he found it, with the rest restored. The need for such drawings from Brunelleschi on is obvious: they served as models for builders or masons who had to be familiarized with a new morphology and a new system of proportions. Yet only someone thoroughly familiar with the conventions of Classical architecture could give through them the necessary information.

Alberti freely admitted that he looked at the remains of Roman architecture in the first place because he wanted to find out whether he could learn from them anything for the present. With this aim in mind, he found ruins of greater interest than ancient authors; he was in fact highly critical of Vitruvius. None of his drawings survive, but from his remarks in *De re aedificatoria* we can reconstruct their character. They seem to

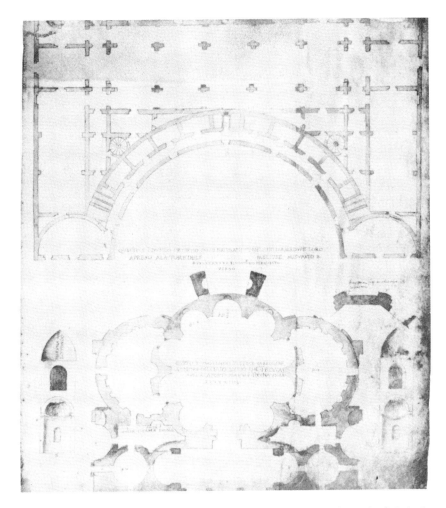

Figure 27. Giuliano da Sangallo, ground plans of the exedra at the end of Trajan's Forum and of the so-called temple of Minerva Medica, both in Rome. Page from a sketchbook now in the Vatican Library. These two measured plans give clear evidence of Giuliano's working method, and of the way in which he combined archaeological studies with the particular interests of the architect. The plan of Trajan's Forum had to be reconstructed from the scant remains visible in his day. The "Minerva Medica" was popular with Renaissance architects on account of its complex layout and vaulting system.

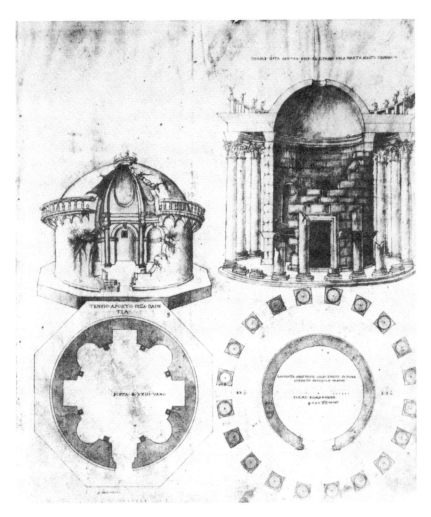

Figure 28. Giuliano da Sangalo, a temple at Porto near Ostia and the so-called temple of Vesta in Rome; page from the Vatican sketchbook. Both these drawings are strange combinations of accurate observation and fancy, particularly striking in the case of the "Vesta" temple. The section gives not the actual state of the building but Giuliano's reconstruction. For the temple at Porto we are given both a proper ground plan and a somewhat romantic view of a ruin.

Figure 29. Codex Escurialensis, view of the Roman Forum; late fifteenth century. This sketchbook, now in the Escorial, Spain, possibly comes from the workshop of the Florentine painter Domenico Ghirlandajo; it contains about 150 drawings after the antique, comprising views, plans and elevations, architectural and decorative details, and a few pieces of sculpture. It served as a pattern book for artists and architects interested in the remains of Classical art.

have been of three markedly different kinds. He noted forms, as for example the various types of capitals, bases, or ornaments. Further he measured what he had found and worked out the proportions of details as well as of whole buildings. Lastly he explored building techniques and demonstrated them graphically as well as verbally.

This "new learning" was presented empirically by draftsmen and theoreticians of the fifteenth century. Giuliano da Sangallo's sketchbook with its free reconstructions has already been mentioned. Another sketchbook, the celebrated *Codex Escurialensis*—so named after the place where it is now kept—mixes drawings after sculpture, ground plans, ornamental motives, views, architectural details, and so forth (Figures 29-30). It was obviously a pattern book, equally of use to painters and to builders. Alberti went a good way toward a rational approach to the many questions raised by contemporary demands and Classical models, but Antonio Averlino, called Filarete (ca. 1400-1469), who wrote his utopian *Trattato di*

Figure 30. Another page from the Codex Escurialensis: a pattern sheet with six capitals. It is likely that this page of the sketchbook was copied from a pattern book, compiled by an architect, which was widely known, since other copies after these capitals are known. While Figure 29 represents a picturesque view of an ancient site, this page is drawn with the accuracy required by masons who had to copy these capitals in stone.

*architettura* about 1460, did little to establish clear guidelines for the new kind of architect. Only in the early sixteenth century with Raphael do we find a rationally worked out approach to the problems facing the Vitruvian architect, that is, the man who had to master both theory and practice.

In spring 1514 Raphael became an assistant to Bramante for the new St. Peter's, and when Bramante died a few months later Raphael, together with Fra Giocondo, then aged eighty, took over the direction of building the new basilica. Fra Giocondo had published in 1511 the first illustrated edition of Vitruvius, and seems to have been a scholar and designer rather than a practicing architect. Neither he nor Raphael was expert in construction, and it is significant that Giuliano da Sangallo, who was appointed with them as chief administrator or co-ordinator, had real experience as a practicing architect. Moreover Giuliano had originally been trained as a joiner and engineer. We may speak in this case of a well-thought-out division of labor.

The same rational manner of working is evident again when, a few years later, Raphael was commissioned by Leo X to record ancient Rome. His report, contained in a famous letter of 1519, speaks of his twofold activities: the measuring and drawing of the monuments, and the interpretation of the visual evidence in the light of Classical authors. The drawings proposed by Raphael were to be of two kinds. There were to be views of the ruins, but, more important, he also suggested true architectural drawings, consisting of plans and elevations. The tradition started by Brunelleschi as essential for architectural practice—and, we may add, for the training of architects—had now reached maturity. For we should not think of Raphael's task as a purely archaeological undertaking. In a period when modern papal Rome was to emulate the capital of the Roman Empire, the practical value of such a record for the builders of the new town was obvious.

Brunelleschi's career is a good example of the profession of the architect during the first half of the fifteenth century. His biographer Manetti tells us: "At a tender age Filippo learned to write, read and calculate, as most boys of good families are expected to do in Florence, and he also had some book learning, since his father was a notary and perhaps planned the same profession for his son" (p. 39). Reading, writing, and calculating were part of the basic education given to Florentine children in the fifteenth century. But, as Michael Baxandall has recently argued, many continued their studies to include mathematics, and "for most middle-class people the mathematical skills of the secondary school were the climax of their intellectual formation and equipment" (p. 86). He adds that the surviving schoolbooks show clearly that the pupils were taught commercial mathematics, of which the study of proportion was an integral part. The application of these skills to architectural design of the fifteenth century is obvious. A fairly general knowledge of this kind of mathematics may also explain why designers sometimes furnished only a ground plan, leaving the working out of the proportional elevation to the master mason in charge of the execution of the design.

But, as his biographer tells us, Brunelleschi from early on showed a great interest in drawing and painting, and his father, recognizing his talent, allowed his son to train as a goldsmith. Such an initial training was undergone by many artists of the period because it included the basic skills required in all the arts. In 1398 Brunelleschi was matriculated in the Arte di Seta, the Silk Manufacturers' Guild, normally joined by goldsmiths, and in 1404 he became a master. He remained a member of this guild even after taking up architecture; as already mentioned, there never was in Florence, or elsewhere in Italy for that matter, an architect's guild. It seems that, like Brunelleschi, the architects of the fifteenth century, if they belonged to any guild at all—Alberti, a scholar, never did join one and would hardly have qualified for membership in any of them—joined the one appropriate to the training they had originally received.

Brunelleschi certainly practiced at least for a while the craft for which he had been trained, and like other goldsmiths of the time he also worked in bronze and wood. His carved *Crucifix* still hangs in S. Maria Novella, and the bronze panel depicting the *Sacrifice of Isaac*, with which he competed for the Baptistery doors, can still be compared with Ghiberti's prize-winning entry (Florence, Bargello). It may be true, as Manetti and Vasari hinted, that failure to win this important commission turned Brunelleschi's mind to the study of ancient architecture, and eventually to the application of the knowledge thus gained.

Brunelleschi's beginnings in a traditional craft are not unusual when we consider the careers of other fifteenth-century Italian archtiects, none of whom came out of a masons' workshop. Michelozzo worked as a sculptor with both Ghiberti and Donatello, and after the mid-thirties he was employed as an architect by Cosimo de' Medici, also succeeding in 1446, upon Brunelleschi's death, as *capo-maestro*—master mason—of the cathedral. Antonio da Sangallo was a carpenter rising step by step in the workshop of Bramante, who himself had first been a painter. Francesco di Giorgio, Raphael, Peruzzi, and Giulio Romano were painters by training. Alberti's background was different, however. Coming from a patrician family, he had had a university education, and to his contemporaries he always was first of all a scholar. In any case, none of these men, who were responsible for so many of the most celebrated Renaissance buildings, were technicians, and they all needed help when it came to problems of structure or building methods. Such help could only come from the practical men, the masons, builders, and joiners. It is possible that Brunelleschi was advised on the complex problems of statics arising in the construction of the cathedral cupola in Florence by his friend the mathematician Paolo Toscanelli, even though his own early schooling had included some mathematics.

The practice of architecture during the fifteenth century was a co-operative enterprise, presided over certainly by a responsible director, who relied in a variety of ways on a number of experts. The construction of the cupola of Sta. Maria del Fiore is an instructive case in point, about which we are fortunately well informed through a wealth of surviving documents covering most of its long building history. As far as the cupola is concerned, Ghiberti, who originally shared the commission with Brunelleschi, has given his side of the story in his autobiography, the *Commentarii*, while Brunelleschi's role is described in great detail—and with many snide remarks about his rival—in Antonio Manetti's life of him.

The story is complicated, and it is by no means true that Brunelleschi designed and constructed the cupola single-handed, as is so often believed. Ghiberti claims: "Few things of importance were made in our city which were not designed or devised by my hand. And especially in the building of the cupola Filippo and I were competitors for eighteen years at the same salary. Thus we executed the said dome" (*Commentarii*, ed. J. v. Schlosser, Berlin, 1912, p. 51). Manetti reverses the proportionate shares of the two masters (p. 77), but the documents tell a rather different story, and surely one which deserves more credence.

As early as 1404 Brunelleschi and Ghiberti were among the nineteen members of a committee, made up of artists and prominent Florentines, called together to advise the *operai*—the building authority of the cathedral—about the faulty construction of one of the choir buttresses. It is characteristic that so technical a matter should be put before a group of laymen; the practice persisted throughout the building history of the cupola and its lantern, and it was common at the time.

Only thirteen years later, in 1416, do we hear again of consultations with Brunelleschi, and this time specifically about the cupola. In 1418 the *operai* held a competition inviting designs and models for its vaulting. Brunelleschi and Ghiberti—both goldsmiths by training—submitted their proposals; of the other masters who competed eight were carpenters and one was a stone-mason. After the *operai* had inspected all the plans they charged Brunelleschi and Ghiberti to prepare a joint final model, and in April 1420 these two were appointed supervisors of the building program together with the master mason of the cathedral workshop, Battista d'Antonio. We do not know why Brunelleschi and Ghiberti were asked to pool their ideas, but the fact that they were put on an equal footing with an experienced master mason is highly significant. However, three years later a document calls Brunelleschi "inventor and chief director of the cupola [*inventor et gubernator major cupolae*]" (Fabriczy, p. 91), and in 1426 he became a full-time employee of the *operai* at an annual salary of one hundred florins, on condition that he would work exclusively on the cupola. Ghiberti was put on a part-time basis, retaining his pay of thirty-six florins per year with the stipulation that his presence on the building site was required for only one hour every day. This can only mean that his role had been reduced to that of a consultant, and that Brunelleschi was now taking full charge of all operations, including contracting. This arrangement

Figure 31. Filippo Brunelleschi, wooden model for the lantern crowning the cupola of Florence Cathedral, ca. 1436; Cathedral Museum, Florence. Of the many models prepared by Brunelleschi showing both the shape and construction of the cupola and its lantern, this is the only one to survive. While the decorative details of the lantern are clearly shown, only the structure of the cupola beneath is indicated.

is spelled out in a minute stating that he was "to provide, arrange, compose, or cause to be arranged and composed all and everything necessary and desirable for building, continuing and completing the cupola" (Fabriczy, p. 93).

In 1434 occurred a bizarre incident, which throws an interesting light on Brunelleschi's status as an architect and the envy he must have aroused among the conservative masons who had hitherto been responsible for all building programs. In August, when the cupola was nearing completion, the heads of the stone-masons' guild (Arte dei maestri di pietre) had Brunelleschi imprisoned on a charge that he had never paid his annual dues to the guild; the "closed shop" policy of trade unions clearly is not an invention of the industrial age. The *operai* of the cathedral retaliated by having the head of the guild thrown into prison, but some accommodation was reached quickly, and both men were released within a few days.

The cupola was completed in 1436, yet in spite of Brunelleschi's by now established pre-eminence as an architect a competition was held for designs of the lantern which was to crown his cupola. Not surprisingly he emerged victorious, and it is likely that the wooden model still preserved in the Cathedral Museum is the one he submitted (Figure 31).

The word "model" constantly occurs in the documents connected with the building of the cathedral during the fourteenth century and with construction of the cupola in the next. Models—as well as designs—were pre-

pared in the first place for the approval of a patron, though they were
rarely faithfully followed. In one of the frescoes which Vasari painted in
the Palazzo Vecchio to celebrate the rise of the Medici he depicted Brunelleschi kneeling before Cosimo il Vecchio and presenting him with the
model of S. Lorenzo (Figure 32). But, of course, models also served the
builders when it came to the execution of a building. Here, as in so much
else, the Renaissance continued a medieval and even earlier usage. Models
were already known in ancient Greece. Designs for the decorative parts
seem often to have been modeled in wax, a practice continued by Roman
architects. The Middle Ages inherited this method of preparing a building; when Arnolfo di Cambio was entrusted with the building of Florence
Cathedral in 1286 he submitted a model, and later several others followed
as the building progressed and was modified. The last of these, made in
1367, must have been a considerable affair, since it was made of brick. A
beautiful wooden model for S. Petronio in Bologna, dating from 1514,
survives, and so does the wooden model of the Palazzo Strozzi made in
1485. But these are really exceptions, and Vasari complained that careless-
ness of those in charge had led to the loss of the models made for Sta.
Maria del Fiore.

Models did no more than give a general idea of the appearance and scale
of a building, and they seem to have lacked details. These, and much else,
were left to discussions between the designer and those responsible for the
execution of designs. It is quite clear that Brunelleschi and others were
invariably expected to give instructions constantly on the building site.

Brunelleschi's cupola models involved a problem not usually encountered by designers. A cupola over the crossing had been envisaged from
the moment Florence Cathedral was first planned, but technical difficulties had made its construction impossible until Brunelleschi suggested
his solution. It seems from the documents and Manetti's biography that
certain models were specifically made in order to explain his vaulting technique. In particular the famous masonry "chains," introduced to insure
the soundness of the structure, were demonstrated before the *operai* in
this way. Manetti has left a revealing account, written at a time when
these models could still be seen: "Filippo's nature, or rather his custom
regarding models, after he had some years' experience in architecture,
was that the models for his buildings were made revealing little about
measurements, but he took care to make the walls, to show the arrangement of some membering, without the ornaments, capitals, architraves,
friezes, cornices, etc." (p. 117).

Figure 32. Brunelleschi presents the model for the church of San Lorenzo to Cosimo de' Medici. Fresco by Giorgio Vasari, 1565, in the Palazzo Vecchio, Florence. Among the decorations commissioned by Duke Cosimo I in the mid sixteenth century is a series telling the story of his family's rise to power. We do not know whether Vasari still knew the actual model, but his representation of the church is fairly accurate. In any case, the fresco illustrates one of the purposes for which such models were made.

We are less well informed about the procedure Brunelleschi followed on his other. buildings. Of the Old Sacristy Manetti says: "He designed the sacristy and confirmed it by advice both from citizens and artisans of a similar trade" (p. 107). This remark, like the story of the cupola, clearly demonstrates the role of the "learned" architect in relation to the "practical" men on the spot. In planning a church Brunelleschi, like other architects of his century, was guided by function and tradition, and the requirements of the liturgy were uppermost in his mind. But the layout was now controlled by a new system of proportions, based on the study of Vitruvius and of Roman remains. As to the forms, they were also new and broke decisively with the Gothic past. These elements must certainly have been indicated in models and drawings, even if there were no detailed "blueprints" of the kind in use today in every architect's office. All this underlines the inevitable need for collaboration between Brunelleschi and his builders or carpenters. In fact, the documents concerning his repeatedly changed models for the cupola make abundantly clear that the masons of the cathedral workshop had to meet in order to sort out the unusual problems posed by his designs.

But things could also go wrong because there was no detailed planning from the outset. This happened, as Manetti tells us (p. 97), while the Foundling Hospital was being built. During an absence Brunelleschi had left verbal instructions with the builders and the committee of the Silk Manufacturers' Guild, the patrons of the hospital. On his return he found to his chagrin that certain decorative details had not been executed in accordance with his instructions. This could not have happened in an age when the architect's studio provided the executants with detailed drawings of every part of a building under construction.

If Brunelleschi may be described as a goldsmith and a student of Roman architecture turned architect, Leone Battista Alberti, who is always named with him as a founding father of Renaissance architecture, must be called a dilettante in the best sense of the word, and it seems that in spite of his designs for ecclesiastical and secular buildings he never pretended to any expertise on the practical side of architecture.

Alberti came from a patrician family of cloth merchants and bankers who played an important role in the political and economic life of Florence. Although he was illegitimate, he received an academic education and was trained in classics and the law. Yet he was also an accomplished writer, of both poetry and philosophy, and he spent many years as an official in the papal bureaucracy. His wide travels all over Italy brought him into contact with wealthy burghers and princes, many of whom he advised in their patronage of building. We should not think of him as a humanist with an interest in the arts who wrote treatises on painting, sculpture, and architecture, nor as an architect who put up the Palazzo Ruccellai, rebuilt S. Francesco in Rimini as a mausoleum for Sigismondo Malatesta, and built S. Andrea in Mantua. He was something different. None of his treatises were handbooks for practitioners, and the one on architecture, *De re aedificatoria*, addresses the patron rather than the builder. It has been rightly said: "He thinks of architecture entirely as a civic activity" (Blunt, p. 7). For him humanism was not simply book learning or acquaintance with ancient monuments, but the application of all knowledge in the public interest; and the structure of the treatise on architecture is determined by this basic belief. It is not a classicist's primer on style, but rather a guide through an ideal city which can offer the best living conditions for the community. In the Preface he writes therefore: "For the service, security, honour and ornament of the public we are exceedingly obliged to the architect, to whom in time of leisure we are indebted for tranquility, pleasure and health, in time of business for assistance and profit, and in both for security and dignity. Let us not therefore deny that he ought to be praised and esteemed, and to be allowed a place, both for the wonderful and ravishing beauty of his works, and for the necessity, serviceableness, and strength of the things which he has invented, among the chief of those who have deserved honour and rewards from mankind" (p. x).

Alberti begins his treatise with technical preliminaries, drawing and designing for architecture, materials, construction. After next discussing in great detail the choice and use of the best site for the town, he turns to the different types of buildings needed in it, both public and private, laying down rules for both their plans and ornaments.

We do not know when he began work on this treatise, but a first version was presented to Pope Nicholas V in 1452. This dedication is significant, for this pontiff wanted to restore to Rome the dignity of the world's capital, and his three most important building projects—the rebuilding of the Constantinian basilica of St. Peter's, a new papal palace at the Vatican, and the urban renewal of the Borgo Leonino adjoining the Vatican—were to be visible signs of his ambition. It is almost certain that Alberti, who was at the time a papal official, acted as an adviser, though the actual planning and designing seems to have been left in the hands of the sculptor-architect Bernardo Rosselino.

It is a well-known fact that Alberti wrote his treatise with that of Vitruvius in mind, but from the point of view of fifteenth-century architectural practice the differences are far more important than the superficial similarities, such as in both cases the division into ten books, or Alberti's retention of at least some of the Roman writer's terminology. Vitruvius, in spite of his protestations about being a scientist as well as a practitioner, really had written a book full of technical advice, and his scholarly pretense was dropped after a somewhat pompous introduction, which even included astronomy among the branches of learning to be mastered by the architect (see above, p. 39). Originally his book must have been illustrated to demonstrate many technical points, but nothing of this survives. Alberti does not seem to have envisaged illustrations, for there are none in the manuscript dedication copy for Nicholas V of 1452, nor are there any in the first printed edition, which appeared in 1485, after the author's death; later editions, which do have illustrations, cannot claim Alberti's authority for them. There really was no need for them, for he had written as a social philosopher, addressing an educated audience who would know something about the morphology of architecture past and present.

Alberti's characteristic role as a scholar-designer and his relationship to the executing practitioner can still be seen in correspondence referring to S. Francesco in Rimini. At the behest of Sigismondo Malatesta Alberti had designed for the simple fourteenth-century friars' church a severe and classical outer casing which seemed to him and his patron more in accord with the splendid mausoleum required by the Lord of Rimini. At some unspecified date during the early fourteen-fifties Alberti wrote from Rome to Matteo dei Pasti, who was in charge of the building operations on the spot. But it should be noted that Matteo was only a kind of middleman, who in his turn needed the assistance of competent masons, as he had been trained in Verona, his native city, as a miniaturist and goldsmith. He was active in Rimini after 1446 as a medallist. In 1447 he was put by Sigismondo in charge of the first two chapels to be rebuilt, but in 1449, when it was decided to refurbish the whole structure, he became Alberti's chief assistant for the construction of the marble exterior.

In the letter just mentioned Alberti informs Matteo curtly that he cannot accept any criticism of the cupola (originally planned to crown the crossing, but never built) because it is based on Roman models. He goes on to say that the measurements of the pilasters on the façade cannot be altered without destroying the essential harmony of the whole. Alberti asserts that the round window to be broken into the façade will not weaken the structure, but nevertheless he advises Matteo to seek proper advice in all matters concerning the structure. And this is precisely what Matteo must have done. Writing to the patron, Sigismondo Malatesta, he refers to Alberti's letter, which had contained sketches for the facade and a capital. He tells Sigismondo that he has shown them to all "the masters and engineers." They, however, had found these proposals in conflict with Alberti's earlier model, and now Sigismondo is called upon to decide which solution he prefers. We learn yet another interesting item from the letter: one of the Riminese masons wants to go to Rome in order to discuss the vaulting of the nave with Alberti, who rather naively had suggested a wooden barrel vault.

This correspondence—and we certainly have only part of it—is of particular interest because it shows vividly that consultation between designer, patron, and masons was an ongoing process, and that, unlike the situation at a later date, many details of appearance and construction were by no means settled by the time a commission was given, in fact not even when building operations were already in progress. We do not know how decisive Sigismondo's say in the shaping of his *tempio* was, but we do know of several Renaissance patrons who must have been expert enough to take on a greater or lesser share of the designing themselves.

Pope Nicholas V is a case in point. Although he almost certainly had the aid of Alberti, at least as a "consultant"—let us remember that *De re aedificatoria* was dedicated to him—his own activities may have gone further than those of other patrons or rulers who wished to embellish their residences and therefore drew the best available talents into their ambience, as did Julius II and Leo X in the early sixteenth century. Of Nicholas' active patronage there is a curious but telling indication in a contemporary biography of him.

Its author, Gianozzo Manetti (not to be confused with Brunelleschi's biographer, Antonio Manetti), was a Florentine scholar who had come to Rome as ambassador of his hometown. He became a close friend of the pope, who made him apostolic secretary. Soon after Nicholas' death in 1455 he wrote his biography. Speaking in it of the pope's plans for the refurbishing of Rome, he makes an interesting comparison with King

Solomon's activities in Jerusalem, saying that just as Hiram of Tyre had not been the actual architect of the Temple, but only a highly skilled supervisor of works, so Nicholas had called to Rome Bernardo Rossellino from Florence, a "master mason," and put him in charge of all building operations for the various enterprises. With regard to St. Peter's Manetti adds: "Only with him [Rossellino] does he communicate about that structure."

Bernardo Rossellino (1409-64) had been trained as a sculptor, but he had collaborated with Alberti, and all the buildings with which he was connected throughout his life—the Palazzo Ruccellai, the restoration of S. Stefano Rotondo in Rome, and even the work in Pienza for Pius II— also show in some way the hand of Alberti. It seems that once again we have evidence of collaboration between a scholar-designer and a man experienced in the practical side of architecture. In papal accounts between 1451 and 1453 Rossellino is described as *ingeniere di palazzo*.

Platina, the biographer of the popes from St. Peter to Sixtus IV, whose librarian he was, says of Nicholas V: "he built magnificently and splendidly, both in the city and on the Vatican." Platina proves this by giving a long list of the buildings the pope either erected or restored, but he does not name a single architect who worked for him. Platina certainly does not want to suggest that the pope was in every case his own architect, and among the buildings listed there are some for which we know the name of the architect involved. Still, the passage gives evidence of an interesting historical phenomenon. Even during the latter part of the fifteenth century an architect, unlike a painter or sculptor, was not always worth mentioning, because he was still, like a mason, thought to be less important than his patron. This is hardly surprising if we consider that at that time many patrons of architecture were in fact educated men, who did leave the imprint of their minds on the buildings put up for them.

In his lives of illustrious men of the fifteenth century, Vespasiano da Bisticci talks at length about Cosimo de' Medici (1389-1464), whom he had known well and admired very much. Summing up Cosimo's character, Vespasiano reports: "It happened that the administrator of his building works cheated him of a large sum of money. Having investigated the business, Cosimo, like the wise man he was, did not fly into a rage, but simply withdrew the commission from him, and told him that he had no further need for his services . . ." (Vespasiano, p. 232). Such a direct link between patron and administrator—rather than architect—is made even more explicit in the account of the villas Cosimo had built outside Florence:

At Careggi he built the greater part of what we see now and the same at Cafaggiulo in the Mugello at a cost of fifteen thousand ducats. These works maintained many a poor man who laboured thereon. There was not a year when he did not expend on building from fifteen to eighteen thousand florins, all of which went to the state. He was most particular as to payment. He gave the contract for the building of Careggi to an experienced master; and by the time it was half done, Cosimo saw that before it was finished the man would lose several thousand florins. So he said to him: "Lorenzo, you have taken this work in hand, and I know that in the end you will be the loser of several thousand florins. That was never my intention, but rather that you should make a profit. Go on with your work. You shall not lose, and whatever may be right I will give you." And he did what he had promised. Most men would have held that after the master had made a contract, he should have kept it, but Cosimo with rare liberality thought otherwise [Vespasiano, p. 222].

Cosimo il Vecchio was certainly an outstanding patron, but he was also a shrewd businessman hardly given to ostentatious gestures of unnecessary liberality, and he must have had sound reasons for offering to make good the builder's deficit at Careggi. Equally he must have been familiar with the details of the work done for him by the man who had swindled him. It is striking that in neither of these stories does Vespasiano mention the name of any architect, normally the middleman between the mason and the patron. Such an omission is, of course, not unusual in the fifteenth century, but in this case it may imply more than flattery for the patron whose wealth had made the works in question a reality.

Cafaggiulo and Careggi were not built from scratch but were in fact only remodeled, and we know from other sources that for both villas Cosimo used the services of Michelozzo, who, it will be remembered, was a sculptor turned architect. He could simply have been the expert who turned his patron's ideas into designs which could be executed by builders. In other words: was Cosimo perhaps his own architect? Vespasiano seems to hint as much: "He had good knowledge of architecture, as may be seen from the buildings he left, none of which were built without consulting him. Moreover all those who were about to build would go to him for advice" (Vespasiano, p. 224).

In his paper "The Early Medici as Patrons of Art" Ernst Gombrich has argued persuasively for such an active role by Cosimo: "It is hardly fanciful to feel something of Cosimo's spirit in the buildings he founded, some-thing of his reticence and lucidity, his seriousness and his restraint" (p. 40). Among the rich materials adduced to support his thesis one in par-ticular is of interest in our context. It is a panegyrical poem written in "execrable elegiacs" in praise of Cosimo by one Giovanni Avogrado of Vercelli. While full of fantasy, as well as of rather unreliable and exag-gerated descriptions of buildings put up by Cosimo, the part dealing with the Badia of Fiesole, his last pious foundation, tells of the genesis of the building and the patron's role in planning it.

Cosimo now wants speedy and skilled masters who should erect the church and the house in his manner. Such a skilled master notes it all down on his papers; he marks the house, here will be the porphyry gates, let there be a wide portico here, and here the first step of a marble stairway. He traces the cloisters, to be so many steps long; in the centre there will be a tree, but it must be cypress. He wants the cloisters to be vaulted and supported by twin columns, the one to be coloured and the companion of snow-white marble . . . let there be a tailor's workshop here and there the chapter, here the ward for the sick. Turn round; here I want a cookhouse worthy of a duke [Gombrich, p. 46].

Two things are remarkable in this lively account, even if fawning flat-tery may make Cosimo's donation seem grander than it was. There is first of all his explicit insistence that the Badia is to be constructed *more suo,* which means according to his precepts. In the second place, whatever Cosimo knew about architecture, unlike Brunelleschi or Alberti he did not make any designs himself, because we are told that a skilled master takes down his instructions. Such a man might well have been a master mason, for no architect's name is mentioned, just as contemporary wit-nesses are silent about Cosimo's architects in other cases.

There is another, and more reliable, account of Cosimo's intervention in the case of a building with which he was even more intimately con-nected than with the Badia: his own parish church of S. Lorenzo, and Gombrich has drawn attention to this one too. It is possible that in 1446, when Brunelleschi died, the final plan or a model had been either not completed or not approved, for we know that Cosimo inspected a model of the cupola to be placed over the crossing, which had been submitted by Brunelleschi's successor, the carpenter Antonio Manetti. Cosimo's criti-cism was detailed and highly technical: he asked whether the cupola was not much too heavy, and how the fenestration would allow enough light for the choir. Whereupon one of Manetti's rivals produced another model, which not only took heed of Cosimo's criticisms of the earlier one, but which was said to be in the manner of Brunelleschi. (Gombrich, p. 43.)

It is more difficult to assess Cosimo's share in his other two great Florentine donations: the restoration of the monastery of S. Marco and the earlier building history of S. Lorenzo. In both cases his concern seems first of all to have been the provision of proper quarters for the monks and only thereafter the rebuilding of the church. At S. Lorenzo there was the added concern with the Old Sacristy as a burial place for his family. But could even a Cosimo de' Medici have instructed Brunelleschi on details of a new church?

For a variety of reasons—partly personal tastes, partly economic pressures—Cosimo's son Piero and his grandson Lorenzo the Magnificent were not notable patrons of architecture, but the latter seems to have shared at least theoretically his grandfather's interest in it. He was an avid reader of Alberti's *De re aedificatoria*, and he ordered a set of the plans of S. Andrea in Mantua. His judgment was sought not only about sculpture and painting, but also in disputes involving rival architectural designs, as was the case with the sacristy of S. Spirito in Florence. (Gombrich, p. 54.) One might suggest that by the last quarter of the fifteenth century, "professional" architects could be found more easily, particularly in Florence, and that an educated man like Lorenzo now played the part of a learned connoisseur who could act as an arbitrator or advisor.

But surely the outstanding figure among later fifteenth-century patron-architects was Frederigo da Montefeltre, Duke of Urbino—ruler, condottiere, collector of precious manuscripts, scholar, patron of painters and sculptors, and an architect in his own right. Vespasiano da Bisticci's account in this respect is too circumstantial to be dismissed as mere flattery.

As to architecture it may be said that no one of his age, high or low, knew it so thoroughly. We may see in all buildings he had constructed the grand style and proper measurements, as he had observed them, particularly in this palace, which has no superior in the buildings of the age, none so well considered, or so full of fine things. Though he had his architects about him, he first always realised the design, and then explained the proportions and all else. Indeed to hear him argue it would seem that the art which he had really made his own was architecture, so well did he know how to expound and carry out his plans. He built not only palaces and the like, but many fortresses in his dominions of a construction much stronger than those of old time [Vespasiano, p. 100].

H. L. Heydenreich has convincingly shown that, at least as far as the Urbino palace is concerned, Vespasiano's claim can be substantiated: "Frederigo spent more than thirty years on building his residence, which both in plan and decoration was executed essentially according to his instructions. This great enterprise accompanied his whole life, grew, as it were with him, and passed through such transformations on its way that it is precisely in them that we recognize the controlling initiative of its patron" (Heydenreich, p. 1).

We cannot say how Frederigo acquired his knowledge of architecture, but we do know that he was on terms of intimate friendship with Leone Battista Alberti, who visited Urbino several times and may even have considered dedicating his treatise on architecture to the duke. (Heydenreich, note 25.) Nor do we know whether he himself really did some designing, as suggested by Vespasiano. But this claim may well be true, for the same author writes that Cosimo il Vecchio, as was pointed out earlier, was content with giving verbal instructions to the men who had to do the actual designing. Perhaps a letter dated June 10th, 1468, appointing the man who was to take charge of all building operations at the Urbino palace, may help us understand the role played by Frederigo da Montefeltre himself.

The letter opens with a flourish: a fulsome rhetorical eulogy of architecture, an art honored by ancients and moderns, an art based on geometry and arithmetic, which are among the Liberal Arts, and finally an art requiring science and skill. Frederigo next emphasizes how much he himself esteems and appreciates architecture, and continues:

We have searched everywhere, and particularly in Tuscany, the source of architects, but we did not find anyone really capable and experienced in this profession. But in the end we heard first by reputation and then saw through our own experience how excellent Master Luciano is in his art. Since we have decided to build in our town of Urbino a beautiful and worthy habitation, as becomes the praiseworthy condition of our forefathers and our own, we have elected and appointed said Master Luciano as engineer and head of all masters engaged in this enterprise [Heydenreich, note 8, for the full Italian text of the letter].

Master Luciano Laurana is a rather shadowy figure; we know very little about him. He came from Dalmatia, he worked in Pesaro—where Frederigo probably came in contact with him—before being called to Urbino in 1468, and he remained in charge of the palace until 1472. Since the duke may have begun remodeling and extending his palace as early as 1447, it is unlikely that Luciano was the designer, though he submitted a model—of which unfortunately we have no details—in 1465. In any case, Renaissance models were frequently the work of masons or carpenters or even architects who had to give tangible expression to a patron's ideas. It should be noted that the duke's letter appointing Luciano as *capomaestro* refers to him as *ingegniero,* mentions the term or title "architect" only in an administrative context, makes no reference to plans he might have submitted to obtain the post, but lists all the duties normally entrusted to a supervisor of building operations. Luciano is made head of the workshop; masons, builders, carpenters, and smiths will work under his directions. All workmen will have to obey his orders, and he is authorized to remove masters or workmen with whom he has reason to be dissatisfied. He may also engage other masters or workmen, either for piece-work or on a day-to-day basis, as he pleases, and it is in this context that right at the end of the letter the term *architettore* is introduced for the first time. Luciano is empowered "to retain salary or provisions of those who do not do their duty, and to do everything else which appertains to an architect and *capomaestro* in charge of a job" (Heydenreich, note 8). This use of the term does not imply any expertise in designing a building or suggesting its decorations. It simply refers to the business of keeping in order all those employed on a building and ensuring that they do their work according to the instructions of the head.

Heydenreich has rightly drawn attention to the many features which the layout and character of the ducal apartments in the palace at Urbino share with the description of the famous villa Laurentinum given by Pliny in one of his letters. These were well known and much studied in the Renaissance. The duke owned a copy which had been specially written for him, and Alberti referred to the Laurentinum in his treatise on architecture. "So the apartment of the Duke . . . should be understood as the result of a threefold co-operation between the patron, the humanist advisor and the executive architect, each of them contributing to the whole with his particular experience and knowledge. The leading spirit, however, was the patron" (Heydenreich, p. 6). While it is true that Alberti's presence in Urbino is well documented, he must have come more in the role of a friend and equal than in that of a consultant. Frederigo, the pupil of Vittorino da Feltre, one of the greatest humanist teachers of the age, knew his classics. At Urbino patron and adviser may well have been one and the same person, while Luciano Laurana executed his orders and looked after the workmen.

The medieval masons' workshop had been a co-operative enterprise combining many skills. The Renaissance inherited this organization, like so much else, from the preceding period. But there was a difference. The medieval *capomaestro*, who had received his training in such a workshop, was familiar from his early days both with the traditional formal vocabulary and with its structural possibilities and limitations. He had his pattern books and he could draw on the experience of generations when it came to methods of building. But early in the fifteenth century the introduction of a novel set of forms, based on the Classical remains, necessarily brought about a division of labor. The designer of a church or palace in the new style knew everything about Classical details and proportions, but was ignorant of the practical side of building since he had not gone through a mason's training. Hence he needed the help of a builder in order to realize his ideas. Normally the builder's job was comparatively simple, since Brunelleschi, Alberti, and others hardly ever changed the customary layout of churches or palaces but only their appearance. In fact, masons and builders adapted themselves more quickly to their new tasks than the designing architects, who took a long while to grasp the structural needs of building. This problem could still arise in the early sixteenth century, and the fate of Bramante's St. Peter's is perhaps the last significant example of that dichotomy, which had arisen a century earlier.

When Bramante died in 1514 there seem to have been no definitive drawings to guide his successor—Raphael—in continuing the construction of the new basilica. This in itself is interesting, for it is in keeping with a practice which we know from the fifteenth century. As for the building itself, only the foundations of the great piers which were to support the cupola had been laid. But they caused trouble, since Bramante—probably originally a painter—lacked understanding of the structural problems involved in putting up so gigantic a structure. His piers were too weak and had to be strengthened to support the weight of the dome. Brunelleschi (who had studied statics and construction before designing the dome of Florence Cathedral), Alberti, Michelozzo, and others had, as it were, clothed old structures in new garments, but with Bramante the new vision had temporarily outrun the technical know-how.

BIBLIOGRAPHICAL NOTES

The only book which treats the architect during the Renaissance in a wider context is still M. Briggs, *The Architect in History* (Oxford, 1927; reprint, 1974). J. S. Ackerman, "Architectural Practice in the Italian Renaissance," *Renaissance Art*, ed. C. Gilbert (New York, 1970), pp. 148-71, is the best available account, though it deals mainly with the sixteenth century. Valuable information can also be found in H. Saalman, "Early Renaissance Architectural Theory and Practice in Antonio Filarete's Trattato di Architettura," *Art Bulletin* 41 (1959), 89-106, and in P. Murray, *The Architecture of the Italian Renaissance* (London, 1963).

R. Krautheimer, "Alberti and Vitruvius," in *Studies in Early Christian, Medieval and Renaissance Art* (New York and London, 1969), pp. 323-32, has given a detailed analysis of these authors' architectural treatises and pointed out Alberti's independence. H. Koch, *Vom Nachleben des Vitruv* (Baden-Baden, 1951), has given a short but sensitive account of the Vitruvian tradition.

E. Mandowsky and C. Mitchell, *Pirro Ligorio's Roman Antiquities* (London, 1963), Ch. II, give a brief account of antiquarian studies in the fifteenth century and list various sketchbooks. C. Hülsen, *Il Libro di Giuliano da Sangallo* (Leipzig, 1910), and H. Egger, *Codex Escurialensis: Ein Skizzenbuch aus der Werkstatt Domenico Ghirlandaios* (Vienna, 1905), are complete publications of two such sketchbooks, both with many architectural drawings. Interesting points are also raised by W. Lotz, "Das Raumbild in der italienischen Architekturzeichnung der Renaissance," *Mitteilungen des kunsthistorischen Instituts in Florenz* 7 (1956), 193-226.

About Brunelleschi relevant documents were assembled by C. von Fabriczy, *Filippo Brunelleschi* (Stuttgart, 1892); a selection in an English translation will be found in I. Hyman, *Brunelleschi in Perspective* (Englewood Cliffs, N.J., 1974). The fifteenth-century biography by A. Manetti, *The Life of Brunelleschi*, ed. H. Saalman, tr. C. Engass (University Park, Pa., and London, 1970), is a critical edition of the original text accompanied by an accurate English translation. Some special problems connected with the building of the cupola are treated by H. Saalman, "Giovanni di Gherardo da Prato's Designs Concerning the Cupola of Santa Maria del Fiore in Florence," *Journal Soc. Arch. Hist.* 18 (1959), 11-20.

L. B. Alberti, *Ten Books on Architecture*, ed. J. Rykwert, tr. J. Leoni (London, 1955), reprints a famous eighteenth-century translation and adds some useful notes. The most concise introduction to Alberti's views is A. Blunt, *Artistic Theory in Italy 1450-1600* (London, 1940), Ch. I. R. Krautheimer's important comparison of Alberti and Vitruvius has already been mentioned (see above).

Our most revealing source about the life, character, and patronage of Cosimo de' Medici is the biography by Vespasiano da Bisticci, *Renaissance*

*Princes, Popes and Prelates*, tr. George and E. Waters (London, 1926; Harper Torchbook, New York, 1963). Cosimo's patronage is discussed by E. H. Gombrich, "The Early Medici as Patrons of Art," in *Norm and Form* (London, 1966), pp. 35-57.

The role of Pope Nicholas has been analyzed by G. Dehio, "Die Bauprojekte Nikolaus und L. B. Alberti," *Repertorium für Kunstwissenschaft* 3 (1880), 241-57, and by T. Magnusson, *Studies in Roman Quattrocento Architecture* (Stockholm, 1958). Nicholas' activities are also treated fully by C. W. Westfall, *In this Most Perfect Paradise: Alberti and Nicholas V, and the Invention of Conscious Urban Planning* (University Park, Pa., and London, 1974).

L. H. Heydenreich, "Frederigo da Montefeltre as a Building Patron," *Studies in Renaissance and Baroque Art presented to Anthony Blunt* (London, 1967), pp. 1-6, is a brief but informative account of Frederigo as his own architect. The same author's entry "Architekturmodell," *Reallexikon zur deutschen Kunstgeschichte*, Vol. I (Stuttgart, 1947), col. 918-40, while mainly concerned with the history of the model in Germany, lists also the most important Italian examples and gives the only serviceable account of a strangely neglected subject.

M. Baxandall, *Painting and Experience in Fifteenth Century Italy: A Primer in the Social History of Pictorial Style* (Oxford, 1972), while ostensibly dealing with painting, touches on a number of problems also relevant to the training of architects.

# 5

## The New Professionalism in the Renaissance

CATHERINE WILKINSON

If the fifteenth century saw the emergence of a new conception of architecture, it took another century for the architect to find, claim, and establish his place in the variegated and rapidly changing social structures of the Renaissance. Alberti had a clear idea of architecture as a vocation for a gentleman with a liberal education and a special knowledge of mathematics and geometry; but his view of architecture as a profession was indistinct. As we have seen in the previous chapter, in *De re aedificatoria*, written about 1450, he expressed the modern view of an architect as the complete designer, capable of planning cities and designing everything from palaces and churches to a humble farmhouse; but he had nothing to say about the training of an architect or about building practice except in the vaguest terms. A century later, Philibert Delorme (1510-70), like Alberti a distinguished writer, was able to envisage a self-governing profession of specialists with accepted standards of training and clearly defined responsibilities and privileges. In his *Premier tome de l'architecture*, published in 1567, he defined the spheres appropriate to the patron, the architect, and the workman and set up guidelines for their working relation. His second book opens with a summary of the aims that inform his treatise:

In the preceding book we have sufficiently advised the architect and the Seigneur, or whoever would like to build, of their positions and duties as the two principal heads of the building enterprise. It remains in this second book to turn our pen to the third class of persons, without whom no building can be perfect. These are the master masons, the stone cutters, and the workmen (whom the architect must always control) who as well must not be deprived of our labor and instruction here, since it has pleased God for us to give it [*Premier tome de l'architecture*, Bk. II, Fol. 31].

What makes Philibert's view of the profession so much more focused than anything before is that he outspokenly contrasted his architect to those who designed buildings but were not, in his view, architects. Patrons, he said, should employ architects instead of turning to "some master mason or master carpenter as is the custom or to some painter, some notary or some other person who is supposed to be qualified but more often than not has no better judgment than the patron himself" (Bk. I, Fol. 6). Most of these would-be architects were really trained for manual work and had no knowledge of the principles of architecture. The others had stopped at book learning and, satisfied with their geometrical demonstrations, they could not apply their theory to the work. What they did was nothing but "a shadow of a real building" (Bk. I, fol. iv, a paraphrase of Vitruvius).

The true architect was something different, a man who combined the practical experience of the master mason with the knowledge of the amateur, a man (as Philibert said) schooled not only in books but in long experience. What gave the architect as a professional man his definition was a set of relationships—both professional and social—with those he came in contact with: the patron, the workmen, and the administrator and officials of the building program. But Philibert's view was partly the consequence of his conflict with the building professionals, who considered themselves capable of devising a building and whose habits and privileges were undermined by the architect.

In separating himself from the mason and the carpenter, Philibert was making a social distinction. The architect was striving to present himself as the practitioner of a Liberal Art. This effort was relatively new in France but it was well established in Italy, where the emergence of the architect in the Renaissance parallels the rise of the painter and sculptor to the status of intellectual. In 1436, when Alberti wrote his dedication for the Italian version of his treatise on painting (*Della pittura*), he pointed to the renewal of the three arts of sculpture, painting, and architecture in Florence and made it clear that this achievement, culminating in the architect Brunelleschi's invention of perspective construction, was not a matter of manual skill but an intellectual feat, a discovery of new laws of art. For Alberti, the architect was an artist and an intellectual whose activity had nothing to do with that of a craftsman. But of the three arts, architecture was the most easily separated from the crafts. Traditionally founded upon geometry and mathematics, architecture was almost a Liberal Art. As we have seen, this idea was clear in Vitruvius' text and survived in late antiquity, but it was only latent in medieval building practice. The architect in Tuscany, since he did not belong to an architect's guild, was more easily distinguished from the craftsman than either the painter or the sculptor. In *De re aedificatoria* Alberti never mentioned the guilds, and his definition of an architect, which was based upon the authority of Vitruvius, was the first modern portrait of the artist-intellectual.

As Alberti had realized, the artist's striving for a higher social status depended upon a new style of patronage. The architect aspired to be educated like a courtier and to behave like one; and between him and his patron was the bond of a shared appreciation of the theory of architecture. *De re aedificatoria* was written to inform the humanist patron rather than the architect (Krautheimer, "Alberti and Vitruvius," p. 328). The distinguished patronage that every architect hoped for was the guarantee of his social status. In the middle of the sixteenth century, Giorgio Vasari was still extremely sensitive to the social position of artists, and he described the career of the Florentine architect Giuliano da Sangallo (1443-1516) as a progression from patron to patron. Giuliano enjoyed the protection and favor of Lorenzo de' Medici, who put him in touch with Alfonso of Naples. The project for Alfonso's palace of Poggio Reale apparently attracted the attention of Cardinal Giuliano della Rovere, later Pope Julius II, and Giuliano became his architect. The truly great patron could maintain an architect: Julius took Giuliano to France, presented him to the king, and called him to Rome when he was elected pope. Giuliano had every reason to expect a great future as papal architect, when Julius abruptly replaced him with Bramante (1444-1514). A patron like Julius with great means and an addiction to building was invaluable to artists, but he could be ruthless with them. Most distinguished architectural careers in the sixteenth century were built around such patrons: Julius II and Bramante, the Gonzaga and Giulio Romano, the Farnese and Antonio da Sangallo the Younger, Philip II and Juan de Herrera. Michelangelo (1475-1564) worked for a succession of great patrons including Julius II, the Medici, and the Farnese.

Philibert Delorme had been fortunate enough to find his first important patron in Cardinal Du Bellay, with whom he was closely associated in Rome and for whom he built the Chateau of St. Maur. Du Bellay passed him on to the French king Henry II, and Philibert's career would have been assured had not Henry's early death deprived him of his position at court. Philibert mourned his loss, but he was sufficiently aware of the vulnerability of an architect entirely at the whim of his patron to suggest some rules for their relationship. The patron's activity, he argued, ought to be confined to the preliminary stage of a project when he was free to request designs from a number of architects and, having selected one, to demand alternatives and revisions. He might go over the smallest details of the project but, once the plans were settled, he ought to withdraw and leave the architect alone.

In fact, this rarely happened, as one might suspect from Philibert's plea. There were few great patrons who did not demand changes, often at a very late stage in the building, and many felt free to torment the architect with their own ideas. Vasari complained that the Villa Giulia, where he himself had worked, could hardly be called anyone's design because Pope Julius III every day invented "some caprice of his own which the architects were obliged to carry out" (Milanesi ed., vol. 7, p. 694).

Most of the exchanges between patron and architect took place in person, and we have few accounts of them; but, occasionally, as when Michelangelo was in Florence designing the Laurentian Library, his negotiations with Pope Clement VII in Rome were conducted by mail. From the papal half of this correspondence that survives one can see that in the nine months between November 1523, when Michelangelo received the commission for the library in Rome, until the digging of the foundations in Florence the following August, the papal secretary wrote to Michelangelo at least once a month (often more), and every time he asked for drawings or responded to studies that had been sent to him—anything from technical studies of the foundations to "qualche nuova fantasia" for the library ceiling.

The behavior of Clement VII corresponds to Alberti's humanist ideal of the educated patron who is capable of discussing the fine points of design with his architect. Clement supervised the initial design of his building with great care, and he continued to follow its progress, approving subsequent designs as they were readied for construction. He was by no means an exception. Philip II of Spain represents this Renaissance patron in his extreme form. Not only did he demand a great number of designs, often from several architects, and have them worked up into synthetic perfect projects, but he went over the smallest details of construction in his administrator's and architects' accounts. I know of no other patron of his stature who would bother to decide with his architect whether a bit of construction should be contracted as a whole or executed by day-labor. Neither Clement VII nor Philip II would have taken such an active part in the design of the buildings they commissioned had they not considered architecture a suitable pastime for a prince, nor could they have involved themselves to this extent without close and constant communication with their architects.

The higher social standing for the architect that resulted from humanist patronage had its negative aspect. Without the protection of an established guild, the architect seems to have had few if any legal safeguards for his practice. A powerful patron might call in other architects at his pleasure or even cancel a project at an advanced stage. The history of Michelangelo's designs for the façade of the church of S. Lorenzo in Florence is almost impenetrable because so many architects seem to have been involved and so many changes made in the program within a relatively short period of time. Michelangelo won the commission and spent nearly two years supervising the quarrying of the marble blocks. But, in the end, Clement VII annulled the contract and the project came to nothing.

The patron might also reduce the building funds so that the architect would find himself in charge of a building he could not execute. This was a favorite device of Philip II when he had lost interest in an old-fashioned building, like the Alcázar in Toledo. It is also true, however, that patrons unwittingly overreached themselves. The vast unfinished pile of the La Pilota Palace in Parma and the fragment of another grandiose palace in Piacenza testify to the ambition of the Farnese, which exceeded their means. Aware of this danger, Philibert counseled achitects as well as patrons to take a realistic view of their finances.

Incidentally, the financial side of architectural practice in the Renaissance is not always clear. Unless an architect was on salary for a large building program, as were the architects for St. Peter's in Rome, it is not always evident how he was paid. The documents of construction generally begin with the assembling of materials and the hiring of contractors and workmen. There are few financial records from the earlier phases. The cost of preparing drawings and models for presentation to the patron was considerable, and the architect may often have borne it himself. Philibert complained that he had spent a great deal of his own money on models.

Architects who were attached to a single patron might be kept on retainer, however. Philibert was given the revenues of two abbeys by Henry II. One of them had stone quarries on its property, and he may have been given it so that he could exploit it directly. In general we know little about this sort of revenue, or about the practice of receiving a percentage from contractors.

Salaries for architects attached to major building programs or employed by city governments were good. Michelangelo was not impoverished by taking over as architect of St. Peter's, in spite of his complaints; and Sansovino did well as architect of the Procuracy of Venice. What we would like to know, however, is how much the designing services of an architect were worth apart from his duties as an official or as the responsible head of a building program. This is difficult to ascertain. Andrea Palladio (1508-80), who never held an official position or enjoyed the protection of a royal patron, never became a rich man. Apparently the designing and building of private palaces and villas was not very lucrative.

Not all of those who could afford to employ an architect could also afford to conduct themselves in a grand style. Patrician patrons were unlikely to require more than one palace or country house and a family chapel; occasionally they might finance a church. They could not keep an architect on retainer, and probably they could not expect to claim very much of his time unless they commissioned a monumental work. Through the sixteenth century, however, the smaller commissions became an increasingly significant part of some architects' practice. Antonio da Sangallo the Younger (1483-1546), who had an established practice in Rome in the 1530s and 1540s, was architect of St. Peter's and the Palazzo Farnese before Michelangelo, but apparently he was also known for more modest palace designs. The career of Palladio, the greatest architect of the later sixteenth century, was based almost entirely upon the Vicenzan and Venetian nobles for whom he designed palaces and country estates that were both elegant houses and practical centers for the farming investments of their owners. His reputation was seemingly established by his successful entry in the 1549 competition to remodel the city council hall in Vicenza—the so-called Basilica—but his numerous villa designs (over twenty are illustrated in his *Quattro libri*, published in Venice in 1570) and palace projects formed the bulk of his practice. The commissions for churches, which were more expensive as well as more prestigious, did not come until his later years.

In some cases, the architect so extended his practice that he had little to do with the execution of the building. Galeazzo Alessi (1512-72) designed the Strada Nuova in Genoa, a new street with palaces for wealthy Genoese banking families. He also designed villas for the same patrons. But he may only have provided rough sketches for many of them, leaving the detailed designing and the supervision of construction to architects and decorators who were loosely associated with him. It would seem that he came to function as what Wolfgang Lotz has aptly called an "architect by remote control" (*Galeazzo Alessi*, p. 10).

The conduct of an architect's practice varied enormously in the sixteenth century, but it is clear from the records that architects like Palladio and Alessi had a larger number of commissions than their predecessors. Neither Palladio nor Alessi was attached to a court or to great patrons, and they were not obliged to supervise the construction of the buildings they designed, although they often did so. This is a notable change from the fifteenth century when, at the time Alberti wrote, there were only a handful of men who might be considered architects according to his definition of the term and only a few patrons with the intellectual pretentions to hire them. By the 1560s, this was no longer the case; and to judge from the number of surviving Roman palaces, it would seem that already in the 1540s it was customary for upper-class families to hire an architect. In France, Philibert Delorme recognized that without the relative security of the guild organization, an architect must support himself by smaller commissions, and he was proud to say that he had designed all kinds of buildings, from magnificent palaces to modest houses. By this time, the architect was well on his way to taking over the last preserve of the craftsman and master-builder.

A new working relationship with the building trades was as necessary to the sixteenth-century architect as was the new style of patronage. Alberti had quite consciously opened a gap between the architect and the craftsman, a gap so eagerly accepted by architects and, by the sixteenth century, already so firmly established in Italy that it was difficult to bridge from either side. It was responsible for the often bitter exchanges between men working as architects but placed on opposite sides of the division between the liberal and the mechanical arts. These debates usually concerned technical competence—the "craftsman-architect" accusing the "dilettante architect" of incompetence and the architect asserting his intellectual superiority over the craftsman. The craftsmen who were to execute the architect's designs were, in Alberti's words, just "an instrument to the architect" (*De re aedificatoria*, Preface). Philibert Delorme took much the same view when he spoke of the "third class of persons . . . the master masons, stone cutters, and workmen whom the architect must always control."

This view of the architect is so close to our own and so easily transposed into the modern relationship between the architect and the building contractor that we are likely to overlook the striking character of Philibert's assertion for its time. In France the situation was different from that in Italy. The masons and carpenters Philibert referred to had been but lately the masters of the royal works in France, men like Gilles le Breton, the powerful Parisian master mason who had been employed under Francis I (see next chapter). Such men were organized in a closely knit system that effectively controlled construction and architectural design. As in the earlier medieval system, a man was trained through formal apprenticeship and, as he worked his way up in the system, each step increased his responsibilities until, as a qualified master mason, he could undertake the design and direction of a building himself. This profession did not acknowledge the distinction between designer and builder; nowhere did it recognize the separate function of an architect in Philibert's sense of the term. Buildings like the chateau of Azay-le-Rideau were designed and built by guild shops. Even as original a masterpiece as Chambord must, in the end, have been built this way, whatever the original involvement of Leonardo and Domenico da Cortona may have been.

In Spain, the building trades appear to have been more dependent upon large building programs and the shops less strictly organized than in France. Master-builders did not belong to a guild, and a man's training took place on the job. He rose in the hierarchy of workmen (usually beginning as a stone-cutter or as a mason if he aspired to become a master) to the position of supervisor or *aparejador*. As such he organized the workmen, estimated costs, and sometimes put up money for building materials. He was a master-builder in the last stage of his training. Then, as master of the works, he would finally be responsible for the design and for the proper execution of the building. The important appointments, for example the *maestro mayor* of any of the cathedrals, were the basis of a solid reputation, and, in principle, a man held only one such position at a time. By the early sixteenth century, however, the master was often absent on other projects, leaving the building in the hands of his supervisor—an indication of the weakening of the system as well as of a more varied practice. By this time, the master of the works was beginning to estrange himself from the rest of his trade and to become an architect in the full sense of the word.

The patron was represented at the works by a separate structure headed by the administrator at the building site and by the notaries and paymaster (if the program was a large one), who prepared the contracts for each major section of building or for expensive piecework like decorative carving, and paid the semi-skilled workmen by the day or week. They also paid the men on salary to the works—themselves, the master, and the contractor. These officials kept precise records of expenses, everything from the large cost for building stone to the price of renting a mule for the master to travel on to consult with the patron.

In Spain, as in France, this system ran smoothly as long as the designer remained the head of the organization of workmen. Obviously, it tolerated outsiders with difficulty, and we shall see that the transition to the new system was not accomplished without some open conflict.

In placing all responsibility for design upon the architect, Philibert removed the most cherished privilege of the master mason. The French guilds had only two means of defense: they could conspire against the architects who were placed over them (as they seem to have intrigued rather successfully against the Italian architect Serlio who had been brought to France by Francis I), or they could adopt the title of architect themselves, as Philibert suggested that they were doing. The use of this new title indicates that the integrity of the traditional system was lost. Henceforth, the position of master mason would no longer guarantee the right to design a building.

Something similar occurred in Spain when, in the reign of Philip II, the master-builders found themselves displaced first by architects imported from Italy and then by the king's courtier and amateur architect, Juan de Herrera (ca. 1530-1597). Herrera, who modeled his career on Alberti's image of the architect, was an accomplished mathematician and geometrician with an interest in Hermetic philosophy and some skill as a diplomat, but he had no practical training in building. That he was able to function as the royal architect was due entirely to the support of Philip II. Against the alliance of patron and architect, the building profession was relatively powerless. It fought back when outsiders were within its reach, but Philip II never placed Herrera in an official position as master of the works. The position remained vacant (as it did at the Escorial) or it was filled by a disciple of Herrera's who did have professional training but could be counted on to follow Herrera's plans (as happened at the Lonja in Seville). Thus the designing phase was removed from the control of the building trade, which without its former privilege and prestige nevertheless continued to function. Certainly, no building program as large as the Escorial could afford to dispense with an organization of craftsmen, and Philip II very sensibly retained the basic structure of organization. In fact, the traditional organization of a large building program was practical and, with certain modifications, it remained stable in western Europe through the seventeenth century. But one result of the appearance of the professional architect was that a stigma was now attached to practical training that prevented men apprenticed in the building trades from becoming architects without some compensating "liberal" education.

The situation is much clearer in France and Spain, where the architect confronted an established building profession, than it is in Italy. In areas where the building trades were well organized, as they appear to have been in Milan in the fifteenth century for example, there was resistance to the newfangled architect. Filarete was appointed by his patron Francesco Sforza to the cathedral works in the 1450s but was soon fired. When put in charge of the duke's vast project for a city hospital, he had great difficulty collaborating with the local builders who were active on the project. The conflict was not only between Filarete's Florentine style and that of the Milanese. As is amply documented in Filarete's *Trattato di architettura*, written about 1465, he took a lofty view of the architect's status and shared Alberti's view of workmen. This image of an architect deploying armies of workmen who toiled obediently under his commands did not sit well with the master-builders who were appointed to assist him. That he seems also to have had a lively contempt for the Milanese did not improve matters.

In provincial centers, the building trades may have been responsible for designing well into the sixteenth century. Palladio was apprenticed to a stone-mason in Padua in 1521, and he worked as a builder in Vicenza until the 1530s. But the building trades seem never to have dominated the practice of architecture in Italy as they did in France and Spain. Architects like Giulio Romano (1499-1546) in Mantua encountered no obstacles to their practice and, in Venice, the sculptor Jacopo Sansovino (1486-1570) was the leading architect.

As we have seen already, there was no architect's guild. Aspirants were obliged to take their training in another craft. Giuliano's father apprenticed him in wood sculpture. In some parts of Italy, as in France and

Spain, the aspiring architect still apprenticed as a stone-mason or in stone sculpture as in the medieval period.

There were certainly architectural workshops in Italy, although we know very little about them. Filarete describes his shop, with its drafting table and his assistants busy about him. The Solari who were associated with him in Milan may have been something like a firm of master-builders. In Florence, Giuliano de Sangallo had a shop of workmen, including stone-carvers, whom he took with him to execute the palace at Savona for Julius II. Vasari mentions that Giuliano's confidence in his shop permitted him to leave the building in their hands and go to France. But these men were apparently not apprentices in architecture. Palladio's training (see below, p. 140) is exceptional for a Renaissance architect; few other Italian architects emerged from his background before the middle of the sixteenth century.

The absence of a powerful building profession in Italy in the Renaissance and the early prominence of architects are both related to the leading role taken by central Italy in architecture as well as the other arts. What was exceptional and precocious about central Italy, and Tuscany particularly, was its tradition of artist-architects. This tradition was founded on the belief (well rooted by the fifteenth century) that any artist could design a building since it was the conception of the work that mattered rather than the construction. This conviction derived from the custom of treating the three arts of painting, sculpture, and architecture as three branches of the same art of design, and it is probably very old in Tuscany. In the fourteenth century, Giotto the painter and Giovanni Pisano the sculptor received important architectural commissions. In fact, the majority of architects before the 1550s in Italy were trained as painters or sculptors; the career of Arnolfo di Cambio was exceptional. Vasari noted this phenomenon and ascribed it to the fact that artists were trained in *disegno*—"the father of our three arts"—which made it possible for them to extend their practice to another field. Developed by Vasari (and others) into a theory of artistic creativity, *disegno* was the foundation of the liberal status of the practice of art, without which it would not have been possible to distinguish painting, sculpture, and architecture from, say, silversmithing or furniture-making, and the artist from the craftsman.

The Florentine idea of *disegno* is discussed in Filarete's *Trattato*, and it was the basis of his image of the artist. Filarete trained himself as a sculptor and metalworker and came to Sforza's court as an architect but probably also as a complete artist. In his treatise, he described the architect as a courtier who devises entertainments for his prince, and designs fresco cycles and monumental sculpture as well as buildings. He imagined the artist in a position much like that which Leonardo da Vinci actually occupied at the Sforza court half a century later.

Practical experience in *disegno*, meaning essentially drawing and perspective, was the only feature of their formal training that Renaissance architects had in common. It was learned during their apprenticeship—as Leonardo certainly learned it in the shop of the sculptor and painter Andrea del Verrocchio. Intarsia workers were also trained in geometry and perspective; this may be why a number of architects, including Baccio d'Agnolo and Vignola, emerged from this craft. The only other shared experience was the architect's self-apprenticeship to the art of antiquity, which he normally served in Rome.

Equipped with a knowledge of perspective and mathematics and of the remains of Roman architecture, an artist could become an architect. This is apparently what Brunelleschi did or was believed to have done. It is probably the path that Filarete followed, because he became an architect only after a lengthy stay in Rome. This line of education is aptly brought out by Vasari in his life of Bramante. Drawn from the beginning to mathematics and geometry, Bramante took his training under a painter specializing in architectural perspective. Then, having decided to become an architect, he went to draw and measure the ancient monuments in Rome and there came to the attention of wealthy patrons. Vasari's picture of a great architect is no doubt distorted by his scheme of the development of the arts, his desire to play up the resemblance to the career of Brunelleschi, the prototypical Renaissance architect, and to play down the buildings of Bramante's first period in Milan. It is also in contrast to the career of a specialized architect like Giuliano da Sangallo, whom Vasari describes as a professional man, not an intellectual or an artist, who is elevated by great patrons. Vasari makes a negative example of Giuliano who, after his long service to Julius II, found himself idle and forced to beg permission to return to Florence while Bramante replaced him as architect in charge of the papal projects.

Vasari's biographies of the Sangallo architects are his only example of a continuing family tradition in central Italian architecture, but he is somewhat dubious about their standing. That he disliked Antonio da Sangallo the Younger and admired Michelangelo (who disliked the Sangallos even more) does not entirely explain his reservations. He emphasized the sound technique and the practical designs of both Giuliano and Antonio but he made it clear that, when it came to the greater projects, they were second-rate compared to geniuses in design like Bramante and Michelangelo. There is no doubt that Bramante and Michelangelo were indeed the greater architects, but Vasari's reluctance to praise the Sangallos as designers may be partly because they lacked a painter's or a sculptor's training, and were not artists in the true and noble sense.

The extent to which the *disegno* tradition and the image of the artist-architect dominated architectural practice in central Italy is remarkable. The architectural careers of Bramante, Raphael, Peruzzi, and Michelangelo all developed from their work as artists. Giulio Romano, who was raised in Raphael's painting studio and who was primarily a painter until 1523, could go to Mantua and become a distinguished architect. His work for the Gonzaga of Mantua shows no inexperience. Jacopo Sansovino, the Florentine sculptor, went to Venice a few years later and became architect to the Procuracy without much practical experience. Such designers seem to have enjoyed a freedom and acceptance that was rare in the fifteenth century. Alberti apparently chose to work closely with someone experienced in architecture, but there is no evidence that Giulio or Sansovino felt the need for such collaboration.

The technical inexperience of the artist-architects of the Renaissance should not be exaggerated. One cannot stand in front of Alberti's facade of San Andrea in Mantua and not recognize the control that the designer exercised over the smallest details of the decorative scheme even if, as in this case, we know very little about how it was done. Bramante, trained as a painter, was an experienced architect when he began to work for Julius II in 1505. In the 1490s, he had been consulted on the model for the crossing tower of Milan Cathedral, which was a technical problem of notorious difficulty. The view, expressed often, that Bramante was a magnificent designer with a poor notion of building technology is a little like saying that Shakespeare was more or less illiterate. The technical faults of Bramante's buildings for Julius II—the poor foundations in the Belvedere and the cracks in the piers of St. Peter's—were due to their unprecedented scale, the frenetic speed with which they were built, and to Bramante's experiments with a new building technique—the revival of Roman concrete construction which made possible, in the piers of new St. Peter's, the vast, molded forms that had not been seen since antiquity. Bramante's technical innovations were introduced in response to the artist's new conception of spatial organization, and even his admirers perceived his handling of structure as "bold rather than well-considered" (Serlio, Book 3).

The Italian artist-architect had no tie with the building trades; yet strictly speaking he was not an amateur, since his status as an artist qualified him as a designer. This image of the architect found its most complete expression in Michelangelo: sculptor, painter, and (as Vasari said) the model for a whole generation of architects. It survived in Italy well into the seventeenth century, when the sculptor and architect Gianlorenzo Bernini astonished his contemporaries with his versatility; but it was essentially a creation of the fifteenth century. One must remember that Bramante was over fifty when he began Saint Peter's in 1506 and that Michelangelo was trained before 1500.

In the sixteenth century, besides the amateur architect and the artist-architect, one also finds a third variety of architect: the specialist who considers himself both a gentleman like the amateur and a designer like the artist but who insists upon his independent status as a professional in his field. It is in this respect that Philibert Delorme's conception of the architect is avant-garde. At the opposite pole from the craftsman he placed "some painter or notary" (by whom he certainly meant Primaticcio, who had replaced him at Fontainebleau, and Pierre Lescot, who was involved at the Louvre). In his view, such a person was no better qualified to be an architect than was the mason. Philibert had no sympathy for those who dabbled in what he considered a serious profession. Confident of his own social status, he did not hesitate to affirm his close contact with the technical and craftsmanly side of architecture. He had been trained as a master mason himself in his father's shop in Lyons, and he was proud to say that he had been designing buildings since he was fifteen. As a man whose career had been made through his contacts with royal patrons in the highest intellectual circles of his day, he felt he could dispense with the trappings of a humanist. Philibert was concerned with designing buildings and with seeing them properly executed. He could see that the architect would have to be able to manage his workmen. Without proper supervision, he warned, the contractor might cheat the architect and build the walls so poorly that they would not support the roof. On the other hand, the architect himself must know what is feasible and not present plans for fantastic projects that could not be executed. Here Philibert was surely referring to Serlio's totally impractical scheme to vault the Salle de Bal at Fontainebleau. Philibert himself solved the problem by a magnificent wooden coffered ceiling designed on a system of his own invention (published in his own *Nouvelles inventions pour bien bastir* in 1561). Philibert had a specialist's admiration for ingenious structural solutions that is characteristically French and is not found in Italy to the same degree. It permitted him to admire Gothic vaulting—"la mode françoise"—which, "although it is out of fashion, is not to be despised," an attitude one does not find stated in Italy until Scamozzi's and Guarino Guarini's writing in the seventeenth century. Vasari, who was Philibert's Italian contemporary, could find no such redeeming virtue in Gothic architecture.

There are signs of the emergence of this kind of professional architect in central Italy, although here the emphases were reversed. Philibert's workshop training gave him professional authority over the master masons that Italian artist-architects like Serlio and Primaticcio lacked. But Antonio da Sangallo the Younger suffered because of his close tie to the trades. Cellini remarked spitefully that one shouldn't expect much from him since he was trained as a carpenter; and we have seen that his practical expertise, although admired by Vasari, did not entirely compensate for his lack of artistic training. It was this that Cellini really held against him: the fact that, as Ackerman has remarked, Antonio was "one of the few architects of his time who never wanted to be anything else" ("Architectural Practice," p. 149). He was a professional existing in an artistic environment that was in principle hostile to him. His own training (whether or not he was really an active carpenter) had come in Bramante's studio, where his uncle had arranged for him to work. He seems to have prepared drawings and supervised construction when Bramante was too infirm to do this himself. He is thus the first major Italian architect to have been professionally trained. He seems also to have been the first central Italian architect to develop a highly organized shop—the *setta sangallesca*, as Vasari called it, which was composed of assistants, draftsmen, and apprentices who owed their livelihood to Antonio's architectural practice.

From his position, Antonio could challenge the right of Michelangelo, a sculptor and a painter, to meddle in the design of the Vatican fortifications, to which Michelangelo is supposed to have replied that, although he didn't know much about painting and sculpture, he had had a lot of experience with fortifications. The joke was half true since Michelangelo had served the Florentine Republic as director of fortifications several years earlier. Without making too much of the anecdote itself (it is reported by Vasari), we do know from Francesco de Hollanda's *Dialogos*, written about this time, that Michelangelo was very much concerned with the Vatican project and, from other accounts, that he quarrelled with Sangallo over the plans. It is certainly characteristic that Antonio offered his challenge as a specialist to an amateur and that Michelangelo responded by asserting his own professional competence.

Nor is it surprising that their exchange concerned fortification design. According to Vasari, this was the area where the young Antonio first distinguished himself. Some years earlier, Pope Leo X had called together a team of military architects to plan the fortifications of Civitavecchia. After several days of discussion and the presentation of numerous schemes, no agreement could be reached until Antonio came up with a synthetic project that satisfied everyone, including the pope and the engineers. By the 1530s Antonio was the leading military architect of central Italy.

Military design, sometimes classed with architecture and sometimes with engineering, was practiced by nearly every major Renaissance architect except Palladio. In the fifteenth century, Filarete and Francisco di Giorgio included it in their treatises, and Leonardo recommended himself to Sforza as a military expert as well as painter, sculptor, and musician. In his brief discussion of the nobility of painting and of the artist in *The Courtier*, Baldassare Castiglione cited the application of drawing to the arts of war. War was a pastime, a serious concern of the nobility, and a fit and necessary object of study for a prince. Perhaps for this reason, a practitioner of military architecture in the Renaissance was a gentleman by consequence of his profession. In the sixteenth century, he was often an independent specialist. Military architecture had its own body of theory, and its practice involved precise calculations and drawings on the part of the designer; but only semi-skilled laborers were required for construction. Unlike medieval castles, Renaissance fortifications were of rough masonry or earth. Military architects dealt with the highest class of patron, with princes and city governments, and their expertise was highly valued. Many of the great military specialists of the period are no longer well known, but the reputations of a number of architects, including Michele Sanmichele in Verona and Galeazzo Alessi, who first appeared as a military architect in Perugia, were based on their military work. Vignola, Michelangelo, and Philibert Delorme could all claim to be experts in fortification design. Michelangelo may not have considered this as exalted a discipline as sculpture or painting, but it was certainly a distinguished profession with no taint of association with the trades.

It is difficult today, when the artist's social standing is high and the profession of the craftsman is nearly atrophied, to appreciate the intense concern of the Italian Renaissance artist to establish his status. His efforts did not stop with learned discourses on the nobility of the arts or with his intimacy with the highest levels of society. In spite of his immense artistic reputation, Michelangelo always insisted upon the nobility of the Buonarroti family; and architects tried whenever they could to bring out the best in their ancestry. The practice of military design was perhaps the most obvious way for an artist to affirm a status on a par with the other professions such as medicine or law. Certainly, it was the first aspect of architectural practice to gain independent recognition.

Andrea Palladio was a professional architect and, of all the great Italians, his career most resembles that of Philibert Delorme in France. He was trained as a stone-mason and worked as a builder, and he advanced his career with the help of a humanist patron; but his career was nevertheless shaped by a characteristically Italian view of the architect. Andrea di Pietro della Gondola was discovered by the humanist Trissino, lifted out of his humble stone-mason's trade, re-educated, and re-christened to emerge as Palladio, the architect. His belated liberal education, as Ackerman has rightly stressed, (*Palladio*, p. 21) was tailor-made for an architect—the study of geometry and proportion, Vitruvius, and Roman monuments. Palladio did not have Alberti's liberal education or an artist's training in *disegno*. He was, as Philibert said of his own training, more "educated in books and long experience." But unlike Philibert, Palladio never made a point of his earlier, humbler career. Although it undoubtedly influenced his approach to architecture, Palladio's apprenticeship as a stone-carver was politely passed over in silence when he became an architect and an associate of humanists and patricians (see his preface to the *Quattro Libri*, Venice, 1570).

It is no coincidence that the most advanced form of the architectural profession was to be found in France and in northern Italy—in provincial centers like Vicenza, where Palladio established his practice, in Genoa, where Alessi did much of his work, or in Verona, where Michele Sanmichele was the leading architect—and not in central Italy, where the artist-architect continued to dominate the scene. Yet even in Rome, there were signs that architecture was slowly becoming a specialist's field. Vasari, in spite of his belief in the unity of the arts of design, faulted the early artist-architects for their ignorance of building, often to the extent of not knowing the technical language. His own technical preface to the *Lives* is concerned with building technology—how to mount an architrave so that it will not crack—and only secondarily with the theory of architecture based upon the symmetry of the human body. In his second edition of the *Lives* (1568), Vasari added in the life of Antonio de Sangallo a story which probably happened later but which illustrates his own attitude. Pope Paul III had opened a competition for the design of the cornice of his palace and Vasari, as he told it, came to present Michelangelo's design with those of the other architects. After reviewing the various projects, the pope turned to Antonio and asked where Melighino's project was. Antonio, who was already humiliated by this competition for the design of part of his own building, had had enough: "Melighino?" he replied, "But really, Holy Father, he's a joke!" Emphatically, the pope reminded Antonio that he wished Melighino (who was a notary turned designer and courtier) to be taken seriously. The story shows that, although the pope might wish to encourage his favorite, an amateur was not taken seriously by professionals like Sangallo and Vasari.

Perhaps the clearest example of the new attitude is Michelangelo himself who, in spite of his own belief in the practice of *disegno*, protested that he was not an architect—by which surely he did not mean that he considered himself incapable of designing a building but that he lacked constructional expertise. From documentary evidence, even this was not quite true. Michelangelo was concerned with the technical aspects of building to a remarkable degree. This is not surprising, since he approached architecture as a sculptor famous for carving marble himself and for allowing only the smallest share of the work to his assistants. He took the execution of his buildings as personally as he took his sculpture, and his ornamental vocabulary was so complex and so idiosyncratic that it must have required both skillful workmen and the closest supervision. In his architectural practice, the result was a concern for building materials and building technology and a professional sense of responsibility for the construction. Although too old to supervise all the work at St. Peter's in person, he watched it carefully. When he was absent from Rome and a bit of unusual vaulting was improperly executed, he had it torn out and re-done, much to his personal "shame and vexation."

Michelangelo treated what we would call technical problems as design problems, and this brings him close to Philibert's view that the architect must concern himself as much with materials and techniques as with the design and ornament of architecture. In fact, this attitude brought them both closer to the craft of building than Alberti had envisioned for his humanist architect a century earlier, although it is merely an extension of the Classical ideal of the fusion of theory and practice. At any rate, by the 1560s, we may say that the architect had achieved full professional status and, like a doctor or a lawyer, he might take full responsibility for all aspects of his practice.

We must remember, however, that this still was not the profession in its modern form, which is a creation of the nineteenth century. As Ackerman has pointed out, the difference lies partly in the fact that in the sixteenth century, and indeed until the Industrial Revolution, every piece of a building was made to order. This created problems of communication. The new architect, who would not be working in the stone yard or be always present at the building site, needed to provide his workmen with precise instructions. An important part of this procedure, the more traditional way of communicating personally and verbally, escapes us today, so that at points we can be puzzled by how things were built at all. On the other hand, new devices were employed in the sixteenth century and old ones re-adjusted to establish communication with patrons and, more importantly, with the executants. The architect came to rely on models and increasingly on drawings to communicate his designs to the builders.

As we have seen, the medieval tradition of model-building in Italy continued in the Renaissance. The model was first of all made for the patron and occasionally for the public—a purpose it still serves. It was also used as a guide for the builders. In the sixteenth century, the character of architectural models seems to have varied considerably. Philibert complained of fancy models that were painted up to conceal a poor design; but models could be impressive. Michelangelo's ten-foot full-scale wooden model of the cornice for the Farnese Palace was hoisted into place so the pope could see how it would look. Such an elaborate and costly affair must also have been intended for the use of the workmen. Working models, usually of wood, were expensive. Sangallo's model for his design of St. Peter's is famous because it cost a fortune. Philibert, who complained of the expense of models, nevertheless advised the patron and the architect to invest in them because detailed models of all the major parts of the building would be justified in the long run. Michelangelo, who left a clay model of the staircase of the Laurentian Library for the workmen to follow when he left Florence, was using scale models for the workmen at St. Peter's many years later.

But, even in the fifteenth century, drawings were beginning to replace models in architectural practice. Filarete describes a type of drawing which he calls a "relief drawing," made on squared paper. From this master plan, further scale drawings of detailed plans could be made. The technique derived from the squaring of a panel for a perspective construction, as Alberti explained it in *Della pittura*, but Filarete seems to have been the first to apply the technique to architectural drawing. The close relation between perspective construction and methods of architectural drafting is essential to an understanding of the development of architectural drawings in the sixteenth century.

To judge from the copies of his treatise, Filarete's drawings were rather primitive (Figure 33), especially when compared with the beautiful architectural drawings that survive from the later Renaissance, when this branch of *disegno* came into its own. Unlike the fifteenth century, the sixteenth century is rich in architectural drawings of all sorts—studies after antiquity and contemporary buildings, sketches of an architect's ideas, and numerous plans and some elevations and sections, as well as perspectives and a great wealth of architectural details. From this collection of material we might expect to be able to read the progress of a building from the architect's first sketches to the final working drawings; but, in fact, the professional use that was made of these drawings is not clear. One problem is that there are seldom enough drawings from any one project to follow its evolution. But there are also consistent gaps in the evidence. As Ackerman has explained,

finished drawings may be classed in two categories: first the large, carefully drawn, and attractively rendered projects that were made for the client; they are rare and they cannot have been much use for construction because they almost never include measurements or a scale. Moreover, they typically show the building that was to have been built rather than the one that was built. . . . The second type of finished drawing was intended for use in construction, but it is limited to details—a window, an entablature—and was intended only to guide masons and carvers ["Architectural Practice," p. 161].

Where are the working drawings that might in some way correspond to the blueprints used in a modern office? One answer is that they are gone, used up on the job; another is that they never existed. Certainly a great number of drawings have perished, but it is puzzling that so few of the drawings that do survive can be identified as working drawings.

Many of the drawings we have were probably made for the patron. These include not only the presentation drawings from an initial phase of a project, but also the studies and sketches that were exchanged when the

Figure 33. Elevation and grid for a church, from Filarete's *Trattato di architettura,* ca. 1465. The scale grid illustrated below the elevation of the church was the basis of Filarete's designs and made it possible for him to provide his patron with a measured view of his entire project.

final plans were being negotiated and construction was actually under way. Such use of drawings is documented in the correspondence between Michelangelo and Pope Clement VII during the work on the Laurentian Library, already mentioned above. A number of drawings may also have been made during the meetings and consultations that were so often held between the patron and several architects. The numerous "ideal" plans of St. Peter's, which exist in a bewildering number of versions by different hands and which are often covered with notations and corrections, do not seem to relate to any identifiable stage of construction but may well be the product of group discussions with the patron. If we recall Vasari's account cited earlier of Sangallo's meeting with Pope Leo X and his military engineers, we realize that this group must have produced a number of drawings within a very few days.

Presumably, once the plans were settled, the approved design was passed on to the workmen for execution. A study for a fresco at the Farnese Palace at Caprarola (Figure 34) shows the architect with some associates (perhaps intended to personify his liberal education) delivering his drawing to the contractor for execution while, in the background, the stone-cutters and masons are busy with the building. Certainly, by the mid sixteenth century, it was possible to build a building without a model. Michelangelo's Laurentian Library must have been largely executed from drawings, since there is no record of a model until he left Florence. But what sort of drawings? The study for the fresco at Caprarola shows the architect holding a plan, and master plans were certainly made. The other type of working drawing is the architectural detail, and it may well be, as Ackerman has suggested, that when the architect was able to supervise construction, these were all that were needed.

There is, however, evidence of a different type of architectural drawing in the Renaissance—the perspective projection, the analytical section and elevation drawing—which is associated with the building of St. Peter's, specifically with the appointment of Raphael in 1514 as chief architect.

The appointment of Raphael (1483-1520) as architect of St. Peter's is the most striking example of the Italian confidence in the genius of the artist. St. Peter's was the most complex building program of the century, and Raphael had very little experience as an architect. His appointment came because of his status as a great painter and apparently on Bramante's recommendation. As Raphael realized himself, his other commitments, as well as his inexperience, made it impossible for him to work as Bramante had done, and we saw in the last chapter that he was given Giuliano da Sangallo and Fra Giocondo as architectural mentors. Raphael welcomed Fra Giocondo gratefully, but since Fra Giocondo was seventy-nine it was hardly to be expected that he would supervise construction for very long; and Giuliano was old and soon returned to Florence. Two years later (1516) Fra Giocondo died, and Raphael asked for another assistant. Antonio da Sangallo was given the job; thus was created the organized building operation at St. Peter's, with Antonio as chief supervisor until 1520 when, on Raphael's death, he became chief architect.

Figure 34. Jacopo Bertoia, *Construction of a Rotunda,* study for the decoration of the villa at Caprarola. The professional architect, accompanied by his scholarly advisors, presents his plans to the manual workers who will carry them out.

There is some reason to believe that Raphael may have shaped the assistants assigned to him into something resembling an architectural office, although how much of it was already established under Bramante before 1514 is still open to debate. One reason to favor Raphael, rather than Bramante, as the organizer of the work at St. Peter's is the character of Raphael's own painting atelier. Raphael's assistants worked as extensions of his own hand, preparing drawings and cartoons from his sketches and ideas as well as executing much of the work. Except perhaps for Giulio Romano, who was chief assistant and shop foreman, these artists were not independent personalities while they were in Raphael's shop, and they are identifiable only occasionally and only in the execution of works, not in their conception. Raphael's painting shop was a remarkable innovation. It is also closer to the modern architectural office than any architectural practice we know from the Renaissance.

Raphael was not a figurehead at St. Peter's; on the contrary, he was so preoccupied by his new responsibilities that contemporaries found him unlike his usual self. In spite of this, there are no drawings of St. Peter's that are certainly by his hand. A new plan of the building was drawn up during this period, and a model was begun. The plan, published by Serlio in 1540, and existing in other versions as well, is considered to be Raphael's design, but the many drawings from his period of office are certainly by others—chiefly Antonio da Sangallo. This suggests that he may have been using Antonio the way he used his painting assistants—to prepare studies from his ideas. He could then rework more finished plans.

If this is true, then Raphael's need for more precise kinds of architectural drawings is obvious. A building on the scale of St. Peter's could have been built from the few plans and details that would serve for a smaller building, but the spatial conception of St. Peter's was far more complex than that of previous buildings. It was too intricate to be held in the mind of the architect or conveyed to the patron and workmen by simple sketches and details. Perspective renderings made the project visible more cheaply and rapidly than a model. They could be revised, and measured sections and elevations could serve to prepare more detailed specifications—all of which could be done by assistants. As mentioned in the last chapter, the famous letter to Leo X concerning the projected "reconstruction drawings" of ancient Rome explained that the illustrations would be accurate and legible. They would show not only the foundations, which one could see from a plan, but also the character of the architecture in space—they would have been a complete application of *disegno* to architecture.

Figure 35. Menicantonio (?), combined elevation and section of an early project for St. Peter's, Rome; undated. The techniques of perspective projection, here applied to architecture, made it possible to represent the complex spaces of the new St. Peter's. Such drawings are the ancestors of the analytical drawings used in the modern office.

None of Raphael's drawings for this reconstruction project has been identified, and there is some question if any were made, but some of the new type of elevation and section drawings made for St. Peter's are preserved in a sketchbook belonging to Paul Mellon (Figure 35). This type of drawing, however, cannot be associated with a new type of architectural practice. Raphael died in 1520, before his organization of the works was firmly established; and although Antonio da Sangallo inherited his position and kept it until his own death in 1546, he seems to have invested most of his energy in the notorious wooden model and to have been satisfied with sketches for his own designing and with plans and details for working drawings. Nor did Michelangelo, who disliked delegating any design functions to others, choose to work as Raphael had. The measured elevation and section drawings which were later made from the model were apparently not used in the actual design process.

In the sixteenth century, however, the set of measured architectural drawings—plan, elevation, and section—did develop into the means of communication between architect and workmen. The Escorial, begun in the 1560s, was built largely from such drawings, although models were also made; a number of elevation and section drawings by Juan Bautista de Toledo and Juan de Herrera survive. Juan Bautista was Michelangelo's assistant at St. Peter's, so perhaps the analytical drawings were used in Italy more than surviving drawings would indicate. In France, Philibert Delorme was perfectly aware of Italian developments in architectural drafting after he returned from Rome in 1536. His copies of the elevation drawings for St. Peter's, which are preserved in Munich, are close to those in the Mellon sketchbook. Philibert, moreover, clearly saw the advantage to using drawings in building, although he was not prepared to give up model-building. He devoted the major part of his treatise to explaining the different types of drawing and illustrating the decorative vocabulary of Classical architecture. In his instructions to the masons, he states that he wishes to demonstrate "what instruments and methods the masons should use for measurement, as much as for the *orthographies* as for the *scenographies*—that is to say for the plans, elevations and facades of buildings— in order that they might have a sound knowledge before proceeding to any drawings or models" (Bk. II, Fol. 31).

Alberti had made it clear that architectural practice without theory was just a trade, not a discipline (*De re aedificatoria*, Bk. IX, Ch. x); but the actual relation between theory and practice in the Renaissance is a matter of debate. Wittkower (*Architectural Principles in the Age of Humanism*) identified humanist theories of proportion and geometry as a serious aspect of real buildings, particularly those by Alberti and Palladio. On the other hand, Krautheimer ("Alberti and Vitruvius") has shown that *De re aedificatoria* was not addressed to practitioners; and Ackerman ("Architectural Practice," p. 153) has observed that architects of the High Renaissance produced little theoretical writing of their own. Although I cannot agree with Ackerman's conclusion (p. 170) that High Renaissance architects were anti-theoretical in outlook, it is true that, in some of the later architectural treatises at least, the theoretical discussion often seems largely rhetorical and lacking in any direct relationship to design. The fact is that, like Vitruvius before them, Renaissance architects were anxious to unite theory with practice because the definition of their profession depended upon it. The development of a professional literature in the sixteenth century was largely the result of their coping with this problem.

Vitruvius' *Libri decem* was the only theoretical work on the fine arts to have survived from antiquity, and this accounts for the independent character of Renaissance architectural writing, which has no parallel in contemporary treatises on painting or sculpture. After *De re aedificatoria*, Vitruvius was the model and vehicle for discussions of architectural theory. Alberti's work was conceived as a modern answer to Vitruvius, but being written in Latin and having no illustrations, it could hardly have been of much use to the builder even after the first printed edition appeared in 1485. The sixteenth-century editions of Vitruvius, beginning with Fra Giocondo's Latin text in 1511, were still addressed to the same, but now more numerous, audience of humanist patrons and educated architects. The number and quality of these editions, both Latin and Italian, testify to the continuing fruitful bond among patrons, scholars, and architects. Daniele Barbaro's splendid edition (Venice, 1556) has an extensive scholarly commentary and illustrations by Palladio. By the end of the century, Vitruvius was accessible in other illustrated Italian editions and in French and German translations. In the commentaries upon Vitruvius' often obscure text, architects could keep abreast of current theories of proportion and composition, and they could study the Orders and reconstructions of some Classical buildings. But this did not make Vitruvius an architectural handbook, nor did the editors attempt to present the current state of architectural practice. Cesariano (edition of Vitruvius, Como, 1521) had used some contemporary buildings—notably the section of the cathedral of Milan and a schematic plan and elevation of Filarete's hospital—to illustrate Vitruvius' points and to assert a relationship between Milanese and Classical style; but he was chiefly interested in publishing his own, rather fanciful, reconstructions of ancient buildings.

The ambitious publications of the Bolognese architect Sebastiano Serlio (1475-1554) were the first to present architectural theory in the form of a professional manual. Serlio published his Book IV in Venice in 1537, the first to appear of seven projected books on architecture (he published five and a sixth appeared after his death; see next chapter). Serlio reduced the inheritance of humanist theory to a systematic presentation of perspective, the Classical Orders, and buildings of antiquity, with which he also included some modern buildings such as Bramante's Tempietto and the project for the dome of St. Peter's (Bk. III, Venice, 1540).

Serlio's theoretical commentary was perfunctory and revealed a certain divorce between a theoretical residue and the aims of a straightforward pattern book. In Book IV, for example, he presented each Vitruvian Order and then moved on to his own designs illustrating how it could be used. His Book V was a collection of his own designs for portals, from doorways to city gates, with no theoretical apparatus and no obvious relation to Vitruvian or Albertian theory. In other books, Serlio illustrated similiar series of variations on a theme such as the palace or private house, none of which is derived from Classical buildings. Serlio relied primarily upon his large woodcuts to demonstrate the principles of proportion and composition of Classical and modern buildings, and he included precise measurements and details. In his legible plans, elevations, and sections, architects could study classical reconstructions more easily than in any edition of Vitruvius, so that Barbaro's and Serlio's collections of designs amounted to a manual of the modern style.

The unprecedented success and enormous influence of Serlio's publications was due to the fact that they were, in large measure, a published version of the Renaissance architectural sketchbook where the architect kept his reference material: drawings after antique and contemporary buildings, and his own projects. As we have seen, the *Codex Escurialensis* is a fine fifteenth-century example, and a number of others survive from the sixteenth century. One can also find a precedent for Serlio's collection of building types in the fifteenth-century manuscripts of Francesco di Giorgio and, as Pedretti (*Leonardo*, p. 5) has observed, in Leonardo's medical illustrations. It would appear that many of Serlio's illustrations were based upon sketchbook drawings by his master Peruzzi.

Serlio's publications entirely superseded a modest little dialogue on the Classical Orders, *Las medidas del romano*, by the Spanish cleric Diego de Sagreda, published in Toledo in 1527—a simple pattern book showing the Orders, ornamental columns and bases, a bit of entablature and a doorway, some of which appear to have been derived from contemporary Italian rather than Classical prototypes; and Serlio's works were the model for the architectural manuals of the later sixteenth century—the specialized treatises on the Orders, the collections of ideal building types, and the manuals of fortification design—all of which relied primarily upon their illustrations. In 1561, Philibert published his *Nouvelles inventions pour bien bastir*, which is an illustrated handbook on wooden construction (Figure 36). Vignola's famous *Regola delli cinque ordini d'architettura* appeared in 1562, and his *Due regole della prospettiva practica*, a manual of illustrations, was published in 1583, after his death, by the learned mathematician Ignazio Danti, who added a biography of Vignola and a theoretical commentary. Like Serlio's books, these works were meant for the widening market of practitioners who needed manuals of Classical and

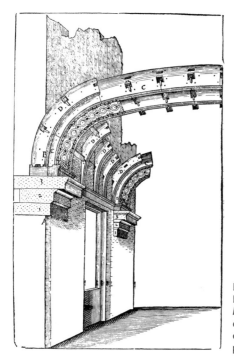

Figure 36. An illustration in Philibert Delorme's *Nouvelles inventions pour bien bastir,* 1561 (Book 2, ch. 6). It demonstrates a new system for making ceiling beams out of several separate pieces of wood.

modern style for their own work. But Serlio was also the model and the license for such extraordinary publications as Wendel Dietterlin's *Architectura*, a collection of ideal projects published in 1593 (Figure 37).

Two major theoretical treatises in the sixteenth century reintegrated theory with the professional approach to architecture found in the manuals. Philibert Delorme's *Premier tome de l'architecture* was a genuinely theoretical work, based upon Vitruvius but recast for contemporary needs and with a partly functionalist point of view. Following Serlio, Philibert published large and beautiful illustrations of the Orders, adding a theoretical commentary; but he also added a sixth "French Order" of his own invention. He justified his expansion of the Classical canon on theoretical grounds: the Orders had originally developed from local building traditions and available materials. Philibert reasoned that, like Corinth, which gave birth to the Corinthian Order, France should have her own national Order which would take into account the character of French building stone and employ decorated column drums rather than the single column shafts that were appropriate to marble. Philibert planned to devote another treatise to the problem of harmonic proportions—evidently to be a reconciliation of Classical theory and Christian number symbolism—but he never wrote it. The great reintegration of humanist theory with contemporary practice is the treatise published two years later: Andrea Palladio's *I quattro libri dell' architettura*, which appeared in Venice in 1570. Palladio demonstrated how theory and practice defined the architect's profession, in a manner so lucid and elegant that his book enjoyed a success that has never been equaled by any writer on architecture.

Like Philibert's, Palladio's theory is based upon Vitruvius, and he too followed Serlio's example and published his own work. But unlike Serlio, Palladio published his commissions. The *Quattro libri* included plans and elevations of twenty executed villas and seven more projects that Palladio did not expect would be built, and he named the place and patron of the executed works, so that, as he said, architects might visit them. As is well known, these buildings were not all built as he published them, and his plans are also ideal types in which the principles of Renaissance composition and theories of harmony are presented in measured plans and elevations. As an architectural theorist Palladio is a close relative of Alberti. But the practicing architect is as evident as the humanist scholar. Palladio presented in concise terms, and with splendid illustrations, the procedure

Figure 37. Design for a doorway from Wendel Dietterlin's *Architectura*, 1598. A virtuoso demonstration of the architect's creative ingenuity. Although it is an architectural fantasy, such a composition could be used as a mine of decorative motifs by other architects.

for building—from choosing the site and materials to planning the heights of rooms and locating the staircase; and, to stress the Classical authority of this architecture, he followed his presentation of each building type with his reconstruction of its Classical model, based upon Vitruvius' text. Thus his illustration of an antique villa demonstrates the same principles as his own designs (Figure 38).

The theoretician and the practitioner coexisted without friction in Palladio because he simply assumed the qualities in the architect that Philibert had insisted upon as separate, if reconcilable, aspects of the profession. Just as Palladio's architecture was a model of contemporary Classicism, so he himself was the model architect: well read in architectural theory, supremely knowledgeable about Roman antiquities, and personally responsible for sound and economical buildings for his clients. His ideas were not all new; many came from Alberti; but his self-portrait as an architect, and his illustrations incorporating the material of the manuals and his own practice in a Classical theoretical structure, defined the range of the architectural profession for years to come. One can follow Palladio's impact in editions, translations, and adaptations through the eighteenth century. The most immediate effect of the *Quattro libri*, however, was to focus the architect's view of his profession (as its delayed effect was to propagate a style). The fragment of Vincenzo Scamozzi's architectural treatise, published as *Idea dell' architettura universale* (Venice, 1615), is based upon Palladio's scheme and designs, although not upon his lovely style of writing. At the beginning, Scamozzi felt obliged to cite all the theoretical works of his predecessors that he could think of—Palladio, Philibert, Vignola, Alberti, and numerous others—before turning to his own exposition of Classical theory. The result is a somewhat undigested accumulation of two centuries of thinking about architecture, but this was its innovative aspect. Scamozzi treated architectural theory as doctrine, but also as the accumulated experience of the architects themselves. This may partly account for his appreciative remarks on some Gothic buildings, which he viewed, not as models of style, but as architecture and therefore interesting.

The most modern aspect of the expanding architectural publication in the sixteenth century is the architectural print. The practice originated in the Roman print trade, which had developed from Raphael's innovative practice of publishing his own painted work in engravings by Marc Antonio Raimondi before 1520. It was anticipated in Serlio's woodcuts of some modern buildings and in the prints after Classical antiquities; but

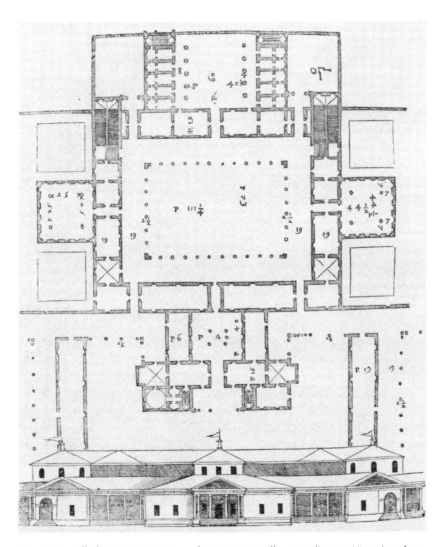

Figure 38. Palladio, reconstruction of an antique villa according to Vitruvius, from his *Quattro libri*, 1570. This reconstruction of a Classical villa, based upon Vitruvius, is also a perfect statement of Palladio's own style. The schematic plan and elevation are sufficient information for laying out a building and for determining the proportions of its major elements.

the publication of buildings was not really under way until the 1450s, when the Spaniard Antonio Salamanca organized the publishing of prints on a large scale in Rome. In 1546, he issued the engravings by Antonio Labacco (born 1495) after Antonio da Sangallo's famous model of St. Peter's—large plan, elevation, and section prints which were the first to be comparable to the earlier publication of Raphael's paintings. These were followed by other prints of modern buildings. An anonymous engraving of the hemicycle of St. Peter's appeared in 1564 and, in 1568-69, a famous series of engravings of the architecture of Michelangelo by the Frenchman Etienne Dupérac (1525-1604). Dupérac was both an architect and an expert on Roman topography, and his magnificent engravings of the elevation, section, and plan of Michelangelo's project for St. Peter's are of sufficient scale and accuracy to be essential for modern reconstructions of Michelangelo's ideas. But Dupérac did not work from elevations and sections by Michelangelo. He compiled his views from the wooden model and from detail drawings. His are essentially reconstructions and, in the case of St. Peter's, his engravings are apparently the only such views of the project that ever existed.

The Frenchman Lafreri published Dupérac's engravings of projects as if they were completed buildings. Like Labacco's prints, they were intended for an audience of specialists anxious to know what was being planned for St. Peter's; not surprisingly, the enterprise was largely in the hands of foreigners, and the prints primarily for export. Single sheets soon developed into the architectural album—the most famous being Jacques Androuet du Cerceau's *Les plus excellents bastiments de France* (Paris, 1576-79), a vast series of plans and views of the major French chateaux. Adapting Dupérac's scheme to the publication of his own building, Juan de Herrera prepared an elaborate set of drawings of the Escorial which were issued in 1589 with a brief, separate text keyed to the prints. *Las estampas* and *El sumario* were, like Luigi Vanvitelli's monumental publication of the royal palace at Caserta in 1759, personal as well as official publications which aimed to place the buildings in the corpus of modern architecture. Dupérac's projects also suggested the notion of publishing an architect's complete oeuvre, first undertaken in the eighteenth century with the *Opus architectorum* of Francesco Borromini (Rome, 1735) and the *Architettura civile* of Guarino Guarini (Turin, 1737).

Such publications were designed for the specialist, whether amateur or professional. Patrons collected the treatises, manuals, and prints; but, by the end of the sixteenth century, most architects also had their own professional libraries. Juan de Herrera in Spain, for example, owned all the major works by sixteenth-century architects (except Palladio) as well as editions of Vitruvius and Alberti.

The change in architectural style which we saw taking place in the fifteenth century implied a new conception of architecture. Alberti's ideal of architectural harmony—the design to which nothing can be added and from which nothing can be taken away without spoiling it—required the architect to be responsible for every detail of his building; but, as a designer, he had no necessary role in the construction. The acceptance of Classical theory meant that architecture could not be learned on the job, it had to be studied. At the same time, the architect was free to design for any building material and to use any technical device that would make his building stand.

This view of architecture has characterized the profession until very recent times, when architects have begun to feel constrained by the image of the omnipotent designer; but, within the broad frame of post-medieval architecture, changes of style did imply some changes in practice. The radical alterations of a building during construction, which we have seen to be characteristic of the sixteenth century, would be inconceivable in a modern building. The modern building is a single form; the Renaissance building was conceived as a harmony of separate parts, each with its own identity. The long-term acceptance of this idea, and of the decorative vocabulary that was meant to express it, made it possible for a building to be designed in a series of stages. This was why Michelangelo could speak of returning to Bramante's forty-year-old plan for St. Peter's and could reshape the parts of the structure then standing—the remodeled fifteenth-century choir, Bramante's piers, and the hemicycle designed by Raphael and re-handled by Antonio da Sangallo the Younger—into his own conception. Michelangelo's modifications of the Palazzo Farnese must be understood in the same way; but his design of the Porta Pia (1561) already shows an eccentric relation among the individual elements, which denies them independence.

The complete submission of individual parts to the whole is, of course, a feature of Baroque architecture. Even as Classicizing a building as Bernini's Sant' Andrea al Quirinale (1658-70) depends upon the orchestration of elements, none of which makes sense without the others. In a façade by Francesco Borromini (1599-1667) the rhythm of the whole dominates to the extent that the Classical vocabulary is deformed or given up entirely.

A natural consequence of this new approach to architecture was an increased emphasis on the designing phase before construction. The number of studies required before a building was begun and the number and complexity of the drawings required to build it now increased. By the seventeenth century, this need was being met by the architectural office, where plans and working drawings were prepared by assistants. These men were not workmen, or even draftsmen, but junior architects, and they had to be capable of designing in the master's style. Borromini, who worked in this capacity for Bernini, deeply resented the subjugation of his own personality to another architect who would take the credit for his work and guide its style. One finds a similar situation in the French office of Jules Hardouin Mansart (1646-1708). The junior architects, who were responsible for detailed designing in an office, often later became independent architects. This did not mean, however, in the case of architects like Bernini or Mansart, that the master's building was not his own.

In 1665, Bernini (then sixty-seven years old) set off from Rome for Paris, where he was to prepare his final projects for the new Louvre of Louis XIV. The commission is discussed in the following chapter; only two things need be noted here: first, that Bernini was not venturing—as Serlio had done more than a century ago—into unknown territory. French architects were there to meet him and, it soon appeared, to challenge his projects with their own. Second, although the personal style of Bernini differed quite profoundly from the French conceptions of Classicism, there is no doubt that Bernini's French colleagues shared his theoretical views on art. As Hibbard (*Bernini* [Baltimore, 1967], p. 174) has pointed out, Bernini's ideas were those of the sixteenth century: a belief in *disegno*, concern for order and proportion in architecture, a respect for antiquity; and these ideas exactly suited the taste of the young French Academy.

Bernini was not alone in stretching the Classical canons to include his own work. Throughout the seventeenth and eighteenth centuries, architects continued to study Vitruvius; to read the treatises of the sixteenth century; and, until the functionalist challenge of the eighteenth century, to conduct their discussions of architectural style in the terms framed by the architects of the Renaissance.

BIBLIOGRAPHICAL NOTES

There is no general study of the architect's profession in the Renaissance. Perhaps because the greatest Renaissance architects are such familiar artistic personalities, scholars have not felt the need to investigate the profession in order to understand the buildings. The brilliant article by J. S. Ackerman, "Architectural Practice in the Italian Renaissance," *Journal of the Society of Architectural Historians* 13 (1954), 3-11, reprinted in *Renaissance Art*, ed. C. Gilbert (New York, 1970), was the first to demonstrate the importance of the subject; but his treatment is limited to the High Renaissance, primarily to the career of Antonio da Sangallo the Younger in Rome. The following works will serve as a guide to further study.

The best place to read about central Italian architects and their careers is Giorgio Vasari's *Vite de' più eccellenti pittori, scultori, ed architettori*, 2d ed. (Florence, 1568), available in a number of modern editions and translations, the best of which is still G. Milanesi's of 1878. The most useful guide to the vast literature on Renaissance architecture is L. Heydenreich and W. Lotz, *Architecture in Italy 1500-1600* (Baltimore, 1973), which also contains the clearest and most recent discussion of the projects for St. Peter's from Bramante to Sangallo. See also the comprehensive bibliography compiled by J. S. Ackerman and J. A. Pinto, *A Bibliography of Renaissance and Baroque Architecture* (Cambridge, Mass., 1974).

The career of the greatest of the artist-architects of the Renaissance, Michelangelo, can be studied in excellent modern scholarship. J. S. Ackerman's *The Architecture of Michelangelo*, 2 vols. (London, 1961), revised edition in one vol. (Baltimore, 1971), contains a wealth of information on architectural practice as well as a classic analysis of Michelangelo's architecture. The following are also well worth reading for what they reveal about Michelangelo's methods of design and the organization of the works at St. Peter's: H. A. Millon and C. H. Smyth, "Michelangelo and St. Peter's—I: Notes on a Plan of the Attic as Originally Built on the South Hemi-Cycle," *Burlington Magazine* 111 (1969), 484-501 (a new interpretation of Michelangelo's design for the attic); and H. Saalman, "Michelangelo: S. Maria del Fiore and St. Peter's," *Art Bulletin* 57 (1975), 374-409 (a study of the dome).

C. L. Frommel, *Der römische Palastbau der Hochrenaissance*, 3 vols. (Tübingen, 1973), is an invaluable source for architectural practice and patronage in Rome. H. Hibbard, *Carlo Maderno and Roman Architecture 1580-1630* (London, 1971), covers the later period. D. Howard, *Jacopo Sansovino: Architecture and Patronage in Renaissance Venice* (New Haven and London, 1975), is a carefully documented study of the Venetian situation. See also J. S. Ackerman, *Palladio* (Baltimore, 1966). C. Pedretti, *Leonardo da Vinci: The Royal Palace at Romorantin* (Cambridge, Mass., 1972), is a convenient study of Leonardo as an architect. I have not discussed Leonardo in this chapter because his career is atypical in so many ways; but, as Pedretti's monograph shows, it was full of implications for the future of architectural practice. Useful material on the many-sided career of Galeazzo Alessi may be found in the Acts of the International Congress in Genoa: *Galeazzo Alessi, e l'architettura del cinquecento* (Genoa, 1974), with an introduction by W. Lotz, pp. 9-12.

Any consideration of the theory of Renaissance architects must begin with R. Wittkower's classic study, *Architectural Principles in the Age of Humanism* (New York, 1965). J. von Schlosser's *La letteratura artistica*, revised edition by O. Kurz (Florence, 1964), is indispensable as a summary of the tradition of architectural writing; and it includes a comprehensive bibliography of architectural treatises. See also R. Krautheimer, "Alberti and Vitruvius," *Acts of the XXth International Congress of the History of Art* (Princeton: N.J., 1963), reprinted in the author's collected essays: *Studies in Early Christian, Medieval, and Renaissance Art* (New York, 1969), pp. 323-32.

No published Renaissance architectural treatise exists in an annotated modern edition, but later reprints and translations, if not the original editions, can be found in larger libraries. Philibert Delorme's *Premier tome de l'architecture* (Paris, 1567) was reprinted together with his *Nouvelles inventions de bien bastir* (Paris, 1561 and 1568) in Paris, 1892. See also A. Blunt, *Philibert Delorme* (London, 1958).

Andrea Palladio's *I quattro libri dell' architettura* (Venice, 1570) exists in numerous later editions and translations, the most accessible being the reprint of Isaac Ware's translation, *The Four Books of Architecture* (London, 1738), with an introduction by A. Placzek (New York, 1965).

Vignola's *Regola delli cinque ordini d'architettura* (Rome, 1562) exists in numerous later editions. His *Due regole della prospettiva practica*, edited by Ignazio Danti (Rome, 1583), was somewhat less popular.

Vincenzo Scamozzi's *Idea dell' architettura universale* (Venice, 1615) should be supplemented by his *Taccuino di viaggio da Parigi a Venezia*, edited by F. Barbieri (Venice and Rome, 1959).

On prints, see: C. Huelsen, "Das 'Speculum romanae magnificentiae' des Antonio Lafreri," in *Festschrift für Leo S. Olschki* (Munich, 1921); but there is no general survey of architectural prints, and they have not been studied in relation to architectural practice. On architectural drawings, W. Lotz's "Das Raumbild in der italienischen Architekturzeichnung der Renaissance," *Mitteilungen des Kunsthistorischen Instituts in Florenz* 7 (1956), 193-226, is fundamental.

For the seventeenth century, see also R. Wittkower's *Gothic Versus Classic: Architectural Projects in Seventeenth-Century Italy* (London, 1974), which contains much valuable information about practice.

I would like to thank James S. Ackerman and Henry Zerner for their helpful criticism.

# 6

## The Royal Building Administration in France from Charles V to Louis XIV

MYRA NAN ROSENFELD

The history of the Royal Building Administration in France is a topic of utmost importance, since this institution influenced the organization of the modern architectural office. Its delegation of the tasks of business administration, drafting, planning, site inspection, and engineering contributed to the way in which architects work today in large offices. Furthermore, the curriculum of the Royal Academy and of its successor, the Ecole des Beaux-Arts, was the basis for the method of instruction used in architectural schools until the advent of the Bauhaus in the twentieth century. Finally, the Royal Building Administration provided the means for the modernization of medieval architectural practice in France through the introduction of the new methods from Italy which have already been investigated in Chapters 4 and 5.

The Royal Building Administration, or, as it was called in French, l'Administration des bâtiments royaux, was the result of many decades of development. Its sources go back to the reign of Charles V (1364-80). At its inception, its structure was simple. It consisted of masons, notaries, and the Master Mason who was its administrator. The creation of the post of Inspector General during the reign of Louis XI (1461-83) placed a business administrator above the Master Mason. Charles VIII (1483-93), who had been to Italy, introduced the position of Royal Architectural Adviser in response to Italian practice of the time. The Royal Architectural Adviser was given authority over the Master Mason. Francis I (1515-47) brought about significant changes when he appointed Sebastiano

Serlio as Royal Architect. Francis, the first French monarch to be interested in the quality of architectural education provided by the Royal Building Administration, commissioned Serlio to write several books on architecture, obviously for the use of the members of the administration. By the time of Louis XIV (1643-1715), there was an increase in the staff which assisted the head architect, as well as in the personnel concerned with business administration. This enlargement was accompanied by a greater hierarchical organization and a greater specialization in the tasks. The head architect was no longer concerned with financial administration or with the actual work on the site. The king himself, through the intermediary of the Inspector General—Finance Minister Colbert—took a more authoritative role in the development of the Royal Building Administration, as we shall see in the case of the East Colonnade of the Louvre. Finally, during the reign of Louis XIV the Royal Academy of Architecture, the first official school of architecture, was created in France; it significantly altered architectural practice. Our knowledge of the Royal Building Administration is based on building contracts from the fourteenth to the eighteenth centuries, the proceedings of the Royal Academy of Architecture during the reign of Louis XIV, and architectural treatises.

The organization of the Royal Building Administration during the reign of Charles V (1364-80) is a concrete example of the working conditions of the French architect during the Gothic period. In Chapter 3 we noted that the medieval architect received his training from the guilds and then rose from the rank of stone-mason to that of head architect who provided the design and directed the work. The hierarchy in the Royal Building Administration parallels that which we find in the workshops of the large cathedrals. The king was a client similar to a bishop, the chapter of a cathedral, or the abbot of a monastery. The administration during the reign of Charles V drew upon Parisian masons for its manpower and the notaries of the Parliament of Paris for its financial administrators. Architects in Paris had been organized into the corporations of stone-masons and carpenters since the middle of the thirteenth century. The specific regulations for their training in a workshop, the length of apprenticeship, and examinations for certification of professional expertise were registered with the Parliament of Paris in the *Livre des métiers d'Etienne Boileau* (Etienne Boileau's Book of Professions). These two corporations had received their charters from the king. The distinction between planning and manual labor was unknown in France during the Middle Ages. The medieval architect learned all the aspects of the profession from stone-cutting and business administration to planning, mathematics and engineering; most masons were trained in family workshops. In France the word "architect" was not used to mean "planner" until Fra Giocondo, an Italian consultant to Charles VIII, was called *architectus regius*, "Royal Architect," by the humanist Guillaume Budé.

Charles V's extensive building program was the consequence of the need to protect his domain from the constant threat of the English, with whom he was at war. He built a new fortification wall around the right bank area of Paris. Within the city, he constructed a large manor, the Hôtel Saint-Pol, and renovated the Louvre. He also renovated his castles at Vincennes, Melun, Montargis, Crueil, Vivier, and Saint-Germain-en-Laye. The king must have played an active role in the direction of the Royal Building Administration. Christine de Pisan described him in her biography, *Le livre des faits et bonnes mœurs de Charles V* (Book of the Reign of Charles V), in 1405 as a "wise artist, true architect, prudent organizer, and a sure planner, since he commissioned beautiful foundations in many places as well as notable, beautiful and noble buildings, not only churches and castles, but also other buildings in Paris and elsewhere. . . ." The head architect of the Royal Building Administration was Raymond du Temple, a mason from Paris, who had the title of Master of the Masonry Works of the King, Maître d'œuvre de maçonnerie du roi. Raymond du Temple produced the initial ideas for the buildings and co-ordinated the work of a large group of masons, carpenters, sculptors, painters, and tapestry-makers. As an administrative architect, he has been compared to Philibert Delorme, the architect of Henry II. Raymond du Temple also held the title of Sergeant at Arms, which may be an indication of activity as a military engineer. He was paid a regular salary for his post as Sergeant at Arms and, in addition, a stipend for each building he supervised.

One of the most important projects of Charles V in Paris was the renovation of the Louvre (Figure 39). This fortified castle had been built during the reign of Philip Augustus (1202-24). Because of the construction of the new wall on the right bank, the Louvre was no longer needed for protection and could be transformed into a more sumptuous residence. Gardens were added and crenelations were torn down. In 1367 Charles decided to transfer his library from his palace on the Ile de la Cité to the northwest tower of the Louvre. He added new royal apartments in the North, West, and South Wings. Work was carried out until 1372 under the direction of Raymond du Temple. Payments to the masons were made

by Gilles Mallet and François Chateprime, two notaries from the Parliament of Paris. The Royal Building Administration included the masons Drouet and Guy de Damartin, two brothers from northeastern France, and the sculptors Jean Saint-Romain, Jean de Liège, and André Beauneveu. The masons were not paid a regular salary but were remunerated for their work according to the amount of masonry that was used for each building. Since most architects in France were also trained as stonemasons, it was not unusual that Guy de Damartin was paid to work both as a sculptor and a mason. He executed the portraits of the royal family on the main staircase of the North Wing, and he also destroyed the crenelations on the South Wing of the Louvre between 1367 and 1369.

During the reign of Charles V, the Royal Building Administration in Paris set a standard in architecture which had an influence in other areas of France and in other strata of society. There was communication between the architectural workshops of Charles V and those of his brothers, the dukes of Berry and Burgundy. In 1370 Guy de Damartin was appointed Master of the Masonry Works of the Duke of Berry. His brother Drouet became Master of the Masonry Works of the Duke of Burgundy in 1384. Finally, André Beauneveu was lent to the Duke of Berry in 1392. In that year, when the castle of Mehun-sur-Yèvre was completed, the Duke of Burgundy sent a delegation headed by Claus Sluter and Drouet de Damartin to the Duke of Berry to inspect it.

Guy de Damartin's career as an architect is an example of how a man might work up through the professional hierarchy. In 1370, when he was appointed by the Duke of Berry, he was given a house in Bourges in order to do site supervision on the projects in the vicinity. Guy was not paid a regular salary but was remunerated according to his activities on each individual building. In 1383 he was paid for having supplied the other masons with ground plans for the palace at Riom. In 1384 he was paid merely for the time spent in supervising the drawing of a plan of the palace at Poitiers by another mason, Jean Gérout. His administrative role did not include the financing of the buildings. We know that for the palace at Riom there was a separate financial administrator, Jean de Sauvignon,

Figure 39. Limbourg brothers, view of the Louvre, *Très riches heures du duc de Berry*, Chantilly, Musée Condé, ca. 1410/16. The Limbourg brothers painted the Louvre just after it had been renovated by Charles V, who added new apartments to the older fortified castle of Philip Augustus which had consisted of a *donjon* surrounded by curtain walls and corner towers.

who had been paying the masons and verifying the contracts since 1376. This separation of financial and architectural planning follows the practice of the Royal Building Administration.

After the death of Charles V in 1380, extensive royal building activity ceased for almost a century because of the Hundred Years War with England. The war officially ended in 1429 with the coronation of Charles VII and the Treaty of Compiègne, but political stability did not return to France until the reigns of Louis XI (1461-83) and Charles VIII (1483-98). Louis XI re-established Paris as the capital of France and centralized the administration of the government. Several major innovations occurred in the organization of the Royal Building Administration. In 1461 Louis XI established the position of Inspector General. He gave Gaspard Bureau, a notary, the title of Réformateur, général, visiteur des œuvres. Gaspard Bureau took over site inspection, which had been the job of the Master Mason. This reform thus placed a financial administrator over the Master Mason, a policy that was continued by all subsequent French monarchs.

The second major innovation in the organization of the Royal Building Administration at this time was the introduction of an architectural advisor who was not burdened by administrative duties. During his expedition against Naples, Charles VIII had been influenced by the role Giuliano da Majano, Francesco di Giorgio, and Giuliano Sangallo played at the court of Alfonso II of Aragon, and of course by the example of Alberti, who had been adviser to Pope Nicholas V and to Sigismondo Malatesta. Charles VIII brought Fra Giocondo to France, as well as Pacello da Mercogliono, a Neapolitan designer of gardens. These Italian architects advised the three French Master Masons of the king, Colin Biart, Guillaume Senault, and Louis Amangeart. Pacello da Mercogliano designed a garden inspired by Roman antiquity for the castle of Amboise, which had been transformed by the three Master Masons into a manor. Fra Giocondo was given the title Deviseur de bâtiments (designer of buildings). He worked mainly as an engineer until he went back to Italy in 1505. In 1499, he advised Colin Biart and Guillaume Senault on the construction of a new bridge to replace the Pont Notre Dame in Paris, which had collapsed. He also designed an underground hydraulic system for the gardens which Pacello da Mercogliano had added to the castle of Blois in the early part of Louis XII's reign (1498-1515).

The reign of Francis I (1515-47) was extremely important for the history of the Royal Building Administration. Like his predecessors, Francis I harbored French dynastic ambitions in Italy. After his return from captivity at the Battle of Pavia against Emperor Charles V in 1528, there was relative peace, and conditions were favorable for building. Until 1536, Francis retained the organization established by his predecessors for the Royal Building Administration. He continued to use Italian architectural advisers. Between 1517 and 1519, Leonardo da Vinci designed a new town at Romorantin near Blois. Francis also employed Domenico da Cortona, who had been adviser to Charles VIII and Louis XII. Domenico da Cortona was head architect for the castle of Chambord (1515) and for the Hôtel de Ville in Paris (1531-49). As before, the Inspector General of the Royal Building Administration was a notary from Paris, Florimond de Champeverne. He held the title of Surintendant (overseer). More personnel was added to the financial department of the administration. Champeverne was aided by several Controllers who traveled to the different buildings to do site inspection and check the execution of the work according to the contracts. These were Nicolas de Neufville, Guillaume de la Tuelle, and Louis Poireau. There was, in addition, a Paymaster, one Nicolas Picart. All these men were notaries from Paris.

Between 1528 and 1547, the Master of the King's Masonry Works was Gilles le Breton. He held the title of Maître général des œuvres de maçonnerie du roi (master of the king's masonry works). He was assigned to Fontainebleau, a fortified castle and convent that Francis I renovated and enlarged (Figure 40). Gilles le Breton's administrative duties with regard to the other royal buildings must have been minimal, since each had its own head architect. Girolamo della Robbia directed the construction of the castle of Madrid; Pierre Chambiges, the castle of Saint-Germain-en-Laye; Jacques and Guillaume le Breton, the castle of Villers-Cotterets. The coordination of these projects was in the hands of the Inspector General, Florimond de Champeverne. The administrative duties of the Master Mason of the King had declined since the reign of Charles V.

Gilles le Breton came from a family of Parisian masons. As in the past, the Royal Building Administration continued to draw on the Parisian corporations for its manpower. Gilles le Breton probably received his early training at the castle of Chambord, since his father was employed there between 1519 and 1524. He did not receive a yearly salary, as did the financial administrators, but was paid for the work he directed according to

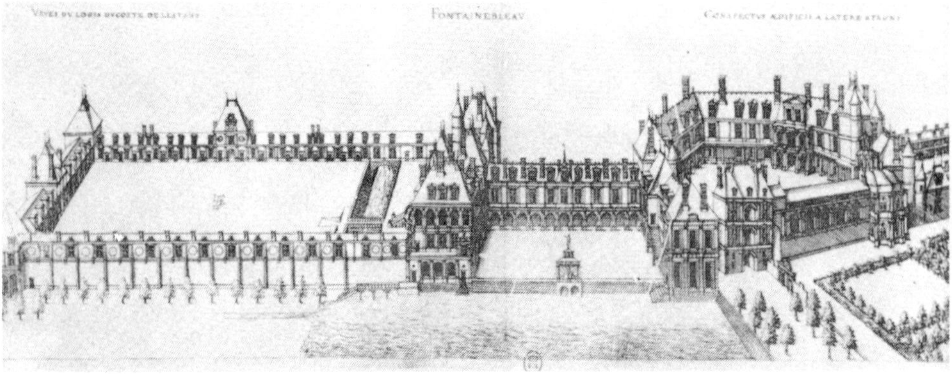

Figure 40. Jacques Androuet du Cerceau, view of the Castle of Fontainebleau, 1579. Francis I renovated the medieval castle of Fontainebleau and established his court there. The Oval Courtyard to the right, as well as the Entry Gate, was built by Gilles le Breton, Master of the King's Masonry Works.

the size of the building and the amount of masonry used in its construction. Le Breton was assisted at Fontainebleau by a large workshop of other masons, the most important of whom were Jean aux Bœufs and Pierre Chambiges, also from Paris. Between 1528 and 1548, Le Breton supervised the design and construction of the Oval Court (the site of the royal apartments), the Gallery of Francis I, the Porte Dorée, the Entry Gate, and the wings around the Lower Courtyard, which contained a library, a chapel, the Ulysses Gallery, and servants' quarters.

Francis I made several important changes in the Royal Building Administration during the last ten years of his reign. His first innovation was the appointment of the Bolognese architect Sebastiano Serlio to be an adviser on both architecture and painting at Fontainebleau. On December 27, 1541, Serlio was given the title of Royal Architect and Painter in charge of the Castle of Fontainebleau. He was paid 400 gold crowns annually. Serlio was commissioned to provide Gilles le Breton with architectural designs and to advise Primaticcio on the interior decoration of the castle. Several of Serlio's designs were executed by Le Breton: his projects for the Salle du Bal or Ballroom (Figure 41), the North Portico of the Oval Courtyard, and the Pine Grotto at the end of the Ulysses Gallery. Serlio also contributed to the design of the fresco decoration in the interior of the Pine Grotto, which was executed by Primaticcio. Serlio's dual appointment as painter and architect was unusual in France, where architects were trained as sculptors rather than painters. It was more usual for Italy, where most of the major architects of the first half of the sixteenth century had been trained as painters like Serlio. Serlio's dual activity is

similar to that of Charles Le Brun later in the Royal Building Administration of Louis XIV.

Another innovation was Serlio's administrative role in the Royal Building Administration. Until this time, the architectural advisor had been
spared administrative duties. But in the contract of 1541, Serlio was paid
an extra 20 pounds per day to visit the other royal castles. He was an architectural supervisor who was to make sure that the royal castles were being designed and constructed according to the principles of sound architecture. In this capacity, Serlio supplied Francis I with designs for the
Louvre in Paris, as well as for several other castles and palaces.

Francis I was also interested in improving the education of the masons
who worked in the Royal Building Administration. A major reason for his
hiring of Serlio was to have him publish his architecture treatise in France.
Serlio had published his Book IV, *On the Roman Orders*, and Book III,

Figure 41. Sebastiano Serlio, the Salle du Bal, Fontainebleau, 1542-45. Serlio brought
to France new methods of building construction and new ideas from Italy. This ballroom was modeled on the loggia of the Villa Madama by Raphael in Rome, ca. 1519.

Figure 42. Sebastiano Serlio, palace façade, Book IV, folio XXXV, Venice, 1537. Serlio's books on architecture were the first manuals printed during the Renaissance that were meant for the practicing architect rather than the patron.

*On Antiquity*, in Venice in 1537 and 1540. These were the first contemporary books on architecture to be printed in a modern language with illustrations and to be destined primarily for the architect, not the patron (Figure 42). In the introduction to the *Third Book*, which was dedicated to Francis I, Serlio stated that he intended to publish ancient and modern French buildings in his future books. For his publishing activities, Serlio was paid a salary of 100 gold crowns per year by Marguerite of Navarra, the sister of Francis I. While he was in France, Serlio published Books I and II, *On Geometry and Perspective*, in 1545; Book V, *On Churches*, in 1547; and the *Extraordinary Book on Doors* in 1551. The inclusion of French translations alongside the Italian text indicates to us that these books were destined for the architects in the Royal Building Administration.

Francis I's final innovation in the structure of the Royal Building Administration was the appointment of his Finance Minister, Philibert de la Bourdaisière, to be Inspector General in 1536 at the death of Champeverne. This was the first time that these two posts had been held by the same person. It was later paralleled by the appointment of Colbert, Louis XIV's Finance Minister, as Inspector General of the Royal Building Administration in 1664. Francis I must have made this appointment so that he could more efficiently divert money from the treasury to the Royal Building Administration.

Francis I died in 1547. During his reign, there had been much confusion in the Royal Building Administration because there were three administrators at its helm: the Inspector General, the Royal Architect, and the Master Mason. Henry II (1547-59) streamlined and centralized the Royal Building Administration by appointing Philibert Delorme, whom we have already met in Chapter 5, to be Inspector General in 1548. Delorme was the first person to hold the dual appointment of Royal Architect and Inspector General. He was given the responsibilities held earlier by Philibert de la Bourdaisière and was commissioned to do site inspection and to verify the contracts of the masons working on the castles of Fontainebleau, Villers-Cotterets, Yerres, and Madrid. In addition, Delorme provided designs for the castle of Anet, the Château Neuf at Saint-Germain-en-Laye, the chapel at Villers-Cotterets, and the castle of Fontainebleau. Henry II probably felt that architectural expertise was needed to handle the financial affairs of the Royal Building Administration. Delorme's experience as Inspector General is reflected in his description of the duties of the architect in his treatise *Le premier tome de l'architecture* of 1567. He recommended that the architect have training in law and finance in addition to the usual professional training. Delorme was aided in his duties by a Controller, Pierre Deshotels, and by a Paymaster, Nicolas Picart. There was a separate administration for the buildings Henry II commissioned in Paris. The Controller was Jean Durand. Pierre Lescot, a notary and member of the Parliament of Paris, directed the construction of the Louvre. He was aided by Jean Goujon, an architect and sculptor, who designed the building. The Royal Building Administration also included a military engineer, Adam de Craponne.

Philibert Delorme's career followed a pattern that we have found earlier in the Middle Ages. Trained as a mason, he worked himself up in the profession to be an administrative architect. Between 1533 and 1536, Delorme accompanied Cardinal Jean du Bellay to Rome while the cardinal was French ambassador at the Vatican. A sketchbook of drawings of Roman buildings in the Munich Staatsbibliothek is an indication of the importance of this trip for his education. When he returned to France, he worked briefly as the Cardinal's architect before he was appointed Inspector General of the Royal Building Administration. His original training as a mason came to the fore when he designed the tomb of Francis I for the

Cathedral of Saint-Denis at the beginning of Henry II's reign. When Henry II died suddenly in 1559, the Royal Building Administration was taken over by a painter, Primaticcio. It would not be under the control of a professionally trained architect again.

In the second half of the sixteenth century, France was plagued by civil war between the Protestants and Catholics. When Henry IV (1594-1610) finally reunited the country in 1594, several changes were made in the Royal Building Administration. The Finance Ministry was given back the control it had lost during the reign of Henry II. Sully, the Finance Minister for Henry IV, was also Inspector General of the Royal Building Administration between 1590 and 1594. Jean de Fourcy, a notary, held the post of Inspector General between 1594 and 1624. The power of the Royal Architect diminished. Salaries indicate the relative importance of the members of the Royal Building Administration. At this time Fourcy received a salary of 6,000 pounds per year, while Louis de Metzéau and Jacques Androuet du Cerceau, the Royal Architects, received only 400 and 800 écus each. More personnel was added to the financial department. Fourcy had an assistant, as well as several Controllers who did site inspection. There was now one Controller for buildings, one for gardens, and one for fountains.

A major innovation in the structure of the Royal Building Administration during the reign of Henry IV was the establishment of royal control over the Parisian masons and carpenters who were still recruited for manpower. In 1597, Henry IV reformed the statutes of the corporations of the carpenters and masons. He appointed a royal Master Mason in Paris to see that the rules about professional qualifications were being enforced. He also decreed that the same standards be applied all over France. In 1607, Henry issued a building code for Paris which established uniform regulations for safe, fireproof construction throughout the city.

In spite of these laws, there were constant disputes between the Royal Architects and the masons recruited in Paris. There were still no definite requirements for the level of expertise required of the masons. The task of hiring them was left to the discretion of each architect. On February 7, 1608, a royal proclamation was issued stating that the architect in charge must check the competence of the masons and contractors, as well as the validity of their price estimates. The architect was admonished to make sure the work of the masons was executed according to the *rules of art*. Despite these efforts by Henry IV to establish special standards, the issue

was solved only later during the reign of Louis XIV, when the Royal
Academy of Architecture was founded. The final contribution of Henry IV
and Sully to the structure of the Royal Building Administration was the
establishment of factories to supply the royal buildings with furniture, fabrics, tapestries, porcelain, and silverware. This was a sector of the Royal
Building Administration that was continued by Louis XIV.

During the reign of Louis XIV, the Royal Building Administration was
enlarged. There was a greater specialization in the jobs and a much more
hierarchical organization. The architects were all made subject to the control of the king and the Inspector General. In 1664, Jean-Baptiste Colbert,
Louis XIV's Finance Minister, was appointed Inspector General. Colbert
centralized the structure of the administration as he had done for the government of France. His most important innovation was the foundation of
the Royal Academy of Architecture in 1671. The king thus gained absolute
control over the architectural profession in France. He determined the
standards for the training of architects, as well as the awarding of commissions. Colbert was the intermediary between the king and architects on all
levels. He worked out the programs of the buildings for the architects and
judged the quality of their work. As Protector of the French Academy
after 1672, Colbert also determined the way in which architects were
trained. A banker, one Louvois, was the Controller of the administration.
He paid the architects, masons, and contractors. Manpower was still recruited from the corporations of masons and carpenters of Paris. Louvois
had six assistants who were called Commissioners and did site inspection.
    Louis Le Vau was appointed Royal Architect in 1654 and continued in
this post until his death in 1670. His father, Louis I Le Vau, had been an
architect in the Royal Building Administration of Louis XIII. Le Vau was
directly responsible to Colbert. He consulted with him and presented him
with ideas for the buildings. Le Vau in turn directed the work of four
other architects who had the title of Inspector. These Inspectors did drafting, drew up specifications, and directed the masons on the actual building
sites. They were François Mansart, Pierre Le Muet, François d'Orbay, and
François Le Vau, Louis Le Vau's brother. Claude Perrault, an authority
on Vitruvius and an engineer, took the place of Mansart after the latter's
death in 1666. In that year, Sebastien le Prestre, Marquis de Vauban, was
appointed architect in charge of fortifications. It is interesting to note that
while Louis Le Vau was Royal Architect, he was also able to work as a
freelance entrepreneur like Inigo Jones and Christopher Wren in Eng-

land. He was involved with his father and brother in the development of the Ile Saint-Louis, where he served as a contractor of numerous stately town houses for members of the king's Financial Administration.

The Royal Building Administration during the reign of Louis XIV also had a historian, André Félibien, and an iconographer, Israel Sylvestre, who executed engravings of the royal monuments. At the bottom of the hierarchy was the Gobelins Factory, whose director was the painter Charles Le Brun. This factory employed over two hundred artisans to produce furnishings for the king's buildings. It was similar to the factories that had been set up by Henry IV, but it now had its own school.

The way in which the Royal Building Administration functioned during the reign of Louis XIV is best illustrated by the competition for the design of the East Wing of the Square Court of the Louvre (Figure 43). We have much contemporary documentation about the relationship between the patrons, Louis XIV and Colbert, and the architects. The Square Court of the Louvre was begun in 1547 with the construction of the West Wing, which contained the apartment of the king. By 1654, the year in which Louis Le Vau became Royal Architect, the South, West, and North Wings of the Square Court had been completed. Le Vau began work on his first project for the remaining East Wing in 1659. By the time his final plan was accepted by the king in 1667, the Royal Building Administration had developed eight different projects. Of the numerous drawings which have come down to us, only twenty can be attributed to Le Vau. This is an indication of his duties as an administrative architect. He did sketchy drawings of initial ideas, but the more detailed, finished plans and elevations were executed by the four Inspectors under his direction.

Between 1659 and 1663, Le Vau presented four projects to the King for the East Wing of the Louvre. Finally, in 1663, his fourth project was accepted. Le Vau had directed the execution of two architectural models for this project. One was made of wood, the other of stucco. There are twelve drawings by François Mansart which show the foundations for this fourth project. However, the building was interrupted in 1664 when Colbert became Inspector General of the Royal Building Administration. Colbert rejected Louis Le Vau's fourth project because he felt that it was not grand enough. He criticized Le Vau's use of half-columns on the façade and the doorways inside the wing, which he thought were not wide enough. In spite of the fact that Louis XIV hardly ever lived in the Louvre, Colbert felt that the palace was important as a symbol of the king's political power in Paris. In 1665, Colbert decided to hold a competition

Figure 43. Paris, Louvre, East Wing, 1667-71. The East Wing was added to the Louvre during the reign of Louis XIV and was the collaborative effort of Louis Le Vau, Charles Perrault, and Charles Le Brun.

for the East Wing of the Louvre in order to obtain a better design. The Royal Building Administration under the direction of Le Vau submitted a fifth project. At the same time, Colbert sent Gian Lorenzo Bernini, Candiani, Carlo Rainaldi, and Pietro da Cortona in Rome a drawing by Le Vau of this fifth project. Colbert also sent these Italian architects detailed requirements for the program of the East Wing. The Wing was supposed to contain several large galleries, kitchens, pantries, storage rooms for silverware for the king and queen's table, and rooms for the servants and guards. The Italian architects sent their drawings back to Colbert. Colbert and the king were judges for the competition; Bernini won it. On June 2, 1665, Bernini made a triumphal entry into Paris and presented the king with two more projects. The king chose the final one, and in the autumn of 1665, the foundations were laid for Bernini's third project.

In 1666 Colbert and the king changed their minds again. Work on Bernini's design was stopped. According to several memoranda that Colbert sent to Bernini, Bernini had not followed the program set by Colbert. Bernini wanted to place the royal apartments in the East Wing. This was considered unsuitable because of the noise and climatic conditions there. Colbert and the king wanted to keep the royal apartments in the South and West Wings.* Secondly, according to Claude Perrault, there was objection to Bernini's unorthodox use of the Roman Orders.

During the year 1666, the Royal Building Administration set up a committee to present its final project to the king. This committee consisted of Charles Le Brun, the king's painter, Louis Le Vau, and Claude Perrault. The composition of the committee is interesting, since Le Vau was the only full-time practicing architect; Perrault had been trained as a doctor. The final project was the result of a collaborative effort by these three men. We have one preliminary chalk drawing by Louis Le Vau for this final project; the façade of the East Wing is shown with a colonnade (Figure 44). There are two ground plans which were executed by the Inspectors of the Royal Building Administration and two drawings by Le Brun for an alternative façade without a colonnade. Since the king's buildings were also conceived as political propaganda, visual symbolism was an important factor in the planning process. It was for this reason that Le Brun, who was in charge of royal iconography, was included in the committee. He may have suggested the idea of the colonnade; Louis XIV was often represented in the guise of Apollo, the Sun God, and in a drawing for the fresco of the Apotheosis of Apollo for the dome of the main salon of the castle of Vaux-le-Vicomte, Le Brun had depicted the palace of Apollo as a colonnade. Claude Perrault was an authority on the interpretation of the Latin text of Vitruvius, and in 1673 he published an illustrated edition of Vitruvius' *Ten Books on Architecture*; he played a role in determining the proportions of the columns on the east façade.

In April 1667, the king and Colbert accepted the eighth project for the East Wing, drawn up by the architects of the Royal Building Administration. That Louis Le Vau continued as administrative director of the project is supported by a plan of the Square Court which he executed in 1668 with the change of the doubled South Wing. The East Wing was finally completed in 1671 after twelve years of negotiations between the patrons and the architects of the Royal Building Administration.

* I would like to thank Joan Draper for this suggestion, presented in a seminar paper on the Louvre at the College of Environmental Design, University of California, Berkeley, in 1974. See Pierre Clément, *Lettres, Instructions et Mémoires de Colbert* (Paris, 1868), pp. 245-65.

Figure 44. Louis Le Vau, preliminary drawing for the East Wing of the Louvre, 1667. Le Vau executed this drawing in red chalk just after work on Gian Lorenzo Bernini's third project was stopped in 1666. It is a good example of an initial sketch in which the architect works out his general ideas for a building.

The most important result, I believe, of the competition for the East Wing of the Louvre was the establishment of the Royal Academy of Architecture in 1671. The French architects had followed the king's directives on the program during the first phase of the competition, but they had not put enough grandeur and majesty into their projects. This was why Colbert decided to turn to Italian architects. Colbert and the king were probably also dissatisfied with the training of the French architects in the theory and aesthetics of architecture. A school was needed where French architects could be trained specifically for the Royal Building Administration. When the academy met for the first time in 1672, the main topic of discussion was a definition of beauty in architecture. For the first time since the Middle Ages, the methods of architectural training were completely changed. In the academy, the architect learned, first, abstract principles of design. Only later, when he entered the Royal Building Administration, did he gain practical experience. On the other hand, in the Parisian workshops from the Middle Ages to the seventeenth century, the architect had learned principles of design and structure through direct practical experience. Learning in the academy was through discussions of specific problems. The architects studied the Roman Orders, works of famous architects of the past and present, the royal buildings, and architectural treatises. The principles of education developed by the Royal Academy were published by its first director, François Blondel, in his *Cours d'architecture*, which appeared in Paris in 1675. The methods of instruction developed by the Royal Academy influenced the way architecture was taught all over Europe in the eighteenth and nineteenth centuries. It was only in the twentieth century, when the Bauhaus was founded in Germany, that this system was finally challenged.

BIBLIOGRAPHICAL NOTES

Pioneering work on the structure of the Royal Building Administration has been done by Louis Hautecoeur, *Histoire de l'architecture classique en France*, Paris, Tome I, Vol. 1, 1963, "Les maîtres maçons," pp. 1-8, "Les guerres d'Italie," pp. 111-34, "Les châteaux royaux," pp. 230-58; Tome I, Vol. 2, 1965, "Naissance de l'architecte et de l'administration des bâtiments royaux," pp. 179-218; Tome I, Vol. 3, 1966, "L'Administration des bâtiments sous Henri IV," pp. 13-25; and Tome II, Vol. 1, 1948, "Colbert et l'administration des bâtiments," pp. 413-25. For the reign of Charles V, see Adolphe Berty, *Topographie historique du vieux Paris*, Tomes I-II, *Région du Louvre et des Tuileries* (Paris, 1866-68); Yves Bottineau, "L'architecture des premiers Valois," *Gazette des beaux-arts* (1974), 237-62; Alfred de Champeaux and Paul Gauchery, *Travaux d'art exécutés pour Jean de France, Duc de Berry* (Paris, 1894); and Paul Gauchery's article, "Influence de Jean de France, Duc de Berry, sur le développement de l'architecture et des arts à la fin du XIV$^e$ siècle et au commencement du XV$^e$ siècle," *Congrès archéologique* 65 (1898), 255-79. General background on the sixteenth and seventeenth centuries is found in Anthony Blunt's book *Art and Architecture in France 1500-1700* (Harmondsworth, 1970). Building documents of the reigns of Francis I and Henry II have been published by L. de Laborde, *Les comptes des bâtiments du roi* (1528-1571), I-II (Paris, 1877-80). For the careers of Philibert Delorme and Serlio, see Blunt, *Philibert Delorme* (London, 1958); W. B. Dinsmoor, "The Literary Remains of Sebastiano Serlio," II, *Art Bulletin* 24 (1942), 130-46, and M. N. Rosenfeld, "Sebastiano Serlio's Late Style in the Avery Library Version of the Sixth Book on Domestic Architecture," *Journal of the Society of Architectural Historians* 28 (1969), 155-74, and "Sebastiano Serlio's Drawings in the Nationalbibliothek in Vienna," *Art Bulletin* 56 (1974), 400-18.

We have the most information on the Royal Building Administration for the reign of Louis XIV. J. Guiffrey, *Comptes des bâtiments du roi sous le règne de Louis XIV*, I-V, (Paris, 1881-1901), has published the building documents. The competition for the Louvre colonnade has been analyzed recently by R. Berger in "Charles Le Brun and the Louvre Colonnade," *Art Bulletin* 52 (1970), 394-403, and by A. Braham and M. Whiteley in "Louis Le Vau's Projects for the Louvre and for the Colonnade," *Gazette des beaux-arts* 64 (1964), 285-96 and 348-62. Insight into the philosophy and curriculum of the Royal Academy of Architecture can be gained from François Blondel's *Cours d'architecture* (Paris, 1675), and H. Lemonnier, *Procès-Verbaux de l'académie royale d'architecture*, I-X (Paris, 1911-22). Much more research is needed on the structure of the Royal Building Administration during the Middle Ages.

# 7

# The Rise of the Professional Architect in England

JOHN WILTON-ELY

The formation of the architectural profession in England is intimately bound up with two major intellectual and social changes over the past four centuries—the transition from medieval to modern processes of thought and the shift from an agrarian to a capitalism-based society through the Industrial Revolution. The inter-disciplinary character of the modern architectural designer is the product of the first change; the professional organization through which he fulfills an increasingly specialist role is the result of the second; and the inherent conflict between these two aspects remains unresolved.

One of the first Englishmen to call himself "architect" was John Shute, who, in 1563, five years after the accession of Elizabeth I, did so in *The First and Chief Groundes of Architecture*. Shute's origins are still uncertain, but he seems to have trained as a painter and been sent to Italy in 1550 by his employer, the Duke of Northumberland. Shute's book not only represents the earliest exposition of the Classical Orders in England but was the first attempt to consider the practice of architecture from a theoretical standpoint. Paraphrasing Vitruvius, Alberti, and Serlio, he advocated the Renaissance ideal of the designer as universal man, not simply proficient in drawing, surveying, geometry, arithmetic, and optics, but also versed in literature, history, and philosophy as well as in medicine and astronomy.

Admittedly, such a conception of the controlling intellect was highly premature in a situation where building remained a largely collaborative process along medieval lines. Although Classical motifs had been introduced to England through the palace constructions of Henry VIII's Office of Works, the Orders continued throughout the century to be regarded as an anthology of decorative ornament, culled from the plates of Serlio, Delorme, de Vries, and others, rather than as a system of modular design.

Shute's ideal did, however, reflect the cultural aspirations of the new architectural patrons of the Post-Reformation era—the landowning politicians, civil servants, and nouveaux-riches like John Thynne of Longleat or the Cecils of Burghley and Hatfield. In Elizabethan England the construction of lavish country houses, as a manifestation of wealth and social status, went hand in hand with the imposition of a foreign and exclusive style, replacing the evolutionary nature of the vernacular Gothic idiom. In collective enterprises, such as the building of Longleat between 1554 and the 1580s, a cultivated landowner like Thynne appears to have been the directing mind, though advised by specialist craftsmen in matters of construction and ornament. Drawings and models as well as printed pattern books now began to play an increasingly important function in circumstances where the medieval fusion of designer and workman no longer operated and where Thynne himself co-ordinated building activities, assisted by his steward, John Dodd, in a supervisory capacity. Similarly at Burghley House over a comparably protracted period, we find Sir William Cecil guiding his mason-foreman, Roger Ward, with the occasional "rude trick" and receiving similar rough sketches for decision from his steward, Peter Kemp, acting somewhat as a clerk of works.

Already within this amateur situation, however, there are signs of an embryonic professional, the surveyor, who increasingly assumed initiative, in construction as well as in design. Several of these figures originated from the Royal Office of Works, often combining government responsibilities with consultations and private commissions. Quite the most remarkable was Robert Smythson, who rose from principal free-mason to being designer of a group of impressive country houses with highly original plans including Wollaton Hall and, probably, Hardwick Hall.

The important group of drawings in the Royal Institute of British Architects (RIBA) Collection connected with Robert Smythson and his son John indicate the growing significance of this mode of communication (Figure 45). While some are merely surveys or records of existing works, many of the original designs include plans drawn to scale, often dimensioned, with the various rooms designated. Certain sheets even have flaps

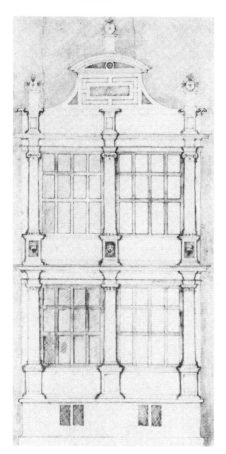

Figure 45. Robert Smythson (ca. 1536-1614), elevational design for a two-storey pilastered bay-window. The advent of the surveyor in sixteenth-century England, controlling design at the expense of the craftsman's traditional initiative, is represented here by a drawing probably connected with Smythson's first documented work at Longleat in the 1570s. Its traditional nature is also reflected by the way the new modular discipline of the Classical Orders, introduced from the Continent, assimilates the window system of Perpendicular Gothic.

provided to indicate alternative solutions to the plan or ornament for the patron's consideration, and others are clearly working drawings. The latter omit the detailed instructions, customary today, which were then often included in the contract along with matters relating to any important roof structures involved.

By the time of his death in 1614, Robert Smythson had acquired property and the status of "gentleman," being described on his memorial tablet as "Architecter and Survayor unto the most worthy house of Wollaton with divers others of great account." By this date, however, suddenly and unexpectedly emerged the first Briton to be immediately recognizable in the full Renaissance sense as architect—Inigo Jones. On his return from a second visit to Italy in 1615, Jones had brought with him an unrivaled understanding of the creative process behind Classical design, derived as much from a first-hand critical examination of antiquity as from the study of Palladio's treatise and buildings. Apart from Jones's key works such as the Queen's House, Greenwich, the Banqueting House, Whitehall, and Covent Garden, his surviving drawings for the court masques as well as for his architecture reveal an artistic personality far beyond the capacities of Shute or even Smythson (Figure 46). In the words of Sir John Summerson, "It is not simply the ability to draw which is significant, but the state of mind, the sense of control of which that ability is the outward sign. It represents, indeed, a revolution in architectural vision, and when we meet it with Inigo Jones's earliest surviving sketches in 1605 we know that we have finally crossed the threshold from the medieval to the modern" (*Architecture in Britain, 1530 to 1830*, p. 62).

Shortly after his return from abroad, Jones was appointed Surveyor of the King's Works; and for the next two hundred years, the Office of Works was to prove an important center for progressive architectural thought. This institution not only established what approximated to the first systematic architectural training, as undergone by Jones's nephew, John Webb, but maintained a continuity of experiment in Classical design through a period when England was increasingly affected by contemporary developments abroad.

Significant as Jones is as the first true architect in the modern sense, his career is unrepresentative of the general current of English architecture until the latter half of the eighteenth century, when the idea of a single figure, responsible for both design and supervision, began to be widely accepted. Until then the architectural scene was characterized by the continuing importance of the gentleman-architect. Such a figure was Sir Roger Pratt, who returned to England in 1649 after extensive travels in northern Europe and Italy. His five country houses, including the ill-fated Coleshill, combine influences from Jones and continental sources together with many indigenous features surviving from the earlier half of the century. Pratt's meticulous comments on architectural practice, surviving in a manuscript for an unpublished treatise, underline the persistence of the collaborative process involving patron, advisers, and craftsmen in an informal relationship. According to his advice to a prospective builder:

First resolve with yourself what house will be answerable to your purse and estate, and after you have pitched upon the number of the rooms and the dimensions of each . . . if you be not able to handsomely contrive it yourself, get some ingenious gentleman who has seen much of that kind abroad

Figure 46. Inigo Jones (1573-1652), alternative façade designs for the Prince's Lodging, Newmarket Palace. Evidence of the first true English architect, in the Renaissance sense, first appears with the drawings of Inigo Jones, reflecting a single intellectual and artistic vision in their searching lines and precise notation of metrical harmonies. In the evolution of the Prince's Lodging around 1619, as demonstrated by these two elevations, Jones takes as his point of departure the villas of Palladio and Scamozzi (above) to arrive at a highly original house type (below) of central importance for English architecture from the mid seventeenth century onwards.

and been somewhat versed in the best authors of Architecture . . . to do it for you, and to give you a design of it in paper, though but roughly drawn . . . and after you have had the advice and heard the discourses of many such [advisers] . . . get a model of wood to be most exactly framed accordingly . . . so go on with your building, or change it till it please you [Gunther, *Pratt*, pp. 60-61].

Other passages underline the comparative simplicity of the building operation and the designer's reliance upon a body of highly competent craftsmen, trained under an exacting apprenticeship, and allowed a considerable margin of initiative in the detailing of ornament.

The career of Sir Christopher Wren, covering the latter half of the seventeenth century, was in certain respects as untypical as Jones's. Unlike that of the latter, however, Wren's direction of the Office of Works and the sheer range of buildings carried out under him had a lasting impact upon the status and responsibilities of the architect as well as upon the organization of the entire building industry. Although only twelve years younger than Pratt, Wren represents, as perhaps never again, the universal competence envisaged by Shute a century earlier. Like his fellow member of the Royal Society, Robert Hooke, Wren applied to architectural design a keenly analytical and empirical mind, frequently more concerned with aspects of technology than with the niceties of formal expression. Wren introduced to architecture unprecedented developments in structural science, often resulting in spatial compositions of a complexity approaching those of continental Baroque designers like Borromini or Guarini. In the course of his forty years as Surveyor-General, Wren's responsibilities included the rebuilding of St. Paul's and fifty-one City churches after the Great Fire of 1666 and palace designs for Winchester, Whitehall, and Hampton Court, as well as the large hospitals at Chelsea and Greenwich. Besides the daily administration of the Office of Works, and assorted duties as a Member of Parliament, Wren's actual performance as an architect comprehended the widest possible range of rôles—surveyor, designer, engineer, businessman, and co-ordinator of an army of craftsmen and artisans by means of an efficiently run office.

Although in many respects Wren never achieved the artistic coherence of Jones in the evolution of a design, his use of visual aids in the form of models reveals much of his experimental approach to composition and the manipulation of form according to technical requirements. He established this three-dimensional medium not only as a design tool but also as a comprehensive means of communication between designer, patron, and crafts-

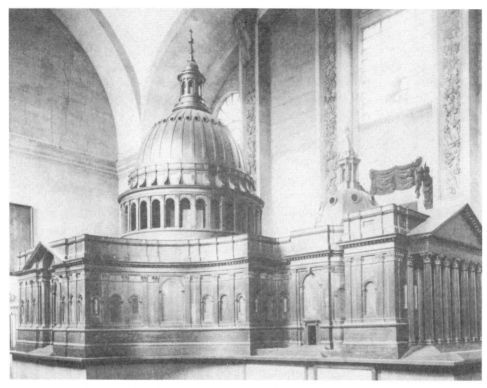

Figure 47. Sir Christopher Wren (1632-1723), the Great Model for St. Paul's Cathedral, London. Wren brought to architectural design a scientific cast of mind that found its expression in such experimental and explanatory aids as models. The Great Model, made by William and Richard Cleer with twelve joiners and a team of specialized craftsmen over a period of nearly ten months in 1673-74, represents the unfettered imagination of the designer. Despite the subseqeunt abandonment of this design, mainly due to the mental climate of post–Civil War England, something of its ideal grandeur was retained in the executed building.

men. The magnificence of his Great Model for St. Paul's, constructed with the greatest precision by a team of specialist craftsmen over ten months, is an eloquent testimony to Wren's unprecedented mastery over the entire architectural process (Figure 47). The abrupt rejection of this noble design without the slightest compensation also serves to illustrate the dependence of even the greatest architect upon the hazards of an informal relationship with the client.

The sheer professionalism of Wren was carried into the early eighteenth century by Nicholas Hawksmoor, trained from the age of eighteen in the Office of Works and largely concerned, while acting as Wren's amanuensis, in evolving a mode of expression as idiosyncratic as it was short-lived, the English Baroque. Great building enterprises such as Castle Howard and Blenheim Palace, in which Hawksmoor collaborated with his colleague in the Office of Works, Sir John Vanbrugh, stemmed directly from the advanced organization and high level of technical competence established by Wren. But it was Vanbrugh, former soldier and successful playwright, rather than Hawksmoor, who was to be more typical of the new century. As Swift's heroic couplet put it at the time:

> Van's genius, without thought or lecture,
> Is hugely turn'd to architecture.*

Making allowances for Vanbrugh's travels in France and Flanders and for his inheritance of Wren's discipline and organization, his sudden arrival on the English architectural scene still reflects something of the social mobility of the age. In fact, well into the last quarter of the century, it is still possible to distinguish three basic categories of designer, often operating side by side, in the form of the gentleman-architect, the artist-architect, and the craftsman-architect.

The Renaissance ideal of the cultivated gentleman, exemplified for the Elizabethans in the pages of Sir Thomas Hoby's translation of Castiglione's *Courtier*, reached its apogee in the Georgian landowner as architect and dilettante. The economic and political stability established under Whig rule found its aesthetic counterpart in the autocratic Palladian Revival, initiated around 1715 by two publications, Colen Campbell's *Vitruvius Britannicus*, Volume 1, and Giacomo Leoni's translation of Palladio's *Quattro libri*. The former title suggests the strongly nationalistic character of the movement in its conscious reaction to the foreign-based expression, as it was seen, of Wren's followers. The preponderance of large country houses illustrated in Campbell's fine engravings indicates the essentially agrarian basis of the architectural system effortlessly adapted from patterns created by Palladio nearly two centuries earlier for the senatorial landowners of the Veneto.

In this context the gentleman-architect, with a Classical education and an Italian bias acquired through the Grand Tour, is epitomized in Robert Boyle, Third Earl of Burlington. His earnest commitment to architecture, rather than his aristocratic status, is stressed in his surviving portraits. The earliest of these shows the earl not only holding the symbolic dividers but supported in the distance by his first architectural work, the Bagnio or

---

* Swift's poem, *The History of Van's House*, 1708, is quoted in full in L. Whistler, *Vanbrugh*, pp. 308-9.

bath-house of his villa at Chiswick (Figure 48). Such professional dedication, approached only by his friend the Earl of Pembroke, earned a magis-
terial rebuke in one of Lord Chesterfield's letters to his son in which the
boy was warned: "for the minute and mechanical parts of it [i.e. architec-
ture], leave them to masons, bricklayers, and Lord Burlington; who has, to
a certain degree, lessened himself, by knowing them too well."*

During the first half of the eighteenth century Burlington's personal example, his patronage and political influence over the Office of Works,
spread the orthodoxy of Palladian rules throughout the nation from mansions like Holkham Hall and Houghton Hall down to the modest terrace
houses of London, Bath, and almost every provincial center. The architectural careers of protegés such as William Kent, originally trained as a
painter, or of Henry Flitcroft and Thomas Ripley, both promoted from
the building trades, indicate the continuing flexibility of entry to the discipline, as well as the high level of competence attained by a thorough
mastery of treatises and textbooks. No less characteristic was the case of
James Gibbs, who exchanged a future in the Catholic priesthood for an
architectural training in the Roman studio of Carlo Fontana. On his subsequent return to Britain, it was only his religion and Scottish nationality,
resulting in his being suspected a Jacobite, which impeded his progress in
the political world of Whig architecture.

The eighteenth century was a Golden Age of architectural publications,
and a veritable hierarchy of treatises and pattern books reflects the percola-
tion of aristocratic taste through the social order. At the top were the
handsome folios of Campbell, Burlington, Kent, and Gibbs, followed by
Isaac Ware's Complete Body of Architecture ("a library on architecture
to the gentleman and builder; supplying the place of all other books"),
and a proliferation of humble manuals produced by enterprising designers
such as Batty Langley and William Halfpenny for provincial masons and
carpenters as well as their middle-class patrons. By this means Palladian
principles also spread rapidly abroad, and Gibbs's Book of Architecture
(1728) enjoyed a particular success in the North American colonies. As
architects acquired an ever-increasing range of patrons through this revolution in communication, so their published designs served as an adver-
tisement of their abilities, gradually emancipating them from dependence
upon the initiative of the aristocracy.

Toward the latter half of the century the operation of new intellectual

---

* The Letters of Philip Dormer Stanhope, Earl of Chesterfield, ed. J. Bradshaw (London, 1926), Vol. 1, p. 259, 17 Oct. 1749.

Figure 48. Jonathan Richardson the Younger (attrib.), Richard Boyle, Third Earl of Burlington (1694-1753). The dilettante as architect, a figure of widespread importance before the emergence of the profession, is uniquely recorded in this early portrait of Lord Burlington, a patron and designer whose aristocratic status and influence contributed to the impact of the Neo-Palladian Revival during the eighteenth century. Subsequently criticized for showing an unseemly expertise for a gentleman, the earl is portrayed holding dividers, with his first building, the Bagnio (1717) in the grounds of his villa at Chiswick, in the background.

as well as economic factors began to threaten the autocratic and agrarian world of Palladian taste, contributing towards the emergence of the professional architect around 1800. Under Neo-Classicism a new historical awareness of the past grew from a gradual shift in emphasis from Rome to Greece, as well as from a growing interest in such non-Classical modes of expression as the Gothic and Oriental styles. Moreover, the standpoint of theorists such as Laugier (*Essai sur l'architecture*, 1753) and Burke (*Enquiry into . . . the Sublime and the Beautiful*, 1756) in favor of Nature as the ultimate source of authority laid greater stress upon the individual aesthetic judgment and upon the designer's obligation to develop an appropriately "modern" style from an eclectic study of the past.

Increasing national prosperity in trade and industry was accompanied by a marked growth in patronage by the upper middle class as represented by bankers like Henry Hoare of Stourhead, merchants like the Elder William Beckford of Fonthill, and brewers like Samuel Whitbread of Southill. Although the Classical styles of aristocratic origin enjoyed an Indian summer during the Regency era, bourgeois taste was reflected increasingly in the cult of the Picturesque on the one hand, and by a more practical application of industry to the arts on the other. The Society for the Encouragement of Arts, Manufactures, and Commerce, founded in 1754, became the forerunner of many literary and philosophical societies established through middle-class initiative throughout the provinces. Urban commissions became the subject of collective decisions in architectural competitions for major public buildings such as the Mansion House, London (1739), the Bank of England (1766), and the Dublin Exchange (1769). As standards of judgment broadened with the activities of building committees and boards of governors or trustees, so the architect was required to play a more closely defined role, "selling" his designs in open rivalry with his colleagues.

Among the leaders of this new breed of professionals were Robert Adam and Sir William Chambers. Despite their sharply divergent viewpoints, characterized by the Adelphi Terrace (1768-72) and Somerset House (1776-86) respectively, they shared the same high standards of design, backed by a formidable business acumen. Each established well-organized offices, negotiated with clients over an accepted scale of fees, and maintained the strictest control over the execution of their works. While foreign travel continued to be regarded as an essential training ("Travelling," according to Chambers, "is to an architect as the university is to a man of letters"), significantly each set out to learn as much from his French and Italian colleagues as from a far-ranging study of the past. Chambers was to maintain his early friendship with leading Parisian designers such as Charles de Wailly and M. J. Peyre. Robert Adam's vivid letters to his brother James from Italy provide a unique insight into his sharply astute yet self-critical character—aware of the necessity to act out the image of the dilettante in cultivating future patrons, yet at the same time anxious to submit to the tutelage of Jacques-Louis Clérisseau and Giovanni Battista Piranesi.

The conscious independence of Chambers and Adam, as opposed to the early eighteenth century's reverence for inherited canons of taste, is also reflected in their theoretical publications. Whereas a late Palladian treatise like Ware's *Complete Body of Architecture* (1756) still amounted to a compendium on the Orders and matters of building science, both Chambers, in his *Treatise on Civil Architecture* (1759), and the Adam brothers, in the prefaces to their *Works in Architecture* (1773-79), advanced personal philosophies of design fashioned by aesthetic judgment from the widest range of visual sources.

As the architectural profession began to assume a distinct identity, various attempts were made to form an organization to protect its interests, improve its social status, and establish a means of formal education. In France, the program of training established under Colbert's Académie de l'architecture in 1671 (see above, p. 173) and extended to its adjunct in Rome in 1720 was augmented by J. F. Blondel's establishment in 1743 of the atelier system through his Ecole des Arts, briefly attended by Chambers himself. In England, however, the only training available in the late eighteenth century was the emerging practice of articled pupilage in an architect's office, as traditionally introduced by Sir Robert Taylor. Additional training in drawing was otherwise gained in the company of painters and sculptors in various improvised art schools, such as the St. Martin's Lane Academy.

A few leading architects had joined the Society of Artists when it was set up in 1761, but Chambers, after quarreling with James Paine, was the prime mover behind the foundation of the Royal Academy of Arts in 1768. Although his personal influence was maintained as Treasurer until his death in 1796, only four of the thirty-six founder members were architects. Their discipline, moreover, was given only a nominal role in the Academy Schools, with a Professor of Architecture whose duties lay in forming "the taste of the students to interest them in the laws and principles of composition," and with only lip-service given to "a critical examination of structures."

Of far greater significance for the future was the Architects' Club, established in 1791 by George Dance, James Wyatt, Henry Holland, and S. P. Cockerell, later joined by Chambers, Adam, and a dozen others. Eligibility was highly exclusive, being restricted to Royal Academicians, holders of the Academy's Gold Medal, and members of distinguished foreign institutions. Among the various topics of discussion over the thirty years of this dining club's existence were professional qualifications, fireproof construction, and professional fees. The pressing need for an improved system of training, however, appears to have been barely considered.

The last decades of the eighteenth century saw various attempts to distinguish between the designer as such and the other traditional roles embraced by architects since the sixteenth century. The historic association between the surveyor and the architect was partially qualified by the setting up of the Surveyors' Club in 1792, mainly involving the new class of professional measurers appointed under the Building Act of 1774. However, in Dr. Johnson's celebrated *Dictionary* of 1755, "surveyor" and "architect" were virtually synonymous terms, and the link was perpetuated in the title of Surveyor-General, held by Chambers as chief government architect until its abolition in the administrative reforms of 1782. The two roles continued to be associated, however, until the foundation of the Surveyors' Institute in 1869, and even then the final break was not made until the 1930s.

The same was true with engineering; despite the foundation of the Society of Civil Engineers in 1771, the Smeatonian Society of 1793, and, ultimately, the Institution of Civil Engineers in 1818, the historic bond between the disciplines survived well into the nineteenth century. Architects like Robert Mylne and Thomas Harrison made important contributions to engineering, especially in bridge construction, during the late eighteenth century. Other designers such as John Smeaton, Thomas Telford, and John Rennie operated with national distinction in both fields during the opening decades of the new century, and as late as 1854, Thomas Hardwick, member of the Institution of Civil Engineers, received the Institute of British Architects' Gold Medal for Architecture.

Undoubtedly the first major act of exclusion and prime move towards professional solidarity occurred in 1834 with the creation of the Institute of British Architects. Its charter of incorporation was received in 1837, and its designation "Royal" was conferred by Queen Victoria in 1866. The Institute was "founded for facilitating the acquirement of architectural knowledge, for the promotion of the different branches of science connected with it, and for establishing an uniformity and respectability of practice in the profession." According to its regulations architects were admitted as Fellows if they had been "engaged as Principals for at least seven successive years in the practice of Civil Architecture" or as Associates if they had reached the age of twenty-one and were "engaged in the study of Civil Architecture" or had been in practice less than seven years. Significantly, Honorary Fellowships were available to noblemen on payment of not less than twenty-five guineas or to any other gentleman "unconnected with any branch of building as a trade or business."

The latter stipulation emphasizes what, by the first decades of the new century, had become a major issue—the relationship between the architectural designer and the rapidly expanding building industry. During the eighteenth century the connection between the architect and the various building trades had been a particularly close and fruitful one, and many distinguished figures such as Chambers, Adam, and Holland had been involved in speculative schemes. This alliance was reflected in Burke's reforms of the Office of Works in 1782, when the posts of Surveyor General and Comptroller were replaced by a single appointment to be held by one "by profession an architect or builder." Ominously, at the same time the official trade appointments such as Master Mason and Master Carpenter were abolished.

The dramatic population explosion between 1800 and 1830, when Britain increased from nine to fourteen million, called for rapid housing and far larger speculative ventures in urban development than had been connected with the leisurely evolution of Georgian London, Bath, or Edinburgh. Accordingly, a new figure entered the architectural scene in the form of the general contractor. Such was Thomas Cubitt, who began his training as a carpenter around 1800 and by the middle of the century was largely concerned in the layout and building of considerable portions of London, such as Camden Town and St. Pancras. Employing all the necessary craftsmen on a permanent basis, these contractors negotiated under competitive tendering in terms of a "lump sum" and thereby replaced almost overnight the traditional costing by piece-work of the master craftsmen. The advent of the general contractor, as essentially a businessman with a financial relationship to design, profoundly affected the historic tripartite relationship between client, designer, and craftsman. It also involved the emerging architectural profession with the fundamental problems of the Industrial Revolution.

The dangers to professional integrity inherent in the activities of the architect-contractor had been recognized early on by Sir John Soane. Justly regarded as the father of the modern profession, Soane did much to promote the high standards of practice by his example as well as through his conscientious teaching as the first active Professor of Architecture at the Academy. It was only because of this latter association, in fact, that he felt unable to accept the Presidency of the Institute of British Architects in 1834, eventually filled by Earl de Grey. In 1788 Soane had given the classic definition of professional responsibility when he stated that:

The business of the architect is to make the designs and estimates, to direct the works and to measure and value the different parts; he is the intermediate agent between the employer, whose honour and interest he is to study, and the mechanic, whose rights he is to defend. His situation implies great trust; he is responsible for the mistakes, negligences, and ignorances of those he employs; and above all, he is to take care that the workmen's bills do not exceed his own estimates. If these are the duties of an architect, with what propriety can his situation and that of the builder, or the contractor be united? [*Plans, Elevations* . . . , p. 7].

Membership in the RIBA continued to regulate the conduct of only a fraction of the architectural profession throughout the nineteenth century, and the liaison between the architect and builder continued in many instances until 1936. There were, however, a number of repercussions arising from the general contractor's activities which were universally felt, particularly in connection with the increasing scale of building operations. For instance, the specialist duties of the quantity surveyor became essential, since costing was no longer calculated on the site or from existing works but was based on bills of quantity. These bills, probably first introduced in the 1830s by Sir Robert Smirke, architect of the British Museum, then under construction, were calculated from detailed abstracts of labor and materials drawn up from the architect's working drawings. Furthermore, as a result of a gradual decline in both skill and initiative among the building crafts through general contracting, greater reliance was now placed on the preparation of detailed specifications, separate from the actual contract. Correspondingly, there was a stronger need than before for a range of more specialized drawings, directed towards different phases and aspects of the building operation. Since the practical nature of design had changed little between Wren and Chambers, there had been only minor distinctions between "presentation" and "working" drawings, the finished appearance of the building being the end in sight. However, with the Industrial Revolution's development of fresh structural techniques, more complex services, and new materials, not to mention the introduction of unfamiliar ornament occasioned by the "Battle of the Styles," architectural draftsmanship became an activity of increasing responsibility and technical skill.

The perfection of elaborate presentation drawings, using the greatest possible gamut of pictorial devices in perspective, coloring, and emotive lighting, also reflected the changes in patronage during the early nineteenth century. The well-informed aristocratic patrons of the previous era, served by an architectural elite sharing the same criteria of judgment, were gradually replaced by building committees of middle-class "laymen" having to be persuaded as well as instructed by a designer who, at times, almost amounted to a purveyor of architectural styles. On occasion these "artist's impressions," such as the spectacular one produced by Joseph Gandy to display Soane's alternative designs for three Commissioners' Churches of the 1818 Act, proved more impressive than the resulting works (Figure 49). In fairness to Soane, however, the difference between these striking images and their meager execution in this instance was expressly due to the Government's parsimony over the funds made available. The pathetic results of the so-called Million Pounds Act were the main target of Augustus Welby Pugin's Gothic wrath in his manifesto of 1836—*Contrasts; or, a Parallel between the Noble Edifices of the Fourteenth and Fifteenth Centuries, and Similar Buildings of the Present Day; showing the Present Decay of Taste*.

Perhaps no other single personality in nineteenth-century England did so much to awaken in the more conscientious architects a sense of social responsibility and active commitment to a philosophy of design. If we set aside Pugin's fervent belief in the Gothic as the only valid form of expression, the criteria laid down in the *Contrasts* and in his later work, *The True Principles of Pointed or Christian Architecture* of 1841, also anticipated much of the concern for functional planning, structural expression, and the nature of materials at the heart of Modern Movement theory. Although much of the soul-less expression and shoddy structures which Pugin bitterly attacked continued to appear throughout the century, a common ground for debate between the articulate profession and an informed public was now established on a far more extensive basis than during the diffusion of Palladian standards in the eighteenth century.

Figure 49. Sir John Soane (1753-1837), specimen designs for churches at Marylebone, Walworth, and Tyringham (by J. M. Gandy). The rising class of professional architects in the early nineteenth century is exemplified by Soane, whose fastidious concern is shown here in a new type of drawing, the "artist's impression," with its pictorial devices and emotive lighting directed at the untutored client. These designs of 1822-24, couched in the ever-widening range of styles, are variations on a basic structure applicable to the niggardly provisions of the "Million Pounds Act" of 1818, ultimately to provoke the wrath of Pugin.

The involvement of an ever-widening public in architectural matters is reflected by the growth of popular education and by the rise of architectural journalism in the nineteenth century. Literature relating to the accelerating force of the Gothic Revival and church reform—from Pugin, via the regular installments from 1841 onwards of *The Ecclesiologist* (journal of the Cambridge Camden Society), to John Ruskin's *Seven Lamps of Architecture* (1849) and *Stones of Venice* (1851-53)—was directed at an unprecedentedly wide lay audience. Large competitions for national buildings became the focus of public debate and lay influence, such as those for the Houses of Parliament (1835), the Government buildings of Whitehall (1856), and the Law Courts (1866-67). Comment appeared not only in the daily press and in journals such as the *Quarterly Review, Punch, Blackwood's Magazine,* and the *Illustrated London News,* but in a number of specialized architectural periodicals. In particular, *The Builder,* subtitled *An illustrated weekly magazine for the Drawing-room, the Studio, the Office, the Workshop, and the Cottage,* began to appear from 1842 onwards, registering every wave of taste from the Late Picturesque to Art Nouveau. Among the various other journals, *The British Architect*, published in Manchester from 1874 onwards, placed greater emphasis on major architectural developments outside London in the rapidly expanding northern centers.

The public and urban concerns of the architect also increased as a result of a mounting quantity of social legislation, such as the Poor Law Act of 1834, the prison and municipal reforms of 1835, and the Interment Act of 1852. Meanwhile the dramatic improvement in communications with the expansion of the railways from the 1840s brought the metropolis into ever-closer contact with the industrial areas of the Midlands and the North. Here commercial prosperity found expression in ambitious civic buildings produced through national competitions, as for example those for St. George's Hall, Liverpool (1836), and the town halls of Leeds (1853) and Manchester (1868).

This unparalleled expansion of professional functions and the introduction of fresh building types such as railway stations, specialized hospitals, offices, and factories, as well as a host of technical innovations in heating, lighting, and drainage, all served to accentuate the broadening gulf between the growing professional organization and the increasingly inadequate training available. In France the technological training established with the Ecole Polytechnique in 1795 had been counterbalanced only two years later by the foundation of the Ecole des Beaux-Arts. This state-directed education was supported by the atelier system, maintaining a salutary contact between students, their teachers, and the practicing profession (see Chapter 8). Yet English architectural education, well into the nineteenth century, still depended largely upon the irregular standards of articled pupilage, augmented by lectures at the Royal Academy and travel abroad. In marked contrast to the official basis of the French system, the world of the enlightened gentleman-architect was, in a sense, perpetuated in privately established and governed bodies such as the Royal Academy and the RIBA—a situation reflecting something of the traditional resistance in English politics to centralized government.

The working of the pupilage system at its best is revealed by a detailed study made of Soane's office between the 1780s and the 1830s (Bolton, *Soane*, appendix C). During this time some thirty pupils in all underwent their training in surveying, measuring, costing, superintendence, and draftsmanship for twelve hours daily over a period of five to seven years. Premiums or fees paid on entry to the office ranged from £50 in Soane's early career to sums between 100 and 175 guineas according to his increasing eminence after 1788, when he was appointed Architect to the Bank of England. Whereas Soane was a model of professional probity and took considerable pains over his teaching, it is clear that the average experience gained was far closer to that described by George Gilbert Scott, who entered the office of a London architect at the age of seventeen only to find himself "a somewhat romantic youth . . . condemned to indulge his taste by building houses at Hackney in the debased style of 1827" (*Personal . . . Recollections*, pp. 55-56). At its worst, the system could plumb the depths only mildly caricatured by Dickens in the office of Martin Chuzzlewit's master, the legendary Pecksniff.

Although in theory the Royal Academy Schools from their inception in 1768 had offered the first formal architectural training in England, teaching there amounted to very little before the conscientious professorship of Soane between 1806 and 1837. Nor, despite much effort by reforming bodies such as the Architectural Society, formed in 1831, did the RIBA itself implement the educational objectives set out at its foundation in 1834. It was only in the 1840s that the first serious attempt was made to provide specialized instruction, particularly in the technical aspects of design, at King's College and University College, London. When in 1841 T. L. Donaldson, first Secretary of the RIBA, was appointed Professor of Architecture at the latter, he gave two courses of lectures for part-time students, on "Architecture as a Science" and "Architecture as an Art"—a symbolic division which was to flaw Victorian architecture throughout the century, producing such confrontations as between George Gilbert Scott's hotel and P. W. Barlow's engine shed at St. Pancras Station.

Since the leaders of the profession continued to be markedly indifferent to the need for educational reform, it was eventually left to the students themselves to make the first major improvement in the best tradition of Victorian "self-help." In 1842 certain junior architects, excluded from the RIBA as not being in practice for the requisite number of years, formed themselves into the Association of Architectural Draftsmen, becoming the Architectural Association in 1847. Teaching was to be conducted by the students among themselves through discussions and criticism of designs prepared under their own initiative. Additional instruction was provided by distinguished visiting lecturers, and, in fact, the purely voluntary basis remained until 1891 when salaried officials and teachers were appointed.

From the start the tone of the AA was as iconoclastic as it was democratic, and its regular papers, reported sympathetically in *The Builder*, provided an essential forum for free-ranging discussion outside the inhibiting atmosphere of the RIBA. A hard-line commitment to the Gothic was resisted equally along with the tyranny of the Five Orders, and various spirited attempts were made by members to respond to T. L. Donaldson's challenge at the inaugural meeting: "The great question is are we to have an architecture of our period, a distinct, individual, palpable style of the 19th century?" (quoted in Summerson, *History of the AA*, p. 6).

Education, however, was the immediate and lasting concern of the Association, and because of its resolute independence, tempered by certain informal links with the RIBA, it was able to exert considerable pressure for reform. In particular, through the AA's campaign for the creation of an equivalent of the French *Diplôme d'architecte*, the Institute was eventually persuaded to hold the first voluntary examination for entry to its Associate Membership in 1863. In return the AA set up a "Voluntary Examination Class," thus establishing for the first time the modern concept of systematic study tested by examination as the basis of the architect's education.

The Victorian profession, however, continued to be more preoccupied with matters of status and business ethics. Among other things the RIBA attempted to impose some uniformity over fees. Following a recommendation of a special committee in 1845, the rate of 5 per cent was adopted, although this did not prevent the Treasury from insisting on 3 per cent for Sir Charles Barry's arduous work on the Houses of Parliament between 1839 and 1852, despite strenuous opposition. Widespread recognition, however, followed the RIBA publication of *Professional Practice and Charges of Architects* in 1862, the rate eventually being increased to 6 per cent after the 1914-18 War.

Equal concern over the glaring mismanagement of national competitions occasioned another RIBA committee in 1838, but this did little to discourage Liverpool Corporation's attempt to combine Harvey Lonsdale Elmes's separate winning designs for St. George's Hall and the Assize Courts into a single building. Nor did it forestall the devious manner in which George Gilbert Scott was awarded the Whitehall scheme, which was subsequently converted from Gothic to a ("Machiavellian") Italianate, more appropriate to current diplomacy, under the influence of Lord Palmerston. Only in 1903 was the RIBA able to restrict its members to recognized competitions, and, in 1938, to impose complete uniformity over the entire profession in this matter.

Even by mid-century the RIBA still represented only 9 per cent of the profession; and the tribulations of one of its most distinguished members, George Edward Street, over the creation of the Law Courts emphasizes the vulnerability of the architect without statutory protection or professional solidarity. Within ten years of moving from Oxford to London in 1855, Street had established an enormous practice as a leading exponent of the Gothic Revival, and in 1866-67 he entered the competition with ten other competitors. After much prevarication, the judges recommended a combination of E. M. Barry's plan and Street's elevations. A strong protest by the disappointed George Gilbert Scott was upheld by the Attorney General, but Street was finally awarded the entire commission in 1868. At that juncture, however, the proposed site on the Strand was abandoned for one on the Thames Embankment. Further protest resulted in the original site being revived in 1870, although by now Street's plan differed considerably from his winning design and was seen to have benefited from Alfred Waterhouse's rejected design. A vigorous controversy ensued in *The Times* and various journals such as *The Architect*, the final design not being put out to tender until 1871. The construction of this highly complex building, according to well over 3000 drawings by the architect, continued right through the decade, and the Law Courts were finally opened in 1882, the year after Street's death. Armstead's impressive memorial to Street in 1886, set within a noble Transitional Gothic arcade in the Central Hall of the Courts, portrays him life-size and seated with metal dividers in his marble hand, concentrating on his labors—a monument of unparalleled prominence for the professional architect (Figure 50).

Six years after Street's election as President of the RIBA in 1881, examinations for its Associate Membership became compulsory, and the profession entered the last phase of the journey towards the objectives outlined at the Institute's foundation in 1834—"uniformity and respectability of practice."

The notion of a specialist profession had met with considerable opposition throughout the century, even from among members of the Institute itself. Ruskin in *The Seven Lamps of Architecture* had attacked "the idea of an independent architectural profession" as "a mere modern fallacy" (2nd ed., 1855, p. xii), and later on in an address to the RIBA in 1865 had expressed a wish "to see the profession of an architect united, not with that of the engineer, but [with that] of the sculptor" (*Complete Works*, ed. Cook and Wedderburn, xix, p. 35). For him, as also for Scott, the crux of the matter lay in the nature of architectural design as the art of decorating structure. Early in the century, however, bold spirits like Owen Jones, a

Figure 50. H. H. Armstead, monument to G. E. Street (1824-81), Central Hall of the Royal Courts of Justice, London. The protracted story of the new Law Courts, between the initial competition of 1866-67 and the eventual completion of Street's complex design in 1882, illustrates the insecurity of the High Victorian profession. Nevertheless, Armstead's monument of 1886 is symbolic of the unparalleled prominence given to the designer and leader of his profession (President of the RIBA in 1881). The group of craftsmen on the plinth relief reflects the late nineteenth century's dream of recovering the intimate connection between design and craft first undermined by the Renaissance.

future organizer of the Great Exhibition, had prophesied that a new architectural style would emerge from the rational use of new materials. As he pointed out to the Architectural Society in 1835, "it is quite evident that if we resist the indolent temptation to imitating the genius of others, invention must result." Even Ruskin himself, only three years before Joseph Paxton's Crystal Palace opened in 1851, had postulated under the Lamp of Truth that "the time is probably near when a new system of architectural laws will be developed, adapted entirely to metallic construction" (*Seven Lamps*, p. 70).

But the development of such a radical and starkly utilitarian system of design appeared for many to threaten the calling and the profession of the architect from several directions. For instance, it appeared to undermine the dignity accorded by the Renaissance to Architecture as the controlling member of the three Fine Arts. It also seemed to assail the barrier of status so carefully erected in the context of industrial society between architect and engineer.

This issue was complicated by a further act of withdrawal by architects from the challenges of industrialization, mainly outside the limits of the organized profession, by means of the Arts and Crafts Movement. Here the impact of Ruskin's teachings was no less profound on the latter half of the century than Pugin's had been on the early Victorians. Under this influence, William Morris and his colleagues, as for example Philip Webb (who like Morris was trained, incidentally, in Street's Oxford office), counteracted what they saw as the corrupting influence of mechanization by reviving the vernacular and craft traditions first demoted by the Renaissance; an attitude reflecting and closely inter-related with the Pre-Raphaelite revolt against Academic art. From these origins were to emerge the "free style" concepts as developed by Norman Shaw and Charles Voysey in domestic design as well as the planning ideals of Ebenezer Howard's Garden-City Movement, both key influences on the course of the Modern Movement.

By the end of the nineteenth century still only 10 per cent of the profession belonged to an organization which *The Times* had dismissed in 1870 as "a highly respectable trades union," and those who remained outside the RIBA included such eminent figures as Philip Webb, William Butterfield, G. F. Bodley, Eden Nesfield, and Norman Shaw. The deciding factor for most of these architects who objected to the compulsory examinations, established by the RIBA through its revised Charter in 1887, lay in the Romantic belief in artistic autonomy. Added to this was the corollary that the essence of architectural design lay in a body of imponderable skills, as elusive of legal definition as they were unassessable by qualifying examinations. Such convictions, however, were beginning to appear something of a luxury in an industrial society where the public had little protection against grave abuses and irregular standards among the less responsible members of the profession. Under these circumstances the Society of Architects was formed in 1884 and promoted a series of Registration Bills before Parliament, one of which in 1891 brought the whole matter to a head. In a letter to *The Times* (March 3rd), addressed to the President and Council of the RIBA, some seventy signatories, including not only leading architects but artists such as Lawrence Alma-Tadema, Edward Burne-Jones, Walter Crane, William Holman Hunt, and William Morris, asserted that a student's "artistic qualifications (which really make the Architect)" could not be "brought to the test of examination, and that a diploma of architecture obtained by such means would be a fallacious distinction, equally useless as a guide to the public and misleading as an object for the efforts of the student." The following year this opinion was defended at length in a collection of essays, edited by Norman Shaw and Sir Thomas Jackson, entitled *Architecture: A Profession or an Art*.

However, it was the need to establish an organized training in accord with the modern era, rather than the debate over artistic capacity or professional status, which finally resolved the issue. During the last decade of the century rapid progress was made in the long-neglected field of architectural education. Already in 1870 the Royal Academy had set up a School of Architecture under Phené Spiers, himself trained at the Ecole des Beaux-Arts. Almost inevitably, however, the most significant developments were to come from the Architectural Association, where a number of innovatory measures were already under way, notably through its unique system of self-instruction related to the RIBA's initial attempts at a qualifying procedure. (According to one of the rules of the Voluntary Examination Class, "each member is expected to acquire information for himself, to be afterwards shared in common with his fellow-students"; quoted in Summerson, p. 20.) By 1887 the RIBA had systematized its examination into three parts—Preliminary, Intermediate, and Final—the first two being voluntary and the third an obligatory qualification for Associateship. This action, together with a considerable increase in the Association's membership during the late 1880s, led to a major reorganization in its structure and reappraisal of its objectives under the presidency of Leonard Stokes. This was to culminate during 1889-91 with the replacement of the "mutual" system of study by a regular curriculum of instruction through paid specialist lecturers according to the "progressive" pattern of the RIBA's examination structure. In this manner the AA was to introduce a form of architectural education which gradually replaced the historic system of articled pupilage and has become the norm today.

The new educational movement accelerated through the 1890s, not without opposition from the "anti-professional" persuasion. A full-time three-year course in architecture was begun in King's College, London, under the redoubtable Professor Banister Fletcher in 1892. Provincial schools followed suit, beginning with Liverpool in 1895, where a B.A. Honours course was established in 1900 and recognized a few years later by the RIBA as exempting students from its Intermediate Examination. Subsequently, in 1920, Liverpool instituted a five-year course giving full exemption from RIBA examinations altogether; it was followed by many other schools between the two World Wars. By then a considerable proportion of entrants to the profession were receiving training in full-time schools rather than under the pupilage system.

By 1900 the battle for a closed profession was largely over—some 15,000 architects by then being members of the RIBA—although a reluctance to legislate over the ability to design continued until 1931 and 1938 when two Architect's Registration Acts were passed, ensuring that John Shute's calling had become a legal title controlled by Parliament.

Very little has survived into the present century of Shute's lofty ideals of universal competence, as exemplified by Wren, and the assured cultural standards of the age of Burlington are equally remote from the modern designer. While, as a professional, the architect would find more in common with Soane and particularly Street, their degree of autonomy in design is no longer possible when often the architect is only one of a team of experts in a multi-faceted organization such as a housing authority or a government department. Nevertheless, in such situations where increasing specialization raises fresh barriers to communication, the architect's historic skills as co-ordinator as well as designer have never been more essential. By means of his inter-disciplinary training he is uniquely equipped to organize a variety of specialized and disparate functions into an intellectually and visually coherent expression. It remains to be seen whether the profession is able to maintain this key integrating role in the face of a crisis of identity as we enter the last quarter of the twentieth century.

BIBLIOGRAPHICAL NOTES

Anyone working in this field must be greatly indebted to the following two complementary studies, F. Jenkins, *Architect and Patron* (London, 1961), and B. Kaye, *The Development of the Architectural Profession in Britain* (London, 1960), as well as to the classic surveys of the earlier part of the story in H. M. Colvin, *A Biographical Dictionary of English Architects 1660-1840*, (London, 1954, now in process of extensive revision), and J. Summerson, *Architecture in Britain, 1530 to 1830* (5th rev. ed., Harmondsworth, 1969).

The principal study of sixteenth-century English architecture remains M. Girouard, *Robert Smythson and the Architecture of the Elizabethan Era* (London, 1966). For two illuminating case-histories see M. Girouard, "The Development of Longleat House, 1546-1572," *Archaeological Journal* 116 (1961), and J. A. Gotch, "The Building of Burghley House," *Trans. of RIBA* (n.s.) 6 (1890), 103ff. Important corpuses of surviving drawings are catalogued and fully illustrated in M. Girouard, "The Smythson Collection of the RIBA," *Architectural History* 5 (1962), and J. Summerson, "The Book of Architecture of John Thorpe," *Walpole Society* 40 (1966). A modern reprint of the 1st edition of John Shute's *First and Chief Groundes of Architecture* (1563) has been published by the Gregg Press, now Gregg International Publishers (Farnborough, Eng., 1964).

The most recent monograph on Inigo Jones is by Sir John Summerson (Harmondsworth, 1966), and an examination of the architect's work for the Crown is provided by the exhibition catalogue, *The King's Arcadia: Inigo Jones and the Stuart Court*, ed. J. Harris, S. Orgel, and R. Strong (Arts Council of Great Britain, London, 1973). For the celebrated Burlington-Devonshire Collection of Jones's designs see J. Harris, *Inigo Jones and John Webb (Catalogue of the Drawings Collection of the RIBA)* (London, 1972). The surviving masque designs in the same collection (still at Chatsworth) are reproduced in *Walpole Society* 12 (1923-24), and are more recently discussed and illustrated along with the relevant *libretti*, in S. Orgel and R. Strong, *Inigo Jones: The Theatre of the Stuart Court* (London, 1973).

Sir Roger Pratt's MS is published in R. T. Gunther, *The Architecture of Sir Roger Pratt . . . from his Note-books* (Oxford, 1928).

Predictably Wren is the subject of a considerable literature, the most recent monographs being by Kerry Downes (Harmondsworth, 1971) and Margaret Whinney (London, 1971). A large proportion of the surviving documents and drawings relating to Wren's career as designer and administrator appears in the *Wren Society* 1-20 (1923-43). For a discussion of the Great Model and model usage in seventeenth-century English architecture see J. Wilton-Ely, "The Architectural Model: English Baroque," *Apollo* 88 (1968), 250ff.

For English Baroque architecture see the survey by K. Downes (London, 1966), who has also contributed two pioneering monographs on Hawksmoor

(London, 1959 and 1969) and is preparing one on Vanbrugh which is certain to supersede the existing work by L. Whistler (London, 1938).

The Neo-Palladian Revival of the eighteenth century, especially Lord Burlington's decisive contribution to its development, is considered in various papers of R. Wittkower, *Palladio and English Palladianism* (London, 1974). A reprint of Campbell's volumes of *Vitruvius Britannicus* (1715-25), with commentary volume by P. Breman and D. Addis, has been published by B. Blom, Inc. (New York, 1967). Aspects of Burlington, including his portraits, are discussed by the present author in the exhibition catalogue, *Lord Burlington and his Circle* (University Gallery, Nottingham, 1973).

For areas of eighteenth-century architectural development involving the changing role of the designer see J. Summerson, *Georgian London* (rev. ed., Harmondsworth, 1962), K. Clark, *The Gothic Revival* (2nd ed., London, 1950), and J. Mordaunt Crook, *The Greek Revival* (London, 1972). For a definitive study of a key figure in the emerging profession see J. Harris, *Sir William Chambers* (London, 1970). Robert Adam's early career is discussed in J. Fleming, *Robert Adam and His Circle in Edinburgh and Rome* (London, 1962), in which the architect's correspondence is quoted extensively. A later phase in Adam's practice is examined in A. Rowan, "After the Adelphi: Forgotten Years in the Adam Brothers' Practice," *Journal of the Society of Arts* 122, no. 5218 (Sept. 1974), 659ff. A comprehensive survey of the Office of Works is being prepared under the general editorship of H. M. Colvin. The only relevant section as yet published is J. Mordaunt Crook and M. H. Port, *The History of the King's Works*, Vol. VI, 1782-1851 (London, 1973).

Sir John Soane's career and his leading part in formulating professional practice are considered in the monographs by Sir John Summerson (London, 1952) and Dorothy Stroud (London, 1961). A. T. Bolton's earlier study, *The Works of Sir John Soane* (London, 1924), remains indispensable for its quotation of letters and documentary material. For Soane's attitude towards the architect's responsibilities, see the preface to his *Plans, Elevations and Sections of Buildings* (London, 1788). For relevant aspects of Soane's practice see G. Carr, "Soane's specimen church designs of 1818: A Reconsideration," *Architectural History* 16 (1973), 37ff, and J. Wilton-Ely, "The Architectural Models of Sir John Soane: A Catalogue," *Architectural History* 12 (1969), 5ff.

Among recent monographs on Soane's teachers and contemporaries are D. Stroud, *Henry Holland* (London, 1966); idem, *George Dance the Younger* (London, 1971); and T. Davis, *John Nash* (London, 1966). See also J. Mordaunt Crook, "The Pre-Victorian Architect: Professionalism and Patronage," *Architectural History* 12 (1969), 62ff, and the same author's casehistory of Smirke's British Museum (London, 1972).

The Victorian architectural scene is the area of a rapidly increasing literature, not least by members of the Victorian Society. Among important surveys are H.-R. Hitchcock, *Early Victorian Architecture in Britain* (New Haven, 1954), idem, *Architecture: Nineteenth and Twentieth Centuries* (3rd ed.,

Harmondsworth, 1968), S. Muthesius, *The High Victorian Movement in Architecture, 1850-1870* (London, 1972). A valuable review of recent research, supported by a rich compendium of visual material, is to be found in the two exhibition catalogues of the Victoria and Albert Museum, *Victorian Church Art*, ed. J. Physick et al. (1971-72), and *Marble Halls: Drawings and Models for Victorian Secular Buildings*, ed. J. Physick and M. Darby (1973). Key aspects of the Victorian achievement are also examined in N. Pevsner, *Studies in Art, Architecture and Design*, II, *Victorian and After* (London, 1968), and J. Summerson, *Victorian Architecture: Four Studies in Evaluation* (New York, 1970). A study of the architect's approach to a particular building-type and life-style throughout the century is provided in M. Girouard, *The Victorian Country House* (Oxford, 1971).

Among recent monographs on nineteenth-century architects and designers, special mention should be made of D. Linstrum, *Sir Jeffry Wyattville* (Oxford, 1972), P. Stanton, *Augustus Welby Pugin* (London, 1971), D. Watkin, *C. R. Cockerell* (London, 1974), G. F. Chadwick, *Sir Joseph Paxton* (London, 1961), and P. Thompson, *William Butterfield* (London, 1971). As regards contemporary writings of the period, Pugin's *Contrasts* (London, 1836) has appeared in a reprint by the Leicester University Press (1973), and Ruskin's various books and papers are to be found in the *Complete Works*, ed. Cook and Wedderburn (London, 1905). Moreover, a useful discussion of Ruskin's attitude towards the discipline and profession is to be found in K. O. Garrigan, *Ruskin on Architecture* (Madison, Wisconsin, 1973). For an inside account of the workings of the High Victorian profession see G. G. Scott, *Personal and Professional Recollections* (London, 1879). Passages from Owen Jones's paper "On the influence of Religion on Art," referred to on p. 202, are quoted in the catalogue *Marble Halls*, p. 10.

For an account of the developing organization of the profession, its institutions and teaching bodies, see F. Jenkins, "The Victorian Architectural Profession," in *Victorian Architecture*, ed. P. Ferriday (London, 1963); B. Kaye, "Early Architectural Societies and the Foundation of the RIBA," *RIBA Journal* 57 (1955), 497ff; J. A. Gotch (ed.), *The Growth and Work of the RIBA* (London, 1934); J. Summerson, *The Architectural Association, 1847-1947* (London, 1947); and C. M. Butler, *The Society of Architects* (London, 1925).

The important role of architectural journalism is reviewed in F. Jenkins, "Nineteenth-Century Architectural Periodicals," in *Concerning Architecture*, ed. J. Summerson (London, 1968), and architectural publications in general in N. Pevsner, *Some Architectural Writers of the Nineteenth Century* (Oxford, 1972). Detailed accounts of specific phases in the growth of the building industry are provided in H. Hobhouse, *Thomas Cubitt: Master Builder* (London, 1971), and in J. Summerson, *The London Building World of the Eighteen-Sixties* (London, 1973).

The saga of G. E. Street's Law Courts is discussed in J. Kinnard, "G. E. Street, the Law Courts and the 'Seventies,'" in Ferriday (ed.), op. cit.; M. H.

Port, "The New Law Courts Competition, 1866-67," *Architectural History* 11 (1968), 75ff; and J. Summerson, "A Victorian Competition: The Royal Courts of Justice," in his *Victorian Architecture*, op. cit., 77ff.

For the English profession in relation to the origins and rise of the Modern Movement before 1900, a considerable amount of research since the last war has appeared in periodicals, in particular the *Architectural Review*, *Journal of the RIBA*, and *AA Quarterly*. Among major contributions to the understanding of the period are Sir Nikolaus Pevsner's classic, *Pioneers of Modern Design* (first published in 1936; reissued, Harmondsworth, 1960), and his various papers reprinted in *Studies in Art, Architecture and Design*, cited above. A more recent appraisal over a wider period is R. Macleod, *Style and Society: Architectural Ideology in Britain, 1835-1914* (London, 1971). Something of the progressive architect's viewpoint during this period is conveyed in W. R. Lethaby, *Architecture* (London, 1911; revised 1929).

In addition to his wife, the author would like to thank Professor Peter Murray, Dr. Norman Summers, and Sir John Summerson for valuable help during the preparation of this paper.

# 8

# The Ecole des Beaux-Arts
# and the Architectural Profession
# in the United States:
# The Case of John Galen Howard

JOAN DRAPER

The Ecole Nationale et Spéciale des Beaux-Arts in Paris was, until it was closed down in 1968, the oldest school of art and architecture north of the Alps. This prestigious institution traced its origins to the classes given by the Academies of Painting and Sculpture and of Architecture which were established under Louis XIV in 1648 and 1671 respectively (see Chapter 6, p. 173). Over the years, political revolutions and changes in taste quite naturally affected the school. Nevertheless, it maintained a remarkable continuity of style and teaching methods throughout the years of its existence. At least until the early twentieth century it kept its reputation as one of the leading academies of the world.

The Ecole des Beaux-Arts served as a model for those Americans who sought to improve the practice of architecture through better education. Its influence became particularly strong in America at the end of the nineteenth century when architects, like many other professionals, felt the need to set higher and more uniform standards for themselves. The Ecole, as it was called, possessed what these concerned people wanted to create in America: a well-organized curriculum, a rational design theory, and government patronage. This long-established French institution seemed a natural source of ideas at a time when American architects were lobbying for state licensing laws, decrying the low quality of public buildings, organizing professional societies, and attempting to found new schools.*

* Weatherhead (pp. 235-36) lists the American architectural schools founded before World War I: Massachusetts Institute of Technology, 1865; Cornell University, 1871;

For many architects who came to maturity between 1865 and 1915, the Ecole provided both the locus of their own advanced training and a prototype for new educational programs which they hoped to establish in the United States.

"Beaux-Arts" was a fitting label for these architects and their reform movement. The phrase means fine arts, and a Beaux-Arts architect was one who firmly believed that architecture was an Art. The identification of the movement with a school is also appropriate, because advocates claimed that universal principles could be rationally perceived, expressed, and then taught systematically to any intelligent person. Americans who went to Paris learned an academic approach to architecture which stressed tradition, not originality. When they returned, they spread this point of view, not only through the example of their work, but through an educational campaign, ranging from popular journalism to the establishment of numerous schools of architecture. They even suggested strengthening government control over education along the lines of the French system by creating a national design school in Washington, D.C., which would be administered by a Bureau of Fine Arts. Although this school never materialized, the Society of Beaux-Arts Architects (founded in 1893) and the Beaux-Arts Institute of Design (organized in 1916) contributed significantly to the standardization of architectural curricula along Ecole lines.

The Ecole itself was a centralized, government-supported school divided into two sections, one for architecture and one for painting and sculpture. Its students progressed along a series of clearly marked steps, from entry examination to becoming *diplômé par le gouvernement*. One advanced by winning design competitions. Aspiring architects who were admitted entered the Second Class, accumulated a set number of points in competitions, and then became members of the First Class. For the diploma, they were required to win more competitions, complete a thesis

---

University of Illinois, 1873; Syracuse University, 1873; Columbia University, 1881; University of Pennsylvania, 1890; George Washington University, 1893; Armour Institute of Technology, 1895; Harvard University, 1895; University of Notre Dame, 1898; Ohio State University, 1899; Washington University, 1904; University of California, 1904 [actually 1903]; Carnegie Institute of Technology, 1905; University of Michigan, 1906; Alabama Polytechnic Institute, 1907; Tulane University, 1908; Georgia School of Technology, 1908; University of Texas, 1909; Catholic University of America, 1911; A. and M. College of Texas, 1912; Rice Institute, 1912; University of Minnesota, 1913; Yale University, 1913; University of Oregon, 1914; University of Washington, 1914; and North Dakota Agricultural College, 1914.

Figure 51. The library of the Ecole des Beaux-Arts, Paris, in a photograph from about 1905. Good libraries were essential to academic, Ecole-trained architects since their designs were based on a thorough study of precedents. Students first became acquainted with the "documents" here in the Library of the Ecole.

project, and gain a year's work experience. Culmination of the process for a select few was the annual Grand Prix de Rome competition, open only to French citizens. The winners were sent to the French Academy in Rome for four years of study and were guaranteed an official government position when they returned.

While the Ecole exerted strong control over the nature of a student's work, it left him or her quite free to choose how and when to do it. Around the turn of the century, the school organized lecture courses, set competition programs, administered juries, and provided a library and a gallery of prints and casts (Figures 51 and 52). But the center of the student's world was the *atelier* or studio where competition projects were worked out (Figure 53). All but three of the twenty or so ateliers were maintained independently by *patrons* (design professors) who were practicing architects. The patron usually came around in the evening to give critiques, but otherwise the atelier was student-run according to time-honored traditions. Students could come to the atelier whenever they wanted, since only a minimum number of projects was required each

Figure 52. Interior court of the Ecole des Beaux-Arts, Paris. The Ecole possessed a huge collection of copies of great works of art for the students to study. Reproductions of paintings, sculpture, and architecture from ancient Greece and Rome and Renaissance Italy, as well as original modern French works, were distributed throughout the complex of buildings and courtyards on the rue Bonaparte. The interior, glass-covered court shown here contained plaster casts of Greek and Roman sculpture, including part of the Parthenon, restored.

year. Advancement through the hierarchy set by the Ecole did, however, require discipline and hard work, and it encouraged individual initiative.

Large numbers of American students went to Paris between 1890 and 1910, hoping to be admitted to the Ecole des Beaux-Arts. They were attracted by the school's reputation for giving rigorous Classical training, free of charge, to all who qualified. Few went to England, where architectural students were apprenticed, not schooled, and the attitude toward professional standards was perhaps more ambivalent than in the United States (see Chapter 7). In nineteenth-century America there were few well-trained architects and only a handful of professional schools. Yet the amount of building in the period following the Civil War was tremendous. American architects felt that one way to improve the quality of this proliferation of structures was to impose stricter technical and artistic standards on the profession. The tradition-bound, hierarchically structured Ecole seemed worth emulating to those architects who were alarmed by the almost total lack of regulation of the American building industry and the architectural profession.

Many Americans were attracted to the Ecole by its intellectual and theoretical approach to design. They yearned for the discipline of Classi-

Figure 53. Atelier of Jean-Louis Pascal, Paris. This widely published photograph shows the atelier of Jean-Louis Pascal, 1866 Grand Prix winner, as it appeared about 1905. Students of the Ecole des Beaux-Arts are gathered in their studio, which shows signs of both work and play. The second young man from the right, who holds the T-square, was the Massier, the treasurer and student in charge of the atelier. The Americans who attended this studio were Herbert M. Baer of New York, Edwin H. Hewitt of Minneapolis, Albert Lansburgh of San Francisco, and Paul Cret, who was born in Lyons, France, but came to Philadelphia shortly after graduating from the Ecole.

cism and the scholarly eclecticism of the French. Both students and practitioners found their immutable design principles—unity, harmony, balance, repose—by studying the great monuments of Greece, Rome, Renaissance Italy, and Baroque France. Ideally, Beaux-Arts architects were creative eclectics who avoided direct copying of ancient or modern buildings. They tried to make new and appropriate compositions with traditional elements drawn from a wide variety of sources. But whether they looked to Augustan Rome or Elizabethan England for motifs, the composition of architectural elements was governed by the Classical principles. Beaux-Arts architects, to a large degree, rejected nineteenth-century picturesque theories based on emotional responses to architecture and on structural expression. Instead, they proposed a revival of Renaissance design ideas for modern use.

Up to the time of the Chicago Fair of 1893, this Academic Classicist point of view was far from common among American architects. The World's Columbian Exposition dramatically awakened America's interest in monumental architecture and urban design. The impressive central section of the Fair grounds was designed by Daniel Burnham, Richard Morris Hunt, Charles McKim, Charles Atwood, and other advocates of the grand French manner. The "White City," as it was dubbed, provided mayors, industrialists, university presidents, and other potential patrons with their first glimpse of unified Classical design on a large scale. Before this event, the Beaux-Arts principles and methods were of interest only to a few architects in New York and Boston. The average person knew little of Academic Classicism, although there was a growing appetite for art and culture throughout the country.

To architects who believed in the primacy of art and scholarship, the situation of their profession in the last third of the nineteenth century was deplorable. From about 1870 onward, such critics began to complain bitterly in the pages of popular and professional journals about the crassness and ignorance of their fellow practitioners. They also blamed clients, who demanded novelty or economy before beauty, for the low level of American architecture.* In response to this situation, a group of concerned architects, many of them former Ecole students, began an educational campaign aimed at the profession and the public. Possessed by an almost missionary zeal, they took time off from the drawing board to teach, write, speak, and organize for their cause.

The ultimate purpose of the Beaux-Arts Movement was to raise the status of the profession. Architects wanted to become recognized as experts with specialized knowledge, obtained through long study. They sought to infuse the profession with a theoretical base and to establish ethical principles of conduct. Doctors and lawyers were also seeking to develop formal educational programs and standards of practice in the nineteenth century. But unlike medicine and law, architecture was not considered one of the learned professions; it was a vocation to be picked up on the job. In 1898 there were only nine professional schools with an enrollment of 384 students (Weatherhead, p. 63), yet the 1900 census reported 10,581 persons calling themselves architects (Noffsinger, p. 49).

---

* Some typical laments on the sad state of American architecture are: A. D. F. Hamlin, "The Battle of the Styles," *Architectural Record* 1 (1891), 265-75; William Nelson Black, "Various Causes of Bad Architecture," *Architectural Record* 2 (1892), 149-63; and the series of which the first article was "Architectural Aberrations, Number 1," *Architectural Record* 1 (1891), 133-34.

Anyone could hang out a shingle, for there were no state licensing laws at all until Illinois set the precedent in 1897. Thus a talented and honest architect could not guarantee the competency or scrupulousness of colleagues. If people were to recognize the need for the professional services the architect offered, they had to be made aware of how the architect differed from the draftsman, builder, or engineer. At a somewhat earlier date, these same problems were faced in Britain, as John Wilton-Ely has explained in Chapter 7.

The lack of professional organization among American architects in the nineteenth century paralleled a laissez-faire mentality in other aspects of life—government, economic competition, health, and safety. Ambitious and clever people without formal training easily found work in the rapidly growing cities and towns. Most architects started their careers as overworked draftsmen. When they had picked up a basic knowledge of drawing, materials, and construction, they set up their own practices. Quite often "architects" were builders or contractors who also designed what they constructed. Many of the better architects reported on the census rolls were immigrants trained in various European academies and technical schools. Few American-born persons before the 1890s had had the benefit of systematic foreign training, and among those who had were the leaders of the profession. Richard Morris Hunt was the first to attend the Ecole, between 1845 and 1853. He was followed by Henry Hobson Richardson, Charles F. McKim, Louis Sullivan, Thomas Hastings, Bernard Maybeck, and others. Russell Sturgis, who studied at the Academy of Fine Arts and Sciences in Munich, was one of the few to go to Germany. However, the average nineteenth-century architect hardly fit the definition of a professional. William Robert Ware, a student of Hunt's and founder of the nation's first architectural school at the Massachusetts Institute of Technology, complained of the situation in 1866 in the outline of the MIT course: "The profession is at present in the hands of mechanics," who might be good at practical matters, but are "ignorant of the higher branches of their calling."

Education was to be a key factor in the professionalization of architecture. In a general way, professional schools inculcated ideals and fostered group identity. On a more formal level, uniform and nationally recognized university degrees and other certificates would give an acknowledged stamp of approval to the young professional, especially if they were to be required for licensing. Around the turn of the century, a serious interest in architectural education marked the emergence of the profession as such. At the 1900 annual convention, members of the American Institute of Architects passed an amendment to their by-laws requiring new candidates for membership after January 1902 to have graduated from an approved school or to have passed a special Institute examination. Its Committee on Education began making detailed annual reports in 1906. Several years later, in 1912, the Association of Collegiate Schools of Architecture was founded to encourage the exchange of information and the setting of high, uniform standards.

The educational activities which resulted from this concern were strongly influenced by the Ecole. Because the goals and methods of the French system seemed to serve American purposes at the time, many new or reformed courses were modeled on it. The architectural schools at public and private universities put increasing emphasis on design instruction, and a number of schools, including MIT, Pennsylvania, and Harvard, brought French Ecole graduates to the United States to teach their new courses. For working draftsmen, competitions and independent ateliers were sponsored by the Society of Beaux-Arts Architects. This group also increased the number of young men attending the Ecole itself by establishing the Paris Prize in 1894. The Architectural League of New York, founded in 1881, performed locally some of the functions of the French national school. It arranged exhibitions of drawings, sponsored design competitions, and established a collection of casts, sketches, and photographs. Planning for an American Academy in Rome and a Rome Prize, modeled on the French Academy in Rome and the Prix de Rome, was initiated in 1894 by the group of architects and artists who had worked together on the Chicago Fair. Behind these educational efforts were two basic goals: the establishment of rules which would raise the general standard of taste and produce a vital national style, and the development of special artistic abilities which would differentiate architects from the technicians of the building industry.

Of course, not all architects were in sympathy with these efforts, nor with the affected elitism of some members of the Beaux-Arts movement. Louis Sullivan, who had studied at the Ecole in 1874, and Frank Lloyd Wright, who turned down Daniel Burnham's offer of four sponsored years in Paris, were the most influential detractors of the school. They called its teachings artificial, superficial, and totally unsuited to American needs. Others whose attitudes toward architecture were less at odds with Beaux-Arts theories were nevertheless annoyed by the mannerisms of the self-conscious and cliquish Beaux-Arts architects who were becoming increasingly popular. Some claimed this was nothing but a "Frenchite" fad among a group of snobs aping Parisian fashions.

Despite such opposition, and whatever one might think of their artistic production, the influence of Beaux-Arts architects on professional education was significant. Their success was due to their ability to adapt elements of the Ecole program to American needs. They realized that they could not blindly copy a system developed in France over a period of three hundred years. Educators such as William Ware of MIT, A. D. F. Hamlin of Columbia, and John Galen Howard of Berkeley worked primarily within the structure of the universities. These institutions were concurrently undergoing a tremendous expansion to meet America's need for better higher education, particularly in the vocational fields. Typically, American architectural schools, like other professional faculties, developed under the wings of the growing universities and not into independent entities as in Europe. The situation necessitated compromises. Studio design instruction, modeled on the project method of the Ecole, had to be integrated with the university lecture and class systems, which broke a curriculum into highly segregated units. In contrast, each student at the Ecole progressed at his or her own pace through a series of one-day- to two-month-long projects. The goal of American schools was to produce, as the AIA's Committee on Education put it, the "gentleman of general culture with special architectural ability" (*Proceedings* [1906], 27-33). The Ecole, while praised for its many apparent virtues, was regarded as too narrowly specialized. Reformers considered the combination of its strong artistic orientation and a healthy dose of the humanities necessary to balance the overly technical curricula of the earlier architectural programs, which had usually been lodged in engineering departments.

The Ecole's major significance in the United States, apart from the introduction of Academic Classicism, lies in the role it played in the professionalization of architecture. John Galen Howard (1864-1931), founder of the school of architecture at the University of California, was an important figure in this process. He was a participant in all phases of the Beaux-Arts Movement, and his experiences and attitudes are excellent indicators of its progress. Howard attended the Ecole between 1891 and 1893. In 1903 he moved to Berkeley, where he became the university's Supervising Architect as well as its first Professor of Architecture. He left behind a large collection of drawings, letters, and memorabilia, now owned by the university, which allows us to probe deeply into the relationship between the architect, the school, and the profession. Howard was typical of the men who dominated the profession in the opening decades of the twentieth century when the Beaux-Arts Movement was at its peak. He was in contact with major personalities and ideas. Through his example, we can see why the Ecole's teachings seemed appropriate for America at that time and exactly how the Beaux-Arts Movement was propagated in the United States.

The course of Howard's education between 1882, when he entered MIT, and 1893, when he set up independent practice, was guided by the example of his teachers and employers and by his own unhappiness with current professional standards. At "Tech" Howard encountered Eugène Létang, the Ecole-trained design instructor. Henry Hobson Richardson, in whose office Howard worked between 1885 and 1887, had attended the Ecole and was, at the time of his death in 1886, the leading architect in the country. Charles McKim, who gave the young man a job in 1889, later made it possible for him to study in Paris. Throughout this training period, Howard seemed motivated by a lofty idealism and a fascination with the artistic rather than the technical or pecuniary aspects of architecture.

Although the School of Architecture at MIT was the oldest in the country, having been founded in 1865, it suffered from the same limitations which plagued other early schools. Courses in construction and the pure sciences dominated the curriculum as opposed to courses in design and the liberal arts. Enrollment was small, and teaching materials such as books and photographs were too meager to allow the full range of studies Ware had desired. In Howard's sophomore year there were only five regular students and about a dozen working draftsmen taking a special two-year course. That same year (1883) an attempt to inaugurate an architectural laboratory in which to illustrate the theory of construction by experiment had to be abandoned for lack of time in the set curriculum. Howard left MIT in 1885 without graduating because of financial reasons and his dissatisfaction with the scientific emphasis of the program.

He found the experience of working in Richardson's office more rewarding. Both the great architect's work and the conduct of his office set high standards not to be found elsewhere. Of Richardson's architecture Howard later wrote, "It was and is to *us* something more than a hopeful and refreshing oasis in the desert of our crude and, till him, uninspired American art" (MS Correspondence and Papers). He spoke warmly of the Brookline office, where he was treated like a student as well as an employee. The younger men, of whom there were four in 1885, were given private alcoves in which to work, a great privilege considering how busy and crowded the office was then. "The old man," who hardly touched a pencil in his last year, walked around the office giving friendly criticism and encouragement to his employees, including the students.

It was one of Mr. Richardson's principles always to have before his draftsmen photographs and casts of all the best old work, as a constant unconscious means of educating their tastes, and architectural affectations—this last no small matter—and each occupant of an alcove was allowed liberty of selection among the large collection of photographs which encircled the office [MS Correspondence and Papers].

Compared to the situation he later found in Los Angeles, this period of Howard's life must have seemed particularly stimulating.

The young architect's first journey to the West Coast was motivated partly by the spirit of adventure and partly by the desire to earn enough money for a trip to Europe. But California was a disappointment. He enjoyed the climate and natural scenery, but loathed the boom-town atmosphere of Los Angeles. Howard felt he was prostituting his talent working for the firm of Caukin and Haas, who specialized in Richardsonian Romanesque. He wrote home:

[They are not] capable of understanding or appreciating me. . . . Men who have scarcely received a rudimentary training in art, whose care and pursuit is solely and finally to make money . . . such men neither understand art so well as I do, nor from the crude untrained lack of taste are so capable of producing good work [Letter dated Sept. 12, 1887, Correspondence and Papers].

Escaping from materialism and ignorance, Howard set sail for Europe in November 1888. He wrote of his aims:

It is not primarily to attend any school . . . that I go; but to come into contact with the noble monuments which other ages have bequeathed our own. . . . I, an architect, turn to Europe, that vast library of architectural knowledge and accomplishment [Letter dated July 10, 1888, Correspondence and Papers].

Similar sentiments must have been voiced by the hundreds of other young American artists—poets and painters, traditionalists and moderns—who flocked in ever-larger numbers to Paris, Munich, and Florence from the 1870s on. They were seeking to define an American culture. That search led them, in one direction, to a rediscovery of America's colonial past and, in the other, to Europe. Nationalism and cosmopolitanism went hand in hand. The architects began to study New England farmhouses and Southern mansions and at the same time felt the need to observe in person the full range of Old World architecture. They wanted to know the real textures and colors, the true scale and proportions of European buildings which they had studied before only through prints, descriptions, photographs, or plaster casts. They hoped to create a vital American architecture by mastering all that Europe had to offer. This was to be no indiscriminate raid, however. The new eclectics rejected the quirky use of ornamental motifs which characterized mid-Victorian architecture and scorned the falsity of iron cornices and wooden gingerbread. Through concentrated study, they hoped to gain literacy and discipline.

Howard's grand tour was short, and the systematic study of "the noble monuments" at the Ecole des Beaux-Arts had to wait for a future visit. But his education, as such, continued. When he returned to the United States, Howard went to work for the firm of McKim, Mead and White, leaders in this American Renaissance. His employers not only set an example for Howard through their own work, but the atelier atmosphere of Richardson's office prevailed in their New York office, too. The firm pioneered the Classical Revival and the return to academic discipline in the United States. Under way when Howard joined them in 1889 were two of the firm's most influential urban monuments designed before the Chicago Fair: the Boston Public Library and Madison Square Garden. Howard worked under Stanford White on the theater and tower of the latter project. Meanwhile he had the run of the large library of books, photographs, and sketches available for study. Here, too he found the company of like-minded men, for New York was the center of the Beaux-Arts Movement.

But Howard stayed in America for less than two years: the message of this architectural reform movement had made its mark. He felt his education was incomplete without the advanced training in design offered by the Ecole des Beaux-Arts. His attendance was made possible by a loan from Charles McKim, who throughout his career gave many young men this same opportunity. McKim's concern for the education of the younger generation was typical of Beaux-Arts architects. In 1857 Richard Morris Hunt had set up an atelier in New York. His students in the few years of its existence included Henry Van Brunt, George B. Post, William Robert Ware, and Frank Furness. Howard carried on the tradition by founding a school of architecture at Berkeley, by sending one of his own sons to the Ecole, and by endowing a traveling fellowship for University of California students.

The Ecole des Beaux-Arts was the ideal finale to the education of student architects of Howard's generation. It taught them what they could not learn at home, namely how to be masters of Academic Classicism. The hope was that the school which produced France's artistic elite would do the same for America. Two aspects of this training most valued by Americans were a command of the design method by which any problem, from a small house to an entire city, could be systematically solved, and fluency in the Classical language of architecture. These were essential skills for those architects who considered themselves serious artists. Academic Classicism was certainly not a mode in which the brilliant but untutored individualist could shine.

Although the Ecole became the American architectural students' mecca, it was a school designed to meet specifically French needs and not one which made any concessions to the presence of its numerous foreign students. Its highly regimented, hierarchical system was organized to produce an elite corps to fill official posts in government departments, particularly the Public Buildings and National Palaces Service, under the direction of the Ministry of Fine Arts. Winners of the Prix de Rome entered government service upon their return from Rome. Their prize-winning designs, which were idealistic exhibition pieces and not plans for real buildings, represented the standard of excellence by which all student competitions were judged. While architects who received diplomas did enter private practice, the Ecole curriculum was not related specifically to the more ordinary aspects of the profession. There were other schools of architecture in the country, and, since there were no licensing laws in France, a formal education was not required for practice. Nevertheless, an Ecole diploma represented the pinnacle of prestige for a French architect.

Ideally, Americans went to Paris to learn the principles of Academic Classicism, not to enter the profession in France or to reproduce its hierarchical organization at home. Some returning enthusiasts, of course, imitated everything French, from *cartouches* and *œils de bœuf* to atelier slang. But among more serious-minded persons, the Ecole served as a graduate design school, of which there was no counterpart at home. Many Americans did not bother to become *diplômé*, a task requiring as many as six years and having little meaning in the United States. Howard attended the Ecole for only two years and left without graduating. He had come to Paris after three years of university training and six years of office experience. Consequently he was able to advance very quickly, amassing half the required First Class values by the time he left in the spring of

1893. Fifteen years later, this difficult and expensive mode of training was already becoming dispensable. Not only had design programs been strengthened in American universities, but the general concept of an appropriate architectural education for America had been formulated. Significantly, after 1908 the numbers of American students attending the Ecole began to drop off, although the number of Americans who graduated rose because of improved prior training.

The American concept of the ideal architectural education was developed from a mixture of French and homegrown ideas and was tempered by experience. In order to understand its formulation, we need to look at the experiences of an Ecole student, such as Howard, who later established an architectural school. Fortunately the extensive set of letters and drawings which he left behind allows us to probe into the development of his educational philosophy in Paris, New York, and Berkeley.

Ecole students had to be well prepared in their field before entering. A highly competitive examination was given twice a year, covering design, drawing, modeling, mathematics, descriptive geometry, and history. When Howard sat for the exams in March and April, 1891, there were 230 aspirants, including fifteen Americans. Only thirty were admitted, including three Americans. Howard was placed fourth overall. His success was due partly to his American training, but also to several months spent making measured drawings in the atelier of Paul-René-Léon Ginain, the 1852 Grand Prix winner and architect of the Ecole de Médecine. Nine or ten other American aspirants shared his corner of the studio, all of them mastering the French language and architectural conventions. There were also special "prep schools" like the one described by Louis Sullivan in *The Autobiography of an Idea*, where students boned up on history and mathematics.

Once admitted to the Ecole, Howard had to make an important decision. Which atelier should he enter? Here was where he would learn design and spend most of his time. Howard chose the atelier of Victor Laloux; nearly a hundred other Americans through the years did likewise because this was a "strong" atelier with lots of esprit de corps and many prizes to its credit.* Like most other patrons, Laloux was a Grand Prix winner (1878), the recipient of many honors, and the architect of large government projects, including the railway station and Hotel de Ville at

---

* Laloux was awarded the Gold Medal by the American Institute of Architects in 1922 for his services to American architecture.

Tours and the Gare d'Orsay at Paris. This was one of the independent ateliers with no official connection to the Ecole.

Whichever atelier they chose, Americans were greatly impressed by the atmosphere they found there. Tales of rowdy parties, mad *charettes*, and lively traditions filled their reminiscences. The key ingredient of atelier spirit was group loyalty. The *patron*'s little band pulled together to defend its honor against the other studios. Everyone, from the greenest *nouveau* to the most advanced *ancien*, helped one another, at the same time maintaining a friendly internecine rivalry. The *anciens* criticized the work of the *nouveaux*, and the *nouveaux* pitched in to help the *anciens* render plates for a big competition. This atmosphere of cooperation and the personal guidance of the *patron* were as important as the more formal aspects of the program.

Howard needed only sixteen months, the minimum period, to earn enough values to move from Second to First Class. Most students took two or three years. This initial stage of his training was intended to teach him the fundamentals of design and the science of construction. In a logical manner, the student moved from the simple to the complex, the small to the large. In design he began with *analytiques*, rendered plates in which he demonstrated his knowledge of the Classical Orders, standard window and door treatments, and small elements of historical buildings. Then he entered several competitions for the design of small structures, such as a primary school, a loggia, and a courtyard. Before taking the year-long construction course, Howard studied descriptive geometry, stereotomy, perspective, and mathematics. The lectures, examinations, and short projects prepared him for the final construction project, which required him to synthesize all he had learned about science and art. In the year 1891-92, Howard's three-month project "include[d] all the construction and calculation relative to sizes of iron, thrusts of vaults, details of trusses—in fact everything that would be necessary for actual construction of a Library and Museum of Sculpture" [Letter dated April 14, 1892, Correspondence and Papers].

Having mastered the fundamentals of historic precedent and construction, Howard became a First Class student. Now he devoted his efforts totally to the art of design, applying the theory and method of the Ecole to original compositions. Again he was free to pick among the *concours* (competitions) set by the Professor of Theory. Each year these included six *esquisses* (sketch projects), six *projets rendus* (two-month projects requiring rendered drawings), and other special competitions. In order to give free rein to the student's imagination, project programs were usually of an idealistic nature. Typical subjects were a festival gallery in a palace, a commemorative monument, and a pantheon, although there were also theaters, schools, and churches. Site conditions and client needs were specified, but only generally. The purpose of these exercises was to train the architect in the fine art of composition. More practical matters, such as site supervision, building law, and professional practice, were learned later in the required year of apprenticeship.

The theory and method of the Ecole, its famous "secrets" of composition, can best be explained by following the course of a typical *projet rendu*. Three drawings and the program for one of Howard's Second Class projects were preserved among his papers (Figures 54, 55, 56) His design for a court of a Ministry of War Building is presented in an *esquisse* (preliminary sketch), a rendered section, and a rendered detail section. The rendered plan is missing. The problem set here was simpler than a First Class project, since the arcades and Orders were specified. Nevertheless, the complicated design process taught through this exercise was the same as that used for a project of any scale, from a student sketch problem to the actual design of large groups of buildings. It served a Beaux-Arts architect throughout his or her career.

Howard's first task in the Ministry of War project was to work out the *parti*, or basic concept of the design, beyond the general outline set for him by the program. He arrived at the Ecole, picked up the program, and was immediately shut up for twelve hours in a little *loge* or alcove to produce from his imagination a sketch plan and section. This was kept on file at the school. The student kept a copy of the *esquisse*, since the rendered project he turned in two months later had to match it. The rationale behind this artificial limitation was twofold. It was considered a substitute for restrictions of client and site encountered in real life, and it forced students to attack the problem in general terms at first, leaving the details for later. Artistic unity and harmony were assured because the student had to pursue one line of development through to completion. Practice, imagination, and knowledge were essential in this system, because the broad lines of development had to be set out quickly and independently.

Above all, the student sought to give the sketch design a suitable character which could be further developed in the weeks to follow. *Caractère*, as introduced in the eighteenth century by Laugier and Blondel, was an important concept in French Neo-Classical theory. The term was never strictly defined, but generally it meant the expression of the qualities of a building. Through manipulation of plan, proportions, and decorations the architect could express the nature of the building's function and site. For example, Howard's arcaded courtyard for a Ministry of War was very dignified and correct, although richly endowed with sculptural decoration; the Roman forms, particularly the figure of Mars, recalled ancient military might. The festive character of a theater or casino might be indicated by lush Baroque decoration. The design of a church might be composed of Gothic or Byzantine forms if appropriate to the situation. By the 1890s, the French had become thoroughly eclectic.

Developing the suitable character of a building involved more than searching for the right sort of decoration. The plan could be equally expressive of *caractère*. In fact, planning was the greatest skill the Ecole bestowed upon its students. Creation of the plan was governed by a set of unwritten principles, developed through the years and transmitted in the atelier from *patron* to *ancien* to *nouveau*. Historian George Gromort ventured to set them down:

assure unity by making the principal element clearly dominate;
sacrifice as many secondary elements as possible to reduce the plan to its most simple expression;
avoid equalities between elements which are not identical;
allow no building or street which is not well lit, let light and air penetrate throughout, and make courtyards ample;
orient whenever possible the entire composition toward the most extended horizon, opening out the body of the building more and more in that direction. [*Histoire*, vol. II. p. 14].

After fixing the character of the *parti*, the student spent about six weeks studying the design and developing the details. Documents were consulted to find suitable precedents. Sketches were made, trying out various compositions of forms. Theoretically, students looked for concepts among the precedents, but more often than not, they simply cribbed from here and there. Sources included P. Letarouilly's *Edifices de Rome Moderne* (Paris, 1840), C. Daly's *Motifs historiques* (Paris, 1880), printed plates of past competition entries, measured drawings sent home by Prix de Rome winners, or any number of volumes in the Ecole's excellent library. Students also studied the school's extensive collection of casts and authentic fragments of historical buildings. The successful design made use of "the les-

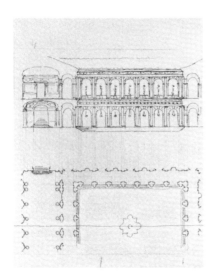

Figures 54, 55, and 56. John Galen Howard, Courtyard of a Ministry of War Building. Student project from the Ecole des Beaux-Arts, 1891. This project is an excellent example of the sort of work the Ecole required. It was a Second Class *rendu,* which tested the student's knowledge of composition at a scale between the single bay and the entire building. Three of the four drawings survive. Figure 54 is the *esquisse* or sketch (11 by 14½ inches), Figure 55 is the rendered section (21¾ by 36¾ inches), and Figure 56 a section of one bay (23¼ by 39¼ inches). The rendered plan is missing. Also preserved among Howard's papers was the program for the competition, which can be translated as follows:

Competition
Analysis of elements
May 8, 1891
2nd Class
Rendered Project

National and Special School of Fine Arts
Architectural Section

The Professor of Theory proposes this subject for a competition: the courtyard of a Ministry of War Building. This courtyard, preceded by a vestibule, is surrounded at ground level and at the first floor by an arcaded portico, with columns engaged to the piers. The ground floor will be of Roman Doric Order and the first floor of the Ionic.

One should work hard to arrange the two Orders to make a perfectly unified whole. The Ionic cornice should crown the entire building.

The courtyard is seven arches long. These arches are spaced 5 meters apart, from pier center to pier center.

The sketches should consist of a plan of the courtyard and vestibule and a longtitudinal section, both at the scale of 1:.0025.

For the renderings, which are due June 27, the plan should be at a scale of 1:.005, the general section at double that. There should also be an elevation at one bay of the portico, consisting of one arch and two entire piers at each level, and a section, at a scale of 1:.04. In this section one should follow the Roman practice of superposition of engaged columns, absolutely avoiding any sort of overhang. The drawings should be washed. Exactitude in delineating shadows is indispensable.

Paris, May 8, 1891
Signed: Guillaume

sons of the past" but still had its own particular quality, determined by the nature of the project and the student's artistic flair.

Quite as important as designing was rendering. About two weeks out of two months were required for this phase of a *projet rendu*. Through exercises of this sort, Ecole students learned to produce exquisite drawings, often in brilliant water-color wash. Critics complained that this was merely cleverness which had nothing to do with real architecture. Beaux-Arts graduates admitted that the school required a degree of rendering facility rarely encountered in practice, at least outside the big competitions. But Howard maintained that the process of carefully calculating forms and shadows forced one to have a real sense of the relationships of solid masses in space. He defended the *point de poché*—the elegant patterns of wall solid, and mosaic which enlivened the floor plans—as a sort of shorthand notation from which one could read the entire building form, rather like a conductor reading a score. But whatever the actual artistic value of these conventions, they did serve a professional purpose. In teaching them, the Ecole provided America with a corps of talented draftsmen, a group notably lacking in the nineteenth and early twentieth centuries.

Howard was able to put his Ecole training to immediate use when he returned to the United States in the spring of 1893. He had performed brilliantly in all aspects of his studies, but he had left without a diploma. His reasons were both personal and professional and had nothing to do with antagonism toward the school. Also, he was twenty-nine years old in 1893. Thirty was the age limit for Ecole students, and it was certainly not too early to set up private practice. Howard settled in New York and seems to have been quite successful in the eight years he spent there as a member of the firm of Howard and Cauldwell. He was the design specialist, his partner the engineer—an increasingly common division of labor, discussed in detail by Bernard Michael Boyle in Chapter 11. The partners' buildings—large houses, hotels, a school, a library—were all skillful essays in the Academic Classical manner; Howard had returned home just at the moment when the Chicago Fair made its profound impact upon the profession and the public. Charles Moore, in his biography of Daniel Burnham, looked back upon this era from the 1920s and remarked:

To the Artists of America, the Fair meant public recognition of their work in conjunction with one another. Standards of achievement and taste had been created. Eclecticism and freakishness, falsely called originality, had been discredited; the treasure-houses of the past opened doors long closed to Americans, because never attempted. Suddenly we became heirs to untold riches in art. Young architects trained at the Beaux-Arts found receptive clients where they had feared to encounter opposition. They no longer spoke a foreign language, but made their appeals to understanding ears [*Burnham*, vol. I, p. 90].

Howard was destined to be an educator as well as a designer. On April 14, 1903, he signed a contract with the Regents of the University of California to become its Supervising Architect and first Professor of Architecture. He had obtained this dual appointment through his participation in the International Competition for the Phoebe Hearst Architectural Plan for the University of California. Howard and Cauldwell were only placed fourth when the final results were announced in September of 1899. But the winner, the Frenchman Emile Bénard, declined to carry out his grandiose scheme, and Howard was eventually chosen to rework the campus plan. Undoubtedly his design ability and friendship with local architects whom he had known from his Los Angeles days helped to secure the position. But equally important were Howard's educational qualifications. The president of the university had stated in his 1900 report that he intended a school of architecture to be developed in conjunction with the new building program based on the Hearst Plan. No doubt university officials were on the lookout for someone with excellent credentials for the joint appointment. Howard was just the man. Not only had he studied at MIT and the Ecole des Beaux-Arts and apprenticed with the country's two leading architectural firms, but he had shown his commitment to education during the years of private practice in New York. He had sat on the Education Committee of the Society of Beaux-Arts Architects, of which he was a founding member. And he had served as a juror for the annual exhibitions of architectural drawings sponsored by the Architectural League of New York and the Philadelphia T-Square Club. Thus, a man whose own education was strongly directed by the Beaux-Arts Movement was now in a position to instill its ideals in the younger generation.

The architectural school Howard established at Berkeley in 1903 was only the thirteenth in the United States and the first west of the Rocky Mountains. Before he came, the university had offered only a few informal courses in architectural drawing, taught by Bernard Maybeck. Aspiring architects from the West Coast had had to content themselves with apprenticeship, take a degree in civil engineering, or go East or abroad for formal training. Howard was asked to create an architectural school practically from scratch. It began as a twelve-student atelier in a corner of the

Supervising Architect's office. By the time he retired in 1928, the department had become an independent school with its own graduate program and a faculty of seven.

Forces and ideas from both within and without shaped the architectural school at the University of California. Through the years, Howard had to reconcile conditions imposed by administrators with his own concept of an ideal course of study. The university system, which had already assumed much of its present form by the early twentieth century, need not concern us here. But the state of architectural education has changed considerably and needs to be discussed. Howard seems to have shared the goals expressed by other leading American educators who sought to raise the standards of the profession by creating schools of high quality. He was keenly aware of the need to create a curriculum balanced between strictly architectural subjects, the liberal arts, and scientific studies. He wanted to lengthen the course of study and did succeed in establishing a graduate program devoted exclusively to professional studies. Also, Howard attempted to introduce an integrated course of design instruction which was not arbitrarily broken up by the unit, grade, and year categories imposed by the university. It was this component of the curriculum—design—which was most strongly influenced by the Ecole des Beaux-Arts.

The content rather than the organization of design instruction resembled that of the Ecole. Only in 1915 was Howard able to institute the "value" system, whereby students proceeded at their own pace through competitively judged projects. This arrangement applied only to the senior and two graduate years and was elective. Otherwise the usual semester course system prevailed, as it did almost everywhere else. Competitions and ateliers were made the bases of all design instruction only at Columbia University, and they remained controversial among educators. Three problems were encountered with the French system: competitions were felt to encourage overly elaborate graphic displays; judges were often accused of bias; and ateliers were difficult to establish because not many architects were willing to take time away from the office to teach.

Given the semester system, Howard set up a program of design instruction which approximated that of the Ecole at least in content. Classicism was taught in an orderly and thoroughly academic manner which changed little during the Howard years. In 1905-6, architecture majors began studying design in their junior year. Lower-division students took general courses and learned drawing techniques—pen and ink; shades, shadows, and perspective; descriptive geometry; stereotomy; and freehand sketching. Juniors began by making simple compositions in the Elements of Architecture course and by attending lectures in architectural history and theory. Seniors studied Planning, at a level approximately equal to the Second Class at the Ecole. Graduate students continued with planning and took Composition and Advanced Design, in which they were given First Class level projects. This pattern remained nearly the same throughout Howard's tenure as head of the School of Architecture, although the design component increased in proportion to other areas as new courses were added. Historical Drawing was separated from History in 1913. The Classical Orders were taught apart from Elements of Architecture after 1917. Drawing the nude, an element of French architectural education, was added only in 1920 when certain influential prudes had died or retired. In 1926, the Theory and Design courses of the third, fourth, fifth, and sixth years were combined into a more demanding series of core courses.

Design projects assigned to University of California students in the early years were modeled on those at the Ecole. Unlike the situation at many other American schools, design instructors were not imported Frenchmen. Teaching in this area was handled by Ecole-trained American architects who were as aware as Howard of the relationship between foreign methods and native practice. Nevertheless, the student projects which these instructors supervised tended to be blatantly archeological. The *analytiques, esquisses,* and *projets rendus* were intended to inculcate the universal principles of architectural composition taught by the Ecole. These were artistic exercises, not essays in sociology or structure. Therefore the programs imposed few practical restrictions and the subjects were sometimes fanciful building types, such as palaces, with little relation to the students' own world. A typical junior-year *analytique* was the Lobby to a Court Room (Figure 57), which illustrated the decorative potential of domes and the Corinthian Order. Between 1912 and 1914, the second-year design students (seniors) were asked to create such things as a railway station for a small town, a villa by Lake Como, a casino at a spa, a city police station, and a garden sculpture loggia. In 1916 a skyscraper was the subject of a senior project (Figure 58). Graduate programs called for an atheneum, a department store, a state capitol, a bank, and a monastery. The further these building types were from the reality of twentieth-century America, the closer student designs resembled published archeological drawings. Their work seems to indicate that the Beaux-Arts Movement's goal of producing a vital national style through creative

Figure 57. Lobby to a Court Room, junior year student project, School of Architecture, University of California, Berkeley, ca. 1913. The purpose of this *analytique* was to teach beginning students the rudiments of Classical composition. A simple room and its decorative details were carefully drawn, with much care being given to the layout of the page.

eclecticism was not viable in a country lacking its own great historical monuments.

Howard did, however, subscribe to the then-common assumption that American architecture could flower by tapping into the still-vital European Classical tradition. He believed that our Georgian past made Classicism the natural stylistic tendency of the nation. In organizing an architectural school, this conviction led of necessity to an emphasis on historical scholarship. Design courses were based upon history and theory courses, which dealt almost exclusively with European buildings and ideas known to students only from books or photographs. Howard gave history slide lectures for twenty-four years—eight cycles of three years each. Bound volumes of his transcribed notes indicate that the "usable past" extended to ca. 1520, with the exception of seventeenth- and eighteenth-century France. Lectures covered ancient, Early Christian, medieval,

Figure 58. Dorothy Wormser, class of 1916, stands beside a senior project done at the University of California, Berkeley. The designer, who later worked for Julia Morgan, recently described the project in a letter to the author. "It was entitled 'Skyscraper for an Old World City.' The class divided itself into Classicists and Gothicists, and the Gothicists placed 1, 2, and 3 in the judgement (I was #2). Yes, mine was supposed to be Gothic, with a nod toward New York's Woolworth Building and Brussels' Hôtel de Ville. In my solution, the former, the tower, held the required offices; the latter, the palace, the restaurant, bank, club, etc."

and Renaissance architecture, but little else. A binder labeled "Modern Architecture" dealt with the High Renaissance. One lecture on the Italian Baroque and Rococo contained the warning that students would find little there to emulate. The only American buildings discussed were Georgian and examples of the Classical Revival.

Theory classes were equally in line with French Academic Classicism. They consisted of Howard's running translation of *Eléments et théories de l'architecture* by Julien Guadet, Professor of Theory at the Ecole since 1894. The book, based on Guadet's own course, is a highly rational discussion of building types and the composition of architectural elements from artistic and practical standpoints. But, as one of Howard's students pointed out, their professor could never quite twist the French building types to fit American patterns, thus limiting the value of Guadet's principles for American students. Although these esoteric studies were far removed from the daily lives of university students, they were taken seriously, because it had become important for an architect to be a competent scholar.

While design was Howard's major interest, technology was not ignored at Berkeley. On the contrary, students were required to take many courses in engineering, mathematics, and physics, particularly in the early years. But the tendency was for these courses to be taken over by the School of Architecture as Howard tried over the years to make it more and more into an autonomous institution. The Ecole des Beaux-Arts had its own construction course. Likewise, Howard, who was fully aware of the latest developments and put them to use in his own practice, wanted to create an integrated program of structural and mechanical engineering instruction especially for architecture students. Civil engineering continued to be taught in the School of Engineering, although special courses for architects were created by a sympathetic dean. Architectural mechanics was put under Howard's control in 1913 with the addition of a new member to the Architecture faculty to teach the courses. In the same year, the Department of Architecture officially became a School, and thus was removed from the control of the School of Engineering, whose faculty had been able to out-vote Architecture by virtue of the fact that it taught such a high proportion of classes required for the major. One further example of Howard's effort to control the technical training of his students was the addition in 1922 of an instructor to teach rendering, which had formerly been given by the Drawing Department. Clearly, the trend was to teach students about the latest advances in building technology, but to do so in a way which subordinated science to art as had been done at the Ecole.

The desire to broaden the student's course of study inevitably led to attempts at lengthening it. Howard and other educators desired to provide sophisticated design instruction, advanced technical training, courses in professional ethics, a background in history, languages, literature, and the fine arts. Their ideal was to produce the "gentleman of general culture with special architectural ability." There was, however, a practical limit to the length of professional education. While the Ecole set stringent entrance requirements, in this country only a high school diploma could reasonably be required of incoming freshmen. No Ecole-style admission examinations were ever instituted at Berkeley or any other school, and the first two years had to be devoted to foundation studies. Graduate programs improved in time as enrollment increased, but such programs were limited to one or two years. The example of the Ecole had influenced American educators in the direction of ever-longer and more sophisticated courses of design instruction, but this was mitigated by the American university's concern with general education rather than intense specialization. Furthermore, American students were under much stronger pressure to leave school in order to work than were French students, whose education was subsidized by the government.

Outside the university, the Ecole's influence on architectural education was less dilute. University extension courses and those offered by the YMCA and various architectural clubs were set up for working drafts-men. Most popular were "bread and butter" courses, such as rendering. It was reported that history, esthetics, and cultural studies, which formed a prominent part of university students' architectural training, were "shunned like the plague" whenever offered. These evening courses for working students were conducted in ateliers set up by the dedicated Beaux-Arts architects, who followed the example set by Richard Morris Hunt fifty years earlier. After 1893, the Beaux-Arts Movement became more organized. Students worked on competition programs sent from New York by the Society of Beaux-Arts Architects, and after 1916 by the Beaux-Arts Institute of Design. Local ateliers competed and held exhibi-tions, then sent the best drawings to New York for national competitions. John Galen Howard confined his teaching activities to the University of California, and he did not use the Beaux-Arts Society's programs as a number of other schools did. According to his 1915 report to the AIA con-vention, however, ateliers were being conducted in San Francisco by a former student and two Ecole-trained associates. These three studios gave design training to sixty-nine young draftsmen that year.

To summarize, the Ecole des Beaux-Arts provided the best available model for these vocational and university programs of professional educa-tion. In the late nineteenth century, when architects had begun to feel a concern and responsibility for the state of their profession, in typical American fashion they fixed upon education as the means of creating great art and high ethical standards. Since there were no precedents for an American architectural education, any more than for an American style, the architects looked abroad. France had a thoroughly organized system of professional education. From it Americans borrowed teaching methods which encouraged the concept of a national Classical style. The extensive array of courses created in America between 1890 and 1915 showed the strong impact of the Ecole, modified by other, specifically American concerns.

BIBLIOGRAPHICAL NOTES

The basic study of American architectural education is Arthur Clason Weatherhead, *The History of Collegiate Education in Architecture in the United States* (Los Angeles, 1941). More discursive and less historical is F. H. Bosworth, Jr., and Roy Childs Jones, *A Study of Architectural Schools* (New York, 1932). Useful for statistics and names is James Philip Noffsinger, *The Influence of the Ecole des Beaux-Arts on the Architects of the United States* (Washington, D.C., 1955), but the work contains no analysis.

The best primary sources of information on trends in architectural education during the period under study are the Reports of the American Institute of Architects' Committee on Education, contained in the *Journals of Proceedings* of the Annual Conventions, beginning with the Fortieth in 1906.

The description of the School of Architecture at the University of California at Berkeley is based on a variety of archival materials and university publications. Howard briefly described the School in the introduction to the Architectural Association of the University of California's *Yearbook* (San Francisco, 1912).

John Galen Howard's papers and drawings are collected in several locations of the University of California campus at Berkeley. His Correspondence and Papers are in the Bancroft Library. The Documents Collection, College of Environmental Design, holds Howard's school work, many working drawings, and several scrapbooks.

Secondary works on other architectural schools and institutions include: Theodore K. Rohdenberg, *A History of the School of Architecture, Columbia University* (New York, 1954); Caroline Shillaber, *Massachusetts Institute of Technology School of Architecture and Planning 1861-1961* (Cambridge, Mass., 1963); University of Pennsylvania, Department of Architecture, *Book of the School* (Philadelphia, 1963); Lucia N. and Alan Valentine, *The American Academy in Rome, 1894-1969* (Charlottesville, Va., 1973).

For contemporary descriptions of schools, see the series "American Schools of Architecture," which began with A. D. F. Hamlin, "Columbia University," *Architectural Record* 21 (1907), 321-26.

The best general study of American universities of the nineteenth and early twentieth centuries is Laurence R. Veysey, *The Emergence of the Modern University* (Chicago, 1965).

Numerous articles on the Ecole des Beaux-Arts and its influence in the United States appeared in turn-of-the-century periodicals. The entire volume of *Architectural Record* 10 suppl. (Jan. 1901) is devoted to the subject. Other articles of interest are: Paul P. Cret, "The Ecole des Beaux-Arts: What Its Architecture Means," *Architectural Record* 23 (1908), 367-71; J. Stewart Barney, "The Ecole des Beaux-Arts: Its Influence on our Architecture," *Architectural Record* 22 (1907), 333-42; John Galen Howard, "The Paris Training," *Architectural Review* (Boston) 5 (1898), 4-7; idem, "The Spirit of Design at the Ecole des Beaux-Arts," *Architectural Review* 5 (1898), 25-27;

and Montgomery Schuyler, "Schools of Architecture and the Paris School," *Scribner's Magazine* 24 (1898), 765-66, reprinted in *American Architecture and Other Writings*, ed. William H. Jordy and Ralph Coe (Cambridge, Mass., 1961), II, 575-78.

American university libraries collected books in French about the Ecole during the period of interest in the school. These included: Henry d'Herville (pseud.), *La section d'architecture à l'Ecole nationale et spéciale des Beaux-Arts, contenant les programmes d'admission, l'exposé pratique de chaque partie de l'examen* . . . (Paris, 1894); Henry Guédy, *L'enseignement a l'Ecole nationale et spéciale des beaux-arts: Section d'architecture* (Paris, 1899); E. Delaire, *Les architectes élèves de l'Ecole des Beaux-Arts* (Paris, 1907); Albert Louvet, *L'art et la profession de l'architecte*, 2 vols. (Paris, 1910-13); M. Alexis Lemaistre, *L'Ecole des Beaux-Arts* (Paris, 1889).

Studies of French architecture in the nineteenth and early twentieth centuries also contain information on the Ecole and its professors. See George R. Gromort, "Architecture," *Histoire général de l'art français de la Révolution à nos jours* (Paris, 1922), II; and Louis Hautecoeur, *Histoire de l'architecture classique en France* (Paris, 1957), VII.

One should also consult the many publications of the Ecole and its professors, such as Institut de France, Académie des Beaux-Arts, *Les Grands Prix de Rome d'Architecture, 1850-1904*, 3 vols. (Paris, ca. 1905); and Julien Guadet, *Eléments et théories de l'architecture*, 7 vols. (Paris, 1902).

Unpublished studies which have contributed to this article were: Alexander R. Butler, "McKim's Renaissance: A Study in the History of the American Architectural Profession" (Ph.D. dissertation, Johns Hopkins University, 1953); Barbara K. Silvergold, "The Education of a Beaux-Arts Architect," paper on Richard Morris Hunt, presented at the 27th Annual Meeting of the Society of Architectural Historians, New Orleans, Louisiana, April 3-8, 1974; Richard Guy Wilson, "Charles F. McKim and the Development of the American Renaissance: A Study in Architecture and Culture" (Ph.D. dissertation, University of Michigan, 1972). Forming the background for this article was the author's "John Galen Howard and the Beaux-Arts Movement in the United States" (M. Arch. thesis, University of California, Berkeley, 1972).

# 9

## Architectural Education in the Thirties and Seventies: A Personal View

JOSEPH ESHERICK

The year 1932 was not quite the bottom of the Depression; things were to get worse before they got better. I entered the University of Pennsylvania Department of Architecture in the School of Fine Arts in the fall of that year. That fall Roosevelt was elected to his first term, and the stock market sank to an all-time low; it was the year of the Veterans' Bonus March in Washington, of record unemployment.

In spite of this apparently grim state of affairs, the entering freshman class in architecture was one of the largest in recent memory and the largest it was to be for many years. Although Pennsylvania is nominally an Ivy League institution, its character was and remains distinctly urban and its students a more polyglot mix, more closely representing what one would expect in the urban centers of the East, than was characteristic of deep Ivy League schools such as Princeton or Yale. In place of "hurrah for the red and the blue," a derisive parody of the Penn anthem in those days sung by opposing spectators at football games substituted "hurrah for the Wops and the Jews."

Penn has always drawn a large number of students from the Philadelphia area, southeastern Pennsylvania, New Jersey, and New York, and the Depression reinforced this natural tendency. If the study of architecture in the thirties was an elite undertaking by a privileged group trained for its role in the private schools and academies of the East, this was not evident in our class. Virtually all of us were products of the public school system, a great many of us from large urban high schools. But it was a real mix—big-city and small-town children of white collar and blue collar, of professionals and merchants—with the merchants far outweighing the professionals. It was mostly men and by design. The policy of the school was explicit:

Women students in Fine Arts, having completed the equivalent of the first two years of the five-year course in architecture, may enter the course in architecture, upon successfully passing the examinations to the upper school; the number of women admitted may not exceed ten per cent of the total enrollment in each class.*

Attrition in the class, severe after the first year, was surprisingly mild considering the times. Seven out of thirty-six in our entering class did not return after their first year, and another three dropped out after their second year. The remaining twenty-six continued on to graduate in a class augmented by transfers and returning short-term dropouts for a year or two, so that the class at graduation (39) was larger than the class when it entered (36).

Penn in the mid thirties was a firmly committed Beaux-Arts architectural school and had been for many years. Its connection with the Ecole des Beaux-Arts was deliberate and of long standing; the school's first head, Warren Powers Laird, had been at work in a Paris atelier when he was asked to take over in 1890. Professor Laird in turn was responsible for bringing Paul Phillipe Cret to the school in 1903. In the mid thirties the majority of the Professors of Design had studied at the Ecole des Beaux-Arts; in the academic year 1934-35 all of the full Professors of Design— Cret, Bickley, Sternfeld, and Dengler—were either architects *diplômé par le gouvernement* or, in the case of Sternfeld, Paris prize winners. In addition Professor Koyl, the dean, was the Rome prize winner for 1911 and Professor Gay, the Professor of Architectural Construction, had been at the Ecole in Cret's old Atelier Pascal. It is not unreasonable, then, to conclude that the Beaux-Arts scheme at Penn was authentic.

Pennsylvania was an affiliate of the Beaux-Arts Institute of Design in New York (later the National Institute of Architectural Education). Along with architectural schools, independent ateliers, and architectural

* *University of Pennsylvania Bulletin, School of Fine Arts Announcement* 1934-1935, pp. 21-22. It would be interesting to know why this was the policy of the school and whether the school seriously thought that it might ever have more than 10 per cent women. Given the general attitudes of the time, as reviewed in the following chapter, it would seem unlikely. In any case it is an issue worth looking into; and any inquiry might usefully go beyond architecture and look into the schools of law, medicine, and business.

clubs all around the country, Pennsylvania used the Institute's architectural programs and the judgment system for architectural design in grades A and B (fifth and fourth years), for archaeology projects required in the architectural curriculum, and for interior design, required both for architecture and the Department of Interior Decoration.

I have referred to "the school." This is how we as students referred to it and I continue to think of it that way, but this is not precisely correct. Architecture was a department in the School of Fine Arts which also included landscape architecture, music, interior decoration, painting and sculpture, mural decoration, illustration, interior design, and applied design. All work, both academic and technical, in architecture, landscape architecture, music, and interior decoration was taken at the University, but technical work in painting, sculpture, mural decoration, and illustrating was taken at the Pennsylvania Academy of Fine Arts, and interior design and applied design at the Pennsylvania Museum School of Industrial Art. But the school was dominated by the Department of Architecture, in terms of numbers of faculty and students as well as resources and facilities. In the academic year 1934-35 ten of twelve professors and 68 per cent of the students were in the Department of Architecture.

Beaux-Arts structure was maintained formally and consciously both by the curriculum and by affiliation with the Beaux-Arts Institute of Design. Beaux-Arts traditions were maintained just as consciously but perhaps less formally by various means: anecdotes or fables, for instance, tossed out during criticism or at smokers and other informal functions where it was certain that at least one faculty member would reminisce about the glories of Paris or Rome.

Three currricula were offered: a special three-year course leading to a professional certificate, a five-year course leading to the degree of bachelor of architecture, and a seven-year combined course in arts and science and architecture wherein the student received his bachelor's degree from the college after his fourth year and his bachelor of architecture degree after his seventh. In spite of the hard times there were very few students in the special program when I was at Penn, and probably because of the hard times none in the seven-year program. There was in addition a graduate course of one year for the holder of a bachelor's degree in architecture, leading to a master's degree. Three options were offered in the graduate program: architectural design, drawing, research in the history of architecture or landscape architecture, or professional practice; architectural history and criticism ("intended for those who desire preparation for re-

search, teaching or criticism in the field of architecture"—*Bulletin,* 1934-
35, p. 31); and architectural construction.

The description of the program in architecture was straightforward and
factual and entirely consistent with the way the faculty thought and
worked.

Architecture is an art and a profession: its practice requires a background
of general cultural knowledge and a nice balance of artistic and practical
ability. The student of architecture must have latent talent, and be willing
to work hard and faithfully to acquire proper training. . . .
Modern problems to be successful must have modern solutions; the proper
approach to modern solutions is through a study of the solutions of the past.
Good design—good proportion and composition—are the growth of past ages
of art. The architect must properly relate the elements required in the solution of a problem; he must choose materials for permanence as well as for
beauty; he must understand mechanical installations; he must administer the
disbursement of funds and supervise the work of the various trades; and
withal, he must care for the best interest of the client whose affairs are in his
trust [*Bulletin,* p. 20].

If anyone had any doubt that what was intended was a straightforward,
strictly professional program, the catalogue went on to describe the
curricula:

To prepare for such practice, the courses in architecture are intended to
provide the fundamentals of architecture; to so present architecture to the student that he will become inspired to distinctive achievement; to teach the student to think for himself; to develop initiative and a sense of responsibility; to
show the student how to solve a problem. From the needs outlined above, have
developed the curricula of cultural or academic subjects, and a modicum of
physical education to safeguard the health of students apt to overwork. The
technical studies, while taught in the several groups of design, construction,
drawing and rendering, and history, being nevertheless interrelated parts of the
single subject, are taught with that singleness of purpose in mind. Draughting is
needed in all of them. Study of elementary architectural forms is concerned with
elementary construction. Construction is the basis of architectural designs and
gives the foundation on which design can be taught . . . [*Bulletin,* pp. 20-21].

And again the catalogue meant just what it said. It described a carefully
coordinated and integrated program with all parts tied together supporting the design courses which dominated the curriculum.

Such flexibility as was offered still demanded coordination and integration: "Progress in those courses in which individual criticism is given in
the atelier or studio (design, freehand, water color) may be as rapid as
the student's talent permits, provided the advance is equal in these several

fields" (*Bulletin*, p. 21). Thus one could not advance in one subject out of step with the rest of the program. Any advance had to be across a fairly broad front.

Professor Laird had been succeeded as Dean in 1931 by George Simpson Koyl. He was a short, wiry man with white hair and a great white moustache, crisp, energetic, formal, and slightly pedantic. But he meant what he said and he said things in a refreshingly simple, unadorned manner. Shortly after he became Dean the architectural alumni society at Penn published a "Book of the School" in 1934. To this Dean Koyl contributed an article entitled "The Policy of the School," in which he set forth the following objectives:

The first objective of a policy is the maintenance of a "superlative technical school"; in other words "quality before quantity" . . . the school is the "gate" to the profession, and we are responsible to it for the type of men we graduate.

The second objective is the maintenance of an "inspired teaching staff." Education is largely self-education through individual effort under guidance; but the school is morally responsible for the type of instruction it offers. . . . The student's natural aptitude and attitude of inquiry must be satisfied by teachers who are themselves students, constant in their research for old truths and new developments, alive to the progress of civilization, and forceful in the presentation of information. . . .

The third objective is the maintenance of a "completely rounded curriculum." We must continue to provide a broad background of selected cultural subjects and a complement of up-to-date technical courses. . . .

The fourth objective is "coordination of instruction." . . . the conception of architecture must be as a unity.

The fifth item of policy is the "stressing of fundamentals." To understand form in light is fundamental and is achieved by training the mind through the eye to perceive. Perception is the basis for knowledge, and through knowledge and will is creation possible . . . [*Book of the School*, pp. 5-6].

With much of this we would agree today: the notions of technical excellence, the stressing of fundamentals, and a broadly rounded curriculum all fit present objectives. The concept that "education is largely self-education" and that teachers are "themselves students" is also fairly generally popular today. Some schools would certainly agree with the expressed relationships and responsibility to the profession, although at Berkeley, which I know best, the responsibility of the school would not be so narrowly defined but would be seen as an extremely broad social commitment. Our current view of what fundamentals are would probably be different, though we would not argue with the idea of stressing fundamentals. Again, we would agree with the "completely rounded curriculum," but there would be vast differences of opinion as to what constitutes roundedness. Coordination of instruction we might not even understand. One of the most highly developed aspects of architectural education before the Second War was the degree to which all course work, both academic and technical, was coordinated to support the studio effort in design. The program was essentially single-minded, focused, and continuous. It was hard-boiled and demanding, frankly a matter of training in a well-established way of doing things. As John F. Harbeson put it, "The purpose of [the Beaux-Arts] training is to impart to each student a method of attacking and studying any problem in architectural design which may be presented" (*The Study of Architectural Design*, p. 9).

Training in established skills, indoctrination into an established profession, and the development of an understanding of commonly held architectural perceptions were explicit formal tasks for the staff; less formal and less explicit was the task of introducing us to a broadly cultured intellectual life. The Ecole in Paris had developed an operating pattern that became, as we saw in Chapter 8, the accepted mode for the Beaux-Arts system in the United States. Walter Cook, in the *Architectural Record* for January 1901, listed the best features of the system as follows: "1st. The division into ateliers. 2d. The tradition of the older pupils helping the younger. 3d. The teaching of design by practising architects [and, we might add here, the judgment of the competition by a trained jury of practicing architects]. 4th. The beginning of the study of design as soon as the student enters the atelier. 5th. The system of the 'esquisse.'" In this country the Beaux-Arts Institute of Design became the administrative body, managing the writing of programs and the conducting of judgments in New York. The schools of architecture were then affiliated with the BAID, as were numerous architectural clubs and private ateliers.

"The tradition of the older pupils helping the younger" was highly formalized, and known then as "niggering." As soon as one was able to show any competence at all in drawing or lettering or running a decent wash, the lower classman sought work with a member of the class next above. Those above had, of course, been observing the lower classmen carefully and might actively recruit a likely "nigger," just as they themselves had been recruited perhaps by the previous class. A moderately formal chain was thus formed through the classes, from the fifth-year man at the top down through to the freshman. Those below performed the tasks assigned—the lower the level the more menial and routine the tasks—while those above might act, in an informal way, as critics or instructors. As a pattern of collaboration it was not at all unlike Gropius' "team work"; he, however, had the good sense to give the system a better name.

At Penn the idea of using practicing architects as teachers was taken seriously. Professors Cret and Sternfeld had sizable practices, Professors Harbeson and Ruhnka were then in the Cret office, and Professors Bickley, Metheny, and Kirkpatrick were all active outside the school. And yet design studios were held every afternoon, generally from two to six, and the instructor was always present for the entire period. How they did it I have no idea.

One began to deal with design immediately on entering the school (I hesitate to say "began to design" because our beginning was largely copying); there was an overriding belief that one had to begin to learn drawing and designing very early on. This broadly accepted point of view was set forth by Leicester B. Holland in an essay, "The Cultural Influence of the Study of Architecture," in *The Book of the School:*

> Not long ago I heard a very eminent professor of Fine Arts, who was not an architect, comment with great approval on the tendency to precede architectural studies by four years of academic work. If he had been talking to me instead of to others, I should have taken issue with him, and perhaps—for he is very intelligent—I could have convinced him that he had the cart before the horse. My argument would have run like this. Four years of college is undoubtedly good, if one has the time and money for it, but the actual studies that one pursues there are of superficial value only, except where they lead directly to postgraduate work and a continuing life of study. . . . The architectural student learns what the academic undergraduate should learn but rarely does, for his is truly a creative education. If the four-year academic course could *follow* that in architecture it would be fine indeed, for the architectural graduate has usually acquired an uncommon capacity for it (pp. 25-26).

The five-year program began with a two-year lower school, on completion of which one took an examination for admission to the upper school. In the lower school "the student is given a course that combines essentials of a liberal education and a technical test in architectural studies that will indicate to the faculty, and to the student, whether he should be chosen for advancement to the professional course in architecture, or be directed to such other course as may be better fitted to his needs and capabilities" (*Bulletin,* 1934-35, p. 22).

What was meant by "essentials of a liberal education" was embarrassingly narrow: English (composition and literature); French (reading, grammar, and composition); mathematics; and one year of history. I am certain that the faculty, particularly the studio faculty who taught the drawing and water color courses, were keenly aware of the meager fare in the humanities. All of the faculty urged us to read widely, to visit the museums and galleries, to attend the symphony, the opera, and the ballet regularly. Their urgings worked and we all did. Were it not for this the school could have become a technical-professional wasteland. But happily it didn't.

The examination for entrance into the upper school was held three times a year and was in design and freehand drawing. The exam could be bypassed and early advancement was possible, at faculty discretion. Although the examination was apparently routine, it was an examination and it was serious and people sometimes didn't make it and were told so. I was one of those who advanced early, going into grade C (third-year design) for the last problem of my second year; thus I did not actually have the experience of the examination.

The first year began with an extraordinarily intense program in drawing: freehand drawing in the studio, a large barn-like wooden structure about three blocks from the school, between the dormitories and the medical school, and architectural drawing and mechanical drawing in a ground-floor drafting room of the School of Fine Arts building. The more technical courses, descriptive geometry, shades and shadows, and perspective were taught by Philip Whitney, Professor of Graphics, and George Baumeister, then an instructor in graphics. We worked at first in pencil on yellow detail paper, beginning very much at the beginning, learning how to sharpen pencils (there was nothing available except wooden pencils that had to be sharpened with a knife in those days), learning to control lines, what kind of eraser to use for what purpose, how to keep a sheet clean by masking or tacking down strips of paper to keep the instruments riding somewhat above the surface, how to rotate the pencil along the triangle and T-square and how to get the correct angle to keep the edge of the instrument clean by preventing the grinding off of lead dust in the line drawing process, and on and on.

There was very little of drawing lines just to learn how to draw lines; one learned how to draw lines while learning orthographic projection, the usual revolutions, intersections, developments of planes and solids, and outs or problem sets, the problems being set out for us on the chalk board. increasingly complex curvature. We had no text or mimeographed hand-
For some, who had had no drawing before, the course was difficult. I

had had mechanical drawing in high school, as well as various shop courses including sheet-metal work, which gives one a real feeling for what's going on in orthographic projection. I was lucky then in being able to concentrate on going as far as I could with the more difficult problems.

John Harbeson taught the architectural drawing course, which began with pencil drawing (this time on *white* paper) and freehand lettering. Lettering exercises were continuous—simple exercises based on the rather elementary study of letter forms, more involved exercises studying inscriptional lettering, drawn mechanically; first just the line structure, later with shadows cast when we had learned something more about controlling washes. The text used was Vignola, the drawing at first being of simple moldings, then more complex assemblies of moldings. We were encouraged to be discriminating about the forms of various moldings, their appropriateness for particular uses, the relationship of particular moldings to particular qualities of light and their weathering characteristics, and we were introduced to the concept of scale, which then was a complete mystery to me and is today only slightly less so. We learned how to use the various instruments, and toward the end of the semester were working almost completely in ink drawing with the spring-type ruling pen.

Learning to run washes began with sepia. We had to learn about papers and how to stretch paper before that. After developing a modest control of sepia washes we graduated to india ink, learning how to grind the ink in a slate mortar and then, sometimes after hours of grinding, to filter it through a wick. Here began conceptions of the perfect ink stick; the ideal appeared to be warmish black which when diluted had a clarity to it that the colder blacks never seemed to have. And probably at this time began all sorts of preferences for proprietary materials. Whatman's was the only water color or ink wash paper, Winsor and Newton were the only water colors, and Castell the only acceptable pencil. But the ink sticks were a mystery, the labels being in Chinese.

While all this was going on in the building (it never had any other name or at least no other name that was ever used, perhaps because it had started life as a dental school), related work but of a different character was going on in the studio—charcoal drawing on white charcoal paper (Strathmore, of course), about 18 by 24 inches. For many of us it was our first experience of working at an easel with the drawing nearly vertical before us. We began merely learning how to control charcoal, to control lines and tones, to use a chamois or a smooth stick, an art gum or a kneaded eraser.

The first objects to be drawn were the usual pile of white painted wooden cubes, pyramids, and spheres that used to fill up most drawing studios. From these we went on to architectural forms, drawing from plaster casts of moldings, ornaments, and of course an infinite number of acanthus leaves.

In addition to the professional subjects we had fourteen semester credits in English, French, mathematics, and history. The English was composition, the French was reading and grammar (we were assumed to have had two years of high school French), and the mathematics was analytical geometry and elementary calculus. History was a large survey course in the history of civilization, which was taken to be Western civilization. All of the academic subjects were taught in the College, but there were special sections for architects, and wherever possible architectural relationships were developed.

Essentially the same subjects, both professional and academic, continued in the second semester. Descriptive geometry went on into shades and shadows and perspective, supplemented by pencil drawings, on yellow detail paper, of full-size wooden mill-work details. Curiously this detail work was the one thing we did that was never drawn into the design education and never capitalized on. It couldn't be, of course, because we never designed anything in a material as ordinary as wood. The assumed material for our first design work in the second year was always marble. After that we got down to brick, concrete, and steel. But never wood, except perhaps in a sketch problem.

The freehand drawing courses continued in charcoal, and our instructors were Colarossi, a graduate of the Pennsylvania Academy, a lively witty man with an almost cockney accent; Josef Gerson, a professional drawing teacher, not an architect; and Jim House, who was also a sculptor and a caricaturist for the Philadelphia and New York papers. I recall work in the studio as always being pleasant and relaxing, in part probably because of the relaxed and witty attitude of our drawing critics. Their criticisms were not mere criticisms in techniques of drawing but were packed with discussion of philosophical or ethical issues, or talk about books or about history or the theatre. I had the feeling that right from the start our drawing and painting critics were trying to expand our point of view and liberate us from what they perhaps regarded as a too-narrow technical existence in the design courses. The studio was a curiously separate world. The studio instructors, while enormously influential, never, that I can recall, participated in criticism of our design work or in any of the juries of that work. On the other hand, they were of enormous value in giving us another sounding board for a different approach to design or a different perspective on structure or form. Jim House, who also taught the later courses in modeling, was particularly helpful and stimulating, full of ideas and questions which, as time went on, became increasingly relevant.

Our studies in "the elements of architecture" continued in the spring semester under John Harbeson. He was a particularly engaging man, with a real sense of the student's point of view, always bright, friendly and positive in his teaching but blunt, quick and unmistakably clear.

By spring we had developed enough skill with drawing techniques to be able to concentrate more on what it was we were drawing, and we launched into a study of the elements of architecture, which in the Beaux-Arts system meant walls, porticos, arcades, doorways, windows, cornices, balustrades. Dealing with these elements required the use of one of the five Orders. These we studied, first from Vignola, later from the classic documents—d'Espouy, Gromort, Letarouilly, and others. Thus began what became a routine, certainly for the first few years, of long hours of study and search in the library.

From the very beginning of the academic year informal evening gatherings, called smokers, were held for the school, a large purpose of which was to introduce the incoming student to the traditions of the school and thus attempt to perpetuate those traditions. The great prizes and scholarships—the Paris prize (Figure 59), Rome prize, the Stewardson Fellowship —assumed to be the goal of all of us, were described in detail. We were urged not only to work harder at our professional and academic courses but also to spend more time outside the school, to become familiar with all the cultural institutions the community offered, and also to participate in such campus activities as campus politics or intercollegiate athletics. Some of this urging rubbed off successfully; we became habitués of the topmost balcony of the Academy of Music and such art galleries as existed in Philadelphia.

As freshmen, however, we were still not considered full citizens of the school. We were relegated to the basement drafting room and only began to venture into the upper levels of the building toward the end of the spring term. Freshmen were not allowed to wear smocks until they had fought the sophomore class for the privilege. If they could succeed in removing the smock from the sophomore "smock man" in a muddy, aimless, and harmless battle, they were then privileged to wear what I gather was the traditional blue smock. How these fights were scheduled and organized and who it was that was in charge of saying "on such and such a day such and such a fight will take place" I have no idea, but it happened and we won the privilege. I can't remember whether anybody went out and bought smocks or not. But I do recall that by then we had won some recognition so that we could enter the upper-floor drafting room to begin our apprenticeship to fellow students in the classes above.

The drafting room was a great hall with a very high ceiling, perhaps twenty-two feet (Figure 60). It was largely glass on the long north wall and on the two end walls facing east and west. Two great semi-circular bays, the province of seniors and graduate students, projected out from the north wall. Artificial light was provided by an incredible array of hanging lamps with green conical shades suspended from a vast array of wires that made the room look like a hops field. This would be our home and the center of our academic and social life for the next four years.

Most of us sought work in the summer of 1933, but I doubt that it occurred to any of us to look for work in an architect's office; there simply was none. Roosevelt had been inaugurated; the bank holiday had come and gone; bread lines, apple men, and Hoovervilles still abounded. In the second year the course work became increasingly professional. In the first year twenty-two semester credits had been in academic subjects, out of forty-four for both terms. In the second year academic subjects were down to ten credits out of forty-eight. This increasing dominance of the professional subjects was to continue, and as time went on the professional subjects would in turn be dominated by design, which in the second year took sixteen, or a third, of the forty-eight credits and in the fifth year thirty-two, or more than two-thirds, of fifty credits. But the actual time spent and the physical and emotional and intellectual concentration must have amounted to at least half of our total effort; it was even more if one counted the time spent working for upperclassmen, for we were now committed to this routine. By contrast, a student in architecture at Berkeley would rarely have more than fifteen credits in design out of about forty-two to fifty-five, and in some years he might have *no* credits in design. Architecture I, or Grade D in the BAID system, is described succinctly in the Announcement of the school as "order problems." The full course description elsewhere in the same Announcement read: "*Design*—Grade D. Problems in elementary design involving the use of the elements." What we did were called *analytiques*. It was customary to begin with a simple, relatively "flat" problem (in our case it was a large, monumental, entrance to a courtyard), then to design building parts of greater depth

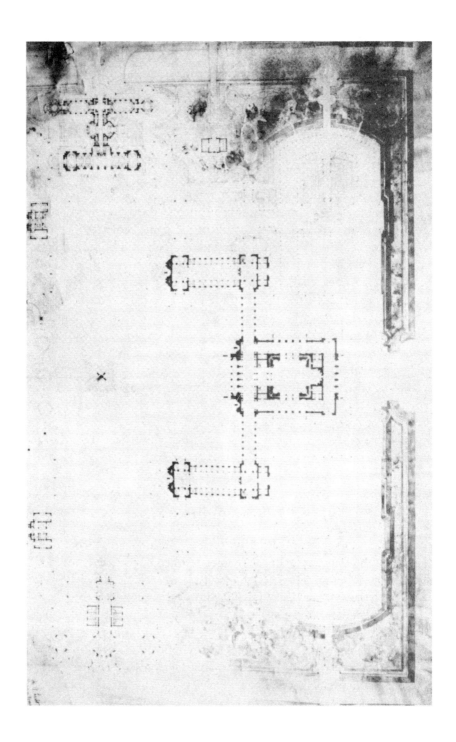

Figure 59. Winning design of the first Paris Prize, 1904. The Paris Prize was awarded to the winner of an extended competition conducted first by the Society of Beaux-Arts Architects and then by the Beaux-Arts Institute of Design. In addition to a stipend sufficient to cover the cost of up to two and a half years' residence in Paris, the winner was admitted without examination to the First Class at the Ecole des Beaux-Arts.

The project, by George A. Licht, is characteristic, both in its general form and in its manner of presentation, of Beaux-Art design, which lasted into the 1940s. The program, in its skeletal form and open suggestiveness, leaving nearly all functional interpretations to the competitor (and, it must be noted, equally to the jury) was also characteristic. The program is so brief that it is worth quoting in full.

"A COLONIAL INSTITUTE" Program by E. L. Masqueray

To be located in Washington, on a lot 800' x 1200' with streets all around, and the long exposure to the north and south. Graduated students of Colonial College would meet there prominent men of this country during their postgraduate course, and would get familiar with the institutions and characteristics of the country. At the same time, people of the United States would get acquainted with the representative people of the tropical dependencies, understand them, and by that mutual acquaintance develop feelings of esteem and friendship so necessary to harmonious and progressive relations.

This institute would consist of three distinct groups of buildings, not necessarily disconnected.

1st—*The Administration*. Residence for President and family. Lodging for two Secretaries. Residence should be large and afford ample room for the accommodation of a few invited guests. The office building should consist of rooms for Secretaries' offices, Information Bureau, Record Rooms, Janitor, one Committee Room, etc.

2nd—*Library-Museum*. Large library room, beautifully decorated; four private studies; two galleries (rooms) to show, in elaborated glass cases, minerals, precious stones, resources of Colonial countries, the walls decorated with tropical views. One large lecture room, seating 1200, to be used also for graduating exercises, etc. Small dressing room for lecturer.

All this part of the Institute to be treated monumentally and so arranged that it could be thrown into one on important occasions.

3rd—*Botanical Garden,* where would be shown plants of the United States, which could be introduced in the Colonies, and large green-houses where tropical plants could be kept and studied. Small aquarium in them for the study of fish. Six class rooms of studies adjoining. The garden does not necessarily need to be a motif by itself. It could be arranged as a setting to the buildings of the institution.

The arrangement of stories, one or several in each part of the institute, is left to the judgment of the competitors. Toilet rooms should be provided where needed. In some prominent location, court or garden, a monument or fountain to "Civilization bringing peace to uncivilized countries" will be located.

For the esquisse give a general plan at 1/64" scale. Facade and Section at the same scale. The esquisse must be done in ink.

For the finished drawings give two plans at 1st and 2nd floors, one main facade, one side facade, and one longitudinal section, all at 1/16' scale; and a detail of the facade at ½" scale to make a drawing about 3' x 4'.

Interesting details to be noted in the design are the almost complete absence of any labels, the designer depending on form and the character of poché to identify spaces or buildings. Note, for example, the two buildings in the lower corners of the drawing, almost identical in plan form, the one on the left implicitly the "Residence for President and family," that on the right, the greenhouses of the "Botanical Garden."

Figure 60. The "Great Drafting Room" at the School of Fine Arts at the University of Pennsylvania in the 1920s. By the 1930s an elaborate grid of wires supported an even more elaborate system of individual cone-shaped metal fixtures for the illumination of the individual drafting tables. Also added were old drafting boards arranged to form cubicles enclosing individual or small groups of desks, used as pin-up boards, as support for shelves, and to give isolation and privacy. The building of the little "loges" was the prerogative only of upperclassmen.

(a monumental portico), then an interior (a large monumental niche with a sarcophagus as the central feature). The final problems were more complete buildings—e.g., a pavilion in a park. The final problem I did not take because I was advanced to Grade C in the spring of my sophomore year. But in any case the idea was to proceed from relatively simple, uncomplicated problems that could be conceived of mostly in a straight elevation, through parts of buildings of greater complexity and greater volume, until the final projects, which were small, more or less complete buildings.

The *analytique* as a teaching device was, at its best, rich, complex, and composed of a wide range of interlocking objectives. Emphasis could be placed in a variety of ways, but generally the problem was one of the assembly of elements, usually specified, sometimes limited (the walls, doorways, windows, cornices, balustrades, etc., we have spoken of above) in some orderly and pleasing fashion—in short a study in composition. Proportion was important, as was scale. Good proportions were generally those similar to the accepted great monuments; scale was always more vaguely defined and was generally taken to be something beyond mere technical feasibility or reasonableness, that is, beyond the sizes determined by the limitations of materials or methods of building or by convenient operation.

To assemble the elements for one's design meant searching through the library for appropriate examples in books or in a large collection of mounted photographs—"documents," they were called. And one was required to have a document for everything one proposed. If it hadn't been done before it couldn't be done now, at least in a Grade D *analytique*, and that was that. Generally it was not considered appropriate simply to copy a single example; it was expected that we would assemble parts from many different examples, thus increasing our "vocabulary," our perception, and our sense of appropriateness, because it was clear that the assembled objects had to go together in a consistent and coherent whole. One learned to see and read, as it were, subtleties of different moldings and ornaments and capitals, and to group various forms by a variety of different systems of compatibility. As I noted above, we began by learning to deal with more or less flat pieces of building and went on to design more completely in the round. While elevation and profile studies dominated throughout, they were far more important in the early stages than in the later ones, where plan and section became increasingly important in studies of space and volume. But we were not only designing buildings, we were also composing a sheet, making a drawing, an *analytique*, which required additionally the disassembly of the general elements of the building and their arrangement on the sheet in a way that explained the whole even more clearly. These elements would be at much larger scale than the drawing of the building itself and would be put together as so many fragments, usually to form a frame through which one looked to see the building itself beyond.

Our first studies were usually done with pencil and tracing paper and concentrated on the building itself. John Harbeson was my principal critic, but I also had extensive criticism from Roy Ruhnka, who was credited (by the students at least) with a great deal of the design of Cret's Folger Shakespeare Library building, and from Don Kirkpatrick, Paris prize winner in 1913. Criticisms were drawn more than talked, particularly by Ruhnka, who barely said a word as he worked over our crude designs. We met in the drafting room every afternoon. Daily criticism was more or less the rule; in a week there would usually be three crits of about an hour each and two shorter ones. To keep up with this pace, that is, just to carry out the work that the critic had laid out, to advance it and refine it to a level where another criticism was warranted, was demanding and meant that all one's spare time was spent in the drafting room.

The drawn criticism was of course freehand, usually with a grease pencil or sometimes with a conté crayon. I have not seen one of these pencils for years—they were short and fat with a black wooden handle, a metal holder for the lead, which was about one-quarter inch in diameter, and a softness somewhere around an HB or a B, something like an Eagle drafting pencil on a cool day. While Harbeson, Ruhnka, and Kirkpatrick could all draw with extraordinary skill, the grease-pencil sketches were still sketches, and it was up to us immediately to take these freehand drawings and harden them up with triangle and T-square. It was rarely our privilege to sketch or do freehand work until we got to the first layouts of the overall sheet composition. Assuming the project would run five weeks, about two weeks before the end we would begin the layout for the final sheet. The sheet size would have been specified, and we would already have studied the elements we were going to use to frame the central design at a fairly large scale—depending on the size of the building, anywhere from ¾ of an inch to 1½ inches to a foot. Sheet composition studies were always in charcoal on tracing paper, usually fairly loosely drawn but with relative values laid in, probably using chalk for the whites at the end of the study. We would be given the same rigorous drawn criticism on the sheet composition as we had had on the building itself.

Some time during this period we would have prepared a board (they were provided by the school) and laid a stretch of a relatively smooth water-color paper. Stretches were always pasted down, the new stapling gun being rare and expensive. It was not a complicated process, but it was filled with subtle variables. A loose stretch would wrinkle too easily with successive washes, or might even wrinkle on a damp day; one too tight might warp the board out of shape or split. Even the process of cutting the stretch off the board when the drawing was finished was not easy and if not done correctly could lead to a tear across the field of the drawing.

From then on it was a matter of drawing furiously over long hours to finish. The various parts of the drawing, the building itself, and the fragments of the building forming the frame of the *analytique* would all have been drawn carefully with about an HB or an F pencil on tracing paper and then reversed and transferred to the final sheet by rubbing. An old silver dollar with nicely rounded edges was a treasure for this purpose, if one could keep it. Otherwise a spoon sufficed. The pencil drawing then had to be inked, usually in a dilute ink, and then the entire sheet carefully erased with an art gum since any grease or graphite on the sheet would make it impossible to run a decent india ink wash. The ink would have been ground, filtered, and decanted into a jar, all by a freshman if one was lucky enough to have one in service. Before one actually began rendering such things as stone joints or shadow, lines might be drawn in with a very hard pencil, but one had to be careful to keep one's hands off the sheet to avoid spoiling the wash.

The freshly ground ink, called "soup," would be cut down into various dilutions and the first large washes laid in. Since the tones were usually built up through successive dilute washes it was important to be extremely careful with the edge of any wash since successive sloppy edges would lead to a messy drawing, and above all else one sought a kind of crispness in detail and luminescence in the wash. Most washes were flat; only details were rendered with graded washes. A good quality paper would take an enormous amount of sponging off of unsatisfactory work, but one had to be extremely careful about erasers, especially if the paper was the least bit damp.

The *analytique* was the central feature of our activities for nearly a year. The entire process was demanding and time-consuming—quite uncompromising in all respects. There was no way to be suggestive or speculative. Hard and precise commitment was called for, and one was continuously pushed to set forth exactly what one intended; and if what one intended was crude or awkward, the methods of presentation exaggerated rather than covered up this crudeness. During the year I worked for, and was helped by, several upperclassmen. But my closest association was with Herb Spigel, an extremely able man with whom I was later to work in George Howe's office—and who would have become one of the country's great architects had he lived beyond his early thirties.

Our academic subjects were now down to English and French-for-Architects, wherein we read primarily architectural documents and wrote about architectural matters. Ten credits for the entire year; not much. Some of the deficiencies were made up by reading, some in museums and galleries, some in the university's evening lecture program, but it was up to us to fill in the gaps, and gap-filling has thus become for me a habit that goes on to this day.

Freehand drawing continued—charcoal drawings of increasingly rich and complex architectural ornaments and fragments, or rather of plaster casts of them in the studio. We were encouraged by our drawing instructors to keep notebooks and to draw whenever we could, particularly buildings or people or animals or trees—anything that interested us. That too became a most useful habit.

Equal in time with the drawing courses was a course in modeling—in clay—under Jim House. It was a relatively new course, brought in, I believe, because of complaints about the lack of experience and training in anything except flat two-dimensional work. We dealt mostly with architectural ornament, mostly relief, and mostly classical forms. I have the feeling that the courses were far more limiting than House would have liked, and I know that his later development of the course was more stimulating and effective. It was, like everything else, a servant course to design and was frankly modeling, not sculpture. Sculpture might have engaged me, modeling did not.

Two other courses ran through the year, one in construction, one in history. The history course was taught (in fact all the history courses were taught) by Professor Gumaer—a round, sedate, vaguely pompous man, trained as an architect but devoted to architectural history. The text was Banister Fletcher, and the methods followed appropriately. History was only Western European history, with enough of the Middle East and Egypt thrown in to form the basis for a mild understanding of Greek architecture. Middle Eastern architecture was there, but the idea was conveyed to us somehow that it was less worthy. Broader social and cultural issues standing behind particular architectural developments were touched on in Professor Gumaer's lectures, I must say more so than in Banister Fletcher, but it was a relatively light touch. A feature of the method was to require careful drawings, one each week, of major historical buildings. The drawings were usually pencil or ink, freehand, and could be traced. By the end of the year we had drawn some thirty or forty monuments.

The construction courses were taught by Harry Parker, with an occasional lecture by Professor Gay. Both men knew building construction extremely well; Professor Gay in particular was an expert in traditional eastern seaboard construction methods. But the first year in construction was mostly Professor Parker's, and he used his own text—*Simplified Engineering for Architects,* which has come to be widely known as "Oversimplified Engineering." His aim, like that of so many teachers of architectural construction, was to knock a bit of engineering into the heads of the distinctly mixed bag in front of him. Although he directed his instruction at those who were weakest in mathematics or physical concepts, he was still available for serious questions about more complex problems, and he did know the subject well. The intention was that the courses in construction would support the courses in design, but they were so elementary and so remote that it simply didn't work. It could only have been made interesting by trying to go quite far beyond the scope of the course; and this, under the circumstances, Professor Parker barely had time to do.

In the spring of my second year I was advanced, early, from Grade D to Grade C. My first critic was James Metheny, a patient and gentle man and an excellent and careful critic. The change was dramatic. We were no longer required to produce a Classic document (that is, a document of any western architectural monument from ancient Greece to the Renaissance, but no later), color was permitted in rendering, and we were designing buildings one could imagine someone using rather than just looking at.

In prior years Grades C and D had had programs prepared by the BAID; but the costs of administering such a vast program had been too great. The BAID was cut down to Grades A and B, and the various schools and ateliers wrote their own programs. But we followed the system and were introduced to the disciplines of the *esquisse*, wherein the student was required, in nine hours of working alone, to produce a small-scale sketch of his proposed scheme which he could not change during the subsequent development of his design.

About a week before a program was to be issued the title alone would be announced, and we would then spend as much time as we could in the library in search of any information related to the subject at hand. This usually meant looking up examples of buildings of a particular type that had actually been built or were projected. At that time there was, in the journals, relatively little analytical work and virtually no research on building types or functions. We would make notes, usually small plan sketches showing the typical schemes that had been used, and we would try to separate these schemes into type-groups and somehow see the broad schematic alternatives that were available. While we never received criticism during an *esquisse*—it was usually a nine-hour continuous process and it was usually "en loge," with the use of documents forbidden—we were given instruction in how to go about taking the *esquisse*.

The rules were simple. First read and reread the program, analyze it, and perhaps break it apart and rewrite it, but at least take some steps to set forth its various categories and criteria, which you could then organize in some useful way. A major problem to be solved early on was that of finding out precisely what *kind* of problem you were working on—that is, a plan problem, a circulation problem, a site plan problem, or an interior problem. If it was a site plan problem this would be immediately evident, probably just a matter of distributing buildings or building blocks around the site according to some logic or system. If it was an interior problem this would be indicated by a relaxation of the requirements for exterior elevations. But to sort out whether it was a plan problem or a circulation problem, or to determine which was dominant, was not always so easy. A plan problem would be characterized by that kind of building where the issue was one of arranging large elements in some orderly relationship to one another (a house, a kindergarten, a church), while a circulation problem would emphasize the paths between these spaces (a factory or shipyard, a railway station, a bus depot). Initially we worried simply about what the writer of the program had in mind, but later on, to a large extent because the system was so competitive, we had to try to guess not only what the writer had in mind but how the jury looking at our work would interpret what the writer had in mind. The residue of such second-guessing persists to this day in most competitions.

Having made some preliminary decisions about the program, we would then begin to draw, at some convenient very small scale, rough schematic plans, concentrating on the idea of developing as many distinct alternatives as possible. These then should, we were told, be studied and compared as to the ways in which they satisfied the program. We might possibly rate them but we would certainly group them into types. We should then devise some orderly scheme for eliminating some of the less likely notions and try to reduce the alternatives to three. These should then be refined as much as one had time for, thumbnail elevations and sections drawn, and every effort made to find impossible and unworkable parts, since whatever we produced at the end of the nine hours we would be stuck with for the next four or five weeks. When a final decision was made it was drawn, in ink, on an 8½-by-11 sheet of tracing paper and turned in. On Monday we were given a print back, but the sheet was retained to be sent forward with our final drawing to the judgment. If the jury felt that the completed project differed significantly (and it was at the jury's discretion to determine what was significant) the project would be declared "hors de concours"; an HC would be crayoned on the drawing, and the jury would then consider it no further.

Harbeson saw the value of the *esquisse* system as mental discipline: "in working on a problem on which one is tied down to an esquisse is as strong and as persistent a corrective as there can be against vague and loose thinking"; and "one of the chief objects of the Beaux-Arts method is to teach a man to confine his efforts to a well defined channel." He also saw it as being representative of a real-life situation: "In actual practice architectural problems are circumscribed by definite conditions, limitations of cost, peculiarities of site or of the client, etc. The esquisse takes the place of these limitations in the classroom" (*The Study of Architectural Design*, p. 8). Cret too saw the *esquisse* as discipline and a means of forcing developmental study.

". . . I found [the *esquisse*] valuable for three reasons, (1) a pupil who begins a problem without a preliminary sketch will spend three-fourths of the time allowed on the problem experimenting on different schemes without ever really studying one; this is missing the aim of school competition which is not to arrive at the best solution of any particular problem, but to learn how to study any problem. (2) In trying to improve a poor scheme, the pupil makes a greater effort than he would if you gave him from the beginning the right solution. (3) The pupils working together and not obliged to keep to their preliminary sketches, arrive after a time all to have the same scheme, which is either that of the most brilliant pupil among them, or the one that the Instructor has pointed out as the best solution. Thus they lose one of the most valuable benefits of the school study, which is to see the different solutions possible under the same program" [T. B. White, ed., *Paul Philippe Cret: Architect and Teacher* (Philadelphia, 1973), p. 27].

The *esquisse* system was difficult, and we (certainly I) rarely produced the number of alternative solutions we were enjoined to produce. But we did practice taking *esquisses*; we looked up old programs in the BAID *Journal* and tried to develop as many alternatives as we could in the shortest possible time. Beginning with Grade C we had, on a quite regular basis, usually better than one every two weeks, sketch problems—the *esquisse-esquisse*—similarly *en loge*, but requiring a completed and rendered single project on a 20 by 30 sheet. The *esquisse-esquisse* was intended to train us both in dealing with the *esquisse* proper and in developing speed in the organization of one's thinking and in presentation. There were usually twelve-hour problems; later twenty-four hours to three days.

Our critics continued to *draw* their criticism, and their crits were just as long and just as frequent. The building types for the various projects in Grade C were usually small (our first was a kindergarten), mostly simple plan or circulation problems, but occasionally a "character" or monumental problem would be thrown in, such as a chapel or a church or a memorial archway. The scale of the buildings was such that they generally ended up as load-bearing masonry-wall structures.

The Beaux-Arts idea of referring back to traditional forms was so strong that there was simply no getting away from it, but a dichotomy arose when the scale of the building became something less than monumental. The response to this was to suggest that we look back at the lesser monuments, the vernacular architecture (no one would ever have said building) of the Old World. An important difference in our use of the library was also that we were now looking for prototypes of buildings for current use in addition to acceptable historic monuments. The library at Penn subscribed to most of the American and European architectural journals, and while most of the American ones told us little about what was going on in anything other than the more accepted traditional ways, the *Architectural Forum* consistently presented what might be called a new point of view (Figure 61).

On our return to school in the fall of 1934, now as juniors, we entered a world increasingly dominated by design and the drafting room culture. Although the drafting room was clearly the center, the library was important both for documents and for the large architectural literature. We were urged to read Guadet (some of Guadet's writing had been introduced in the French-for-Architects course), and we began to read Le Corbusier and Sullivan and Wright on our own.

Our other courses seemed now to have more immediate relevance. Professor Gay's course in construction methods (using Gay's own text, *Materials and Methods of Construction*) was particularly useful because it dealt with structures and materials that we were actually trying to use in our designs. Professor Gay taught the course in a simple, straightforward, descriptive manner, very sound, practical, perhaps more qualitative than quantitative. He was not an exciting lecturer but was such a thoroughly nice and likeable man, so intensely interested in his own subject, that one could not help but be engaged.

Our studio courses in drawing and water color also became more interesting because by now we had enough skill in drawing to begin to see and think about what the sculptor of the piece we were drawing was trying to do in the first place. It became a major element in the teaching, I'm certain quite consciously. The ideas followed through in our water color courses, and drawing or painting from nature became under Professor Dawson partly courses in botany. George Walter Dawson was a large and

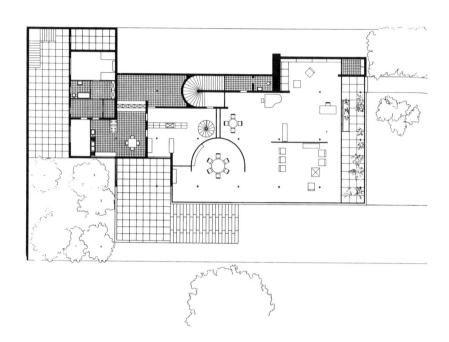

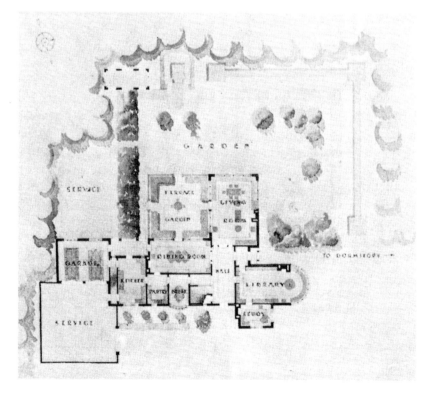

gentle man, very much a New England type; he was an excellent water colorist and one of those extraordinarily able teachers who could either explain something or demonstrate it. He was addicted to European summers, as was Professor Gumaer (who went to Ragusa each year; Professor Dawson went to Ravello). I can imagine him there to this day, an E. M. Forster–like character painting some idyllic sunlit scene. He was also addicted to the *Book of Tea* and was so persuasive about it that it was probably a standard part of the kit of every Pennsylvania architectural student of the time.

Our design courses, although now focused on buildings that could be conceived of as having real and current use, still followed Beaux-Arts criteria. Character was important—not just the character of the façade or ornament but also the character of the plan. The manner of drawing plans was so well established, and had been for such a long time, that the drawing could indicate to the initiated such notions as hospitality or dignity or lightness or gaiety; and we were taught, in our handling of poché and the "mosaic" treatment of plans, to express such ideas. That such notions could only be inventions coming from within the system and have little relationship to any external or communicable reality didn't seem to occur to anyone. Nevertheless it was just such an insistence that contributed to the "paper" quality of Beaux-Arts architecture—and "paper architecture" became one of the dominant issues in a developing concern about the system.

On the good side, however, this intensive study of the plan as essentially a diagram of spaces was important, and I still tend to "read" a building from the plan and in my mind construct from it a conception of the spaces. Sections then become important as adjuncts to the plan diagram, and elevations are imagined directly from the plan and the section. Drawn elevations become a kind of subsidiary summary that one does for some-

Figure 61. Two approximately contemporary plans, the Tugendhat House by Ludwig Mies van der Rohe in Czechoslovakia, 1929 (above), and a Beaux-Arts Institute of Design student project, "A Residence for a College Dean," by W. J. Kreps, Carnegie Institute of Technology, 1935. Beaux-Arts planning continued to conceive of buildings as linked arrangements or sequences of separate and individually identifiable (almost independent) spaces closed by wall systems, implicitly of masonry. This approach dominated Beaux-Arts planning well into the 1940s, and although projects might be submitted reflecting the influence of an open, fluid planning scheme contained in a simply expressed, regular framing system (such as the Tugendhat House), such designs were not premiated and therefore do not appear in the *Bulletin* of the BAID.

body else and unimportant in the sense that they have already been done by the plan and the sections. (My critics will say they always thought so.) Paul Cret, to whom I am indebted as much as I am indebted to anyone for this way of conceiving a building, might have agreed. In the *Book of the School* he wrote: "A good plan is one from which may rise good rooms in a good sequence; its test, therefore, lies in the sections resulting from its lines. The sections are the diagram of the whole composition, and ought to be its source" (p. 29).

It would be unfair to imply that we were working in a kind of vacuum, protected by the shell of the Beaux-Arts. The urging to study examples of building types was serious, and we were also urged, in fact directed, not only to look at buildings of the kind we were dealing with in the design course but to talk to people who used the buildings or who worked in them. Thus if the problem was a restaurant, we were urged to observe how the restaurant worked from the patron's point of view, and to talk to the owner, the waiters, the cook, the dishwasher, and the janitor. We were to take notes, make measured drawings and sketches, and try as much as possible to be familiar with the functional and operational side of what we were doing.

Curiously, though, we were never given problems with real sites. The nature of the site, its physical characteristics and general appearance, might be described, but it was never a real site one could go to and look at and stomp around on. That the sites in the programs issued by the BAID in New York should all be hypothetical is understandable because the programs were being distributed all around the country, but such was not the case in Grade C, where the programs were written at the school and worked on only there.

We were expected to be thinking about real materials in our designs and of course to think of color—the color of materials and applied color. Consequently our presentation and the rendering of final drawings were inevitably in color. Water color was, possibly because of the time it took, less popular than tempera, and Frank Brangwin or H. van Buren Magonigle became the models. Spray guns were rare, simply because they cost more than most of us could afford; but their use was to become an increasingly popular technique. Hugh Ferriss had influence only on rendering techniques for sketch problems, and although Ernest Born's work was greatly admired, it too was more easily adapted to sketch problems. Perspective drawing was only rarely required, and models were almost unheard of.

In the spring I was again advanced early to the next grade, for the last problem. Toward the end of my year in Grade C I had become increasingly interested in a less derivative approach. I resisted the proposals of my critics to decorate my designs with applied ornament, derived or invented. At the same time the undecorated but essentially decorative work that became popular with the Century of Progress in Chicago in the summer of 1933 and its more serious and permanent counterparts like Harrison and Fouilhoux's Rockefeller Center I instinctively rejected. Howe and Lescaze's great Philadelphia Saving Fund Society Building had been finished several years earlier, and we visited it innumerable times (Figure 62). The work of Neutra was becoming better known, Schindler's work was being published, if infrequently, and we saw either in reality or in the magazines other work of Howe and Lescaze. But Le Corbusier, not only in his buildings and projects and drawings but also in his writing, became a major influence, and I and several others devoured everything we could get our hands on.

My first Grade B project was with Harry Sternfeld, probably the most demanding taskmaster in the entire school, harsh in his criticism and definite in his ideas. I argued with him for a year. But he was a wonderful man, he tolerated my arguments, and although I didn't and don't agree with his point of view, it was clear, explainable, and consistent, never arbitrary, and rarely personal. As tough as it was it was a fruitful experience.

I can never forget that first problem. It was a bridge in a park and my *esquisse* had shown a single bowstring arch (Figure 63). I had an idea of a very pure and unadorned concrete structure with even such things as the lighting built into the curb to avoid anything extraneous. I spent a great deal of time in the Towne School of Engineering opposite our building, hounding engineering professors for help and attempting to be as realistic as possible. I would produce a hard drawing and a mass of calculations which Professor Sternfeld would then suggest softening with stone facings or great abutments at the intersection of the arch and the roadway, into which were built half-round decorative lights. The next day I would respond with the same plain structure, advanced a little in detail, and he would respond with more specific drawings of the stone facing and the abutments. At the judgment of the projects in New York, Sternie had the best of it. I ended up with a half mention. Most of the premiated projects were stone-faced.

In the fourth year we continued with Professor Gay in the mechanical equipment courses, and Professor Parker took over the construction

Figure 62. The Philadelphia Saving Fund Society Building, popularly known as PSFS, by Howe and Lescaze, architects, 1932. This building, important and exciting to students, was curiously ignored as a vehicle for teaching or discussion by the regular faculty at Pennsylvania. PSFS and Wharton Esherick's work were, to those students who knew both, two enormously appealing and exciting possible directions.

courses. Professor Koyl taught the two practice courses, Professional Ethics and Practice, and Specifications. Drawing was still charcoal, this time with Paul Domville and Jim House, entirely from casts of antique figures—Roman or Renaissance sculpture. Jim House in particular was interested in anatomy and made of the course an elementary human anatomy course. It was a valuable and useful introduction to the functional derivation of form. House was good at it and not only knew what he was up to but was a first-rate teacher, a great storyteller, and an unusually stimulating man. He encouraged us to draw, not for drawing's sake but to learn about things and to learn how to see. Water color continued with Professor Dawson—still life, or architectural scenes from a great supply of mounted photographs in the studio. This I found unbelievably dull and had to get permission to go outside and try to paint real buildings or landscapes.

In the first term I managed to squeeze in the time to take a course offered in the Landscape Architecture Department on the Principles of City and Regional Planning, historically oriented to a large extent but useful in that it introduced us to the then-available literature. It was really site planning on a large scale but did give us an opportunity to study older cities from primary documents in the Pennsylvania library (I worked on eighteenth-century London).

By this time I was beginning to get a fair idea of the direction in which I wanted to go—pretty much toward Le Corbusier. But, either because I was influenced more by his writings or because I was not sufficiently adept at perceiving or copying stylistic ideas, what I did didn't *look* like Le Corbusier; certainly he would never have recognized any similarities. I was also influenced by both the ideas and the independence of my uncle, Wharton Esherick. Wharton had been teaching me things since I was about twelve, encouraging me to draw, helping me build furniture, showing me something about woodcuts and block printing. His own studio, which he had started in 1926 and added on to several times at later dates, I consider one of the greatest buildings in the country; certainly the best house (Figure 64). Wharton had only one fixed idea about architecture, and that was that the triangle and T-square should be banned. He believed in the simple direct approach, what he called the dumb way to do it. He believed that there were natural, almost organic ways of solving problems which were always better than the more sophisticated ways. A favorite question was, "How would a farmer do it?" He provided Louis Kahn with some of his better one-liners.

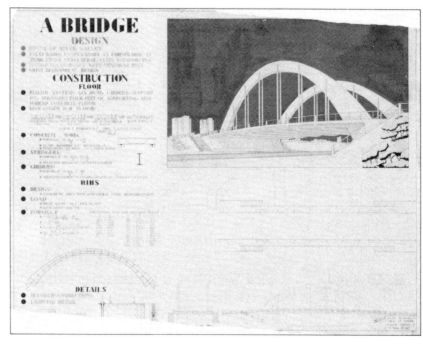

With some of these ideas both Professors Metheny and Bickley were sympathetic, but it was all too vague for Professor Sternfeld. Two of the Grade B problems, "An Artist's Summer Colony" and "The Nave End of a Church," could reasonably fit into the fuzzy mélange of ideas in my head and still be acceptable to my critics. Another, "A Canning Factory," could be made into a simplified version of a Brinkmann and van der Vlugt or Albert Kahn factory and still be acceptable to everybody. But for "A Small Public Library" I attempted to design a building on a radiating plan with the control desk at center, working out a very simple structure of round columns supporting a flat slab on a regular (but radial) framing system, then making the walls Gunite and glass-block curtain walls, all curved, going where they had to go. Absolute outrage. Grant Simon, who had won the Paris Prize in 1913 and who was a good friend of my father's, was out at our house after the judgment, in which he had participated, and he was still sputtering and fuming and the only thing he could say was "Nothing but a diagram. Not a building at all."

Although in the eyes of the school I was clearly not a good student in design (C+), I was still advanced to Grade A for the last problem in the spring. It was more of the same. That summer I drove west with a friend. We picked up a little money doing odd jobs and as much as possible visited his relatives. It was my first venture west of about Paoli. In Los Angeles we saw Neutra and Wright and Schindler buildings, in San Francisco some of Wurster's and Mike Goodman's work, and in Portland Belluschi's work for A. E. Doyle. In spite of the stimulus of the trip I seriously considered quitting school and apprenticing myself either to Wharton or to a sculptor. My father, who was an engineer and a very

Figure 63. Two designs for "A Park Bridge": above, the project of H. E. Zazzi, Atelier Gnerre, first mention; below, that of J. Esherick, University of Pennsylvania, half mention. Gerald A. Holmes, reporting to the jury, wrote: "This problem, extremely simple in its requirements, demanded for a satisfactory solution a feeling for proportion and rhythm and the wisdom to refrain from display of meretricious architectural forms and details." And went on: "The one design Placed, by H. E. Zazzi, Atelier Gnerre, besides being a well proportioned, restrained and mature piece of work, seemed to strike exactly the right note in style and presentation." Of submittals similar to and perhaps including that shown below, the jury commented: "Among the Half Mentions were many very creditable solutions, some representing considerable engineering research, which it is our duty to point out must be subservient to artistic composition and to harmony with the landscape indicated in the program." If one were generous the calculations on the left of the lower figure might be described as polemical; one less generous would describe them as cosmetic.

Figure 64. The oak stair in Wharton Esherick's studio. This remarkable building in Paoli, Pennsylvania, now a museum, needs to be better known, as does Esherick, the sculptor, cabinet-maker, and sometime architect. He and George Howe and Louis I. Kahn were friends and occasional collaborators, and his ideological influence, especially on Kahn, needs to be documented.

practical man, suggested that I finish. "A degree might be useful some day," he said.

The summer between my upper junior and senior years was the only summer I did not work. All of us worked summers if we were lucky enough, and I had been lucky. I had taught swimming at a boy's camp, day-labored ($20 for a sixty-hour week), clerked, and been a dynamiter's assistant. The only thing I did that came remotely close to architecture was drawing isometrics of utility systems going through manholes for a Philadelphia utility company. Fascinating. My first four years I had been fairly active outside the school and was accustomed to trying to fit more things in than I properly had time for. I had been on the swimming team and captain of the water polo team, chairman of the undergraduate council, president of the senior class—the most interesting part about the latter two duties being working with students of the left who were organizing against Nazi and Fascist movements and promoting support of the Lincoln Brigade. I remember that the university administration seemed uncommonly fearful of student political activity, a situation which puzzled me then as much as it does now.

I had decided to follow my father's advice and finish, but I was also determined to follow my own inclinations and work as much as I could in sculpture. Since I then conceived anatomy to be implicitly essential to sculpture, I got a job as an anatomical draftsman in the gross anatomy laboratory of the Graduate School of Medicine, working for Dr. Oscar Batson. It was unpaid, and I exchanged drawings for the opportunity to dissect and to learn from Dr. Batson. I had a couple of cadavers to tend, and I learned more about structure and the interrelationships of function and form than in any other way I can conceive. I also apprenticed myself to Jim House, who was working on a large wooden sculpture, and I worked with him on that through most of the year.

In our senior year design was more dominant than ever. Life drawing was taught two evenings a week, by House and Domville; water color again was George Walter Dawson. A large part of that work was painting objects in the university museum, a wonderful opportunity because of the vast collection of Mayan and Asian sculptures there. Tang horses and camels were extremely popular.

Professor Cret had in the past taught the course in theory, but his voice was going and it was too much for him: he died in 1945 of cancer of the throat. The course was taken over by Professors Harbeson and Gumaer and dealt seriously with conflicts of long standing between the Beaux-Arts point of view and other emerging points of view. George Howe, on many occasions a guest lecturer, was the principal representative of what could then be confidently called modern architecture. Diffident and urbane on the surface, he was a heroic, gentlemanly anti-hero. He was witty and incisive and much more deeply concerned than he seemed to want to let on. The experience for all of us was invaluable.

Otto Faelton was my critic in Grade A design. He was a designer in James Gamble Rogers' office at the time and had taught for some years at Yale. He was an extraordinarily clever man and ideal for training people to win prizes in Beaux-Arts competitions. He was flexible (he could be very flexible; it was our understanding that he had designed Davenport College at Yale, which is collegiate Gothic in stone on one street and brick and Georgian Colonial on the interior courts and another street), but he was an observant and quick critic. He was given to as much good living as one could conceive and enjoyed enormously parties with the students. I remember once being in the Dean's office (I was often there for a variety of reasons) when Faelton walked in with an enormously heavy overstuffed briefcase, which he swung up onto the Dean's desk with the announcement "Documents for the boys, Dean." After a few words he struggled off with his load, and Dean Koyl turned to me and said "Wonderful man, Mr. Faelton, wonderful man." At the end of my meeting with the Dean I went up to the drafting room, where Faelton was opening his great briefcase of documents. It was filled with Scotch.

I can think of no better way to give a feeling for the way the BAID saw the world from its Olympian heights than to list the titles of the projects and *esquisse-esquisses* given that year:

*Projects*

A Summer Hotel
A Public Garden for Refreshments and Music
A Banquet and Ballroom
A Building to Enshrine the Chalice of Antioch

*Esquisse-Esquisses*

The Decoration of a Gymnasium for a Celebration
A National School of Drama
A Pyrotechnic Display
A Ski Club
An Amusement Park

I cannot avoid the feeling that at least one of the reasons for our disenchantment lay simply in the kinds of problems we were given. It is impossible to understand now and it was difficult to understand then how anyone could, in 1937, become deeply concerned about a building to enshrine the chalice of Antioch.

I could take seriously the first Grade A project given in the fall of my fifth year—a summer hotel. I recall that I designed it as a wooden pole structure with a simple warehouse-like frame with partitions and walls, also of wood, floating around independent of the frame—Le Corbusier again. I had worked hard and seriously on the project and had managed a mention at the New York judgment, high for me. But when I saw in the BAID *Journal* the premiated designs I realized that I would never make it, and I suspect that this confirmed my pursuit of other interests.

In spite of an attitude that was no doubt seen by the school, quite fairly, as negative, I was selected as one of a very small group to do the Rome Collaborative Competition under Professor Cret. It was a team design project, teams consisting of a painter, a sculptor, a landscape architect, and an architect. Our collaborators were students from the Pennsylvania Academy. There were about five teams, and we worked separately, each in a large basement room. The problem was an art museum on an island, and I felt that solving the problem of interior lighting was central; but beyond that I saw flexibility as being important and had convinced myself that a loose, rather plastic arrangement was more suitable than a strongly axial or formal one. An obvious advantage of a more formal or symmetrical scheme would be that there would be no question as to where the sculpture and murals of my collaborating artist colleagues would go. Mr. Cret kept prodding me in this direction, unsuccessfully. His voice was fading then and it was difficult for him to speak; he therefore drew his criticisms probably more than usual, but there was no question about his intent and I understood exactly what he meant. Finally, after several weeks of his trying to persuade me and my coming back with the same plastic informal notion, he looked at me and sighed, and said, shaking his head, "Ah, Esherick," and then proceeded really to show me how to do it in the way I had been trying. It was a memorable experience.

The last year was spent trying to learn how to design in a commonsense, rational, and purposeful way. Cret's criticism, working with Jim House as an apprentice, and listening to Oscar Batson talk about anatomy and George Howe talk about architecture stand out as being of the greatest importance. But the debates and differences with the Beaux-Arts faculty were important too. The faculty was demanding and we were made to work hard; and when they argued they argued from a clear, well-defined point of view with no vagueness or mushiness about it. What now seems to me most central was that design was at the heart, that one learned design by designing, and that one had to start early. "We learn through our own mistakes much more than through the best advice of others. C'est en forgeant qu'on devient forgeron," Cret wrote in the *Book of the School*. Further, there was a belief that architecture was a fine art, and the faculty was uneasy about any other connections. Cret, again in the *Book of the School*, wrote:

All education in Fine Arts (and it is not out of place here to reaffirm one's belief that architecture is primarily a fine art, and not a branch of engineering, of real estate, or of a more or less hazy sociology) has for its main object the development of the artist's personality. A consequence is that such a result can be accomplished only through personal effort and not through a perusal of textbooks [p. 31].

The school at Pennsylvania had an abiding faith that its students would develop into broadly cultured men through and because of the study of design. Leicester B. Holland wrote, in the *Book of the School*, "Architecture is the most unspecialized, or rather polyspecialized of the professions. It is an art and a science, its practice demands imagination, organization, administration and diplomacy" (p. 22). He went on:

And above all, there is no academic course that gives such unremitting attention to the practice of speculative reason as does the study of Architectural Design. For the study of Design inculcates an orderly intellectual technique of investigation, apprehension, analysis, logical deduction, and imaginative synthesis, in the solution of all sorts of unfamiliar problems; it provides a repeated drill in philosophic exercise such as is not offered by any other field of study, academic or professional, in our undergraduate curricula today. . . . there is no group in our society—with the possible exception of the better grade of teachers—which, as a whole, shows such broad and enduring interest in art and science and "impractical" fields outside its professional milieu as do the architects" [pp. 23-25].

Design and designing were central, and so powerful that the architect would automatically, almost instinctively, pursue those additional studies necessary for a responsible life of community service.

Certainly similarities exist between the educational programs of the thirties and the seventies. Design, although not now given the emphasis it had in the thirties, is taught in a manner not, I suspect, quite so radically new and different as might be comforting to think. Careful analysis, the development of alternatives, the devising of criteria to select among alternatives, sometimes thought of as latter-day inventions, are cases in point. History, particularly architectural history, is acknowledged in each case. Technology—that is, engineering and building construction—were strongly emphasized at Pennsylvania, and although the content in some respects would today seem simple or naive, the time commitment was a major one. Social and economic issues and the representation of the users' point of view were acknowledged, but there was no formal course work in these; it is only quite recently that such specialized course work for architects and planners has been developed. It may be said that the commitment to some of the social and economic concepts was less strong than it is now; certainly it was less loud and the expectations may have been more modest, but the point is that there was an awareness of these issues on the part of the faculty.

It would appear to me that the greatest contrasts are, on the one hand, the insistence in the thirties that architecture's primary alliance was with art, and in the seventies that the alliance is with the social sciences; and, on the other hand, the belief in the thirties that design and designing were central and that everything else could and would be picked up by the student on his own as needed, possibly later, and the implicit belief in the seventies that it is perhaps quite the other way around and that it is design and designing that will be picked up. But this is not strictly true and is not the point of view of everyone, nor does it seem likely that this point of view will prevail. And this brings us to what is perhaps the greatest contrast: that there was in the thirties a relatively consistent and homogeneous, if not exactly monolithic, point of view. The Beaux-Arts system tried as best it could to accommodate itself to other points of view from time to time, but I suspect the very rigidity of those competing points of view made the Beaux-Arts system more rigid in response.

Today the situation is one of enormous diversity, which I can only regard as healthy. The only danger I see is that one or some combination of the emerging new directions may consolidate and solidify a particular direction in such a way as to seek to dominate the scene with a monolithic structure. We would then be back where we were. If we get there I can only hope that the men in charge will be as intelligent, as cultured, as responsible as their Beaux-Arts predecessors. But I hope we don't get there.

The above has been written mostly from memory and recollection, and I have probably made some mistakes because I kept no journal to which I could refer. In spite of my efforts not to do so I have probably romanticized my experience just like any architect explaining what he was trying to do in a project after he has done it. I have gone into detail about what I did, not because I thought what I did was important, but merely to try to give someone the feeling of what it was like. If I were to summarize, I would merely say we developed a capacity to pursue many interests, for ourselves and for others.

And we did learn to draw.

BIBLIOGRAPHICAL NOTES

For a picture of the United States in the twenties and thirties—that is, just before and during the Depression following the crash of 1929—Frederick Lewis Allen's *Only Yesterday* (New York, 1931) and *Since Yesterday* (New York, 1940) and Dixon Wecter's *The Age of the Great Depression* (New York, 1948) are excellent places to begin, not analytical but journalistic and topical. Details of the programs at the University of Pennsylvania are to be found in *The University of Pennsylvania Bulletin: The School of Fine Arts Announcement*, published annually by the university in Philadelphia. For a broader and yet more explicit view of the history of the school in Pennsylvania and its objectives, see *The Book of the School* (University of Pennsylvania Press, 1934). For more detail about the architectural programs at the University of California, Berkeley, it is instructive to begin with the *Announcement* of the College of Architecture, published annually starting in 1956 and continuing year by year (the name changed to the College of Environmental Design in 1959) to the present. Obvious changes will be noted, both in the broader preliminary statements of objectives and in program details and academic requirements.

The best source on how the Beaux-Arts design studio worked in detail is John Harbeson's excellent *The Study of Architectural Design* (New York, 1926). It is a very explicit how-to-do-it book, particularly good in its description of the *analytique* and such arcane matters as the use of mosaic to express the character of the plan. A more personal and therefore richer expression of the Beaux-Arts approach, along with many interesting personal experiences, is contained in *Golden Jubilee Journal Commemorating the Fiftieth Paris Prize Award* (published by the National Institute of Architectural Education; New York, 1964). Among the many essays by former winners of the Paris Prize is a particularly important one by Harry Sternfeld containing a considerable amount of useful detail on the highly competitive system in earlier days (it was essentially the same in the thirties), as well as a strong and sometimes biting latter-day defense of the Beaux-Arts. Sternfeld's wonderful capacity for sarcasm will be obvious, and it will take little imagination for the architect to grasp what his studio criticism were like.

For specific information on design projects offered by the BAID, see the

*Bulletin of the Beaux-Arts Institute of Design*, published monthly except August and September, which contains the design programs, critiques by the jury, and illustrations of premiated work. It is essential for understanding the Beaux-Arts system, but it is incomplete in that it does not show anything except premiated work; thus it is difficult to get a feeling for anything other than the official point of view, but that is made eminently clear. Note that in the July journal of each year is a calendar for the entire year's work, giving the dates of issue of programs and the due dates. The BAID was ultimately succeeded by the National Institute of Architectural Education, monthly publication gave way to annual, and the succeeding document is *National Institute for Architectural Education Yearbook: Scholarships, Fellowships, Awards*. The remarkable stability of the Beaux-Arts system is made even clearer by consulting *Winning Designs 1904-1927: Paris Prize in Architecture* (New York: Pencil Points Press, 1928). This contains not only the winning designs but also the programs. For subsequent designs, see *NAIE Winning Designs 1904-1963: Paris Prize in Architecture*. Unfortunately this does not contain any of the programs.

An understanding of what the BAID was doing would be incomplete if one did not also consult what was happening at the mother school in Paris—just as any student would have been doing in the thirties. This information was published annually in *Les concours d'architecture de l'année scolaire*, Ecole Nationale Supérieure des Beaux-Arts. This also contains the issuing and due dates of the projects, the programs, and illustrations of the premiated designs. A study of the formal structure of the program and the resistance of this structure to change is worthwhile, as would be a study of the history of building programming. It may well be that the extraordinarily oversimplified programs so commonly used for actual buildings up to about ten or fifteen years ago were the direct descendants of the BAID and Ecole des Beaux-Arts oversimplified programs. I know of no study examining these relationships or the abrupt change in recent years to programs which fifteen years ago might have contained several hundred words but now may contain several hundred *pages*.

There is no comprehensive study of Wharton Esherick's work, and the best approach, therefore, is to visit the Wharton Esherick Museum in Paoli, Pennsylvania.

The architectural student at Pennsylvania in the thirties would have been encouraged to consult a quite specific group of documents. He would have had as a text for the first year of study of the elements of architecture a copy of *The American Vignola*, possibly the International Textbook edition published in Scranton, Pennsylvania. Line drawings of the orders and various moldings, together with geometric relationships and proportions, followed the general pattern of Vignole, *Traité élémentaire pratique d'architecture*, but the quality of the drawings is not nearly so elegant as the earlier Paris editions, and the discerning student would soon have preferred the original.

As soon as the student had an elementary grasp of the orders he would probably abandon Vignola for other standard documents. G. Gromort, *L'architecture classique—parallèle d'ordres grecs et romains* (Paris, 1927) would have been an important source during the study of the *analytique*, particularly for proportions, the use of moldings, the organization of elements, etc. However the basic document would have been H. D'Espouy, *Fragments d'architecture antique, d'après les relevés et restaurations des anciens pensionnaires de l'Académie de France à Rome* (Paris, 1905). The elegance and perfection of both the line and the wash drawing set a standard for the student that was nothing less than intimidating. The accepted bible for rendering was *Architectural Rendering in Wash* by H. van Buren Magonigle (New York, 1928), a very straightforward, clear, and explicit how-to-do-it book.

As the study of the *analytique* advanced and the subjects of study became more like buildings, other documents would have been used: Charles Percier, *Palais, maisons, et autres édifices modernes* (Paris, 1798); A. Grandjean de Montigny et A. Famin, *Architecture toscane* (Paris, 1815); and J.-N.-L. Durand, *Recueil et parallèle des édifices en tout genre, anciens et modernes* (Paris, 1800/01), would all have been used for larger parts of buildings, and particularly for the beginning studies of parts of plans and parts of sections.

Later studies of *analytiques* permitted the inclusion of documents from the Renaissance, and we would have looked at H. D'Espouy, *Fragments d'architecture;* P.-M. Letarouilly, *Edifices de Rome moderne,* 3 vols. (Paris, 1840-57); and César Daly, *Motifs historiques—décorations extérieures* (Paris, 1881), and *Motifs historiques—décorations intérieures* (Paris, 1880). It was easy to fall in love with the elegance of the plans in Letarouilly, and one could not help but be engaged by the explicitness of Daly and the fact that in these drawings exactly how something was put together became clearer.

For still larger-scale work we would have studied *Italian Gardens of the Renaissance* by J. C. Shepherd and G. A. Jellicoe (London, 1925) and *Baroque Gardens of Austria* by Jellicoe (London, 1932)—for the elegant handling of long sections and elevations, for the remarkably simple means of indication, and for the extremely well-drawn bird's-eye perspectives, to say nothing of what was to be gained by the study of the designs themselves.

In our history courses we would have consulted G. Gromort, *L'Architecture romane,* 3 vols. (Paris, 1928-31); A. Choisy, *Histoire de l'architecture,* 2 vols. (Paris, 1899), and his *L'Art de bâtir chez les romains* (Paris, 1873), *L'Art de bâtir chez les byzantins* (Paris, 1883), and *L'art de bâtir chez les égyptiens* (Paris, 1904); but the guiding document would have been J. Guadet, *Eléments et théorie de l'architecture,* 7 vols. (Paris, 1902). Choisy is also useful for his manner of using isometrics, drawings of which Louis Kahn was particularly fond. Guadet is instructive both for understanding the Beaux-Arts approach and for ways of looking at buildings. It is also interesting to read Guadet and Kahn (who studied at Penn in the early twenties with essentially the same interests I had) in parallel; the source of many of Louis Kahn's ideas will become more apparent.

A great deal of the stability of the Beaux-Arts system may have been due to the strength and consistency of the images the above documents produced and to the fact that there was relatively little competition (compared to today) for attention from the magazines and journals. Therefore to obtain a more complete understanding of the setting in which the student worked, one might look at the magazines of the twenties and thirties.

Finally, it is unfortunate that no study has as yet been made relating the particular students whom the Beaux-Arts institutions premiated with their later effectiveness in actual practice as architects. Certainly it would seem reasonable to expect, if the system were effective, that those students who did best in school would emerge as the better architects. I have been able to discover no useful correlations. The BAID *Journal,* in addition to photographs of premiated projects, appends full lists of all grades awarded, from half-mention up. It would be a monumental project to trace *all* students, but some short-listing system will come to mind.

# 10
## On the Fringe of the Profession: Women in American Architecture

GWENDOLYN WRIGHT

> Women are as imaginative as men; they just have the wrong kind of imagination for architecture. BRUCE GOFF

> The more elaborate the home, the more labour is required to keep it fit . . . ; the more labour required, the greater the wear and tear on both the heads of the family. CHARLOTTE PERKINS GILMAN

American architects defined their profession between the mid-nineteenth century and the early 1900s, and women in this scheme were a conspicuous minority with a restricted set of available jobs. Bernard M. Boyle discusses in Chapter 11 the emergence of a male-dominated Beaux-Arts atelier tradition in the schools of the period. Successful offices, such as McKim, Mead and White or Burnham and Root, became highly specialized commercial enterprises serving ambitious businessmen. Those few women who were able to take part seldom challenged these tendencies or competed with the men who dominated architectural practice; instead they took up the slack where they could, performing the jobs and concentrating on the services which their male colleagues either put aside or treated only peripherally.

A spattering of "women's fields," namely, domestic architecture and especially interiors, evolved as areas of specialization where it was permissible for women to practice, since here they were dealing with other women's needs. Such rigid categorization, by giving women a place in the corner of an occasional office, avoided the tension between accepted female sex roles and women's rights to equal opportunities within the profession. In 1939, the Institute of Women's Professional Relations still supported segregated work roles, emphasizing that "women must be directed into occupations for which they are [peculiarly] adapted." As late as 1969 Dr. Benjamin Spock was saying that "if they [women] had careers in medicine or architecture, for instance, they should be able to make distinctly feminine contributions to the advancement of these fields, rather than compete with men in the usual manly tradition of these professions" (*Decent and Undecent: Our Personal and Political Behavior* [New York, 1969], p. 57).

The limited tolerance made women's lot in the profession an ambiguous one. To many people, their minute numbers and low status in schools and offices seemed to prove the narrow range of their abilities. Such attitudes then rationalized educational discrimination, kept their salaries low, and further restricted their options for advancement within offices. By relegating certain fields to only a very few women, the profession, in effect, neglected both the women and their assigned responsibilities, namely, reform in domestic planning and attention to the needs of the user.

On the surface, the reasons for the association between women and domestic architecture were obvious. Women's tending to the needs of home and family seemed both a universal and a stabilizing social phenomenon. But the profession also actively discouraged women from specializing in areas other than housing. The specialization of women in domestic architecture was not an overt decision, but offices, schools, and the press were adamant about the connection. And, since the late nineteenth century was a time when controlled graduate curricula and a professional organization in architecture were being established, and specialization instituted in most schools and offices, both the association and the discrimination it fostered, had the weight of policy.

The issue of women's place in architectural practice was obviously influenced by Victorian society's rigid sexual stereotypes. Increasingly, the home and the business world were seen not simply as distinct from each other but as polar opposites, morally and environmentally. In the middle-class cult of domesticity, spirituality and sensitivity were personified by the woman—as long as she stayed in the home; the competitive philosophy of laissez-faire encouraged masculine assertiveness in the commercial environment. The architecture of home and office lent physical support to these moral differences. So if a woman—that is, a middle- or upper-class woman—did leave the home, she was only supposed to concern herself with matters pertaining to domestic life. A few such women, and some of their male compatriots as well, did want to apply "female virtues" and "feminine aesthetics" to building, but of course, only to domestic building. Since women managed the home, the reasoning went, they therefore understood how houses functioned; if they did indeed possess a higher moral sense, they should apply that sensibility to the design of better houses. This stand was scarcely a demand for equality of the sexes.

Women were asking for a stronger voice, and men were echoing their appeal, in an area which both assumed to be the female domain: the Home.

Calvert Vaux presented the case as early as 1857:

There can be no doubt that the study of domestic architecture is well suited to a feminine taste, for if we even allow the objections . . . such as the necessity of their climbing ladders, mingling with the mechanics and laborers during the progress of the works . . . we must, nevertheless, see at once that there is nothing in the world, except want of inclination and opportunity, to prevent many of them from being thoroughly expert in architectural drawing, or from designing excellent furniture . . . [*Villas and Cottages* (New York, 1857), p. 236].

E. C. Gardner, a popular writer and architectural theorist, backed the women's cause in 1875:

The world is gone woefully astray . . . vain and sick and useless, all because homes and housekeeping are on a false basis. I can see no way out of the wilderness till some saintly woman who knows the suffering and the need of humanity shall . . . place domestic architecture in the sight of all as the essential foundation of a sound social system [*Illustrated Homes* . . . (Boston, 1875), p. 149-50].

Lulu Stoughton Beem spoke for the women themselves in the *Inland Architect* of October 1884:

Women are naturally better judges of color, better in the blending of fabrics, besides knowing intuitively what is wanted about a house—wants too small for men to perceive [p. 40].

Despite such entreaties, a professional double standard was already clear. On September 30, 1876, the fledgling *American Architect and Building News* published an adamant editorial on the "woman issue":

First, the planning of houses, at least so far as the convenience of their arrangement is concerned, though a very necessary part of an architect's duty, is not architecture at all; and the ability to arrange a house conveniently does not in the least make an architect. There are thousands of people who can adjust the plans of houses to their own perfect satisfaction and convenience, and to those of others, and who do it, but who yet are not architects; just as there are millions of people who know their multiplication-table thoroughly, and use it constantly, and yet are not mathematicians [p. 313].

This statement, issued some time after the founding of the American Institute of Architects in 1857, signified a major schism in opportunities for the sexes and in architectural practice itself. Not only was the division of labor between men and women clearly stated, but there was the implicit dismissal of most domestic architecture as too lowly for professional consideration. The profession would favor theory over practicality, theoretician over user, monument over common building, as well as men over women.

With so articulate a policy, it is not surprising that few women became architects, nor that most women interested in architecture specialized in private housing. The field was inherently conservative, the scale of building usually determined by individual needs and conservative practice, and the financial base relatively modest, which further reduced their range of options. The educator Henry Frost explained the reason for the clustering in a publication of 1936:

Their [women's] professional work, both in architecture and landscape architecture, is likely, though this is by no means always true, to be in domestic fields. The sentimental reasons for this can be ignored. The true reason is that women practitioners thus far are more likely to be commissioned by individuals than by corporations and organizations [cited in D. Cole, p. 81].

From the late 1800s on, women and housing were both on the periphery of the increasingly corporate network of professional concerns.

THE QUANDARY OF ROLES

Those women who became architects recognized the unstable nature of their position. They did not emerge as a group demanding radical changes in housing policy or design. Nor did they present a united front on other issues, not even that of their own treatment. Faced with documented discrimination in hiring, salaries, and advancement, most persisted in their allegiance to the system that had at least tentatively accepted their presence as individual workers.

In order to appear successful, each woman architect had to stand apart from other women, both from her few peers and from the many beneath her in the hierarchy. To band together with others facing similar difficulties would be to acknowledge that women, generically, were subordinate, and that the system was discriminatory. Professional ambition relied upon a belief in personal choice and creative freedom, so each individual wanted to become a success "on her own merits." Furthermore, the professional woman faced personal role conflicts, for the qualities which she and the world considered to belong to her femininity were inappropriate in a professional context. The usual response was to employ, or perhaps create, variations on the female's traditional social function of dealing with emotions, either by the kind of work she did or the way she went about it. Still, the pressure to succeed as an individual and these conflicts of sexual identity created a tension that made most women believe that the problems they encountered were probably of their own making.

Women had four modes of coping with these problems at work, four variations of acceptable female roles to resolve the contradiction with their professional roles. Some strove to become *exceptional women*—just like successful men and more so: more dedicated, more determined, more prolific, giving themselves over totally to their work and professional role. Most women, however, followed a somewhat less consuming path: they were *anonymous designers* who tolerated discrimination and less than their share of recognition in offices and in the press in order to be able to design. Even then, the female architect was seldom able to accommodate a wife-and-mother role with professional demands; whereas the majority of male professionals have been married, the woman who wanted both a family and a career often found that there was not enough time or energy to apply herself sufficiently to both tasks. (Jane Addams' autobiography of 1920 noted that 75 per cent of the women professionals in her day were unmarried; even today, only an estimated half of women architects are married.) Many women who were concerned with the social aspects of the built environment chose not to follow the orthodox path of a formal architectural practice; they became *adjuncts* to the profession: planners, programmers, critics, writers, journalists. This is the role in which women have been best known and most accepted. Finally, there have been numerous women, altogether outside the profession, who were *reformers* dedicated to creating alternatives, either by advocating legislative reform or by building new kinds of domestic institutions. Their concern with reforming the social environment overrode their preoccupation with aesthetics or professional status. Their design process was often collective; their programs, conscious integrations of layperson and expert, work environment and home life. These women wanted to expand the available options for other women, and architectural innovation was one of their means for doing so.

## THE EXCEPTIONAL WOMAN

The names of two women appear in most inclusive histories of American architecture: Catharine Beecher and Julia Morgan. Each devoted herself to her work and made significant contributions to our domestic environment. The lives they chose may seem overly ascetic and self-denying to most women today. Yet, because of their success, the records of these exceptional women have become the ideal against which other women are measured, both for the quantity of their work (Morgan designed some eight hundred buildings during just under fifty years of practice) and for their innovative concepts (Beecher gave us the forerunner of the modern suburban house's technological system and its organization).

As recently as 1955, in a piece called, "Should You Be an Architect?", Pietro Belluschi counseled:

I cannot in whole conscience recommend architecture as a profession for girls. It takes an exceptional girl to make a go of it. If she insisted on becoming an architect, I would try to dissuade her. If then she was still determined . . . she would be *that exceptional one* [emphasis added].

Catharine Beecher (1800-1878) appears in studies of American housing as the foremother of the contemporary suburban house. Her major architectural work, *The American Woman's Home*, was written with her sister, the novelist Harriet Beecher Stowe, and published in 1869. Here was the first visual presentation of the model with which we are now familiar: mechanical services concentrated in the center of the house, making the kitchen–work area prominent in the plan; the surrounding spaces left open and undefined; the facade, relieved of services, free to express any whimsy or fantasy.

Beecher had a strong philosophical rationale for her domestic design. Intrigued since the early nineteenth century with the possibility of professionalized housekeeping, she had traveled and lectured throughout New England and the Midwest, bent on improving women's educational institutions. However, she did not advocate education and professional skills so that women could enter the public world; she promoted a separate-but-equal system whereby they would exercise complete control over the home. Housekeeping could be on a par with male businesses, but only if the proper methods were demonstrated and houses properly organized. To further these ends, she set herself to redesigning the domestic environment, but on paper, so that the ideas would have the widest possible circulation among women themselves.

In *The American Woman's Home*, Beecher defined the house according to a paradigm of professional efficiency in which techniques, tools, and training determined form. Her reforms emphasized the principles of convenience, compactness, and flexibility, and she modified every area of the house to adhere to these precepts. The dominant element was the mechanical core, consisting of a sophisticated heating and ventilating system and an essentially modern plumbing system. Room arrangement accentuated the benefits of the mechanical system. The kitchen moved from solitary confinement at the back of the house to a pivotal position in the center, where it opened into the multi-purpose dining area (the "family room" or "home space") on one side and the drawing room on the other. A "cooking form" converted isolated cupboards and tabletops into a streamlined continuous surface, with explicit containers for every culinary item within easy reach. The living spaces applied the principles to more generalized use, with furnishings either built-in or mounted on rollers to become portable screens and room dividers. The "close packing of conveniences" determined the layout of every room and of the overall plan.

Beecher concentrated on the single-family house in an isolated setting, reflecting the romantic taste of her time and her own desire to segregate the home from outside influences. The façades of her model houses were picturesque Greek Revival or Gothic, evocative of a serene Arcadian existence; the façade was, however, stylized, while the interior was truly innovative. Occasionally she did consider other housing types, including an urban "tenement" or apartment house and a site plan for a suburban neighborhood (Figure 65). The tenement unit could accommodate a family of ten in a minimal space by using sofas, closets, and dual-purpose furniture, all built-in. The community plan included centralized, cooperative housekeeping and common laundries, bakehouses, and stables, so that such services could be eliminated in individual households, rather than simply improved.

Beecher's book was a best-seller, and its proposals were based on feasible equipment for the time, even though most of her suggestions were not incorporated by the market until well into the twentieth century. Although not herself an architect, she proposed significant technical and social innovations for domestic environments. Yet architects of her day and many historians since then have relegated her to the lesser ranks of "lady writers," rather than acknowledge her contributions to architectural theory and technology. Her innovations did not appear in actual commissioned designs; she addressed the housewives themselves, rather than a select group of architects and their clients. Beecher was an exceptional

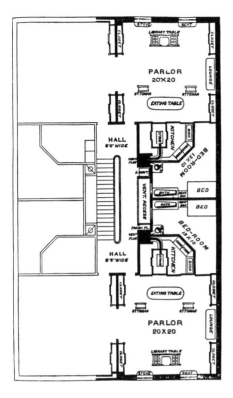

Figure 65. Catharine Beecher and Harriet Beecher Stowe, plans for a model tenement. Early tenements were multiple dwellings, not necessarily for the poor. The Beechers envisioned this arrangement for "young married persons with frugal and benevolent tastes." Each unit was designed to accommodate four persons, and a family of ten could use the flat by converting one of the kitchens into another bedroom. In these apartments, as in Catharine Beecher's model single-family houses, the mechanical core dominates the floor plan.

woman, but neither her prominence nor her insights brought her professional recognition.

Family ties and a reputation for designing livable houses brought a phenomenal number of commissions to the tiny office of Julia Morgan (1872-1957). Her single-family residences, scattered throughout California's Bay Area, and her understated public facilities combined an elegant, restrained style with homey comfort. Morgan was, in all these qualities, a "lady," with an upper-class feminine style.

Morgan never really pushed her career. Her background and her personal inclination determined it. She was graduated from the University of California at Berkeley in engineering in 1894 (apparently the first woman to receive a degree from this school) and was given a certificate of completion by the Ecole des Beaux-Arts in Paris in 1901. The connections of her prosperous Oakland family supported her practice during its early years and during the Depression, although her most famous client, Phoebe Apperson Hearst, engaged her when Morgan was a draftswoman for John Galen Howard's office in 1903. When she went outside this circle of acquaintances, Morgan frequently took on commissions from women's organizations for club and sorority houses, retirement houses, women's dormitories and schools, a women's gymnasium, and a number of YWCAs. In every case, whoever the client, the restraint, taste, and refined simplicity, the comfort and adaptability of traditional forms are more constant than any overtly stylistic belief or any form used as a signature.

Morgan never attempted to publicize herself or her work in the architectural press or even through elaborate designs. Her success undoubtedly inspired younger women, and she openly encouraged those in her office. As one female employee later said: "Morgan was always trying to develop a woman. She'd give you as much work and advice as you could handle. But her devotion was total, and she demanded the same thing from us. I don't know of any men who worked that hard." She seems to have wanted other women to share her success, but believed that hers were the only terms on which to achieve it.

Most historians have assumed that Morgan did not think of herself as a "woman architect," since she never spoke out on feminist issues. But she did not speak out on any other issues either. Nor can she be called a crusader simply because of the number of women-oriented buildings she designed. Whatever Morgan's personal position on women's issues, it was not as significant as the way in which historians have treated it. Some have called the recurrent domestic theme and scale of her work a sign of weakness in her record as an architect, saying that she stayed with a few safe, small types and never moved on to large-scale projects. Yet the criticism arises only because this particular type of association is rare for a prominent architect. All architectural firms must establish ties to corporations, local governments, or at least groups and classes, in order to assure themselves of a continuing practice. A connection such as Morgan's, to women's groups as clients and to domestic architecture as a prototypical form, was no more dependent a relationship than those of male architects to certain clients and preferred forms.

But were the women's groups who commissioned her looking for a particular style? In contrast to the other celebrated architects of her time, certainly to Bernard Maybeck and Ernest Coxhead, Morgan was vehemently opposed to showiness in façade and interior. Yet each building was different and quietly reflected the special qualities of its particular site, function, and users, rather than displaying Morgan's own hand. Her main interests seem to have been the Classicism of detail and proportion, the needs and tastes of her clients, and the fit of the building in its neighborhood and in the life of the group who would use it. While such outward-directed attitudes are, in part, the legacy of the Bay Area Style itself, Morgan interpreted that style with her own subtlety. A pinch of economy, a restraint in form or materials, always kept the house a backdrop—rather than a compelling stage—for social interaction.

Morgan's undramatic style was, to the historian, almost exasperatingly open-minded. She seems to have had no personal predilection toward a certain period, or toward experimentation, or even toward a certain range of materials. She handled shingles and concrete with equal aplomb, and accepted small commissions and renovations as freely as large jobs like the Hearst estate at San Simeon, California. (This point is noteworthy, since Morgan reportedly did the design work on every project in the office, at least through the 1930s.) Morgan even had an explicit technique for eliciting the tastes and preferences of her clients. Her office kept a veritable Sears' catalogue of historical prototypes in its extensive library, from which clients could pick the styles and details they liked. Morgan would then incorporate their pastiche of forms into a coherent whole. If her style does not seem as personal as, say, Maybeck's, it is in part because she kept a low profile in designing with her clients. The resulting variety suggests why less than half of her estimated eight hundred buildings have been identified. Her techniques and their results were by no means arbitrary or the sign of a lack of creativity, however, for Morgan openly criticized architects who resented clients for "imposing" on their forms. Her policies were clear antecedents of today's user-needs criteria and client-participation.

Nonetheless, Morgan's work and her beliefs raise thorny issues about the validity of "women's design" as a liberating concept. Comfort and familiarity are certainly important values, but they can also formalize acceptance of "the way things are"; fit can become a rigid container for a narrow way of life, enclosing people in environments so burdened with role associations that any change seems out of keeping. Such conservatism—at times stodginess would not be an excessive description—is evident in many of Morgan's houses. It is as if professional success was not compatible with forms that might reflect new life-styles for her clients.

Still, it is the *success*, not the beliefs, of exceptional women like Morgan and Beecher which determines criteria for women architects. One woman who worked for years in San Francisco offices, designing a number of buildings, describes the poignant self-image she had internalized:

I was probably dilletantish; I didn't have my nose to the grindstone enough, you see, since I also wanted to have a family and have my own life. . . . I can't really call myself an architect, since I didn't always work full-time, so I could travel and be with my family. . . . Why, I should have paid him [Henry Gutterson, one of her employers] for working there, since I enjoyed myself so!

This woman considered that acclaim and total commitment to a role were indications of professionalism and consequently considered herself unprofessional. Morgan and Beecher represent the compromises that had to accompany professional success for many women—specialism in domestic architecture, environments supportive of traditional middle-class family structure and sex roles, and a restrained, ladylike personal life; in sum, a highly conservative identity. Not even the few successful women architects questioned the precepts that had for so long defined the status of their sex, neither as models for their own behavior nor as models for their clients. Home was the woman's place, and those who left it were sometimes especially adamant on this point, for their "exceptional" status implied that women did not generally qualify to be professionals.

ANONYMOUS ARCHITECTS

Women did make contributions to domestic architecture and occasionally had successful practices of their own. But their names almost all dropped from the course of architectural history, even those who received notice in the press of their own time. The example of Josephine Wright Chapman illustrates the dilemma of anonymity for the female architect. The only reference to her apparently successful career is in a women's magazine: a *Ladies' Home Journal* article of October 1914 entitled "The Real New Woman: A Woman Who Builds Houses." According to this account, Chapman had had a flourishing practice in Boston, designing a number of public buildings, when, in 1905, she suddenly decided that "a woman's work is to design houses. Hereafter I am going to design [only] homes." By adapting to an acceptable role for a woman, she did receive some public attention, but attention as a role model, not as a designer. The article stressed Chapman's philosophy of "home life," not her functional approach; it praised the moderation of her public role, rather than the merit or innovation of her work. Her conclusion was that dedication to domestic architecture, after a period of experiments with other, less feminine types of buildings, "proves a professional woman can be feminine and not be a feminist."

Neither Chapman's early public success nor her conversion to professional pursuits more appropriate for a woman qualified her for coverage in the architectural press. But her career was still remarkable, for few women had the financial independence to experiment with their own offices. They were usually dependent on working their way up through apprenticeships. This was a difficult progression, since office work was generally considered unsuitable for a lady because of the demanding conditions, the necessity of dealing with "crude workmen," abrasive business practices, and the awkwardness of bending over drafting boards and climbing scaffolding in conventional female clothing. Rather than stir up prejudice and censure by being too forward, most women stayed in the background in order to learn. And, for the most part, they had to stay put if they wanted to keep designing.

There were almost no alternatives. Families were seldom likely to sponsor a daughter financially if she wanted to pursue an architectural career. The colleges funded under the Merrill Land-Grant Act of 1862 (nine of which included architecture schools by 1898) were by law co-educational, but they pointedly discouraged women. Private schools, with no such obligations to equality, openly refused to admit women into their architecture programs. Even into the 1930s, according to Joseph Esherick's account of policy at the University of Pennsylvania, a quota system there restricted the number of women students (see above, p. 239). In office or school, it was considered improper, and even unhealthy, for women to work under the conditions which male students and practitioners accepted.

These openly discriminatory policies led to the establishment of a unique school that was only for women: the Cambridge School of Architecture and Landscape Architecture, an institution admirably documented by Doris Cole. Founded by Henry Frost in 1915 in his Cambridge, Massachusetts, office, the school graduated more than one hundred women professionals over its twenty-seven-year history. Each woman was trained in a joint program that combined architecture and landscape, theory and practice, with an emphasis on domestic environments. In 1942, when the school was taken over by Harvard's Graduate School of Design, both the director and many students were uncertain whether or not to see the in-

tegration as an advance, for they saw that Harvard was as much motivated by the financial precariousness of low wartime enrollment as by a
commitment to women.

Three of the more familiar twentieth-century American women architects were graduates of the Cambridge School. Jean Fletcher and Sarah
Harkness, together with their husbands, were partners in The Architects'
Collaborative from its inception in 1945. Their office was a rarity in its
collective organization and in its consequent support of women as equals.
(See Chapter 11 for a discussion of these policies, in theory and in practice.) Fletcher and Harkness could work part-time, even as principals,
during the years when they were raising their families. (Such partnerships
—working in tandem or as a team with husbands in the same profession—have been fairly successful as the model for professional women who
also wanted to have families, since their husbands understood both sets
of demands.)

Eleanor Raymond, another Cambridge School graduate, was Frost's
partner from 1919 to 1935, after which she started her own office. Her
work did receive praise in the press, in particular her simple houses which
made use of innovative building materials and systems: an all-Masonite
house in Dover, Massachusetts, in 1933; a design in Belmont, Massachusetts, which the Architectural Forum in November 1933 called the first
modern house in the state; and another house in Dover, built in 1948
and designed jointly with the owner, Dr. Maria Telkes, using solar energy
(Figure 66).

Frost had recognized a particular emphasis among the students of the
Cambridge School, and wanted to encourage the profession along this
line. Because a woman's "interest in her profession embraces its social
and human implications," he proposed, in a letter of 1941, the reorganization of the school's program around "research and design in the direction
of (for want of a better word) socialized architecture." Frost had a particular goal for the school. He wanted to forge new professional ideals by
preparing the graduates, "perhaps as no other school does at present, for
positions of responsibility on the planning boards of cities and towns, and
in other organizations having to do with social welfare."

Women had indeed, from their earliest entry into the profession, shown
a commitment to "socialized architecture," whether they were involved
with the comforts of the affluent or the needs of the working class. One
example of such a reform-minded philosophy, unusual for a practicing
architect of the time, was that of Margaret Hicks, who in 1878 was the

Figure 66. Eleanor Raymond, Dr. Maria Telkes house, Dover, Massachusetts, 1948. Raymond (right) designed the Telkes residence as an experimental venture, in conjunction with a team of MIT scientists interested in the feasibility of solar heating for small-scale projects. The system they employed—which consisted of roof collectors (accounting for the 57-degree angle of the roof), attic storage tanks, a suspended radiant ceiling, and 10-foot-high double glass panels along the south wall of the house—was developed by Telkes herself. The two women worked together to have the design complement the mechanical system, emphasizing the simple beauty of the equipment, yet presenting a "homelike" image to the surrounding community.

first woman to graduate from Cornell's architecture school. That same year the *American Architect and Building News* published her student project: a "Workman's Cottage," a scaled-down, pared-down replica of the suburban houses her fellow students were designing for the wealthy (Figure 67). Hicks believed that her professional training should not be the private property of a single class and went on to do "tenement architecture" for the growing numbers of immigrants in New York City. Phebe Hannaford in 1883 commended her as one of the few "to have remembered that houses must have light and air, closets and bedrooms" (*Daughters of America* [Boston, 1883], p. 286). At a time when most architects designed for the wealthy, and when builders promoted dumbbell tenements as a reform, Hicks applied the benefits and sensitivity of formal architectural training to housing for the poor.

The strain was great for those women architects who wanted to expand the horizons of traditional architectural practice or established Classical design themes. Sophia Hayden, the young designer of the Woman's Building at the World's Columbian Exposition in Chicago in 1893, did successfully integrate two aesthetic and social philosophies (Figure 68). Her building's façade was grandly Neo-Classical, perfectly adapting to Burnham's master plan, while the 80,000-square-foot interior was an unencumbered industrial space, most of it two stories high. Here she emphasized flexibility and functionalism, downplaying architectural detailing in order to focus attention on the exhibits of household technology and women's

Figure 67. Margaret Hicks, Workman's Cottage, student project from Cornell University School of Architecture. Hicks was the first woman to graduate in architecture from Cornell, a school that was required, under the Merrill Land-Grant Act, to provide co-education. *American Architect and Building News* published her student work in the year of her graduation, but gave no explanation about why it included this small plain cottage among the many elaborate Shingle Style "cottages" for the wealthy. The house is strangely placeless, suspended without any neighborhood context. There are also no provisions for the extended family or boarders, common phenomena in working-class groups. However, despite the strong nuclear-family model, this would be a convenient house for a busy woman to maintain.

Figure 68. Sophia Hayden, the Woman's Building, World's Columbian Exposition, Chicago, 1893. The competition for the Woman's Building was announced on February 3, 1891; less than two months later, Hayden's entry was declared the winner among several other projects designed by women. The twenty-one-year-old architect, who had been graduated from MIT only a year before, described the building as "the result of careful training in classical design and the expression of what I felt and liked." The exterior of the structure reflects the interior subdivisions: a central exhibition area surrounded by a mezzanine and secondary exhibition rooms in symmetrical wings. The contents of the building, however, described other, powerful images: of science, technology, and more worldly roles for women.

art, a model hospital and model kindergarten, displays of charity organizations and settlement houses. Yet not only was her success hard-earned—she suffered a breakdown after the commission was completed—but it did not insure a career. Hayden went on to find work in Boston as an interior designer and then disappeared from the scene.

Women architects who wanted to do something specific about social conditions could not easily take a stand from within their profession. Most professional architects were not directly involved with furthering social change, but instead affected a neutral and intellectual position as experts on physical design. Rather than contend with the ethics of neutrality, some women chose to become "gray ladies" to architecture, "wives" to the profession. In this capacity it was appropriate for them to offer advice and explain the social reality that many architects seemed to ignore.

A number of women have affected the architectural profession by speaking from outside the field, affiliating themselves as consultants on social aspects of design. As planners, programmers, writers, and "household technologists," they have provided architects with important social information. Others have addressed the subject in a more popular vein as authors or journalists. Most of the women in both categories have wanted to protect traditional professionalism and traditional domesticity by improving them. A smaller group has sought to institute change through radical housing reforms and the dissemination of professional knowledge.

The impact of these women's views was felt most during the Progressive period, especially the teens, and again during the Depression of the thirties. During the teens many women, wives of middle-class businessmen or professionals and college-educated single women, sought "self-fulfillment" in jobs, club work, and municipal reform organizations. Many became professionals (in fact, the percentage of women who practiced as professionals dropped in every succeeding decade from the teens through the sixties), but professional and philanthropist alike were intent on reforming the domestic environment and the kind of family life it enclosed. During the thirties, environmental reform was important for other reasons: emotionally, the home offered security; economically, even minor renovations would offer some relief to the stagnant building industry. These conditions meant some work for women as architectural consultants, but on the whole jobs were particularly scarce for them, since a number of cities passed injunctions prohibiting married women from competing for work. Nonetheless, housing did become an issue, for architects and for society. It was no longer simply a "women's field"; women and men took a collective stand on housing matters, putting aside the question of women's special sensitivity to the domestic environment.

Both periods produced a spate of books and magazines for professionals and laywomen, publications that proposed "necessary changes" in housing—either toward communal services or back to more traditional, reassuring imagery. The precedent for women's writing on the subject lay in the domestic manuals of the nineteenth century. Through these books of household information and interior design, educated women (Beecher, for instance) had explained to other housewives the basic skills of home planning and upkeep. The injection of professionalism in authorship at the turn of the century paralleled a new emphasis in content as well. In the fascination with Frederick W. Taylor's principles of scientific management, domestic guides began to preach "household engineering" for the "home management expert." The scientific approach, while practically useful, was a way of laminating the glamor of professionalism onto old duties and routine environments. At the same time, it did give a new legitimacy to the domestic interior: the elevation earned only a brief mention in most of these publications, while the house plan was thoroughly analyzed, with special attention to the convenient layout of rooms and useful arrangement of equipment. The authors and their public—almost all women in both cases—shared a new sense of pride in the merits and mastery of a practical domestic interior. Greta Gray boasted in 1923 that "the truly American part of the house has been studied first, without much thought for the exterior."

Gray held an architectural degree from MIT and a Master's degree in Household Arts from Columbia. Her first book, *House and Home* (Philadelphia, 1923), gave its readers practical information and social theory (Figure 69). A model housing treatise, it addressed the general reader without architectural knowledge, offering information on buying, building, and simply keeping up a house. Alongside the standard sanitary admonitions of scientific management, Gray suggested improvements that would ease the housewife's workday and strain. Concerned with health and with the house as a "protective agent," she understood that a poor environment could harm the psyche as well as the body. Threats to family health, in her estimate, included "fatigue and strain which may be in some measure avoided by well-thought-out arrangements, mental depression which cheerless surroundings and lack of sunshine frequently include, and others, equally as important, perhaps, but less tangible" (p. 3). Gray did not restrict herself to issues of single-family housing. She argued that concern for the home meant attention to the needs of different kinds of families and different individuals. She insisted on the relevance of financing reform and low-income housing provisions as part of a model housing program. Her last chapter outlined what she believed were the necessary developments for the future: cooperatives, state-financed developments, wholesale production of homes, prefabrication, and town-plan-

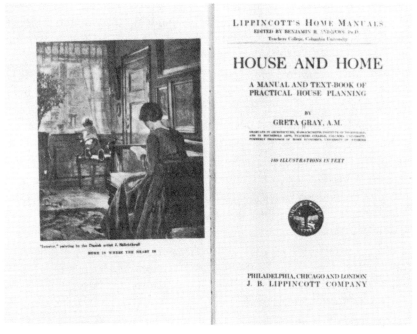

Figure 69. Greta Gray, frontispiece and title page of *House and Home,* 1923. Gray, a graduate of MIT and Columbia University, was versed in the profession and aware of its effects. Her book showed a solid understanding of construction, circulation, services, and human response to the environment. She suggested innovations at every scale, from flooring over a concrete slab in the laundry so that the housewife would not feel the cold and damp, to proposals for town-planning and tenement reform.

ning. Gray's book, while not a radical challenge to the traditional home or the established profession, did present the house as a complex environment and the woman as an effective, active link between the institutions of home and community.

During the early decades of the century even the women's magazines, ordinarily bastions of conservative opinion, began to publish advice for working women and environments designed to meet their needs. The proposals were frequently the work of women architects on the magazines' staffs, including Helen Lukens Gaut and Una Nixson Hopkins for the *Ladies' Home Journal.* In these articles, even women who were not employed outside the home learned to apply the principles of scientific management to their domestic chores. The most popular series in the genre was entitled "The New Housekeeping: How It Helps the Woman Who

Does Her Own Work." (The declining number of domestic servants—or the larger number of middle-class aspirants who wanted servants—was an important factor in promoting new domestic facilities.) In this *Ladies' Home Journal* series of 1912, and then in her book, *Household Engineering: Scientific Management in the Home* of 1915, Christine Frederick defined the kitchen as a modern laboratory where "Tools are not as important as Methods." Frederick's reforms, however, exemplify a major flaw in the progressive infatuation with scientific management. In the rush to improve conditions, there was little analysis of the fundamental problems besetting domestic life; therefore "solutions" tended to be immediate substitutions of one set of goods or dimensions for another, at an exceedingly small scale, and with an even smaller social impact.

The reform movement cooled, even before the Depression, with the heightened individualism of the 1920s. Most domestic guides insisted that the country should return to traditional family life and traditional houses rather than contend with *any* model for progressive change. Emily Post's *The Personality of a House* (New York, 1930, 1933) and Marcia Mead's *Homes of Character* (New York, 1926) criticized the hodgepodge environments of the suburbs. They wanted individuals to make over their surroundings along conservative lines in order to stabilize the social order. Mead provokingly asked, "Are we pleased with ourselves as we look at the piles of tortured building materials, jazzing signs and restless, defiant, unneighborly roof lines? What is our character, judging by these tell-tale evidences . . . ?" (p. 1). These eclectics wanted to replace the disorder they scorned with picturesque houses that were replicas of better days in the past. They did not address the economic difficulties of their own time or the need for a range of different housing types. Their solution to an increasingly severe housing crisis was a duplication of older architectural styles and idealized nuclear families.

While some concerned themselves with traditional imagery for the façade, most of the popular architectural writers concentrated on the domestic interior. In 1933 the Brooklyn Gas Company commissioned Lilian Moller Gilbreth, an industrial designer interested in the psychological implications of environments, to perform a series of efficiency studies for kitchen design. Her proposed changes, which were widely published, were designed to stimulate consumption, in that they emphasized the need for improved kitchen equipment. Her standard of reference was the efficiency of a single worker rather than the well-being of women in general or those who worked outside the home in particular. She apparently never considered that some women might not be in the home for most of the day; never asked why individual women did all the work, only how well it was being performed.

Two women who were active in the 1930s did take a radical approach, integrating interior comfort, community scale, and a recognition of real family patterns in their plans. Elisabeth Coit carried out housing studies for the AIA in the early 1940s in which she outlined adequate standards for size and number of rooms, for air, sunlight, privacy, outdoor space, and group facilities. In addition to clarifying these guidelines, Coit explained that there were limitations to the notion of a "typical family unit" and insisted on varying guidelines for the many "non-typical families." Her work described the particular circumstances of extended families, of families in high-rises and those with large numbers of children, of single mothers, working parents, and the aged. She broke down the accepted myth of the universal family that had generated standardized housing solutions for every domestic situation—all planned around the woman being in the home.

Of all the writers in this century, Catherine Bauer (1905-64) provided the sharpest analysis of American housing, ranging from the stylistic to the political, from individual rooms to national housing policy (Figure 70). *Modern Housing*, published in 1934, was a landmark in her career as a planner and in housing literature. It was an eloquent dissection of housing conditions and attitudes in Europe, the Soviet Union, and the United States that enunciated minimum standards for low-income housing and attacked the isolationism of American architects. Housing, Bauer contended, was a social and political situation that ought to be organized around function, convenience, and wider availability. Even aesthetics, which ought to be a secondary concern, was based on arbitrary fancy detailing rather than on the expression of good workmanship, the desire for good health, and adequate open space. Most people in this country, whatever their class, had to tolerate poor-quality and inefficient planning. Discussing standards, Bauer pointed to the differences between Europe's garden cities, with their concept of standardization "as public utility . . . as community unit . . . as modern architecture," and the uninspired American notions of square-footage requirements and modernistic façades, with little concern for human use of the spaces or the right to adequate housing for one's family. Our architects, she charged, aped the styles of European modernism, but they neglected the social concepts that had generated such styles in the first place.

Figure 70. Catherine Bauer (Wurster). By the early 1930s Catherine Bauer was already a well-known and outspoken authority on housing. While specific about quantitative issues, she insisted that all standards be translated into human terms as well, terms that related to the experience of living in houses and neighborhoods. We needed guidelines, Bauer insisted, "for the cliff dweller (residents of apartment houses) as well as for the slum dweller—and not merely 'minimum standards' that sacrifice space and privacy to better plumbing." Her suggestions ranged from provisions for light and ventilation in an individual unit to the "standard of neighborhood facilities," which would include shops, schools, nurseries, playgrounds, libraries, clinics, and meeting rooms within easy walking distance of every unit—a problem in suburbia as it was in the city tenement.

## THE COLLECTIVE ALTERNATIVE

Bauer, as a planner, was outside the profession of architecture. From this position, she was able to criticize its failings and affect her colleagues in the design fields. Another category of women who were never affiliated with the profession affected the domestic environment by addressing its users themselves, speaking woman-to-woman of their common experiences. They saw conditions change—if only for their own small groups, and sometimes only in terms of awareness. Although the various groups I will discuss did not pretend to work in unison (indeed, they seldom knew of one another's existence), common themes do relate their beliefs and their practice: reliance on basic skills that were easy to teach, rather than professional expertise, and on collectivity instead of individualism; proposals to break down women's isolation in their work; and an appeal to women as the users of the domestic environment rather than to a professional elite as its theorists.

A strong spokeswoman for a radical view of domesticity was Charlotte Perkins Gilman (1860-1935), the grand-niece of Catharine Beecher. A dedicated feminist and socialist, she lectured and wrote about necessary changes in the home *and* the political system that would give women more equality. Her two most famous books, *Women and Economics*

(1898) and *The Home: Its Work and Influence* (1902), lambasted the sentimental image of the home as a center of purity and comfort; instead, she charged, most houses were inefficient, unsanitary, and demoralizing. Neither the work nor the products necessary for keeping up the average home were economical or intrinsically rewarding, so inevitably there was friction between servants and employers, and between husbands and wives; since they all assumed that the house ought to be both modern and restful, it had to be someone's fault if that was not the case. Gilman concluded that the disparity between the image of the home as a perfected institution and the reality of the housewife's frustrations was based on misconceptions about how the home functioned and whom it helped.

Like most reformers of the period, Gilman believed in the inevitability of progress. To create alternatives to the unhappy traditional system, she wanted to professionalize domestic duties—by which she meant their centralization. There would be kitchenless houses and laundryless ones, for such services would be provided through citywide businesses with neighborhood outlets. The city would provide extensive networks of supervised playgrounds and day-nurseries to relieve continuous child-care demands on mothers. Families and single persons could give up the illusion of privacy and self-sufficiency in detached units for the convenience of residence hotels, apartments, and connecting houses. Even more than square footage or stylistic reform, she explained, it would be the conversion to the necessary cooperative or professionalized housekeeping that would provide the motivation for efficient domestic reorganization; after all, people would then be paying for the labor that had always been taken for granted in housekeeping.

While Gilman was not an architect and did not draw up explicit plans, she did present important concepts and clear descriptions of possible alternatives around which feminists of the time could organize. The central issue she raised was that people should have a real choice about how they would live, among real options, not superficial differences. Architecture, she insisted, had a responsibility to provide such options. As Gilman wrote in *The Home:*

The home is a human institution. All human institutions are open to improvement. This specially dear and ancient one, however, we have successfully kept shut, and so it has not improved as have some others [p. 4].

Gilman's strength and success as an individual critic were unusual. Most women who advocated domestic reform preferred to work within the supportive structure of an organization. And even the collective structure varied considerably: one solution was a retreat, usually to the country, by a group who wanted to form an alternative society; the other, the formation of civic associations and community clubs, usually of a philanthropic nature, by middle-class women in urban areas.

The nineteenth century witnessed several waves of communitarian activity, during which more than 300 groups set up their own model societies. Each recognized their environment to be both a vehicle for social change and the physical representation of the group's beliefs. Many of these groups advocated a more equal status for women. The resulting architectural considerations included improved working conditions and labor-saving devices in kitchen and laundry areas, the integration of these facilities so that work was more efficient and more communal, ease of maintenance through carefully chosen materials, furnishings, and detailing in every area, and centralized provisions for child care. And some of them turned to women members for designs—Alice Constance Austin at Llano del Rio, California, and Katherine Tingley at the Theosophist Society near San Diego, for example.

Only one communitarian group was composed almost entirely of women. The Woman's Commonwealth originated in Belton, Texas, in 1866, under the leadership of Martha McWhirter (1827-1904). When the group's social and religious beliefs began to separate them from their families, the thirty women decided to build their own houses and share domestic work. Soon their numbers increased, and they moved into a communal structure in the center of town. Over the years they built additions and moved their smaller houses onto the lot. Eventually the building became a public facility—the Central Hotel—and took in guests. Despite a year-long boycott, it became a financial and social success and was always filled with guests and townspeople. When the group decided to retire to Washington, D.C., in 1899, the town begged it to stay on (Figure 71).

In almost every way, the Commonwealth's Central Hotel reflected an uncommon set of values. The façade was unpretentious, since the group did not believe in decoration. The interior broke with the established Victorian house plan, which dictated a separate room for each function, isolating people and activities. In contrast, the Commonwealth's rooms each incorporated several uses and opened into adjoining spaces and outdoor areas. The women formulated their designs through group discussion and decision-making and through investigation into efficient methods and

Figure 71. Members of the Woman's Commonwealth in the yard of their Central Hotel, Belton, Texas, ca. 1895. McWhirter is seated second from the left. The Woman's Commonwealth functioned as a predominantly female communitarian experiment for some forty years during the late nineteenth century. The group designed and built a number of small houses for itself, and a sizable hotel complex, and affected the pattern of growth of the surrounding town.

user preferences, to which they added an element of mysticism. Even the construction work they did collectively. And, unlike the majority of communal societies, then as now, this group chose to integrate their way of life into the existing social structure around them, rather than moving to the country. Their environment and the beliefs it represented were an alternative that was open to anyone, not only to a select few.

At the close of the nineteenth century, urban women became active in their own reform efforts by affiliating with the Progressive Movement. Women's clubs and philanthropies advocated improvements in prisons, schools, factories, hospitals, and especially in housing and neighborhoods in all parts of the city. The settlement houses exemplify their collective philosophy: the belief in social change through environmental action, the emphasis on home and family life, the conspicuous values of the middle class. Jane Addams, the venerable founder of Chicago's Hull House in 1889, envisioned the settlements as bases for community and reform. Although her early lectures called for environments that would "satisfy" cultural deprivation, her work soon shifted toward dealing with specific physical problems in working-class life. She expanded the facilities of Hull House to include a diet kitchen for invalids, a kindergarten for working mothers in the neighborhood, a gymnasium, bathing facilities, and nursing services. At the same time, Addams and other settlement-house workers—Lillian Wald and Florence Kelley, for instance—felt it important that a single building not encompass all necessary services. Enlisting the support of architects, labor leaders, educators, and politicians, they promoted programs in schools, factories, and family homes that would bring social services directly to the recipients.

In contrast to Hull House, most women's organizations—including the American Federation of Women's Clubs and the majority of the 400 settlement houses—were romantic in their philosophies, conservative in their goals, and isolated from professional or political power. The organizations gave meaning to the lives of restless, educated, unemployed women, but were not always conscious of the real needs of immigrant families. And as power in the Progressive Movement came to be centered in the new professional class of "scientific" social services, which was predominantly male, most of these women remained volunteers. When, as individuals, through local clubs or settlements, or even as social workers themselves, women did propose environmental reforms—urban landscaping, playgrounds and parks, day-nurseries, working girls' clubs, sanitation provisions in tenement homes—they tended to emphasize the moral good of these improvements, instead of their political import. Consequently, when their reform efforts came up against resistance, they had little political weight with which to fight.

The historian Richard Hofstadter has suggested that the Progressive reforms evolved because middle-class intellectuals, suddenly cut off from the power and authority of American society, were more able to identify with the powerlessness of the poor. The argument deprecates the sense of real concern and responsibility among this group, whatever the psychological motivation, but it does have a special validity in the case of women reformers. Women were marginal and insecure, not only because of their class, but also because of prejudice in the professions and in the political arena. Their sympathies with other "outsiders" do reflect a desire to compensate for a power imbalance which they seldom acknowledged, together with a desire not to overturn the system that had found some place for them as individuals. Lacking a sense of their own solidarity, separated from other women by strong class identification, women reformers seldom organized politically around environmental problems and had no unified policy for change. Thus they never posed an alternative to the professional *system*, only to its products.

In various capacities, women have taken on the task of "softening" or "humanizing" the domestic environment, occasionally bolstering their efforts with the status of the professional architect. This bent for reform seems to have arisen as much from their own marginality as women as from their socialization. While they have frequently been criticized for the traditional nature of their built forms, those who proposed alternative domestic settings have usually had to confine their work to paper. It has been inappropriate for them, being women, to be as flamboyant as the eccentric artists, as competitive as the businessmen, as bold as the daring engineers who are the master architects. Women have had to resort to their own, less conspicuous roles in order to secure a place: the isolated exceptional woman, if she had connections, could give her all; the majority accepted the inferior status of anonymous designer in order to belong to the architectural elite; many attached themselves as adjuncts in other fields and proposed necessary reforms; and an outspoken few called for changes in the social structure (including the professional structure) by describing alternative environments.

Despite such efforts, the inequalities still exist, and the corporate-institutional affiliations of the profession have grown all the more powerful. Other minority groups are facing identity conflicts similar to those of women, caught between being assimilated into the professional class and responding to the special needs of their constituencies. It is difficult for the individual to reconcile the two on her—or his—own. As long as architects, male and female, continue to deny the biases of their profession, individuals can only hope to offer adaptations and small-scale improvements.

BIBLIOGRAPHICAL NOTES

General histories of professionalism in America describe the trends toward specialization and legitimization that isolated women in every field. The most useful are Robert Wiebe, *The Search for Order* (New York, 1967) and Daniel H. Calhoun, *Professional Lives in America* (Cambridge, Mass., 1965). On architecture, see Arthur Weatherhead, *The History of Collegiate Education in Architecture* (Los Angeles, 1941). The unpublished master's thesis of Lian Hurst, "Building Shelters in a Corporate Society: Toward a Political

Economy of Architectural Practice in the United States" (University of California, Berkeley, 1974), gives valuable information about the economic base of the profession.

A number of books on women's history emphasize their position in the labor force and their social expectations as workers. This general information is applicable to women architects. Ronald W. Hogeland, ed., *Women and Womanhood in America* (Lexington, Mass., 1973), especially the essay by Barbara Welter, "The Cult of True Womanhood, 1820-1860" (reprinted from *American Quarterly*, Summer 1966), presents a broad range of attitudes toward women, and touches on differences in class and race. Edith Hoshino Altbach, *Women in America* (Lexington, Mass., 1974), summarizes a variety of attitudes and experiences of women in the home and in the work force, as does William H. Chafe, *The American Woman: Her Changing Social, Economic, and Political Roles, 1920-1970* (New York, 1972). The classic is Robert W. Smuts, *Women and Work in America* (New York, 1959). Jessie Bernard, *Women and the Public Interest* (Chicago, 1971), analyzes the prevailing "supportive function" of women's work and the "career patterning" of professional women into certain fields. Cynthia Fuchs Epstein, *Woman's Place* (Berkeley, 1970), discusses professional models and images as well. Richard Jensen's "Family, Career, and Reform: Women Leaders of the Progressive Era," in Michael Gordon, ed., *The American Family in Social-Historical Perspective* (New York, 1973), notes the emergence of the "female role" in early professionalism, and the implications of this course on each profession and for women themselves.

More recent research on women in the architectural profession includes: Ellen Perry Berkeley, "Women in Architecture," *Architectural Forum* (December 1972), Adele Chatfield-Taylor, "Hitting Home," *Architectural Forum* (March 1973), the "Women and the Arts" issue of *Arts in Society* 11 (Spring-Summer 1974). *Status of Women in the Architectural Profession* (Washington, D.C., 1975) is the report of the AIA Task Force on Women in Architecture, Judith Edelman, chairperson. Doris Cole, *From Tipi to Skyscraper* (Boston, 1973), is an overview of women's impact on American architecture. Dolores Hayden and Gwendolyn Wright provide an annotated bibliography of recent work on women as architects and users of the built environment, both past and present, in their "Review Essay" for *Signs: Journal of Women in Culture and Society* 1 (Summer 1976). The Belluschi quote on p. 285 is from "Should You Be an Architect?," no. 7 in a series by New York Life Insurance Company (1955), reprinted in *Scholastic Magazine* (April 1971).

Material on Beecher is from *The American Woman's Home* (New York, 1869) and *Treatise on Domestic Economy* (Boston, 1843). Kathryn Kish Sklar, *Catharine Beecher: A Study in American Domesticity* (New Haven, 1973), provides a thorough biography. For the section on Morgan, I relied principally on Richard Longstreth's unpublished paper "Julia Morgan (1872-1957): Some Introductory Notes" (University of California, Berkeley, 1972), the November 1918 issue of *Architect and Engineer* which was devoted to her work, and a helpful interview with Dorothy Coblentz, a former employee of Morgan's. A two-part article in *Architectural Record*, "A Thousand Women in Architecture" (March and June 1948), noted the number of women who were still practicing after the war and cited the work of the most successful. *Dwelling, Place, and Architecture: Women in American Architecture and Design*, edited by Susana Torré (New York, 1976), documents the history of women as designers, builders, and users of the domestic environment. There are chapters on Beecher, Morgan, Raymond, Hayden, and Bauer, and extensive material on contemporary practice and theory.

Planners have received more individual attention. The major writings of Elisabeth Coit include "Notes on the Design and Construction of the Dwelling Unit for the Lower-Income Family," *Octagon* (October and November 1941), and "Housing from the Tenant's Viewpoint," *Architectural Record* (April 1942). A sampling of the work by Catherine Bauer includes: *Modern Housing* (Boston/New York, 1934), *A Citizen's Guide to Public Housing* (Poughkeepsie, N.Y., 1940), *Social Questions in Housing and Town Planning* (London, 1952), and "Slums Aren't Necessary," *American Mercury* (March 1934), from which the quote on p. 300 is taken.

In its early stages the adjunct role of the woman architect was closely associated with scientific management and reformism. Fascination with both ideas was pervasive; see Samuel Haber, *Efficiency and Uplift: Scientific Management in the Progressive Era, 1890-1915* (Chicago, 1964). Two influential books on the subject by home economists are Martha B. Bensley and Robert Bruère, *Increasing Home Efficiency* (New York, 1916), and Margaret G. Reid, *Economics of Household Production* (New York/London, 1934). Dolores Hayden's *Seven American Utopias: The Architecture of Communitarian Socialism* (Cambridge, Mass., 1976) describes the innovations and the limitations of that approach. For further discussion of the Commonwealth, see Gwendolyn Wright, "The Woman's Commonwealth: Separatism, Self and Sharing," *Architectural Association Quarterly* 6 (Fall-Winter 1974), pp. 36-43.

Literature on the women's clubs and settlement houses points out the paradoxical nature of these reform movements: William O'Neill, *Everyone Was Brave* (Chicago, 1969), Allen F. Davis, *American Heroine: The Life and Legend of Jane Addams* (New York, 1973) and *Spearheads to Reform: The Settlement House* (New York, 1967), and Jane Addams, *Twenty Years at Hull-House* (New York, 1910). The reference to R. Hofstadter on p. ooo applies to *The Age of Reform* (New York, 1955). Christopher Lasch, *The New Radicalism in America, 1889-1963* (New York, 1965), points out that such self-interested motivation does not negate the reality of the environmental problems which these women sought to allay.

I would like to thank Marvin Lazerson and Lian Hurst for their helpful comments.

# 11

## Architectural Practice in America, 1865-1965—Ideal and Reality

BERNARD MICHAEL BOYLE

The history of the architectural profession in America before the beginning of the twentieth century is both episodic and incomplete. For most of the nineteenth century, any who so chose could call themselves architects and could engage in professional activities with whatever level of involvement and sense of responsibility they saw fit. No doubt this was, for one thing, because the establishment of formal educational curricula and standards for architects came late in the nineteenth century, with the founding of the first programs in architecture at the Massachusetts Institute of Technology (1868), Cornell University (1871), and the University of Illinois (1873). Further, it was for a long time unnecessary for those claiming to be architects to have had any professional education at all, let alone a formal and technical one. Registration of architects by the states, which usually mandated educational qualifications and carried with it the exclusive right to the title of architect, came even later than the founding of the first schools. The first registration law for architects was enacted in 1897, in Illinois.

In most cases, and throughout most of the nineteenth century, prospective architects acquired the rudiments of a professional background—it could hardly be called an education—by working and learning in the offices of those already in practice. They remained in these situations for differing periods, either as pupils or as junior employees, before setting up for themselves—a training method resembling closely the system of apprenticeship common in England at the same time. Many architects then worked alone or with no more than a small staff, and the organization of practice was frequently as informal as the training. The profession itself was ill-defined and unorganized, and few architectural offices survived the retirement or death of their principals. Understandably enough in such circumstances, there was little continuity between one generation and the next. Not before the return from Europe of the first Americans who had studied at the Ecole des Beaux-Arts in Paris did the older methods of training begin to be replaced, and architects begin to organize themselves into a professional body.

The educational program of the Ecole des Beaux-Arts, which has been described in detail in Chapter 8, had a number of obvious failings: standards were quite restrictive, while instruction was largely unregulated, and the ruling philosophy was generally conservative if not entirely reactionary. Yet by comparison with the American situation at the time, where instruction was paltry and standards were non-existent, it was a model of order, discipline, and excellence. The first Paris-trained American architect was R. M. Hunt, and he was followed by numerous others, among them H. H. Richardson, who returned from Europe in 1865. They were the two most influential practicing architects in America in the 1870s and 1880s, and each established an office which drew on his French experience. Their example had a great effect on the development of architectural training and practice in America from that time forward.

The first American atelier was established by Hunt in New York in 1857, and it became known as a center of progressive architectural education according to the standards of the day. Richardson began practice in 1866, and he strove not only to introduce French methods into his office, but to make it as well a source of training and education for younger men. To those who knew and worked with him, Richardson gave personal as well as professional inspiration, and what he had learned in the French ateliers was reflected in large part in his own practice. The experiences of his student years in Paris remained a vivid memory throughout his life, and the esprit of the atelier was communicated to his associates in the recounting of lively anecdotes:

Many were his recollections of the wild gayety of his friends when some difficult task, left for completion to last hurried hours of all-night work, had been finished and displayed, and the *atelier*—through some one of its members in whose success all the others felt they had a right to share—had triumphed over rival studios in a general *concours* of the School [Van Rensselaer, *Henry Hobson Richardson and His Works*, p. 15].

Figure 72. H. H. Richardson's assistants in his library, ca. 1886. An influential model for American architectural offices of the late nineteenth century was the Parisian atelier, with its characteristic atmosphere of brotherhood and collaboration.

Many of his contemporaries testified later to the influence on their own professional activities of Richardson's notion of the atelier system, how his dynamic personality had made the ideal a living one in his office, and how they had aspired to practice and lead in the same way in their turn (Figure 72). Nor was Richardson's contribution to American architectural practice limited to his enthusiasm for the atelier system, for it is significant that Richardson's personal version of the atelier combined training with practice, in distinction from the French method. In the French situation, the master's office and his atelier were usually separate in location as well as in function. The atelier was often a source of some income to the master, but at the same time it was a semi-independent unit of the educational program of the Ecole des Beaux-Arts. The master's main support came from his architectural commissions, which were executed by his professional office. A student from the atelier might become the master's employee, as did Richardson, for one, but in that case he would not also be a full-time student. This was the method followed by Hunt, whose atelier and professional office were separate entities. By contrast, Richardson's office and atelier were one and the same; there was in America at that time no institution like the Ecole, and it is understandable that Richardson took the whole burden of educating young architects on himself, and he was an inspiring leader:

[Richardson's office] was filled with a score of workers ranging in age and grade from the boyish novice up to the capable, experienced artist, all fraternally bound together and loyally devoted to their chief, all laboring together on work which had a single inspiration and a common accent, and each feeling a personal pride in results which the world knew as the master's only [Van Rensselaer, p. 123].

Another aspect of Richardson's office practice is revealed by this comment, namely, the emphasis placed upon collaboration among the office staff. The collaborative effort which had typified Richardson's Parisian atelier experiences was transposed by him to the field of office practice, again in distinction from the French method. Until ill health restricted his activities, Richardson himself participated in every part of the work of his office, and encouraged a similar degree of participation by his associates. The members of Richardson's office were a team, and all participated in the work, from the highest to the lowest, the older and more experienced helping the younger and less skillful, and deliberately infusing the work process with a sense of fraternity and sharing. Furthermore, Richardson encouraged the equal collaboration of other professionals and artists, e.g., the painter John La Farge and the landscape architect F. L. Olmsted, giving the work of such fellow artists as much independence as his own.

Among those who owed their early training to H. H. Richardson, and later achieved professional distinction on their own, were C. F. McKim and Stanford White. The office of McKim, Mead and White, founded in 1879, in its earlier years continued the educational mission embodied in Richardson's practice, and McKim in particular was said to have succeeded in training and inspiring many younger men. It is clear that an effort was made in their office to maintain the style of the atelier:

I never can forget that when I knew the old quarters at 57 Broadway in which McKim, Mead and White were doing so much to make over American architecture they had the characteristics and atmosphere of an *atelier* . . . that *atelier* became famous across a continent. An immense amount of architectural evangelism . . . proceeded from that fount [R. Cortissoz, in *The American Architect* (1926)].

A sense of participation by all in the work of the office was encouraged by the principals, and White's dynamic personality left a lasting impression on his associates: " 'He was extremely optimistic and enthusiastic, and invariably conveyed his enthusiasm to all about him, whether clients, draughtsmen or builders. . . . He was a born leader and superintendent' " [F. L. V. Hoppin, in Baldwin, *Stanford White*, p. 263]. McKim, like Richardson a student of the Ecole des Beaux-Arts, included painters and sculptors as collaborators in his architectural endeavors wherever possible. Further, McKim's personal commitment to architectural education was indicated by his untiring efforts toward the founding of an American School in Rome, in imitation of the French Academy. Success in this project came after several years, when the American Academy in Rome was founded in 1897, admitting students in painting and sculpture as well as architecture. It replaced the American School of Architecture in Rome, which had been founded by McKim and a few friends in 1895, which in turn had been the realization of McKim's project of 1894 for an Architectural Atelier. In other words, the idea of the atelier was a continuing inspiration in the minds of leading figures in nineteenth-century American architecture, and as long as their offices remained relatively small there was no doubt that the shared experiences of the atelier could be the reality as much as the ideal. American architectural offices did not all remain small, however, and the office of McKim, Mead and White was to become one of the largest.

In his autobiography, R. A. Cram recalled his first professional experiences in the office of Rotch and Tilden in Boston, where he spent five years: "When I began my study of architecture with Rotch and Tilden in 1881, an office that had ten draughtsmen was a big and imposing affair" (*My Life in Architecture*, p. 41). By the time of McKim's death in 1909, the office staff list of McKim, Mead and White contained no less than 89 names; and the total, including unlisted non-professional staff, most probably exceeded 100. An office of such a size was considered very large by the standards of 1950, and must have seemed huge in 1909; and it is not surprising that a new type of office organization developed insensibly in response to the needs of what was in fact a new type of office. At first, the three principals had shared all responsibilities; but later McKim came to be most involved with large planning projects and with client relationships, i.e., obtaining jobs through his extensive social contacts, while Mead took responsibility for management and production, and White for detailed design. Their office was so large because of its success in capturing the largest commissions of the day, but its great size cannot have failed finally to destroy or at least substantially to diminish the old intimacy of small scale. Despite the testimony of friends and colleagues to the inspiring leadership and ubiquitous participation of Stanford White, for example, it seems clear that no single person, no matter how energetic, could have involved himself directly in every stage of every one of the office's numerous jobs. It became necessary for the principals not only to divide the responsibility for various areas of work among themselves, but to delegate authority extensively as well.

The office of Cram and Wentworth provides an even clearer example of the trend in office organization in the late nineteenth century. In his description of the founding of the office, Cram noted, "As I considered myself as the designing factor in a putative architectural firm, I must have a practical partner" (Cram, p. 69); and this was at the beginning of his professional career. Here it was established at once that there would be division of responsibility, even though the office at first comprised no more than the two principals. Cram was in charge of all design, later taking large-scale design and planning to himself and leaving detailed design to B. G. Goodhue, while C. F. Wentworth, later to be replaced by F. W. Ferguson, was responsible for office management, structures, and supervision. According to Cram, who himself had no professional education, such an arrangement reflected logically the skills and predispositions of the participants, and there appeared here a pattern of organization from the first quite unlike Richardson's atelier. Division of responsibility plainly never hindered the office's growth and success, which were considerable, yet Cram's recollections were only of "a closely knit architectural unity, even when the members amounted to forty or more," where there were "assistants who were friends as well as employees" (Cram, p. 81). Beside this may be set a memory of McKim, who was said to have "regarded his assistants as participators in the creation and treated them as equals. The office had an inspiring atmosphere, due largely to Mr. McKim's ideals. Men were glad to be associated with him" (W. A. Boring, in Moore, *The Life and Times of Charles Follen McKim*, p. 57). Whatever the value of such reminiscences, it seems to have been true that for Cram, as much as for McKim, fraternity and participation remained meaningful as ideals even as their offices in fact came to embody those ideals little or not at all; and in at least one famous example, ideals were absent from the start.

Perhaps most well-known of the large offices of the later nineteenth and early twentieth centuries was the office of D. H. Burnham in Chicago, founded in 1873 as Burnham and Root. Like Cram, Burnham lacked formal professional education, while J. W. Root was a graduate of the engineering school of New York University. Root had professional office experience as well, and played a major role in the growth of the office's reputation. Yet it was after Root's death in 1891, and primarily through Burnham's promotional and managerial skills, that the office achieved its greatest success. The late-nineteenth-century building boom in Chicago and the Columbian Exposition of 1893 provided enormous opportunities for architects, and Burnham was uniquely prepared to take advantage of the moment. As he told Louis Sullivan on their first meeting, Burnham had a clear idea of the nature of architectural practice, and of where his own direction lay: "My idea is to work up to a big business, to handle big things, deal with big businessmen, and to build a big organization, for you can't handle big things unless you have an organization" (Sullivan, *Autobiography of an Idea*, pp. 285-86).

After Root's death, Burnham logically enough sought out and hired men with the professional skills he himself lacked, and which were essential to the maintenance of a large office. In 1912, at its greatest extent, Burnham's office had 180 employees, as well as small branch offices in New York and San Francisco. The main office in Chicago was run by a managing partner who had under him three senior associates, each of whom was in charge of one of the work areas of design, production, and supervision. Such an arrangement left Burnham free to pursue client relationships, always his main concern, and stood as a much-admired model of office organization at the time. Again it was Sullivan who, looking back on the last decades of the nineteenth century, pointed to the larger significance of Burnham's office organization:

During this period there was well under way the formation of mergers, combinations and trusts in the industrial world. The only architect in Chicago to catch the significance of this movement was Daniel Burnham, for in its tendency toward bigness, organization, delegation, and intense commercialism, he sensed the reciprocal workings of his own mind [Sullivan, p. 314].

In other words, Burnham's office organization reflected general tendencies in American society at the time, and in this it was a model of a new order in architectural practice, one destined to become as dominant there as in the world outside the profession.

How great was the effect of the new order can be seen by returning to the example with which we began: the office of H. H. Richardson. For it seems that notwithstanding his leadership and influence during his lifetime, Richardson's untimely death brought on the decline of his methods not only in the offices of the next generation, but among his own successors as well; even there, in the home of collaborative effort, the principle of participation was converted imperceptibly into the practice of separated responsibilities. Control of the work areas of design, structures, and management in Richardson's office was divided on his death in 1886 among three men, J. Shepley, C. Rutan, and C. A. Coolidge. Not unexpectedly, Richardson's sometime atelier came soon to resemble other well-known offices of the late nineteenth century in its methods of work and organization. Indeed, Richardson's most recent biographer attributed the declining level of artistic achievement of the office under Richardson's successors, at least in part, to the organizational changes that followed Richardson's death. Whatever the reasons for the quality of the work of Shepley, Rutan, and Coolidge, it was certainly true that large architectural offices in America were soon to be marked by a firm, not to say rigid, internal structure characterized by separation of responsibility and division of labor.

Few outside the profession could have been expected to observe that the large office represented something quite new for architectural practice. Yet if the common notion of the architect remained the traditional one of the individual artist-practitioner, the change in methods of practice brought by the coming of the large office was not unnoticed within the profession. Addressing a group of fellow professionals in 1902, a New Jersey architect suggested that it was time for the discrepancy between the reality of architectural practice and the public view of it to be removed, for, as he pointed out, "Instead of our successful architects as a whole constituting a class of befogged dreamers they are in reality fully as keen and of as large capacity in the business of money getting as any other constituency in American affairs." Again, admitting that there were still some dissemblers who affected to believe that all achievement in architecture sprang from unique artistic genius while knowing well it did not, he noted the existence of others "who with great sincerity make not the slightest pretense that their successes are founded upon anything other than superior business ability. . . . They were and are business men engaged in gaining money by practising the business of architecture." Further, he concluded that the change in the nature of architectural practice was both inevitable and permanent, justifying his conclusion with logic as effective now as it was then: "The architectural opportunities fall to those who are preëminent for business rather than artistic ability, and thus it is they who build the architecture of the country, good, bad or indifferent. The architect must be a business man first and an artist afterwards" (J. F. Harder, in *The Brickbuilder* [1902]). It should be emphasized that there was nothing prophetic in these observations, for they were describing the professional situation as it was actually perceived from the inside in 1902. If they still seem notably timely, that can only be evidence of the persistence of the misapprehensions about architectural practice against which they were directed.

Although a purposely brief survey of only a few of the more well-known examples, this discussion has intended to show that the large office was an established fact of American architectural practice by the end of the nineteenth century. It should be noted as well that many of those large offices continued a successful professional life without interruption into the twentieth century, often in spite of the replacement of their principals; and a few of them are still in practice today. There was in the example of such offices as those of Cram and Ferguson, and McKim, Mead and White a continuity unknown to the previous century and even unfamiliar to the whole history of the architectural profession. The continuation of the work of an architect in earlier periods was not infrequently undertaken by an assistant or successor, but typically it was the program of the patron which continued rather than the practice of the architect. By contrast, the large architectural office has seemed to become a self-sustaining phenomenon in America since the beginning of this century. It is not surprising that the style of office organization first developed in the early large offices has continued to be used, with increasing precision, by the large offices which have grown up in more recent years.

Organization for practice in the twentieth century soon had to respond to the demands of increased job size and work complexity. Very large numbers of skilled professionals drawn from various fields were needed for projects such as the Empire State Building and Rockefeller Center, for example, both built in New York in the 1930s. The activities of architects, structural and mechanical engineers, construction companies, and materials suppliers, as well as many others, all had to be coordinated in ways both precise and all-encompassing. Diagrams of the organizations formed to carry out these great enterprises were extraordinarily detailed and also extraordinarily complicated. So many decisions had to be made during the progress of a very large project, any one of which might have had an effect on the whole quite out of proportion to its own apparent significance, that it became essential for every decision to be integrated with the rest.

The means chosen to achieve this end was the separation of the decision-making from the other aspects of the work, and the appointment of particular individuals to take charge of it, whose responsibility it then became to coordinate the separate work areas. If separation of the traditionally joint components of architectural practice tended to diminish the participation of the individual worker in the whole, it nonetheless seemed to be an unavoidable result of the demands of the work, ultimately developing its own rationale. What was at first a separation of responsibility and division of labor resulting more from the growing needs of growing offices than from deliberate intention, soon became a basic principle of organization; and it was applied not only to large offices but even, in some cases, to small ones as well.

In 1950 the American Institute of Architects sponsored a survey of the profession in America. The report which analyzed and commented on the results of the survey concluded that three types of office were typical of architectural practice in America: small, meaning less than ten employees; medium, meaning from ten to fifty employees; and large, meaning more than fifty employees. Diagrams showed the organizational patterns of the three types of office. As might be expected, in the small office the work of each employee might range over the whole field of activity found in the office, including design and presentation, production, supervision, and so forth. Above the scale of the small office, however, separation of work into distinct professional or skill areas appeared, and the diagrams of organization of the medium and the large office were different only in degree and not in kind. The coordination of the work made necessary by its separation into skill areas was accomplished by a special level of employee, inserted between the principals and the other employees, whose sole task it was to supervise the work process itself, a function unrelated to any traditional or modern skill area. Even the small office, as the report noted, was capable of being subjected to the organizational pattern of the large, for small and medium were commonly regarded as evolutionary stages in the history of an individual office, whose professional destiny it was to grow to the largest possible size.

It is not difficult to see that the historical development of the structure of the large office, leading first to separation of the various aspects and stages of the work and second to separation of the decision-making from the work itself, led in turn to specialization on the part of the workers and their separation one from another. An employee in a small office would be expected to participate in all office activities, but such general competence was not required in a large office, and was even perhaps a little detrimental to the individual's ability to give an undiluted contribution to the large office's specialized needs. Thus it began to follow that in the large office different employees might well not only become specialists in different activities, such as design or production, but might also spend, and even expect to spend, all of their professional careers engaged in those activities alone.

Specialization of role within the office structure was paralleled to some extent by specialization of practice in general. The survey reported that nearly half of the offices responding considered themselves specialists in one or more areas of professional activity, e.g., religious buildings, hospitals, schools; and some offices specialized in other ways, e.g., in very large projects, such as governmental buildings, or small projects, such as private houses. But whatever area or scale of specialization an office attempted, or whether it aimed at no specialization at all, the pattern of organization found in the large office had by 1950 come to be very widely followed in American practice.

Architectural education in late-nineteenth-century America took a direction similar to that of office practice. At first, Americans desirous of receiving the best available education went to Paris, but it soon became apparent that it would be simpler and more effective to set up formal programs of architectural education in America. The influence of men such as Hunt, Richardson, and McKim extended beyond their offices to the establishment of formal education for architects. As their offices were modeled more or less on the French ateliers, so it was natural for the educational programs they supported to be modeled more or less on that of the Ecole des Beaux-Arts. Mention has already been made of McKim's efforts toward the founding of the American Academy in Rome. At home, dependence on French methods went beyond imitation of curriculum to the importation of Frenchmen as teachers. The first of the imported pedagogs was Eugène Letang, who arrived at the Massachusetts Institute of Technology in 1872. He was followed by a growing stream of others, which continued unabated until well into the twentieth century and long after the Ecole had ceased to be at the forefront of architectural education in Europe—where by the beginning of the century a new theory of design had matured after more than fifty years of discussion and experiment.

The history of that development was traced by Nikolaus Pevsner in a seminal work, *Pioneers of Modern Design*, published first in 1936, in which were demonstrated the connections between artistic hostility toward machine technology in 1850 and acceptance of it after 1900. The nature of those connections will be discussed later, but at this point it will be enough to say that one of the effects of that historical process was a new theory of design education derived from the new theory of design. Not the first, but from the point of view of architectural education, the most important figure in the development and implementation of the new theory of design education was the German architect Walter Gropius (1883-1969; Figure 73). Himself the product of a rigorous formal education, Gropius after 1900 appeared as a leader of the avant-garde in architectural design, and after the First World War became a leader in progressive architectural education as well. From 1919 onwards, Gropius published numerous explanations and justifications of his theory of design education. In almost every statement he emphasized the need for a spiritual awakening in modern society to parallel the social consciousness aroused by the First World War, for "not until the political revolution is perfected in the spiritual revolution can we become free"; only after the spiritual revolution "will the people again join together in building the great art work of their time . . . the freedom cathedral of the future." It was the spiritual unity of medieval society which had made possible the magnificent achievements of the Gothic builders, the same unity of work and spirit which had characterized the life of the medieval craft guilds. Modern society had to rediscover that unity, and "the relationship of man to man, the spirit of small communities, must conquer again. Small fruitful communities, secret societies, brotherhoods . . . building guilds as in the golden age of cathedrals" (Lane, *Architecture and Politics in Germany, 1918-1945*, pp. 49-50).

Yet for all his medieval analogies, Gropius did not envision a return to a preindustrial Eden. On the contrary, full acceptance of the realities of the modern industrial world was fundamental to his approach. His program was given its first practical expression in the Bauhaus, which Gropius and his associates refashioned from top to bottom as the embodiment of his new theories of education and design.

When Walter Gropius took up the directorship of the Staatliches Bau-

Figure 73. The revolution in design theory which took place in the 1920s was largely under the direction of German artists and architects, of whom the most influential was Walter Gropius, shown here in Dessau, 1927.

haus in Weimar in 1919, he set out to create a school of design and crafts that would be responsive to the challenges and opportunities of the twentieth century. The Bauhaus had been formerly a crafts school of traditional type, but under Gropius' leadership it was to become a center of experimentation in the bringing together of machine technology on the one hand and modern design theory on the other. Gropius came to the Bauhaus from a career in architecture, and in fact he viewed all design as architectonic in basic character. With this understanding, Gropius approached all design problems as basically similar, and thus considered it necessary for all designers to have the same basic education. In a series of publications Gropius enunciated his theory of unified design training, emphasizing its major features:

. . . The Bauhaus was inaugurated in 1919 with the specific object of realizing a modern architectonic art, which like human nature was meant to be all-embracing in its scope. Experiment once more became the center of architecture, and that demands a broad, co-ordinating mind, not the narrow specialist" [Gropius, *Scope of Total Architecture*, pp. 19-20].

Gropius' modern architectonic art included all artistic activity as well as all design problems: "What the Bauhaus preached in practice was the common citizenship of all forms of creative work, and their logical interdependence on one another in the modern world" (p. 20); and the educational program was intended to remove the academic distinction between the so-called fine arts and so-called applied arts or crafts.

The Bauhaus aimed at the training of people possessing artistic talents as designers in industry and handicrafts, as sculptors, painters and architects. A complete co-ordinated training of all handicrafts, in technique and in form, with the object of teamwork in building, served as the basis [p. 23].

The curriculum of the Bauhaus was designed to demonstrate the similarity of method common to the solution of all design problems, beginning with a basic course through which all students had to pass before they entered the workshops, where they confronted the problems of working with actual materials. The basic course was not only a pedagogical device intended to make the student think broadly; it represented as well an essential part of Gropius' theory, namely, the rational basis of design:

The spiritual implications of art in society are to be redefined and, with the help of the scientists and using their methods of precision, the social and psychological components of art—not only the technical ones—are to be determined by a distinct order of values and meanings [p. 51].

That there was to be found a scientific language of design, independent of subjective human variables, so to speak, Gropius had no doubt:

Basic order in design needs first of all a denominator common to all, derived from facts . . . today, a new language of vision is slowly replacing individualistic terms like "taste" or "feeling" with terms of objective validity. Based on biological facts—both physical and psychological—it seeks to represent the impersonal cumulative experience of successive generations [p. 51].

There was to be a new order and a new visual language, in which "scientific" experimentation would discover the "objective" facts on which would be based "rational" design. The means to this end were clear, for the scientists had shown the way to a new and unbiased perception of reality; perceptual psychology would provide the facts for the unified approach. "If we can establish a common basis for the understanding of design—a denominator reached through objective findings rather than through personal interpretation—it should apply to any type of design" (p. 30); for it was the subjective nature of traditional design theory that was to be replaced, and "if we can understand the nature of what we see and the way we perceive it, then we will know more about the potential influence of man-made design on human feeling and thinking" (p. 30).

It was objective human responses that the new design would accommodate: "I consider the psychological problems, in fact, as basic and primary, whereas the technical components of design are our intellectual auxiliaries to realize the intangible through the tangible" (p. 30). All Gropius' statements on education were consistent with those two points: at bottom all design problems would submit to a single method of approach, and the tool of that method was an objectivity founded on the truths of experimental science.

Application of Gropius' theory followed two further principles, demanding unification of diverse skills and collaboration of diverse individuals. Not only should there be a unification of all the arts and crafts under the single head of design, but as well all other areas of knowledge and experiment should be drawn upon, for "good architecture should be a projection of life itself and that implies an intimate knowledge of biological, social, technical and artistic problems." Unity of purpose was the essential theme of the educational program, pointing toward the needs of man in society: "Man is to be the focus; his spiritual and material needs in relation to the life of the community should determine all stages of the student's training" (p. 56). Translated into the school program, the aim of a unified education influenced the choice of teaching method, namely that

students should be trained to work in teams—also with students of related techniques—in order to learn methods of collaboration with others. This will prepare them for their vital task of becoming co-ordinators of the many individuals involved in the conception and execution of planning and building projects [p. 57].

The principle of cooperative teamwork could be seen as a distinct contrast to the competitive system of the Ecole des Beaux-Arts, but for Gropius it had other benefits, of more general significance: "I consider this co-operative principle particularly promising, and very appropriate to the spirit of our age; especially when these groups include engineers and economists" (p. 64). Collaboration would tend toward the goal of unified activity in building: "If [the architect] will build up a closely co-operating team together with the engineer, the scientist and the builder, then design, construction and economy may again become an entity—a fusion of art, science and business" (p. 74); and beyond this, collaboration pointed to the social unity which Gropius sought to invoke through architecture.

. . . I tried to put the emphasis of my work on integration and co-ordination, inclusiveness, not exclusiveness, for I felt that the art of building is contingent upon the co-ordinated teamwork of a band of active collaborators whose co-operation symbolizes the co-operative organism of what we call society [p. 19].

The role of the architect was to be a "co-ordinator" who would "unify the many social, technical, economic and artistic problems," and in this the modern architect was reassimilated to the past, for "the historical mission of the architect has always been to achieve the complete co-ordination of all efforts in building up man's physical surroundings" (p. 76); and "in all great creative periods, architecture in its highest embodiment has been the dominating mother of all arts, has been a social art" (p. 47).

Collaboration and teamwork were necessary and logical responses to the perceived realities of modern industrial society, but their usefulness did not end there. Collaborative effort would not only bring diverse skills and viewpoints together in design solutions made more consequent because more inclusive; collaboration would also, and perhaps more importantly, diminish the role of the individual in the final result. The common insight behind Gropius' principles was that it was subjective individualism which lay at the root of the problems of modern design education. Only universals, objectively arrived at, could rescue architecture and design from the morass of historicist obfuscation and sentimentality, for "only the collaboration of many can succeed in finding solutions which transcend the individual aspect" (p. 28); immortal art would be the product not of the individual but of the group. In other words, as the profession of architecture fulfilled itself by satisfying the needs of society, society in turn would fulfill itself through revolution in the profession of architecture.

Gropius' theories gradually found toleration, if not total acceptance, in the Germany of the 1920s, but his practice at the Bauhaus, first in Weimar and later in Dessau, encountered increasing opposition. At first the opposition was purely local, but in the later years of the decade Gropius and other progressive architects in Germany became involved increasingly in the political turmoil of the time, willingly or unwillingly. Many of them ultimately became victims of that turmoil, and left Germany for other European countries or emigrated to America, thereby spreading the methods and ideals of modern German architecture through much of the world. Gropius himself left Germany for England in 1934 and England for America in 1937.

Before Walter Gropius came to America, the work of the Bauhaus and its theory of education were little known to Americans. Apart from the efforts of a few lonely pioneers such as George Howe and immigrants such as Walter Lescaze, Richard Neutra, and R. M. Schindler, and the publications of H.-R. Hitchcock, Americans had little information about the new architecture of Europe. Knowledge of European practice and theory was mostly limited to the contacts of individual Americans with the Ecole des Beaux-Arts, the presence in American architectural schools of imported French teachers, and curricula modeled to various degrees on the French original. With the arrival of Gropius at Harvard University in 1937, and the immigration to America of others who had been associated with the Bauhaus, the new European ways were established as it were overnight, and their supplanting of the old methods became only a matter of time. It is not an exaggeration to say that ten years after his arrival, Gropius had made the school of architecture at Harvard into the best known and most admired, not just in America, but throughout much of the world. The old ways died slowly, but very little was left of the Beaux-Arts domination of the American architectural curriculum by 1950.

At the same time the influence of the new ideas was being felt outside the schools. Proof of that was provided by Lever House (Skidmore, Owings and Merrill, New York, 1952), applauded at the time as evidence of the victory of the progressive European ideas in design. Whether that building symbolized a similar victory for the new ideas in American office practice was another question. For some time past, the dominant institution in professional activity had been the large office, and the office that produced Lever House was shortly to become the largest of all.

By 1950, the office of Skidmore, Owings and Merrill had become the outstanding example of the particular style of architectural practice that had developed in America since the beginning of the twentieth century. The office was founded in Chicago in 1936 by Louis Skidmore and Nathaniel A. Owings, both architects, who were joined by John O. Merrill, an engineer, in 1939. According to Owings' own account, the partners intended from the first to follow a definite program which aimed at success and recognition, for themselves and for the profession, and respect for the architect's skills and services. The organization of the office followed a plan for achieving the goal of respect, for "to gain the respect of the client, SOM had to be powerful, had to have national coverage. . . . To accomplish this coverage we used a very old ethic: the master builder system based on the anonymous Gothic builders of the Middle Ages" (Owings, *The Spaces in Between*, p. ix). Beyond respect however, there was a larger aim, namely, the influencing and alteration of the physical condition of society: "We were not after jobs as such. We were after leverage to influence social and environmental conditions." Beyond that was another aim, yet larger: "To work, we must have volume. An efficient set of master builders can eat up a lot of work. Volume meant power. We would try to change men's minds" (Owings, p. 66).

If the office's program seemed to contain internal conflicts, and to carry implications of social engineering as much as of architecture, it had a certain logic nonetheless. Even leaving aside obvious differences in work methods and building technology, it is hard to see any similarities between the practices of Gothic builders and the modern construction industry. Yet it is certainly possible to see another connection, namely, between Owings' description of his office's program and what Gropius had written from 1918 onwards about modern architecture and society. It is perhaps unlikely that Owings was familiar with Gropius' earliest writings, which had appeared only in Europe, and in any case he did not mention them, but there were clear reflections of Gropius' basic ideas in Owings' words. The analogy of the Gothic builders, anonymity, teamwork, and the social motivation of architecture, all were present. For Gropius there was "spiritual revolution," while for Owings there was the "ethic" of the "master builder," though it must be admitted that it was not clear what Owings understood the term "ethic" to mean in the modern American context. To begin with, architect and builder were members of the same group in the Middle Ages, while they are separated in modern practice. Owings' meaning was perhaps expressed by another statement on the office's program, in which the partners pledged "to offer a multi-disciplined service competent to design and build the multiplicity of shelters needed for man's habitat" (Owings, p. 66).

Skidmore, Owings and Merrill set out to provide every kind of professional service within a single frame, including not only the usual design, structural, and production services, but also interior design, graphics, all types of presentation, technical research, and mechanical and other engineering specialties. The office aimed at giving its clients a total in-house package of design and related services, and no doubt it was that aspect of the office's practice that was thought to resemble the medieval builders' guild. The impact of this concept of service was felt as the office grew larger, for as the office developed new needs, new personnel were sought to fill them. It is not hard to imagine that an individual's usefulness to the office was measured partly by his ability to fill a predetermined position in the office structure. In addition to the founding partners, whose activities came to be primarily managerial and entrepreneurial, later partners were specialists in general design, in housing, hospitals, prefabrication, and so on.

The other logical element in the office program was the realization that there had always been in America a visible relationship between the amount of work handled by an office and the recognition and respect the office could expect to receive in return. There were exceptions to that general rule, and a small office could be famous while a large office was unknown, but the reverse was more common. As Skidmore, Owings and Merrill grew larger their work and clientele became national in scope, and offices in San Francisco and Portland were added to those already existing in Chicago and New York. In 1958 the office was a national operation under the direction of fourteen general partners, fifteen associate partners, and thirty-nine participating associates, with more than a thousand employees altogether.

The four regional offices were organized in the same way, so that each office would be capable of handling most jobs on its own. That is, each office represented all the skills found in the others, with full-service capacity. Several benefits derived from that system of organization. For one thing, providing all related professional services within a single office not only made coordination easier and more convenient, but made direct supervisory control of the product easier as well. For another, the more areas of professional activity that came under one roof, the greater were the opportunities for increasing efficiency and productivity. Again, division of the office into several units, each self-sufficient, provided benefits similar to those of diversification in industry: when one unit had a small amount of work, jobs in the other units could keep the entire operation running at a profit. Skidmore, Owings and Merrill was finally not only one of the largest offices in America, but also one of the most all-embracing in professional terms and the most integrated in terms of business operations. Horizontal integration was provided by the four units around the country, while vertical integration was accomplished by the inclusive package of design and design-related services. Although Owings made much of the fact that the office never became incorporated as a business, its style of organization and operation was essentially that of any corporation of national scope.

As each regional office offered a similar service to the others, so all were run in much the same way. Each office had a management group whose members were responsible for the major divisions of the office, e.g., design, interiors, production, etc. Within each division, responsibility for individual jobs was delegated to job captains, each of whom was in charge of a group assigned to a particular task. When the group's work was done, the task would be carried on by the next division in the order of work, and assigned to a particular group within that division. Continuity in a single project was provided by the supervisor, who was a member of the management group, and followed the project through the various work stages. Overall co-ordination of the work of the office, assignment of personnel from job to job and even from office to office, and also ultimate design control, were the province of the general partners at the top of the office hierarchy. The general partners circulated among the four offices as necessary, acting essentially as a further management level (Figure 74). Apparently this arrangement did not differ greatly from the typical large office system discussed earlier, except for its greater size and more sophisticated management, but there were significant differences at the lower levels of office practice.

Such a large, or in this case enormous, office predicated a very firm internal structure, and the more precise the aims of the office, the firmer the structure had to be. As has been seen, Skidmore, Owings and Merrill from the first had very precise aims, and intended to reach those aims by providing a total design service to their clients. Now total design service was not a new idea, for it was found in the work and even more in the theory of the Bauhaus, and its origins along with those of other aspects of Gropius' work lay in the nineteenth century. William Morris and his circle extended their talents to every field of design, and many later figures, such as Peter Behrens in Germany and F. L. Wright in America, did the same when the opportunity arose. What marked out the quality of total design service in the practice of Skidmore, Owings and Merrill was that here, as in other aspects of the office's organization, total design was conceived as a device of control as much as of service, a constituent of the service package which was the office's product. The more areas of design decision the office could draw under its control, the more the decisions themselves could be made subject to the general aims of the office; from which it followed that the more decisions the office controlled, the more firmly the control had to be exercised, in order to provide the client with that high if unvaried level of design and service on which the office based its success. It was this that explained the separation of the various management levels from one another, and from the lower levels of the work force. While there was representation within the office of all the neces-

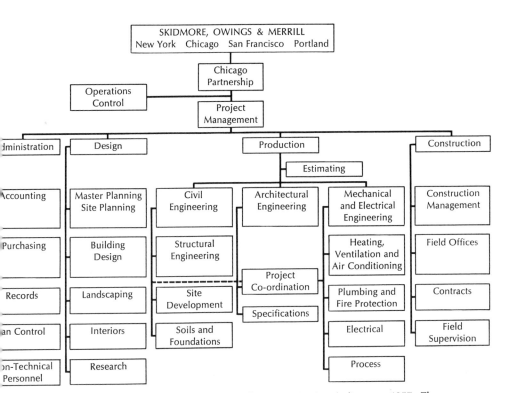

Figure 74. Skidmore, Owings and Merrill, office organizational diagram, 1957. The large American architectural office of the twentieth century was typified by a style of organization both complex and rigidly structured.

sary specialties, they were rigidly segregated according to task and specialty. While there were teams of workers, each team was made up of identical members, e.g., all designers, all engineers, and so on, and rarely if ever would a team of designers come into contact with a team in another work area.

It should be emphasized that this kind of teamwork in no way resembled the ideal enunciated by Gropius. The team of different skills bringing their different views and insights to a single problem, and working from initiation to final solution as a team all of whose members participated in all stages of the work, was not the reality of work in a huge office like Skidmore, Owings and Merrill. There the work passed from team to team, as from one individual to another on a factory production line, and the final product tended to be a replica of all the other products of the office, or factory, representing the original impulse but containing no input from the various production stages. In fact no such input was desired, because the products of the system were intentionally standardized and anonymous, not unlike the way in which one automobile necessarily resembles another from the same line. It is even possible to suggest that Skidmore, Owings and Merrill's success with large corporate clients was owed to the two special characteristics of their office practice: efficient and therefore reliable management, together with uniform and therefore predictable products.

This considerable achievement was not without its consequences in terms of other things than service and efficiency, and the success of their style of practice was to be questioned ultimately even by its originators. In Owings' words: "it might be argued that as SOM grew larger and older the firm became more rigid," and while declaring that "the practice of architecture is essentially the getting and executing of jobs," he also asked, "What had we become? Certainly not designers in the classic sense. We were entrepreneurs, promoters, expediters, financiers, diplomats; we were men of too many trades and masters of none" (Owings, p. 99).

Yet the final form of the office was no more than the logical result of the initial program, which had identified great size and great success as the twin supports of the plan to "change men's minds," and it was surely the very managerial skill which had made the office so successful that had created the paradox. The anonymous "set of master builders" of Skidmore, Owings and Merrill had in common with those of the Middle Ages only their anonymity, for the methods of the new type of architectural office did not resemble at all the methods of any prior age. In the past, individuality could find an outlet at many levels, but individual initiative was invisible in the final products of the modern set of master builders, which were notable mostly for their uniformity. Large architectural offices in the twentieth century had many characteristics in common with large private corporations and public bureaus, and a similar inherent logic of behavior: "[bureaucratic] organizations are not communities, but structures of power and interest. What they produce is designed to further the ends served by the organization."*

It might be concluded that from H. H. Richardson to Skidmore, Owings and Merrill the organization of the large architectural office in America moved from generalization to specialization, while at the same time the method of work moved from collaboration to division. As the large office gradually included more and more specialists in an attempt to maintain

* Sheldon S. Wolin, review of B. J. Wattenberg, *The Real America* (Garden City, N.Y., 1974), in *The New York Review of Books* 22(1) (February 6, 1975), 15.

the generalist character traditional to architectural practice, paradoxically the team of workers progressively lost its original identifying characteristic of collaboration as the coordinating function was taken over by a new level of management. Put another way, as the professional activity became more inclusive, it simultaneously became more exclusive. Furthermore, the transformation in the nature of architectural practice was general throughout the profession by the middle of the century.

Such an organization should not be thought of as imposed arbitrarily on the real nature of office practice in the modern age, for at least two reasons. Firstly, there is no ideal method or organization in the modern architectural profession. The older forms of guild, apprenticeship, and atelier all survived vestigially in the building trades, at least until recently, but are no longer widely found in architecture, if at all. If there is any ideal preserved in the image of the modern architect, it is the somewhat anachronistic one of the romantic hero struggling against the unheeding forces of philistine society to fulfill his unique and prophetic destiny. The antisocial egotism, to give it its least offensive coloring, which has often characterized the architect in contemporary fiction is the familiar if largely implausible reflection of that historical type. To the influence of the older literary image must be added the effect of the preservation into the modern day of earlier historical methods, such as history as biography, which are no longer considered primary in historical writing in general but are still found in the history of art and even more in popular writing. The seemingly limitless number of biographies of the great figures of modern architecture, which represent the history of architecture implicitly as the history of the individual, maintain this bias. Every major building is put forward as the product of the inspiration of a single and thus necessarily major individual. Only the general public ignorance of what really goes on in an architectural office permitted the continuation of that idealized but quite inaccurate vision of the profession. The individual architect did not disappear in the twentieth century, but his role in the profession became something less than it had once been.

The discussion so far has been concerned with the large architectural office alone, but it cannot be ignored that not all architectural work was done by large offices. In fact, large offices formed only a fraction of the total number of offices, bureaus, and other institutions active in the professional field. Yet there are justifications for that restricted emphasis. First, as noted before, large projects could be handled only by large offices, and so it followed that the sphere of major professional undertakings was dominated easily by the large office. But there is another justification, equally significant, namely, the relationship of the architect (by which is meant, specifically, registered practitioner), to the whole body of the profession in America. Just as it was not always noted that large offices exercised a dominance over the professional activity out of proportion to their numbers, so it was not always noted that registered practicing architects exercised a somewhat similar domination over other members of the profession, and also out of proportion to their actual numbers. For it was not necessary to be a registered practitioner to work in the profession of architecture. What this meant can be seen by looking again at the report of the 1950 survey of the profession.

According to the report, there were just over 19,000 registered architects in America in 1950. As the report also showed, the 19,000 registered architects were greatly outnumbered by the 90,000 unregistered professional employees in architectural offices. When to the numbers of registered architects and unregistered professional employees were added the numbers for associated professional and non-professional workers, the total of those engaged in all professional activities was just over 140,000. Clearly enough, registered practitioners made up no more than one-seventh of the professional body in 1950. What is not quite so clear is that even this small minority was not distributed uniformly throughout the whole field of professional activity. The second observation, while the less obvious, was the more significant for the profession.

In 1950, about one-tenth of all registered architects were engaged in one-man practices. The remaining nine-tenths were principals or employees in some 9,000 private offices and about 1,500 public bureaus and other large institutions. However, about one-half of the 9,000 private offices were very small, i.e., with no more than four employees. When the one-man practices and the very small offices were taken together, it appeared then that almost three-fifths of all registered architects, together with all their employees, accounted for only about one-tenth of the whole professional body. By contrast, the remaining two-fifths of registered architects, together with all their employees, accounted for the remaining nine-tenths of the profession. The significance of the figures became even clearer when the average sizes of offices in the two segments of the profession were compared. The larger group of registered architects practiced in very small offices, averaging less than three persons (including the principal), while the average office size for the smaller group was about ten times as large. Although the very small office was the norm for more than half of all registered architects, it was plain that the remainder, with their much larger offices, controlled a disproportionately large part of the professional activity. In fact, by every professional measure—number and size of projects undertaken, value of contracts, number of employees—the large offices effectively dominated the field.

Above the very smallest scale, the economics of professional work in architecture and the range of required technical skills made it impossible that a single individual could comprise all knowledge and competence in himself. Not only does no architect have all the knowledge and experience in the variety of disciplines necessary for the design and construction of large projects, but no single individual has the time to do all the necessary physical tasks that must be completed before a building project can begin. Little would be built above the scale of the single-family house if all the architectural work were to be done by lone individuals. On the contrary, the larger the project, the larger will be the professional work force required for design and all other stages of the work, as a rule; this led to the second justification for the organizational nature of the modern architectural office.

The economics of scale in industry as a whole were found, with certain reservations, in building also. Line and mass production, specialization of labor, prefabrication, and so on, all were applied to building. Management and planning became quite sophisticated, since the building industry was to some extent competitive, and profitability was a continuing concern to any business. In turn, some of the characteristics of the construction company were found in the architectural office, more or less as a natural outgrowth of the demands of the work. Large-scale building projects required the services of large architectural offices as much as of large construction companies. Large architectural offices tended to be organized in ways that would facilitate work flow, and the demands of work production in the office were in some ways very like what was found in industry. Division and specialization of labor within the building industry were not-unexpected results of modern business accounting methods, which emphasized sectional accountability within any business made up of diverse elements. If the ruthless pursuit of efficiency, productivity, and profits did not exactly describe the workings of the large architectural office, that might have resulted from less sophisticated management and less submissive employees than in business generally, to name only two possibilities, for the principle in operation was the same. In other words, the profit motive, held to be the key to the operation of any business, underlay the workings of the large architectural office as well, and drew with it consequences similar to those in the business world. In order to survive and maintain itself, any large business had to keep the work coming in, and there had to be enough of it to keep the organization running at maximum efficiency, for from that followed maximum productivity and maximum profits. Thus the logic of business organization, not at all surprisingly, imposed itself on professional architecture, and professional activity, once defined as a business, had a natural tendency to remain one, for the effects of the relationship between work and production tended to be self-reinforcing.

If the consequences of treating architecture as a business were destructive of its own self-image, particularly for those individuals who entered the profession with high ideals, they were much more destructive of the social idealism, not to say utopianism, represented in that great tradition described by Pevsner. To the aggressive privatism of the early industrial world, social prophets and idealistic teachers from William Morris to Walter Gropius opposed a vision of a society both well-designed and just. The place of the architect in society was not well defined before the modern era; the architect historically was indistinguishable from other members of the building trades, until Alberti gave architecture a theory of its own and the architect came to be seen as someone special. Even then, in public estimation the architect continued to occupy an uneasy position halfway between the unscrupulous contractor and the feckless artist. The profession of architecture as it is understood today was created in the nineteenth century, in imitation of medicine and the law, then as now the dominant professional occupations. The ideals of the traditional architect were the ideals of society; like the older professions it imitated, the new profession of architecture replaced the ideals of society with the ideals of the profession itself. For the ideals of the profession, the modern architectural office in its turn substituted service to the firm, as in other modern businesses.

In his numerous writings over several decades, Gropius outlined his ideas on the relation of the architect to society and the nature of the profession in the age of industry, offered an ideal of service, and drew a diagram of the professional team which would form itself in a logical response to the complex needs of the modern world. The team would include as many skills as the job at hand demanded, all the efforts to be co-ordinated by the architect, who would be *primus inter pares* rather than *magister operis*. The architect's skills would still be exercised in design, but even more would he or she possess a capacity for co-ordination, compromise, and negotiation, the ability to balance competing demands and needs and to appreciate the points of view of other professionals with their own desires. To the new role of team co-ordinator, the architect would bring also a developed social conscience and a mission of service to society. Specifically, the new architect was to seek out society's needs, identify and propose solutions for them, bring together the necessary skills, and operate as a member of a team all of whose contributors would see their roles in the same light.

In 1945, a group of young architects, three of them graduates of the Harvard School of Design, decided to form a partnership. They approached Gropius with the suggestion that he join with them in a group practice, which would be run according to the principles of teamwork and participation which Gropius had advocated to his students for many years. Gropius accepted the challenge to put his ideas into practice in the American situation, and the result was The Architects' Collaborative (TAC), still active today. Twenty years after its founding, the group published a collection of the office's projects, together with statements by the founders giving the rationale for the group and the principles of operation to be applied in the joint venture. Among the statements Gropius' oft-enunciated ideas occupy a dominant position, as might be expected:

The architect's scope must be broad, for design and planning are of vast complexity. They embrace civilized life in all its major aspects, the destiny of the land, the cities and the countryside, the knowledge of man through biology, sociology and psychology, law, government and economics, art, architecture and engineering. All are interdependent; we cannot consider them separately in compartments [Gropius, et al., *The Architects Collaborative*, p. 20].

Along with the broad range of disciplines brought to bear on the problems of architecture went the necessity for collaboration, for

As we cannot inform ourselves simultaneously in all directions, a member of a team benefits from the different interests and attitudes of the other members during their collaborative meetings. The technical, social and economic data, gathered individually and then presented to the others, reaches them already humanized by personal interpretation and, since all members of a team are apt to add their own different reactions, the new information is more easily seen in its proper perspective and its potential value [p. 24].

Since the first principle of teamwork was collaboration of differing interests, it might be supposed that a psychologist, a sociologist, an engineer, and an economist, for example, would have been members of The Architects' Collaborative from the start, but that seems not to have been the case. The founders were without exception all architects, and, judging from their professional biographies, represented among themselves no special qualifications in other disciplines. The virtual exclusion of other professionals from the office remained a feature of The Architects' Collaborative through twenty years of operation. By 1965, the office had a total of 175 employees (not counting the founding partners), divided among 126 professional employees and 49 non-professional employees. Of the professional employees, 108 were architects, while the remaining 18 were in related areas of professional activity, e.g., landscape architecture, planning. Further, within the total employee group, such differentiation as occurred was apparently not related to differences in professional skills, but to the more familiar separation of roles found in the average office. Eight employees were identified as Senior Associates (seven architects, one non-professional), and ten as Associates (eight architects, one landscape architect, one supervisor); and all of the principals were architects, as noted before. Out of eight founding partners, eight Senior Associates and ten Associates, twenty-six in all, only one was clearly a non-professional member of the office (comptroller). Whatever collaboration took place within the office structure presumably did not cross the boundaries of professional architecture.

The second principle of teamwork was shared responsibility, meaning the subsuming of the individual within the team, all of whose members collaborated towards an ultimately anonymous result. The very name of the office recalled the principle, yet the demands of work had their effects, or so it appeared:

To safeguard design-coherence and impact, the right of making the final decision must therefore be left to the one member who happens to be responsible for a specific job, even though his decision should run counter to the opinion of the other members, for the freedom of the designer in charge must be paramount [Gropius, et al., p. 24].

The divergence between principle and practice revealed in that statement describing the relation of the individual to the group was matched by the description of the office as a whole.

TAC is not a partnership of specialists. . . . Nonetheless, over the years as the volume of work increased, respect for specialization has grown. Currently, several of the associates concentrate on business aspects; others primarily concern themselves with design and presentation. There are also groups within the office specializing in specifications, landscape architecture, city planning, building supervision, model making, and information research [p. 14].

Specialization into groups within the office, marked though it was, did not extend to even the most closely related professional areas, again in spite of announced goals, for "TAC, having no structural and mechanical engineering departments, works on a job-to-job basis with outside firms." The description of the office organization implied unavoidably that its practice, whatever its character when it was founded, had grown to be indistinguishable from that of any other large office in America. There was in the descriptions of The Architects' Collaborative at work little sign of interdisciplinary collaboration, nor much of sharing or participation. Division of labor and separation of responsibility apparently characterized the operations of The Architects' Collaborative as much as the operations of Skidmore, Owings and Merrill.

The explanation might be offered that the seeming failure of The Architects' Collaborative to embody in practice its own stated principles was an ineluctable consequence of the office's success. Growing success brought growth in size—the number of employees by 1965 made The Architects' Collaborative a very large office—and largeness necessitated an organizational structure, there as elsewhere. Again, it might be suggested in extenuation that the absence of other than architectural training in the backgrounds of the founding partners tended naturally and from the first to reduce the group's capacity for interdisciplinary collaboration. But if attempts were made to redress the balance of practice in favor of principle, they were of slight effect, for they were not visible in the office's organization at the end of twenty years of practice. It is difficult to avoid the conclusion that the pervasive effects of the business orientation of the large office had extended ultimately even to the work of Gropius, exposing at last an essential conflict between theoretical ideals and practical realities.

What was revealed was the unresolved question: Was the architect alone to integrate all necessary knowledge, or was the architect to be a member of a team which integrated all necessary knowledge through its components? And the corollary of that question was: Would the architect be sole master of all areas of decision in the building process, or would decision-making be shared with others?

If the architect were to be sole master, then he would have to have something more than minimal competence in the many technical areas of architectural practice and building technology. Since the single individual, as has been said before, could not comprise all the necessary areas of knowledge at more than the most superficial level, the deficiencies of the individual would have to be made up by others. The others could be either architects who had become specialists in particular areas, or they could be non-architects trained in those areas, with full professional competence of their own. The integration of other disciplines into architecture had been one of the basic principles of Gropius' theory; and his answer to the question was the team. In practice, the architectural profession chose to break architecture itself into specialties, even though that choice ran contrary to the program of modern architectural education, which aimed at generalism.

One reason for the contradiction of modern theory by modern practice may well have been that independently trained professionals, such as engineers, sociologists, or psychologists, were indeed inclined to be independent, and to demand for themselves that full share of decision-making which their professionalism had earned for them. By contrast architects, whose education did not equip them to be specialists in anything at all, could be compelled much more easily, by the pressures of the economic system within which twentieth-century architecture existed, to abandon the image of the architect as generalist and master, accepting in its place the reality of the architect first as a specialist like other specialists, and finally as an employee like other employees. Unideal though that situation was, it matched exactly the facts of architectural practice for the great majority of the graduates of modern architectural schools. Theory and practice in modern architecture were not merely divided, they were contrary, both in intention and in fact. The only way in which modern architects could have sole mastery was to control all the processes of building, and the only way they could do that was to control the people who had the technical knowledge they relied on. Since independent professionals could not be expected to yield all power to architects, the architects developed specialized capacities within their own profession, and thus kept control to themselves in the areas of building. As the 1950 survey of the profession made plain, actual control lay in the hands of a very small porportion of the total professional body, and was by no means shared universally. In truth, Gropius' ideal of teamwork was a myth; the profession of architecture had become not a free collaboration of equals, but a business of employer and employee.

From William Morris to Walter Gropius, Pevsner traced a group of continuing themes linking nineteenth-century with twentieth-century design theory. Central to the concerns of those two men and the many other contributors to the theory were a number of stated premises: the need for an art that would be humane and truthful; the extension of that art into all areas of design activity; and the benefiting of all men with inexpensive, well-designed objects of every kind. Other concerns, not quite so clearly stated, lay behind these: the betterment of man's physical condition and the desire for a rational, democratic society. But Morris and Gropius, while sharing a concern for the social function of art and perhaps also a desire for a democratic society, did not share ideas on how this was to be accomplished. Morris' judgment on the industrial world of the 1850s was that it was essentially bad; bad in that it destroyed the old handicrafts, bad in that it produced instead ugly and vicious objects, bad in that it diminished the role of ordinary men in making and shaping their own lives. His solution to what he saw as the overriding problem of his day was to turn his back on the machine, in an attempt to restore the dignity of labor and pride in handiwork which previous ages had known. To be sure, Morris was not himself an architect, and for the development of the new theory in architecture credit must go to John Ruskin, the architectural polemicist, and especially to that great polemical architect, A. N. Welby Pugin (1812-52; Figure 75). Following the lead of these and others, Morris identified the late Middle Ages as the last period in European history in which men had been able to make their own world in a personally meaningful way, and sought there the inspiration for the new art.

Fifty years later, and in another country, Walter Gropius was one of a group of men who were responsible for the creation of a new art, an art for all men and for all circumstances, which aimed at a new humaneness and a new truth. How different that new art's products were from those of Morris and his followers is well known; for it was an art based upon acceptance, not rejection, of the machine, an art aiming at mass-production, not handcraftsmanship. Where Morris had rejected the present and looked to the past, Gropius accepted the present and looked to the future. Nonetheless, as Pevsner showed and as Gropius himself acknowledged, the European (and particularly the German) artists and theorists who

Figure 75. The roots of early-twentieth-century design theory extended back into the nineteenth century, in particular to the work and thought of artists and designers in England. One of the first of these was the architect and writer A. N. Welby Pugin.

created the new art at the beginning of the twentieth century owed a great debt to the artists and theorists, designers and craftsmen (particularly the English) of the century before. The connection between Morris and Gropius lay in their equal intention to create an art for all men, and their equal insistence on truthfulness in the use of all materials.

There was still another area of difference between Morris and Gropius, a difference in some ways as important as their areas of agreement. It was not their contrasting and indeed opposed attitudes toward the machine, because for Morris it was as logical to turn away from the machine to other alternatives still viable in 1850, as it was logical for Gropius to welcome machine technology in 1900 as the only means of production feasible in the modern world. Morris could not have been expected to foresee the future of industrialization from the viewpoint of 1850, any more than anyone else in that day. The difference between the theories of Morris and Gropius was much deeper than the simple question of technical means, for it concerned ultimate ends.

Morris' purpose was not alone the search for truth through art, but the improvement of man's lot. Upon the improvement of the life and work of the individual rested the improvement of society in general. The goal was the good of the individual, and handcraftsmanship and pride in labor were only means to that end. Good design would not only improve man's physical circumstances, but would contribute as well to his social and spiritual betterment, for as Morris saw it, " 'It is not possible to dissociate art from morality, politics and religion' " (Pevsner, *Pioneers of Modern Design*, p. 23). It was there that Morris' thought connected most obviously with that of Pugin and Ruskin, both of whom were moralistic and religious to a high degree. However, while the products of handcraftsmanship were morally pure and socially valuable, they could never be made available to all, for they were too costly and in too short supply. It was his rejection of the machine that was "the decisive antagonism in Morris's life and teaching" (Pevsner, p. 24); and it was the generation of Gropius which was to resolve that antagonism by "discovering the immense, untried possibilities of machine art" (Pevsner, p. 38). But for Gropius' generation, discarding traditional artistic hostility to the machine was only part of their program, for discarded as well was the connection between art and morality, that is, morality as traditional religion, as Morris, Ruskin, and Pugin had understood that term. The secularism of the twentieth century affected art as much as life.

This is not to say that there was no spiritual element in Gropius' theory, for Gropius had spoken of the need for a "spiritual revolution," and had insisted that

the idea of rationalization, which many people aver is the outstanding characteristic of the new architecture, is only its purifying role. The other aspect, the satisfaction of the human soul, is just as important as the material [Gropius, p. 60].

But it seemed that what Gropius meant by "spiritual revolution" and the "satisfaction of the human soul" was "the intellectual achievement which has made possible a new spatial vision"; in the modern world "a new conception of building, based on realities, has developed; and with it has come a new and changed perception of space" (p. 60). Just as personal subjectivity in design had been replaced by the rational products of the anonymous group, so subjective attitudes in society at large would be replaced too, by the new *Sachlichkeit*, or objectivity. While art aimed as before at social betterment, the rules it followed to achieve its aims were not those of moral philosophy, but those of science.

Again and again Gropius wrote of the need to make the architect a coordinator of social, psychological, and economic facts, as much as an artist and technologist. But the social facts Gropius referred to were the facts of behaviorism; the psychological facts were the facts of perceptual psychology; and the economic facts were the facts of industry, mass production, and commerce. Ethics for Gropius meant truth in the use of materials, not general morality; social betterment was equated with healthy living conditions, not political liberty; economics meant efficiency in production, not the welfare of the individual in industrial society; and for traditional religious belief Gropius substituted a "new spatial vision" whose power to persuade was less transcendental than "intellectual" and "objective."

As this brief history has tried to show, architects in modern America indeed came to terms with the facts of industry and commerce, but typically at the cost of their ethical responsibilities as independent professionals. The ethics of the individual architect were replaced by the ethics of the architectural office, and the more the architectural office resembled businesses in general, the more did its ethics resemble those of the business world. Accepting the realities of industrialization was no more than a logical consequence of accepting Gropius' theories of modern architecture, but it resulted in the contradiction between theory and practice noted before. To the extent that secular, rationalist objectivity has shown itself able to solve or at least to ameliorate the problems of the industrialized world, to that extent Gropius' generation was right, and the program they followed was a sound one. On the other hand, reasonable men might well conclude that architectural theory today is as far from solutions to society's problems as it was in the time of Walter Gropius, and in that of Morris and Pugin before him; and that between Gropius' call for a spiritual awakening on one hand and his faith in scientific objectivity on the other, there existed an antagonism as deep and ultimately as disabling as in the theory of his great precursors.

BIBLIOGRAPHICAL NOTES

The biographies of America's famous architects generally have concentrated on the public projects and inspirational qualities of their subjects, and it is difficult to uncover precise information on the workings of their offices. Nonetheless, in many cases it is possible to draw together enough fragments to construct a rough outline of office organization, although the details are often lacking.

For the office of H. H. Richardson, eyewitness accounts are given in M. G. Van Rensselaer, *Henry Hobson Richardson and His Works* (Boston, 1888; reprinted Park Forest, Ill., 1967, and New York, 1969); for more comprehensive information, see now J. F. O'Gorman, *H. H. Richardson and His Office: Selected Drawings* (Cambridge, Mass., 1974); for the office under Richardson's successors, see H.-R. Hitchcock, *The Architecture of H. H. Richardson and His Times* (2nd ed., Hamden, Conn., 1961).

There is no complete study of the office of McKim, Mead and White. The eyewitness account of R. Cortissoz appeared in his "Fifty Years of American Architecture," *The American Architect* 129.2488 (January 5, 1926), 1-5; for other details, see C. Moore, *The Life and Times of Charles Follen McKim* (Boston and New York, 1929), and the essentially anecdotal account of C. C. Baldwin, *Stanford White* (New York, 1931).

R. A. Cram was an indefatigable self-publicist; for the details of the office of Cram and Ferguson, see his autobiography, *My Life in Architecture* (Boston, 1936).

The career of D. H. Burnham has been described most effectively in T. S. Hines, *Burnham of Chicago: Architect and Planner* (New York, 1974), which largely replaced the earlier biography of C. Moore, *Daniel H. Burnham: Architect, Planner of Cities*, 2 vols. (Boston and New York, 1921; reprinted New York, 1968), although the latter contains some eyewitness reports, as also does L. H. Sullivan, *Autobiography of an Idea* (New York, 1924; reprinted 1949, 1956).

Twentieth-century architectural practice was discussed extensively in professional journals, from which there was cited here the account of J. F. Harder, "Architectural Practice—An Art and a Business," *The Brickbuilder* 11.4 (April, 1902) 74-77; for the most comprehensive study, see T. C. Bannister, ed., *The Architect at Mid-Century: Evolution and Achievement* (New York, 1954; = *Report of the Commission for the Survey of Education and Registration of the American Institute of Architects*, Vol. I); more recent, though considerably less useful, is Case and Company, Inc., *1973 Survey of the Profession—Individual Members* (San Francisco, 1974; for the American Institute of Architects).

In contrast to the sparseness of information about office practice before 1900, there were ample descriptions of architectural education; for the earliest programs, see "Architectural Education in the United States," *American Architect and Building News* 24.658 (August 4, 1888), 47-49 (MIT); 24.662 (September 1, 1888), 95-97 (Illinois); 24.667 (October 6, 1888), 155-57 (Cornell); 24.675 (December 1, 1888), 251-52 (Columbia); the major sources are cited in the bibliographical notes to Chapter 8.

For the history of design theory up to 1914, see N. Pevsner, *Pioneers of Modern Design: From William Morris to Walter Gropius* (rev. ed., Harmondsworth, 1960); for the first part of the twentieth century, see R. Banham, *Theory and Design in the First Machine Age* (New York, 1960); the most comprehensive survey is that by P. Collins, *Changing Ideals in Modern Architecture, 1750-1950* (London, 1965). The essential source for Gropius' early writings is B. M. Lane, *Architecture and Politics in Germany, 1918-1945* (Cambridge, Mass., 1968); also useful is M. Franciscono, *Walter Gropius and the Creation of the Bauhaus in Weimar* (Urbana/Chicago/London, 1971);

Gropius' later statements were collected in his *Scope of Total Architecture* (New York, 1955); for a cumulative bibliography of writings by and about Gropius, see American Association of Architectural Bibliographers, *Papers* 1 (1965), 23-43, 3 (1966; entire issue), 9 (1972), 1-27.

The office of Skidmore, Owings and Merrill in the 1950s was described briefly in S. Giedion, "The Experiment of S.O.M.," *Bauen und Wohnen* 12.4 (April, 1957), 113-14; W. E. Hartmann, "S.O.M. Organization," *Bauen und Wohnen* 12.4 (April, 1957), 116; "The Architects from 'Skid's Row,' " *Fortune*, 57.1 (January, 1958), 137-40, 210, 212, 215; H.-R. Hitchcock, "Introduction," in E. Danz, *Architecture of Skidmore, Owings and Merrill, 1950-1962* (New York, 1963); for a more general, if somewhat episodic description, see N. A. Owings, *The Spaces in Between: An Architect's Journey* (Boston, 1973).

The work of The Architects' Collaborative, with statements by the principals, appeared in W. Gropius et al., eds., *The Architects' Collaborative* (New York, 1966); and in conclusion, for enthusiastic advice on compiling this note, grateful acknowledgement is extended to Richard W. Longstreth.

# Epilogue: Still Practicing

Technological developments in the past three decades have wrought radical changes upon American life, business, and minds. From the overwhelming complexity of information networks to the breakneck rate of change, every school child is aware that these are times like no other. The American architectural profession is not immune, and has moved an immeasurable distance in the last thirty five years since Bernard Michael Boyle summed up a hundred years ending in 1965. The intervening years were characterized by dramatic change not only in architectural offices but also to architecture itself. Architecture offices, schools, and the professional organizations such as the American Institute of Architects or the National Architectural Accrediting Board have evolved at different rates. Given the shifting terrain beneath architectural practice, schools and professional organizations exhibit a striking evolutionary sluggishness. They remain oddly similar to the form they assumed in the postwar period over fifty years ago, largely because they are indifferent to market pressures. Architectural offices, on the other hand, have responded to the changing context for work with entrepreneurial acumen, tenaciously retaining certain elements while strategically adopting new practices.

In order to understand the ways architecture has changed in the past thirty years, one strategy would be to observe architectural firms, as I did in the eighties (see Cuff, 1991). By watching what architects do and listening to what they say they do, we gain ethnographic insight into not only the everyday workings of architecture, but the larger context that structures it. But this presumes we hold a common interpretive frame of reference, or that the frame of reference is known to the actors who can in turn communicate it to others. Perhaps that common base of operations was always more social agreement than fact and we merely have little agreement any longer. Instead of a common frame of reference, architects share an uncertain future, the absence of set relations with clients, perpetual economic and political restructuring, and media-dominated identity. The increasing complexities of the architectural profession's larger context have grown virtually unintelligible.

While information abounds about transformations of a global nature that affect architecture, it rarely leads to an answer to the simple question posed by ethnographers: What is going on here? I can offer only a partial response to this question. Most changes we see in practice are the direct result of three fundamental forces that have altered the context for architectural work. They are: digital technology, environmental concerns, technological change in the building sciences, and globalization. Moreover, these three fields interact to exaggerate and intensify more complex outcomes. A survey of the architectural profession's evolution over the past three and a half decades requires explanation of these sweeping transformations and an examination of their impact upon practice. Since the first edition of this book was published, architecture's historic course has been fundamentally altered by these contextual forces which, though culturally systemic, influence architects in highly specific ways. It is striking that such definitive forces of contemporary society were barely glimpsed in 1965, at the close of Boyle's examination of the architectural profession.

## Digital Technology

In 1967, Boyd Auger designed the aluminum Gyrotron exhibited at Montreal's Expo, then the largest single space frame. Its computer analysis took two hours of computer time, measured as the equivalent of 30,000 lifetimes of hand calculation. In 1968, a microchip was developed that held a "kilobit" or 1024 bits of information. In the 1970s, the first microcomputer was developed to rival the mainframe computers of the 1950s (Wilson, 1987). By the late 1970s the first Apple computer was available for popular consumption and in 1981, the IBM PC was born (Ervin, 1999). At the time of this writing, Apple claims the GA processor on its personal computer is a supercomputer on a chip, IBM just developed the world's fastest computer, performing three trillion calculations per second, and the comparison to hand calculation is no longer relevant.

Any brief description of the impact of computation and electronic information risks trivializing this sea change in architecture. As immediate communication eliminates space, and with it time, firms across the globe collaborate almost seamlessly on projects of great complexity. Computation has expanded beyond grasp the available information relevant to any task. Expertise in the current developments of computer capabilities is held by the most recent graduates of schools of architecture, thus unraveling the relationship between experience and wisdom. The static nature of architecture is challenged by a transforming, animate notion of building. Complex geometries can be calculated, visualized, and detailed for construction so that unforeseen architectural forms are both imaginable and buildable. Intervening steps between conception and production are eliminated.

## Environmentalism and Building Sciences

Environmental awareness has seeped into nearly every occupation in the past four decades including architecture, where energy conserving design initiated the larger field of environmental building technology. Two rather independent sources of action and science emerged in the 1960s to shape environmental building technology: postwar high-tech architecture and the environmental movement. While postwar modernist technology experimented with industrialized production, it also reinforced the belief that technology could resolve complex problems, both intimate and large scale. Issues ranging from comfort levels to global warming became linked through building technology. Air conditioning, for example, was a technological solution to increase comfort and its use expanded nearly one hundredfold in the postwar period between 1948 and 1962 (Wilson, 1987). In the early seventies, the energy crisis reversed this course and through alternative technologies an energy conserving architecture developed which, in turn, laid the groundwork for the broad ideals of sustainability.

Developments in environmental building technology have gone hand in hand with progress in the building sciences in general. When Joseph Esherick wrote his chapter for this volume, he recalled architectural education in the 1930s. At that point, "construction" was taught in the Department of Architecture at the University of Pennsylvania, and structure was to be faced in stone and decorated with applied ornament. In Esherick's own office of some thirty professionals in the early 1980s, there was a materials library that was catalogued by a single librarian. Architects might differ as to when the ongoing expansion of materials and building systems became unmanageable, but that expansion continues. At present, product manufacturers continue to send catalog updates, but the most current information is garnered from websites on the Internet. New materials, such as high performance plastics like polycarbonates, structural glass, and high-density concrete, are developing quickly enough to preclude any architect's full knowledge of their capabilities. In the past, experiments were usually the product of ongoing research into some material and method of construction, as with Richard Meier's preoccupation with porcelain glazed panels. Innovations under such conditions is incremental, versus the leaps someone like Frank Gehry has taken in his explorations of materials, means of production, documentation, and design.

Since 1965 when Boyle's survey ends, the field of environmental building technology has evolved both in the United States and abroad, particularly in the Scandinavian countries. Described as eco-tech, green building, or sustainability, environmental concerns have entered architectural consciousness. The building industry has been affected in cities across the world that have formulated eco-regulations concerning renewable resources, energy consumption, sick buildings, smart buildings, recycled materials, and sustainability (see Rush, 1999). Present estimates indicate that over 60% of all energy consumption in the US and 50% in Europe is building-related (Slessor, 1997). These figures alone are evidence that environmental building technology will grow in importance over the coming years.

## Globalization

In 1958, when Skidmore, Owings and Merrill comprised four offices across America with over a thousand employees, it represented the height of corporate logic. The firm was driven by its sheer size, with internal division of labor, regional distribution, full in-house service, and organizational hierarchy. Regional offices managed the projects in their geographic area. By the time *The Architect* was published in 1977, the big firm was in decline (Blau, 1984) and multi-firm, international markets for services were on the rise. While big firms still control the lion's share of international work, small firms are newly able to conduct cross-regional business at scales far surpassing their own, largely due to digital technology. Aided by electronic information systems, projects can be accomplished by teams of geographically dispersed firms, whether consultants, engineers, or other architects (Cuff, 1992). Drawings, initially shipped back and forth in mailing tubes, were later sliced into strips to be fed through fax machines. Now not only the image but its component data is shared instantly, electronically. The immediacy of communications has eliminated distance, permitting round-the-clock project schedules by architects in different time zones. Building materials and systems as well as labor pools are internationally accessible; only the building site remains geographically fixed.

Globalization implies more than internationalism. It embodies the deterioration of a sequestered nationalism, a new dialectic between the global and the local, a shared substructure of information and knowledge, and the reorganization of a national economy to a transnational or world economy. While limited work boundaries remain the norm in architecture (a full 90% of all firms practice only within their own region), offices are just as likely to have a national practice as an international practice (each at 5% of all firms), and there is a striking rise in the size of overseas billing by American firms, from about 5% of all billings in 1990 to 20.2% by 1996 (AIA, 1997).

## Contemporary Changes

Architectural practice around the world has been dramatically transformed in the three and a half decades since 1965, when Michael Boyle assessed the previous century, with an increasing momentum of change in the last decade of the twentieth century. Robert Gutman's seminal text *Architectural Practice: A Critical View*, published in 1988, suggested that there were ten trends at the end of the eighties that characterized the profession's evolution. In order to assess the state of architectural practice in 2000, I will reexamine several of Gutman's primary observations in light of digital technology, environmentalism, and globalization.

Gutman provides the following summary of the ten trends he identified in the book:

"(1) the expanding demand for architectural services; (2) changes in the structure of the demand; (3) the oversupply, or potential oversupply, of entrants into the profession; (4) the increased size and complexity of buildings; (5) the consolidation and professionalization of the construction industry; (6) the greater rationality and sophistication of client organizations; (7) the more intense competition between architects and other professions; (8) the greater competition within the profession; (9) the continuing economic difficulties of practice; and (10) changing expectations of architecture among the public." (p 1).

I will not discuss these trends individually, but will group them into categories concerning demand (trends 1,2), bigness (4,5), competitive edge (7,8), and the consumers, which I have titled "not in your backyard" (6,10). The issue of an oversupply of architects has not materialized, in part because of the expanding demand for architectural services and the large scale economic boom since the time of Gutman's writing.

## Demand for Services

The demand for architectural services continues to expand and to be restructured. Somewhere between 15–25 percent of the members of the American Institute of Architects are practicing in nontraditional settings: in construction management, within corporations or public institutions, as facilities or construction managers, or in design-build arrangements. This figure will surely increase, though probably not to 50 percent before the end of the decade as some suggest (see for example, LeFevre, 1998). According to a 1997 survey by the AIA, practitioners are asked to perform a widening range of services with ever higher degrees of professional competency. This creates a contradiction resolved through collaborative teams of firms (Cuff, 1992) or through the old Skidmore, Owings & Merrill model of large firms of specialists (see *World Architecture*, 1999).

The expansion in services goes hand in hand with the continuing increases in complexity of buildings and building types. Simultaneously, there is an assumption (a narrowing expectation or risk-averse stance) by clients, that the successful competitor for a commission will be the architect with the most directly-related past experience. One sees announcements for jobs—for example, from a school district looking for an architect who has experience relocating portable classrooms, or a city seeking applications from architects who have 5–10 years experience with toxic recycling centers—that range from the mundane to the impossible. The idea of perfect fit has gained strength by virtue of enhanced communication and boundary-free practice. Thus, through Internet advertising, the architect of a recycling facility in one state can apply in another state to build a similar facility. Digitized and globalized, architectural practices become more accessible, yet more narrowly defined. Such a tightly tailored team is in reality an aspect of what Gutman called "the deskilling of architectural labor." To those within the profession without the time or resources to get up to speed on new materials, new legal restrictions, computational techniques, and so on, the increasing range of services often translates to new, elastic collaborations and the concomitant new complexities of project management.

Lastly, one development in the demand for services directly connected to globalization concerns the expanding market for identity-conscious design. Whether by means of a famous designer's reputation or by the creation of themed environments, clients seek architects who can establish a building's identity so that it functions in extended ways. That was the fulfilled expectation of Frank Gehry's Guggenheim in Bilbao, which is helping revitalize the region's economy. Alternatively, the architects Hodgetts and Fung operate more like art directors for creating places, than designers for buildings. In both public and commercial projects, creating identity through architecture is a fundamental function in a global economy.

## Bigness

Scale has always been a critical construct within architecture, both with regard to the size of the firm or the client and to the scale of the building project. Boyle, along with other observers of the modern profession, focussed much of his attention on the issue of office scale. The rise of the large, corporate architectural office in the middle of the twentieth century implied the seeming assimilation of architecture into the broader trends of the service sector. Just like the corporate clients they served, large offices dominated the building economy. Bigness equated with power, an association not overlooked by SOM's partners. Nat Owings reflected in 1973 upon the motives driving him and his partners: "We were not after jobs as such. We were after leverage to influence social and environmental conditions. . . . . To work, we must have volume. An efficient set of master builders can eat up a lot of work. Volume meant power. We would try to change men's minds." (Kostof, p 325–6).

But today power comes in a variety of packages. Size of firm is but one mechanism in a global economy, where information networks and commodification extend the reaches of even very small firms. Consider the recent issue of *Architecture* Magazine (May 2000) on "power." One section, dedicated to notably powerful individuals, sketches a current profile of practice, for example: Rem Koolhaas, global architect-theorist, David Rockwell, themed-environment designer, Andres Duany, suburban evangelist, and Frank Gehry, who writes on the force of Bilbao's economic recovery. Only Art Gensler fits the description SOM supposedly prefigured of architectural practice and the power of the large firm. SOM itself took another path: the architecture firm's recently appointed president is not an architect but a CEO from General Electric.

Gutman argued that the building industry's constituent elements were increasingly consolidated. The term "consolidation" may have misleading connotations of permanence; instead, many firms employ project-based strategies dependent upon the stock market, interest rates, client or project type. Today, I would argue that the building industry is being increasingly restructured. Architects have explored new types of firm and project structures in which they also operate as real estate developers, facilities managers, builders, or investors. In the emergent pan-European economy, transnational "firms" have begun to operate in ways that challenge the very notion of the firm and, with it, its scale. Relatively loosely associated architects in different regions of western Europe are offered incentives to undertake projects collectively. Project teams are organized to match client demand and regional requirements, disbanding when the commission is complete. Although Judith Blau's study (1984) indicated that smaller firms were more flexible and thus capable of restructuring, this need not remain the case given the possibilities of electronic data management and communication. Indeed, another persistent trend is the fluctuating growth and shrinkage in individual offices, which I described elsewhere as elasticity (Cuff, 1992).

Scale has also been part of the environmental agenda, with its maxim that "small is beautiful." In contradiction, it has been argued that large is inevitable (Koolhaas, 1995) and in some ways, the sustainability movement must operate at a large enough scale that the spectrum of environmental forces can be dealt with simultaneously in order to be effective. The interconnections are ever more apparent between the global and the local, the super-sized and the extra-small, the concept and the detail.

## Competitive Edge

In spite of many changes, new models of practice in the United States remain at the margins around a core of offices that can be described in rather traditional terms. Small firms, a full third (33%) of which are sole proprietorships, dominate architectural practice. Another quarter (26%) is made up of two- to four-person firms, half of which have only one licensed architect. Fewer than 20% of firms employ more than ten people, and only 3% have more than fifty employees (Source: 1997 AIA Firm Survey). This basic breakdown of office size has not varied much in past decades, even though the way work is done has changed significantly, particularly in relation to computing. In spite of triumphs by small firms, the dominance of the large firm persists in the U.S. and these firms now operate around the world. Asian and European firms find themselves competing unsuccessfully against globalized, corporate American offices. The U.S. firms that employ fifty or more people, while just three percent of the total, control a disproportionate share of the overall construction billings in the U.S. The larger the firm, the more likely it is to be doing international work; the smaller the firm, the more likely it will be doing work only within its metropolitan area and state.

There is also a kind of competition within the office that has always occurred but that takes a new form because of digital technology. Particularly in times when the building industry is economically strong, the competition for recent computer-savvy graduates is intense. Those employees within the office who know the newest software and can use to its fullest potential will hold a distinct advantage over their peers. For an already-employed architect, it is very difficult to find the time necessary to do more than become adept at the programs in use. Blau (1984) found that this same phenomenon occurred in the early seventies with recent graduates who had energy expertise. Within the office, they were more likely to have access to the firm's principals and associates, and thus to power. This is now the case for young architects well trained in computation.

As Gutman noted, competition continues to intensify among architects and between architects and others in the construction industry. Engineers are increasingly specialized; along with planners and some landscape architects, they have assumed primary responsibility for environmental concerns. Architects have had to retool to deal competently with such issues as brown fields, energy regulations, life-cycle costing, environmental remediation, and sustainability guidelines. During the recession of the early nineties, the portions of the construction industry that suffered most were those working above ground, including architects. By contrast, those professionals (primarily engineers) thrived who were engaged with environmental impact studies and publicly-funded infrastructure.

Between the 1960s and the present, we witnessed the rise of what has been called the "boutique" office—small firms hired for their good name and good design. In an age of increasing anonymity, establishing identity is perhaps the most difficult challenge for architects. They need to create a unique identity that will both secure a market for services and ink in the professional journals. Architects such as Zaha Hadid, Rem Koolhaas, Ben van Berkel, Glenn Murcutt, and Thom Mayne, each in a very different way, have established distinct public identities based only in part on their talents and the qualities of their projects.

Creating an identity is an issue for all firms, not only because of digital technology and globalization, but also because the traffic in images has swept architects along with the rest. Intensified visual stimuli characterize all aspects of postmodern life, from the design of athletic shoes to the marketing of milk to the creation of urban identity through unique architecture. Architects must trade in images, both of themselves and for their clients.

## Not in Your Back Yard

Although the demand for architectural services continues to grow, the demand has developed in conflicting ways. One one hand, prestigious commissions carry heightened imagery and expectations, as described above. On the other hand, an increasingly development-wary public expects civic buildings to drop unnoticed into the background. The latter trend is characterized by the general rise of public review in the design and planning processes. From Prince Charles's vocal stance against the modern, to the neighborhood design board, architects are more constrained than ever before by the will of those who are stakeholders but not owners. What seemed oppressive under the rubric of "not in my back yard" became outrageous in the form of "not in your back yard" either.

Both the general public and clients have assumed new power in the design process. Although Gutman attributed much of that power to the democratic welfare state, it was after the publication of his book that the welfare state's dismantling gained undeniable momentum with the result that the arts of architecture and design have lost state support while public regulation of design has increased substantially. In turn, this has extended the time frame of every project in an office, so that firms must now carry more projects in order to maintain the same work load. The increased scrutiny of designs has also worked as a counterforce to globalization, since back yards are highly localized. By that, I mean that the politics of construction has a geographically specific face. New buildings must be negotiated with city councils, neighbors, county supervisors, environmental activists, and local citizen groups. One consequence is that construction, design, and development have grown more contentious in the past three decades. Architects have tended to respond to these new conditions defensively rather than creatively. Liability, for example, was a key concern in discussions about the new handbook the AIA created in the eighties. *The Handbook of Professional Practice*—while primarily used as a set of reference volumes within offices, particularly for its standard contracts—is an important portrayal of the professional organization's self image at any point in time. In the rewriting of the *Handbook of Professional Practice*, undertaken first in the 1980s and revised at the end of the 1990s, risk and liability were at the fore. Lawsuits had increased in the seventies and eighties and as a result, architects seemed more than ever governed by the advice of their lawyers. This paralleled the expansion of split commissions, which divided the design phases from the construction document phase.

## Conclusion

The clients that plagued Boyle were the large corporations with questionable ethics and unmistakable power. They seem tame now, by comparison to the twenty-something dot-com millionaires, the software developers, and the entertainment gurus. What they do and make is as ephemeral as the spaces they tend to occupy. At the other extreme are the gigantic urban projects undertaken recently such as mixed-use developments in Tokyo, the Getty Museum in Los Angeles, and the whole of Lille, France. These clients need new types of space, space which is temporary, transparent, shifting, provisional, and which creates a "brand identity" in quite different ways from the former corporate headquarters.

Globalization, environmental and building sciences, and digital technology are changing how we think about architecture and architectural practice. It is not only a matter of how we go about the business of architecture, but what it is we think we should be doing, and what we might be creating. Thus our finances, our ethics, and our art are all implicated. Professional standards which tacitly and explicitly have governed the profession are under siege: computers have undermined the role of the author, the need for technical competence requires that firms collaborate, the market insures the success of aggressive entrepreneurs, generalist practices must be packaged for the media. To cope and thrive under such conditions, which fundamentally contradict traditional values, practitioners must reconsider the persistent but outdated notion of professionalism.

This is already occurring as individual architects and firms respond to forceful new directions set by the context for work. The kinds of changes that are transpiring in piecemeal fashion within architectural practices will only proliferate in the coming decades. Both local politics as well as increasing global trade will undermine the current notions of professional licensure. Professional unity will be further challenged by the increasing diversity among practitioners who call themselves architects. Unless the profession's leadership consciously and creatively adapts to change rather than reasserts the typical resistance, the profession will be weakened by these changes.

Although there has always been tension between schools of architecture and the professional organization, it is likely to intensify in the coming decade. The proverbial gap between schools and practice will widen to new extremes, causing much discomfort. The gap will be particularly acute with regard to computation, since students and their prospective employers expect training in the latest versions of CAD, which is either beyond or beneath the capabilities of higher education, depending on the institution. Because universities can support an infrastructure of hardware and software far beyond that available to offices, the cutting edge in digital technology will emerge at a great distance from current architectural practices. On the other side, schools continue in their resistance to the entrepreneurial demands of contemporary practice. New academic models are most likely to emerge from smaller institutions in major urban centers, because they can respond more flexibly than their more encumbered brethren. The accrediting process, which monitors standardized professional education, is going to be tested repeatedly in the coming decades as practice and schools diverge, both threatening to leave the professional organizations behind.

These projections are coupled with the observation that architecture is in a prime position to establish a stronger role in contemporary culture. The architectural profession can benefit from the increasing influence of the visual in our world; appreciation and enhancement of the local can counterbalance despatialized global flows; green building and planning offer a concrete response to complex environmental problems; urban identity and tourism depend upon effective architectural design; architecture perhaps more than any other occupation is advancing the use of digital technology. The potential for the future of the practice of architecture is vast, as are the pitfalls of promoting the status quo. The most recent past of our profession does not give us much hope that we can avoid the pitfalls. But here is where Spiro Kostof's volume becomes invaluable: from the ancient Egyptians and Greeks to nineteenth–century England and France, history demonstrates architecture's ambitious responses to widespread changes in the world.

BIBLIOGRAPHY

American Institute of Architects. *1997 AIA Firm Survey*. Washington, D.C.: The American Institute of Architects, 1997.

Blau, Judith. *Architects and Firms*. Cambridge: MIT Press, 1984.

Crosbie, Michael. "The Schools: How They're Failing the Profession." *Progressive Architecture*, September 1995, pp 47–51, 94, 96.

Cuff, Dana. *Architecture: The Story of Practice*. Cambridge: MIT Press, 1991.

Cuff, Dana. "Fragmented Dreams, Flexible Practices." *Architecture*. Vol 81, No 5, May 1992. 80–83.

Cuff, D. "Community Property: Enter the Architect." in Bell, Michael and S. T. Leong (eds.) *Slow Space*. New York: Monacelli, 1998. pp 120–140.

Ervin, Stephen M. "The Three Computer Revolutions in landscape Architecture." *Landscape Architecture*, Nov 1999, p 56.

Gutman, Robert. *Architectural Practice: A Critical View*. New York: Princeton Architectural Press, 1988.

Koolhaas, Rem and Bruce Mau (Jennifer Sigler, ed). *S,M,L,XL*. New York: Monacelli Press, 1995.

Kroloff, Reed. "How the Profession is Failing the Schools." *Architecture*, August 1996, pp 92–93.

LeFevre, Camille. "Charting Alternatives." *Architecture Minnesota*, Jan/Feb 1998, vol 24, No 1, pp 17, 60).

Rush, Richard D. "Sustainformation." *Urban Land*, Nov/Dec 1999, pp 62–65, 110.

Sassen, Saskia. "Globalization and the Formation of Claims." In Copject, Joan and Michael Sorkin (Eds). *Giving Ground: The Politics of Propinquity*. London: Verso, 1999. pp 86–105.

Sheehan, Tony. "Advanced Construction Materials." *Architects' Journal*, July 13, 1995. pp 37–41

Slessor, Catherine. *Eco-Tech: Sustainable Architecture and High Technology*. London: Thames and Hudson, 1997.

Wilson, Forrest. "A Time of Relentless Technological Change". In *Architecture*, December 1987, pp 115–119.

*World Architecture*. "Ch-ch-ch-ch-changes." No 78, July/Aug 1999, pp 58–59.

# Illustrations

1. Side elevation for a shrine, Egyptian papyrus drawing from Ghorab, probably XVIII Dynasty; Museo egiziano, Turin. Line drawing by R. Tobias.
2. Bird's-eye view of an Amarna palace in a painting from the tomb of Mery-Re, high priest of Aten; XVIII Dynasty. From N. de G. Davies, *The Rock Tombs of El Amarna*, I (London, 1903), pl. XXVI.
3. Portrait statue of the architect Senmut, XVIII Dynasty; Louvre, Paris. Photo: Réunion des musées nationaux.
4. The naval arsenal at Piraeus, by Philon and Euthydemos, 340-330 B.C.; reconstruction drawing. From V. Marstrand, *Arsenalet i Piraeus, og Oldtidens Byggeregler* (Copenhagen, 1922), Plan IV.
5. Clay tablet from Tell Asmar (Iraq), later third millennium B.C. Courtesy of the Oriental Institute, University of Chicago.
6. Casts of architects' tomb inscriptions in the Museo della civiltà romana, EUR, Rome. Photo: W. L. MacDonald.
7. Fragment of a marble plan of Rome, ca. A.D. 200. Photo: Smith College, Slide and Photograph Collection.
8. Fragment of a Roman bath plan in mosaic. From G. Carettoni et al., *La pianta marmorea di Roma antica*, I (Rome, 1960), p. 209.
9. Detail of a painted wall from the Boscoreale cubiculum; Metropolitan Museum of Art, New York. Photo: Smith College, Slide and Photograph Collection.
10. Mosaic of an architect and his assistants; Bardo Museum, Tunis. Courtesy of the Museum.
11. Wall painting from the tomb of Trebius Justus, Rome. Photo: Fototeca Unione, Rome.
12. Casts of Roman brickstamps of the first and second centuries A.D.; Museo della civiltà romana, EUR, Rome. Photo: W. L. MacDonald.
13. Plan of Timgad, Algeria. Photo: Smith College, Slide and Photograph Collection.
14. Trajanic bridge, Alcántara, Spain. Photo: W. L. MacDonald.
15. Apollodorus' Danube bridge as seen on the Column of Trajan, Rome. Photo: Smith College, Slide and Photograph Collection.

# Notes on Contributors

Bernard Michael Boyle, Professor Emeritus of Architecture and Humanities at Arizona State University, has taught as well at Smith College, Dartmouth College, the University of California, Berkeley, and the Southern California Institute of Architecture. He is author or editor of *Materials in the Architecture of Arizona, 1870–1920* (1976), *Blaine Drake, Forty Years of Architecture in Arizona* (1991), *Constructions: Buildings in Arizona by Alfred Newman Beadle* (1992), *Wright in Arizona: The Early Photographs of Pedro E. Guerrero* (1995).

Dana Cuff is Professor of Architecture and Urban Design at the University of California, Los Angeles, and author of *Architecture: The Story of Practice* (1991) and *The Provisional City* (2000). She received her Ph.D. in Architecture from the University of California, Berkeley.

Joan Draper has a M.Arch. and a Ph.D. from the University of California, Berkeley. She has taught architectural history at Montana State University and the University of Illinois. Since 1985, she has been on the faculties of the University of Colorado at Boulder and at Denver. Her published research deals with American architecture and urban planning.

Joseph Esherick taught architecture at the University of California, Berkeley, from 1952 to 1985, while also carrying on an active practice. He was made a Fellow of the American Institute of Architects in 1965. Among his better known buildings are Adlai Stevenson College, University of California, Santa Cruz; the Cannery, San Francisco; Church of Christ the Saviour, San Francisco; and Wurster Hall, University of California, Berkeley (with V. DeMars and D. Olsen).

L. D. Ettlinger taught the history of art at the University of California, Berkeley, from 1970 to 1980. From 1959 to 1970 he was Durning Lawrence Professor of Art, University College, University of London. His books include *The Sistine Chapel Before Michelangelo* (1965), *Albrecht Dürer* (1966), and *Caspar David Friedrich* (1967).

Spiro Kostof was Professor of Architectural History at the University of California, Berkeley, and he also taught at Yale University and the Massachusetts Institute of Technology. Among his books are *America by Design* (1987), *The City Shaped: Urban Patterns and Meanings through History* (1993), and *A History of Architecture: Settings and Rituals,* second edition (1995).

William L. MacDonald, educated at Harvard and in Rome, is a former A. P. Brown Professor at Smith College and the author of several books of architectural history, among them *The Architecture of the Roman Empire,* 2 vols. (1982, 1986), *The Pantheon* (1976), and *Hadrian's Villa and Its Legacy,* written with John A. Pinto (1995) and published in Italy as *La Villa Adriana* (1997). He is Fellow of the American Academy of Arts and Sciences.

Myra Nan Rosenfeld is an independent art historian in Montreal. She holds a Ph.D. in Fine Arts from Harvard University and is the author of *Sebastiano Serlio on Domestic Architecture* (New York, Architectural History Foundation, 1978; reprinted Dover Publications, 1997) which won the Alice Davis Hitchcock Award of the Society of Architectural Historians in 1979. Myra Nan Rosenfeld was Senior Research Curator at the Canadian Centre for Architecture from 1985 to 1999. She is presently writing a book on the Hôtel de Cluny in Paris.

Catherine Wilkinson Zerner, educated at Yale, teaches history of art at Brown University. She has also taught at the University of California, Berkeley and at Stanford University and Centre d'Etudes Superieures de la Renaissance in Tours. Her published work deals with Spanish Renaissance architecture.

John Wilton-Ely was educated at Cambridge, the Courtauld Institute of Art, and London University. Among his books are *The Mind and Art of Piranesi* (1988), *Piranesi as Architect and Designer* (1993) and *Giovanni Battista Piranesi: The Complete Etchings,* 2 vols. (1994).

Gwendolyn Wright is Professor of Architecture, Planning and Preservation and Professor of History at Columbia University, where she was also the founding director of the Buell Center for Research in American Architecture. She is the author of *Making the Model Home: Domestic Architecture and Cultural Conflicts in Chicago, 1873–1913* (1978) and *Building the Dream: A Social History of Housing in America* (1981), among other publications on housing, museum collections, and the practice of architectural history in the United States. Her latest book is *The Politics of Design in French Colonial Urbanism, 1880–1930.*

# Index

Aachen: palace of, 73; Palatine chapel, 71
abbey, 62, 69, 73, 74, 75, 77, 80, 81, 129
Academic Classicism, 213-14, 217, 221, 228
Ackerman, James, 142, 145; cited, 138, 140, 143, 149
Adam, James, 191
Adam, Robert, 190, 192, 193
Addams, Jane, 304-5; cited, 284
Adelphi Terrace (London), 190
*Administration des bâtiments royaux*, 161
*aedificatio*, 20
Agamedes, 25
Agathanor, 15
Aigina (Greece), 12
Airard, Abbot, 75
Akhenaten, 5, 18
Alamaddin Qaisar, 64
Alan of Lille, cited, 79
Alberti, Leone Battista, 29, 89, 97, 100, 103, 105, 106, 111-14, 115, 117, 118, 119, 120, 121, 124, 125, 126, 127, 133, 136, 140, 141, 143, 150, 153, 154, 157, 166, 334; cited, 98, 112, 130-31, 149, 180
Alcantara (Spain), Trajanic bridge, 46 (Fig. 14), 47
Alessi, Galeazzo, 130, 139, 140
Alexander, brother of Anthemius, 53
Alexander the Great, 17, 19, 20
Alexandria (Egypt), 17, 20, 40, 53, 63
Alfonso of Naples, 126

Alfonso II of Aragon, 166
Alma-Tadema, Lawrence, 203
Alps, the, 68, 209
Amangeart, Louis, 166
Amarna (Egypt), 18; palace, 9
Amboise (France), 166
*American Federation of Women's Clubs*, 305
American Institute of Architects, 282, 300, 318; Committee on Education, 217; conventions of, 216, 235
*American Woman's Home, The*, 285
Amiens (France), cathedral, 78, 81
amphitheatre, 46
*anagrapheis*, 12
*analytique*, 223, 231, 232 (Fig. 57), 249, 253, 254, 255, 256
*ancien*, 223, 225
Anet (France), 171
Anjou (France), 76
Anthemius of Tralles, 44, 53, 55, 56, 62, 63
Antioch (Syria), 17; chalice of, 272, 273
Antonio da Sangallo (the Younger), 97, 106, 126, 129, 135, 136, 138, 139, 141, 142, 145, 147, 148, 156, 157
*aparejador*, 131
apartment house, 286, 287 (Fig. 65), 300, 301 (Fig. 70), 302
Apollo, 18, 176
Apollodorus of Damascus, 29, 39, 44, 45, 46, 47 (Fig. 15), 48 (Fig. 16), 49 (Fig. 17), 50, 51, 56, 68